DATE DUE			

European of Yesterday

A BIOGRAPHY OF

STEFAN ZWEIG

STEFAN ZWEIG, about 1940

European of Yesterday

A BIOGRAPHY OF

STEFAN ZWEIG

D. A. PRATER

OXFORD
AT THE CLARENDON PRESS
1972

Oxford University Press, Ely House, London W. 1
GLASGOW NEW YORK TORONTO MELBOURNE WELLINGTON
CAPE TOWN IBADAN NAIROBI DAR ES SALAAM LUSAKA ADDIS ABABA
DELHI BOMBAY CALCUTTA MADRAS KARACHI LAHORE DACCA
KUALA LUMPUR SINGAPORE HONG KONG TOKYO

PRINTED IN GREAT BRITAIN
AT THE UNIVERSITY PRESS, OXFORD
BY VIVIAN RIDLER
PRINTER TO THE UNIVERSITY

TO

FRIDERIKE ZWEIG

Gefährtin seines Lebens

Preface

> *'I profess to write not his panegyrick, which must be all praise, but his Life; which, great and good as he was, must not be supposed to be entirely perfect. . . . In every picture there should be shade as well as light.'*
>
> Boswell, *Life of Johnson*

During his life, Stefan Zweig—poet, dramatist, essayist, writer of *Novellen*, biographer, librettist—enjoyed a literary success granted to few. Between the turn of the century and the advent of Hitler in 1933 his works reached a steadily growing public, not only in the German-speaking lands but also in translation in most other countries of the world. Before the First World War he had made a modest name for himself in Austria and Germany with two volumes of not very distinguished verse, a collection of *Novellen*, two dramas, and his translation of the works of the Belgian poet Émile Verhaeren. Regarding himself as a European rather than an Austrian, he worked hard as a *Mittler*, a mediator in the world of European letters, and as would-be architect of the intellectual unity of Europe: the essay trilogy *Three Masters* (Balzac, Dickens, Dostoevsky), his studies of Rimbaud and Verlaine, and his biography of Romain Rolland, all published soon after the war, were manifestations of these efforts. But the extraordinary fame he achieved in the twenties and early thirties, with (for those days) outstanding sales figures, rested first on his *Novellen* of passion and conflict (*Amok, Letter from an Unknown Woman, Fear, Twenty-Four Hours in a Woman's Life, Episode in the Early Life of Privy Councillor D.*), and then on his biographies, or rather, historical novels (*Fouché, Marie Antoinette*). As a result, there was an assured public for his more solid works—the further essay volumes on

Stendhal, Casanova, Tolstoy; Hölderlin, Kleist, Nietzsche; Freud, Mesmer, Mary Baker-Eddy; and the series of historical miniatures, *The Tide of Fortune*. For some years he was the most translated author of Europe, with works available in nearly forty languages. Even after 1933, when he was forced to publish first in Austria and then with the *émigré* houses in Amsterdam and Stockholm, the reception accorded his *Erasmus*, a thorough and highly topical study of the great humanist, his *Mary Queen of Scots* and *Magellan* biographies, and his only novel, *Beware of Pity*, kept him well to the fore. The last *Novelle*, *The Royal Game*, and his autobiography, *The World of Yesterday*, were both bestsellers in England and America.

Yet today, not thirty years since his tragic death by his own hand in Brazil, we may search in vain for more than a brief mention of Zweig in the current histories published in English of modern German literature. Though his works, in print again in Germany since the Second World War, maintain steady sales there and in Austria, and are available in French, Portuguese, and a few other languages, they have virtually disappeared from the Anglo-Saxon market. It is true that the translations into English, made hurriedly at the height of his popularity, leave a great deal to be desired, and that those works which once commanded large editions were sometimes the less deserving. But the swing of the pendulum to the other extreme has plunged into unwarranted obscurity some which merit inclusion with the greatest twentieth-century German literature. He was a professional whose best prose stands well above that of the gifted amateur Hans Carossa: but the student today, even inside Germany, will find twenty studies of *Doctor Gion* for every one of *Beware of Pity*.

It is the purpose of the present book to attempt to restore the balance, not so much by renewing a study of Zweig's works, as by relating, for the first time in the detail it merits, the life-story of a sensitive, unusually interesting, and extraordinarily complicated personality, and a great European. For it is above all his place in the intellectual life of Europe that today needs to be reassessed—today, when 'Europe' is on everyone's lips, the word itself appearing, like a new Tower of Babel, in scaffolding on the postage stamps of the associated countries. The ideals for which he strove, unobtrusively and, as he thought, unsuccessfully—peace, the liberty of the individual, the moral unity of Europe and the world—are still before us, one day to be attained; and the story of this latter-day Erasmus has a lesson still for us. I have written this book in the form of a chronological narrative, in the hope that the more important parts of the evidence about him thus assembled will make it possible for those more competent than I to form a judgement, and for others not yet familiar with him to look for the first time at his works.

'He who undertakes a biography', Freud once wrote, 'commits himself to lies, dissimulation, hypocrisy, embellishment, even the concealment of his own lack of comprehension: for biographical truth is not to be had, and even if one did attain it, it would be of no value.'[1] Though I had this harsh judgement very much in mind—every man *is* an island unto himself, and Zweig more than most—I refused to be discouraged by it. I have striven for accuracy where good sources were available, and to avoid speculation where they were not.

My story can make no claim to be definitive. Zweig was one of the most prolific correspondents this century has seen, and although I have made use of the two volumes of *Briefwechsel* so far published, and have been fortunate to have had access to a considerable proportion of his unpublished letters, their world-wide scatter has made it impossible to see them all. On the other hand, I have, I think, seen and used most of the secondary literature of importance—the numerous memoirs, essays on certain aspects of his life and works, attempts to explain his success and death—which appeared, some during his lifetime, but for the most part in the decade after 1942, notably in the collections edited by Hanns Arens; and these are acknowledged in the Bibliography and footnotes. Quotations are in my own translation, from the German of the first edition or the manuscript in each case, with the exception of those from *Die Welt von Gestern*, which are taken from the S. Fischer edition, Frankfurt am Main, 1955, 80.–90. Tausend.

1 Letter to Arnold Zweig, 31 May 1936 (Freud *Br* 423).

Earlier biographical studies were helpful in varying degrees: his own sketch and the appreciation by Hanns Martin Elster in 1922, that by Richard Specht in 1927, Erwin Rieger's biography of 1928 (Zweig's forty-sixth year), and the little books by Professor Hans Hellwig in 1948 and Arnold Bauer in 1961. Robert Dumont's *Stefan Zweig et la France* was of capital importance, containing as it does the first full study of the Zweig/Rolland correspondence, and I am greatly indebted to Dr. Dumont's thorough research.

For personal memories, and other assistance of great value, I am indebted to Dr. Richard Friedenthal, Zweig's literary executor; Herr Hermann Kesten; Mr. Heinrich Eisemann; the late Dr. Franz Theodor Csokor; Sr. Abrão Koogan, Zweig's publisher in Brazil; the late Professor Jethro Bithell; Dr. Ferdinand Burger and Sr. Erich Eichner, both of Rio de Janeiro; Mrs. Margarida Banfield, Rabbi Dr. Lemle, and Sr. Leopoldo Stern, also of Rio; Helene Freifrau von Ledebur; Dr. Herbert Lewandowski (Lee van Dovski), Geneva; Dr. Melvin Horwith, New York; and Sr. Isaac Goichmann and the members of the B'nai B'rith 'Loja Stefan Zweig', Penha.

I would like especially to thank Stefan Zweig's heirs in London for granting me access to the papers of the Zweig Estate, and for their permission not only to make use of this extensive material but also to quote from letters by Zweig located elsewhere. For access to, and, where appropriate, permission to publish from, their archives my gratitude must also go to: the Home Office, London (papers affecting Zweig's British naturalization); the Director of the Stadtbibliothek, Vienna, Dr. Albert Mitringer, and his colleague Dr. Karl Gladt (Zweig's correspondence, in particular covering his early years); Dr. Walther Migge, of the Schiller Nationalmuseum, Marbach (Zweig's correspondence, in particular letters to Anton Kippenberg, Victor Fleischer, Paul Zech, Emil Ludwig, and Viktor Wittkowski); Frau Katia Mann, and Dr. Wysling of the Thomas-Mann-Archiv, Zürich (correspondence between Zweig and Mann); Dr. Olof von Feilitzen, of the Kungliga Bibliotek, Stockholm (Zweig's letters to Ellen Key); and Sra. Ida Geiger, Venice (Zweig's letters to Benno

Geiger). Where any of this material has been used or directly quoted, specific acknowledgement will be found in the Notes.

It goes without saying that none of the above-named bears any responsibility for my interpretation or for the opinions I have expressed.

My research over the years was enormously facilitated by the active interest, advice, and help shown me by Professor Harry Zohn, of Brandeis University; Professor Randolph J. Klawiter, of Notre Dame University; Dr. Joseph Suschitzky, of *Libris*, London; Dr. Lionel Steiman, of Manitoba University; and Herr Erich Fitzbauer, lately Secretary of the International Stefan Zweig Society, Vienna: I hope they will feel this result rewards their kindness. I am very grateful also to Mrs. Susanne Hoeller for permission to reproduce two of her photographs, and to Mrs. H. E. Wyatt and Sra. Nicia Kahl, who allowed me to look over Zweig's houses in Bath and Petropolis.

My foremost debt, however, is to Professor Friderike M. Zweig, not only for her edition of the correspondence with Stefan and her own invaluable book on him, but also for her ready help with documentary material, photographs, and personal memories; above all, for her unflagging interest, penetrating comments, and encouragement as she read my first drafts.

'Zum Eingang schreibe ich dankbar ihren Namen.'

Contents

List of Plates

Abbreviations

(For full titles, refer to Sources and Bibliography, p. 364)

Arens[1]	*Zweig: Sein Leben, sein Werk*, 1949
Arens[2]	*Der grosse Europäer . . . Zweig*, 1956
Arens[3]	*Zweig im Zeugnis seiner Freunde*, 1968
Ausst	*Katalog der Gedächtnisausstellung Stefan Zweig*, 1961 (ed. Fitzbauer)
Baudouin	*Éclaircie sur l'Europe*, 1944
Bauer	*Zweig*, 1961
BdFr	*Buch der Freunde* (Ebermayer), 1960
Bildb	*Zweig: eine Bildbiographie* (Friderike Zweig), 1961
Brod	*Streitbares Leben: Autobiographie*, 1960
BrW	*Briefwechsel* (Stefan and Friderike Zweig), 1951
Cahn	Zweig letters to Alfredo Cahn, etc.
DDh	*Zweig (Deutsche Dichterhandschriften)* (ed. Elster), 1922
De Souza	*Os Ultimos Dias de Stefan Zweig*, 1942
Dichter	*Dichter im Café* (Kesten), 1965
Dum	*Zweig et la France* (Dumont), 1967
Exil	*Deutsche Literatur im Exil* (Kesten), 1964
Flower	*Just as it Happened*, 1950
Fr	*Zweig: Wie ich ihn erlebte* (Friderike Zweig), 1947
Fr[2]	*Spiegelungen des Lebens* (Friderike Zweig), 1964
Freud *Br*	*Briefe, 1873–1939*, 1961
Freud/Zw *BrW*	*Briefwechsel* Freud/Arnold Zweig, 1968
Ged	*Zweig: eine Gedenkschrift* (Zech), 1943
Geiger	*Memorie di un Veneziano*, 1958
Grasberger	*Der Strom der Töne trug mich fort . . .*, 1967
H	*Zweig* (Hellwig), 1948
Heute	*Denn heute gehört uns Deutschland . . .* (Ebermayer), 1959
Homeyer	*Deutsche Juden als Bibliophilen und Antiquare*, 1963
IAusst	*Eine Ausstellung . . .* (*Die Insel*), 1965
Jouve	*Romain Rolland Vivant*, 1920
Jugend	*Jugend in Wien* (Müller-Einigen), 1948
K	Zweig letters to Abrão Koogan
KB	Zweig letters in the Ellen Key Archive, Stockholm

Kl	*Zweig: a Bibliography* (Klawiter), 1965
Leftwich	'Zweig and the World of Yesterday', 1958
Liber Amic	*Liber Amicorum Friderike Zweig* (ed. Zohn), 1952
Licht	*Das Licht der Welt: . . .* (Felix Braun), 1949
LM	Zweig letters to Liesl Monath
Mann *Br*	*Briefe*: I (*1889–1936*) and II (*1937–1947*)
Mus Land	*Das musische Land* (Felix Braun), 1952
Neumann	*Ein leichtes Leben: . . .*, 1963
Parandowski	'Erinnerungen an Stefan Zweig', 1961
Poeten	*Meine Freunde die Poeten* (Kesten), 1959
R	*Zweig* (Rieger), 1928
Roth	Zweig letters to Joseph Roth
S	*Zweig* (Specht), 1927
Sch	Zweig letters in the Schiller Nationalmuseum
Sp	*Zweig: Spiegelungen . . .* (ed. Fitzbauer), 1959
StB	Zweig letters in the Stadtbibliothek, Vienna
Stern	*La Mort de Stefan Zweig*, 1942
Str	*Strauss/Zweig: Briefwechsel* (ed. Schuh), 1957
Suche	*Auf der Suche nach einem Weg* (Klaus Mann), 1931
TMArch	Correspondence between Zweig and Thomas Mann
Treb	*Chronicle of a Life* (Trebitsch), 1953
UB	*Zweig: Unbekannte Briefe . . .* (Selden-Goth), 1964
Uhlman	*The Making of an Englishman*, 1960
Vallentin	'Stefan Zweig', 1947
Wendepunkt	*Der Wendepunkt: . . .* (Klaus Mann), 1960
Wolff	*Briefwechsel eines Verlegers*, 1966
Wulf	*Literatur und Dichtung im Dritten Reich*, 1966
WvG	*Die Welt von Gestern* (Stefan Zweig)
Zuckmayer	*Als wär's ein Stück von mir: Erinnerungen*, 1966
ZE	Correspondence received by Zweig (Zweig Estate, London)
ZwV	*Zwischen den Völkern: . . .* (Rolland), 1954

'Your written works are only a third of yourself'
Friderike to Stefan Zweig, July 1930

'The greatest thing in the world is to know how to be for oneself'
Montaigne, I. xxxviii

I. The Golden Age of Security 1881–1904

'Nowhere was it easier to be a European, and I know that it is this city, which already in the time of Marcus Aurelius had defended the Roman, the universal spirit, that taught me early to prize the conception of the community as the highest ideal of my life.' *Die Welt von Gestern*

'It was easier then! Everything was secure. Every stone lay in its allotted place. The streets of life were well paved. The secure roofs rested on the walls of the houses. But today . . . the stones lie on the streets askew and tumbled and in dangerous piles, and the roofs have holes in them, and every man has to find out for himself which road to take and which house to enter.'
Joseph Roth, *Radetzkymarsch*

I

'Everything had its norm, its allotted measure and weight.' *Die Welt von Gestern*

The Vienna into which Stefan Zweig was born on 28 November 1881 seemed the essence of stability and security. The *großer Krach*, the great financial crisis of 1873, just at the time of the Vienna World Exhibition, was very much a thing of the past, and a prosperous society at the heart of a Europe at peace turned its attention away from politics and towards lighter things.

Franz-Josef at the hunt near Gödöllö; *Phèdre* with Charlotte Wolter in the Burgtheater; Johann Strauss's new operetta *Der lustige Krieg* at the Theater an der Wien, with the new discovery Alexander Girardi; the Gallmeyer's skit *Sarah und Bernhardt* coming hard on the heels of the great tragedienne's personal appearance in Vienna—these were more important to the newspaper readers of the day than the petty difficulties of the Taaffe Ministry at home, or, further afield, the complications of the Danube Question. The theatre, music, the opera; the fiacres in spring along the chestnut alley of the Prater; the city, which under Franz-Josef's guidance had burst its medieval bonds only twenty years before, spreading fast north, west, and south, already with a million inhabitants, its Ring the symbol of an era of peaceful pomp, the centre and capital of an Imperium uniting the most diverse of peoples with the minimum of strife—it was the last phase of Vienna's existence as an Imperial city, to end in the catastrophe of 1914, but small wonder that at the time it promised to last for ever.

The boom at the beginning of the seventies had attracted to the capital many businessmen from the provinces, among them Joseph Brettauer. His family, originally from Germany, had followed banking and business success to many corners of Europe; and he himself, born in Hohenems in the Vorarlberg, had lived about twenty years in Ancona (where his second daughter Ida was born, and the Vatican had been numbered among his clients) before moving to Vienna. He took one of the splendid houses between the Hofburg and the Mariahilferstrasse, opposite the Kunsthistorisches Museum, then under construction on the Ring. A hard, strong face shows in the photograph taken a few years before his death in 1881, the simple black frock-coat over baggy trousers and wrinkled boots giving little hint of the wealth he had gradually acquired, and which provided an ample dowry for Ida on her marriage, soon after their arrival in Vienna, to Moritz Zweig.

The Zweig apartment at 14 Schottenring showed perhaps more sign of prosperity. Moritz, the son of a trader in finished goods, came from a Jewish community in Moravia which, unlike the Jews of Galicia, had emerged from the isolation of the ghetto and become 'progressive'. He himself had started, in his thirtieth year, a small weaving mill in Reichenberg in Bohemia, which, under his slow and methodical direction, developed over the years into one of the great undertakings of the Bohemian textile industry that dominated all Austria and the Balkans. Like his father-in-law, he was a careful, safety-first businessman, becoming rich not by exploitation of boom conditions but by quiet living and judicious ploughing-back of his accumulating capital. 'His greatest pride in his lifetime was that no-one had ever seen his name on a promissory note or a draft, and that his accounts were always on the credit side of the ledger in the Creditanstalt—'needless to say, the safest of all banks', wrote his son many years later. But his wife, of the more cosmopolitan Brettauer stock, flightier in her ways perhaps from her early years in Italy, brought a racier, more social atmosphere to the Schottenring flat, where Stefan, the second son, was born, and later to their larger apartment at 17 Rathausstrasse. Now a millionaire in one of the more stable currencies of Europe, Moritz Zweig had changed his way of life but little. He was well educated, spoke both French and English, played the piano well, and was socially more presentable than many of his colleagues, but he neither sought nor accepted any title or office, honour or dignity. Comfort without ostentation, to possess wealth but not to show it, was the principle of his life. The contrast with his wife is clearly shown in a photograph of the eighties: the neat and sober black coat and striped trousers beside the lace-trimmed black satin, jewellery, fan, and elaborate hairstyle of the handsome Ida. It was a contrast Stefan was to use (intensified almost to the point of caricature) in his *Novelle, Untergang eines Herzens*.

Fashion and social life played a great part in his mother's existence in Vienna, and Stefan, by nature more inclined to his father's outlook, and his elder brother Alfred were often the victims of her whims over their dress. The amused, almost cynical tolerance his father showed towards her was not calculated to instil in Stefan an attitude of respect. An early menopause, shortly after Stefan's birth, and the deafness with which she was afflicted while still quite young, tended to confirm her determination to get her own way, and to strengthen the obstinacy which Stefan inherited from her. It is not hard to understand the attraction for him in later years of the ideal of a 'silent woman', or his preference for light, careless, and comfortable clothing.

The Zweig ménage was in many ways typical of the Jewish upper middle classes of Vienna. The city's tradition was a cosmopolitan one, and it had been for centuries the confluence of the streams of European culture; now, in the days of awakening liberalism and of financial upsurge, the great Jewish money houses—Fries, Arnstein, Pereira—had taken a place of honour in the new society, and were closely followed by the wealthy Jewish families of the middle class. From its beginnings in banking, the Brettauer clan had spread over the world—Paris, Italy, New York, Vienna—and now included not merely small merchants or commission brokers but prominent lawyers, directors, bankers, and doctors. Security, solidity, provision for the future were the virtues of this family, as of the Zweigs; but neither thought merely of money-making. Wealth to them was a stepping-stone to the 'culture' of the upper classes. Though it was often superficial, this culture assumed for families like the Zweigs enormous importance as a status symbol, an importance that was decisive for Stefan's vocation as a writer. Had he been the elder of the two sons, he would certainly have been expected to succeed to the business: but his early promise as a writer, sealed when he was twenty with a piece in the leading Vienna daily, the *Neue Freie Presse*, probably weighed more with his father than would have any competence in office or factory. Imperial Vienna, peaceful, politically unambitious, assimilating the most contrasting cultures, was a particularly favourable ground for this strong trait in the Jewish character, the urge to rise above mere money.

It was a well-protected life for the two Zweig boys. Stefan, the less obedient, given to sometimes uncontrollable tantrums, was, it is true, in frequent conflict with his self-willed mother. As so often happens, he was closer to his grandmother Brettauer, who had moved in with the Zweigs after the death of her husband in 1881. There was little room, however, in their well-ordered lives for bad behaviour (though one of Stefan's friends recalled

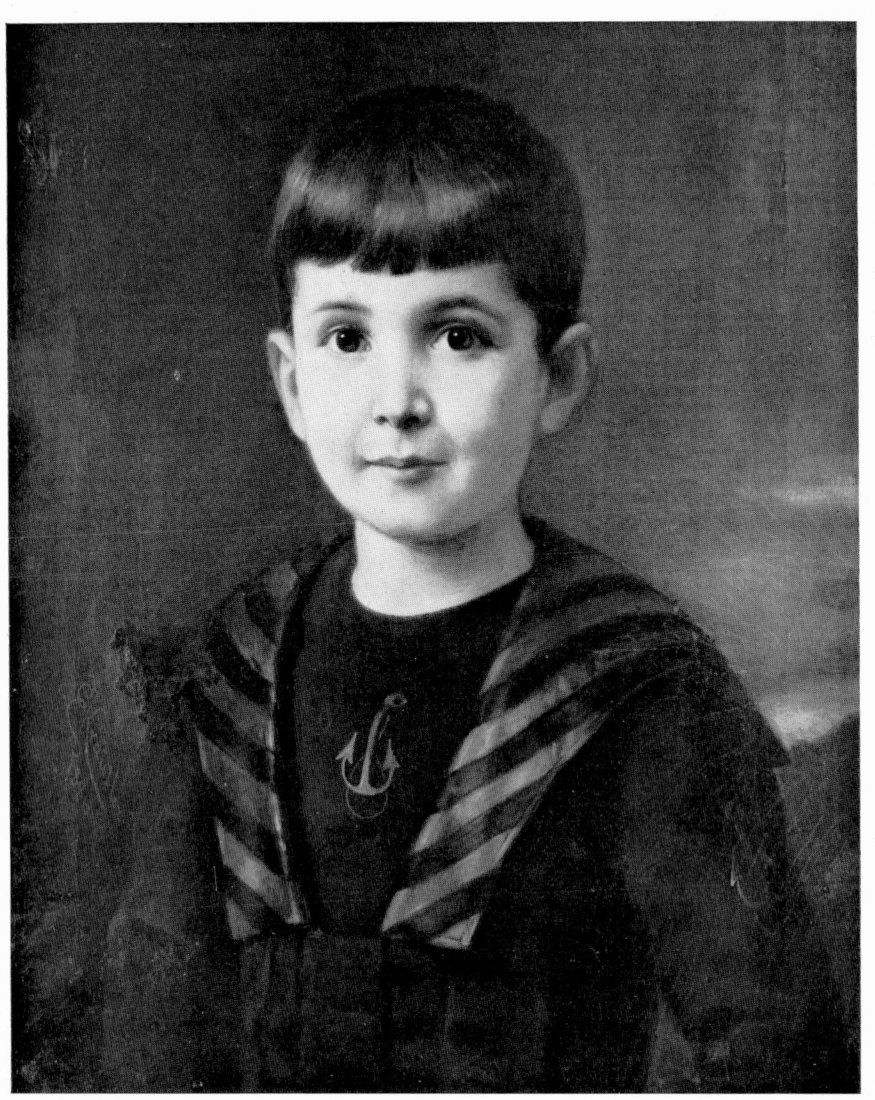

STEFAN ZWEIG, aged four

once discovering the brothers on the floor of the parental carriage playing cards).[1] School, governesses, disciplined walks in the park, a drive with their parents in the afternoon (his father remembered with pride the day when the Crown Princess herself stopped in the Prater to chat to the attractive little lad); in summer to 'the country'—a fashionable inland spa like Marienbad, one of the big hotels in the Austrian Alps, or a smaller lakeside resort like Pörtschach on the Wörthersee (where in 1889 Stefan's path crossed for the first time that of his future wife Friderike). A long way removed from real life, in fact; and it is easy to understand his feeling of relief when as a university student in Vienna and Berlin he was able to escape from this hothouse atmosphere. It was a life of great loneliness, cut off from the freedom usual today, a life of inhibitions and prohibitions, speaking when spoken to, in a world set apart from that of the adults. (He pointed out forty years later to Friderike, not without some bitterness, the modest eating-houses in Marienbad to which the children of those days were taken by their governesses, while their parents enjoyed the expensive restaurants.)

It was conducive all the same to great precociousness—'I can recall how natural it was to change from one language to another at my aunt's table in Paris'[2]—and a devouring eagerness to discover the world outside. There is a good deal of Stefan in the lawyer's son Edgar, in his *Novelle*, *Brennendes Geheimnis*: running away from his mother at Semmering and taking the train for the first time alone, he suddenly realizes the atmosphere of comfort to which he has been accustomed. All around him there are dark abysses his gaze has never reached before, and he looks with different eyes out of the compartment, as though seeing reality for the first time: those houses flying by have people in them, rich, poor, happy, unhappy, with longings and desires like his; the railwaymen by the line are not the mere toys he thought them before, but human beings, each with a destiny. Children with this background ('ten or twenty thousand families like my parents lived in Vienna in that last century of assured values')[3] developed

[1] Letter to Friderike Zweig from Felix Frankl, 14 Mar. 1942.

[2] *WvG* 21.

[3] *WvG* 17.

early and grew impatient of the parental regime and of a society which seemed to have no time for youth.

Above all, families like the Zweigs and the Brettauers were European in their outlook, and had largely lost their specifically Jewish character. For the greater part of his life Stefan Zweig regarded his Jewishness as of secondary importance, and his Austrian nationality as scarcely more than an administrative formality. There was no religion in his home, and nothing of nationalism. For no one was it easier for Europe to become both faith and fatherland.

2

> '*We formed as it were the last generation of that fanaticism for art which is today hardly to be reconstructed. . . . Hard on our heels this passion transformed itself among the younger people to one for sport, exercise, they have become stronger, more capable than we, but I do not envy them for it.*'
> *Autobiographische Skizze*, 1922

Despite his father's wealth, Stefan seems to have had no special schooling. There were governesses at home, but they were more nannies than tutors; and after five years at a normal elementary school he entered the Maximilian Gymnasium in the Wasagasse (now the Wasagymnasium) at the age of ten. Of his eight years in this 'treadmill of learning' he wrote in bitter terms in his autobiography. An academic education was considered essential for the children of well-to-do families then, but the road to the university and the coveted doctorate was long and hard. The classics, English, French, Italian, geometry, physics, and the rest left very little time for bodily development, sport or walks, or indeed any recreation as it is known today. Zweig at the end of his life could not avoid a feeling of envy at the enormously greater freedom, happiness, and independence enjoyed then by children at school; it was scarcely credible to him

> how naturally they chat as equals with their teachers, how they hurry to school without a care, whereas we were constantly filled with a feeling of inadequacy; how they may freely express the desires and inclinations of their young and curious souls both at home and in

school . . . whereas we, as soon as we stepped into the hated buildings, were forced to cringe lest we strike our foreheads against an invisible yoke.

For him and his fellows school was 'compulsion, ennui, dreariness, a place where we had to assimilate the "science of the not-worth-knowing" in exactly measured proportions'.[1] It seemed to him part of the system of society of those days: the old State, ruled by an aged emperor and almost equally aged ministers, was instinctively against youth, with its desire for haste and radical change, and the young man who wished to get on was compelled to try every trick in the endeavour to appear older than he was. At school the teachers represented the authority by which youth had to be held in check, totally lacking in contact with the pupils. At sixty Zweig found himself quite unable to remember either their names or their faces.

When the fiftieth anniversary of this institution was to be celebrated in 1922, and he was asked, as a now distinguished Old Boy, to deliver the address of honour, he declined: he felt no reason for gratitude to this school, and every word in such a eulogy would have been a lie.[2] Although he sent a few verses for the *Festschrift* published on the occasion, neatly expressing the customary clichés about schooldays (it seemed a prison at the time, but the stricter disciplines of later life make us look back with longing to those days, and so forth),[3] he was probably far more honest when he wrote later 'the only true moment of happiness for which I have to thank my school was the day when I was able to shut the door on it for ever'.

He was self-willed and obstinate, and even in his very early years his gentle nature could often be transformed by sudden fits of temper. This rebelliousness showed itself, of course, also in school, though his brother was usually able to prevent the teachers' complaints from reaching their father. The discipline there, the whole educational regime, was a constant pressure towards conformism: 'not to form us inwardly but to fit us with as little

[1] *WvG* 38. [2] *WvG* 39.

[3] 'Wir sagten Schule . . .', in *Wasagymnasium: 50 Jahre einer Wiener Mittelschule, Festschrift*, 1922, 7 (*Ausst* 36).

opposition as possible into the ordered scheme, not to increase our energy but to discipline it and level it off'.[1] It was probably no mere chance that the concept of the inferiority complex was first formulated by men who had themselves gone through the Austrian education of those days. For Zweig, it was to this very pressure that he felt he owed the early emergence of a passion to be free, 'vehement to a degree scarcely known to present-day youth'[2]—and a hatred for all forms of authority which lasted to his death.

Sport—'the scourge of the coming generation', as Hermann Bahr put it about the turn of the century[3]—was virtually unknown to Zweig's contemporaries. *Mens sana in corpore sano* was thought to be adequately catered for by a ten-minute pause after four or five hours in the class-room, or an odd spell in an unventilated gymnasium. Stefan was in any case of no particular physique, and to him, as to many of his friends, bodily activity seemed a pure waste of time. He gave up skating, and even the money his parents allowed him for dancing lessons he spent on books. It was the arts that fired the enthusiasm of these lads as they reached fourteen and fifteen, and the dull curriculum of rote-learning began to bore them. Outside the dreary walls of the Gymnasium lay the exciting city, with its theatres, bookshops, university, and music; and the discovery in themselves, by Stefan and two or three others in his class, of literary or musical aptitudes and interests quickly infected the rest. Although chance might have led this schoolboy enthusiasm in other directions, like philately or socialism, such interest in and passion for the theatre, art, and literature was perhaps natural in the Vienna of those days. The Opera and the Burgtheater were the subjects of constant discussion among these boys' elders, and the newspapers gave special space to cultural events, their front pages, indeed, showing equal favour to the *feuilleton* and to the news of the day. Moreover, here there was no opposition from 'authority'. Literature and the theatre, unlike cards or girls, were regarded as innocent passions.

And their passion became a mania—in Stefan's case probably decisive for his future development. They missed no *première* at

[1] *WvG* 43. [2] *WvG* 44. [3] *Jugend* 60.

the Burgtheater, standing in line from three in the afternoon to secure their *Stehplätze* (it says much for the indifference of their teachers not to have remarked the suspicious frequency with which simultaneous illness would strike down the majority of the class). They watched for the famous on the street, collected their autographs, had their hair cut at the theatre barber's to amass gossip about Sonnenthal or the Wolter, even (through the connections of one of their number) penetrated to the stage during rehearsals ('the thrill of treading those boards exceeded that of Dante when he ascended into the holy circles of Paradise').[1] They read everything they could get hold of, in a fever to know all that had occurred in every field of art. It remained a surprise for Zweig, as he looked back at the end of his life, how much they learned through this exaggerated literary passion, 'how prematurely we acquired a faculty of critical discernment through our endless discussion and analysis'.[1] In school, while their literature master Adolf Lichtenheld droned through his lecture on 'Naive und Sentimentalische Dichtung', they read Nietzsche and Strindberg under the desk; Rilke's poems were between the covers of their Latin grammars; and in their mathematics notebooks they copied out poems from borrowed books. The public libraries were their hunting-ground and the cafés their club, where they ferreted out and discussed the latest.

For it was the latest, the newest, the most unusual, the most extravagant that was their special quest and the subject of their eager discussion. Of the small early editions of the works of Stefan George and Rilke, for example, not more than a few copies could have been in Vienna then, and none of the official literary critics had even mentioned Rilke's name: but every word and line was known to these schoolboys, the ideal audience for a poet with their curiosity, critical understanding, and quickness to rapture. Thanks to the newspapers and magazines available to them in rich diversity in the cafés they haunted (the *Revue de France* alongside the *Burlington Magazine* and the *Neue Rundschau*), their horizons were of the widest. They heard of every new book as soon as it was published and every production wherever it

[1] *WvG* 49.

occurred. Baudelaire, Walt Whitman, Paul Valéry twenty years before he was known in France, were familiar to them at sixteen and seventeen.

Like all young people, they sought out the new because it was new, but there was more to this passion than that. They sensed the changes in values the turn of the century was to bring; and above all, the irresistible attraction of the new art for them was that it was the work of young men. They had living proof that it was not necessary to be advanced in years to be great in achievement. Gustav Mahler had been made Director of the Opera at thirty-eight, Gerhart Hauptmann dominated the German theatre at thirty. In Vienna itself the group called 'Young Vienna' was forming—Arthur Schnitzler, Peter Altenberg, Hermann Bahr, and Richard Beer-Hofmann among them; the satire of Karl Kraus had just begun to pour out in *Die Fackel* ('may our torch shine forth in a land on which—unlike the Empire of Charles the Fifth—the sun never rises').[1] And, before them all, the 'wonder child', Hugo von Hofmannsthal, whose early verses, written under the pseudonym 'Loris' while he was still at school, had astounded Bahr and Schnitzler: 'unique mastery of form', as Schnitzler said to Zweig, coupled with a knowledge of the world 'which could only have come from a magical intuition' in so callow a boy.[2]

3

'In a small way I have already experienced what it is to write with set teeth.'

Zweig to Franzos

Like most of his class-mates, Zweig began early in these school years to scribble. By the time he was sixteen he had had his first poems printed in *Die Gesellschaft* in Berlin, the leading magazine of the Moderns, and in Maximilian Harden's *Zukunft*. Early in 1898 he was in correspondence with Karl-Emil Franzos, editor of *Deutsche Dichtung*, also in Berlin, over contributions of verse and occasional pieces for that periodical. 'The sweetest smell on earth—sweeter than the oil of the Rose of Shiraz—was the smell of

[1] Kraus in the first issue of *Die Fackel*, 1899. [2] *WvG* 54.

printer's ink';[1] and in his last two years at school he was indefatigable in sending in his poems to a whole range of journals and newspapers—*Berliner Morgenpost, Prager Tageblatt, Magazin für Literatur, Südwestdeutsche Rundschau, Badische Landeszeitung*—many of which accepted and published them. He tried his hand also at short stories and *Novellen*, though here he seems to have exercised a greater critical faculty, and it was not until a year or two later, during his time at university, that he felt able to risk their appearance in print.

One indeed, called *Peter der Dichter*, which by June 1899 had reached almost book proportions, he offered to Franzos for *Deutsche Dichtung*, in which he thought it might take up twenty-five columns: the story of a worker-poet who is lionized by society, but finds he cannot take the burden of the world of fashion and returns to his former condition.[2] Neither the manuscript nor the comments of Franzos have been preserved, but it seems clear from his remarks the following year to the editor (who had just refused a later work, a *Wiener Novelle*, the first version of *Erika Ewald*) that his own critical appraisal of his efforts was no less stringent than that of Franzos.

> I realize . . . that this Novelle, as with most of my pieces, is slapdash and over-hasty, but . . . I find that when the last word is written I can make no more corrections, in fact I do not even check through for spelling and punctuation. This is a silly and obstinate way to go about things, and it is completely clear to me that it will prevent me from ever achieving anything great. I do not know the art of being conscientious and diligent. . . . I have burned hundreds of my manuscripts—but I have never altered or rewritten a single line. It is a misfortune not easily to be altered, since it is not a purely external thing but probably lies deep in my character.[3]

He could in fact hardly have been wider of the mark, for nothing is more characteristic of his later works than the tremendous process of distillation through which they have passed: scarcely a line of the original version remains unchanged, and his pride, especially in the biographies and critical studies, was to conceal

[1] *WvG* 96. [2] Letter to Franzos, 21 June 1899 (StB).

[3] Letter to Franzos, 3 July 1900 (StB).

more than he revealed. But at nineteen, with an already remarkable output of published verse to his credit, he really seemed to remain sceptical about his powers. Indeed, as he continued in the same letter to Franzos, he thought it lucky that writing was not to be his career, and that he had never thought for one moment of becoming famous, or even known.

> I have written under five or six pseudonyms, always different. Perhaps if I had not done so, my name would now be known a little; but this would not have given me much pleasure. I really publish only as a spur to further work and to avoid being merely a dilettante: certainly not out of a desire for fame, for I am completely convinced that at best my talent is a small one, for the sketch or the lyric, by no means original and still rather dependent on my reading.[1]

He may have been disingenuous here, but from what is still available of his work of those early years there would seem ample justification for this judgement, wrong though it was to prove. The modest tone of the letter, with its disavowal of any hankering after fame, was at any rate characteristic of him.

Another interest began to emerge during his schooldays, one which was to absorb him in later years: the collection of autographs and manuscripts. Like all enthusiastic boys he found great satisfaction in securing the signatures of those he revered (Brahms was one of his victims on a Vienna street-corner), and had begun his collection in this run-of-the-mill fashion when he was fourteen. It then happened (we have no details of when or how) that someone made him a present of a few autograph manuscripts, most of which he in turn gave away, keeping only those of authors he really loved, and restricting his collection from then on to original manuscripts of poems, prose works, and music rather than mere signatures, letters, or ephemera. An early acquisition was a small manuscript of Hebbel's. In February 1898, in one of his earliest extant letters, he writes to Franzos: 'In view of your great reputation as a collector of autographs, which will soon approach that accorded you as a poet, I take the liberty of sending you one or two rather interesting letters, which are of small

[1] Letter to Franzos, 3 July 1900 (StB).

value to me since I collect only manuscripts and original poems'—asking of Franzos in return something of his. He adds that he also possesses autographs of Goethe, Wieland, Anzengruber, and Beethoven.[1] It was the beginning of a collection which by 1930 had become unique and immensely valuable, and whose fascination for Zweig was its illustration of great minds at their moments of creation, the instant of the first committing to paper, and then the process of correction and amendment: to show, in Goethe's words, that 'in art as in life nothing stays finished, there is only the infinite in movement'.

4

'The day had four-and-twenty hours, and each of them belonged to me.' *Die Welt von Gestern*

When in 1899 the long-desired moment finally came and he was able to slam the door of the hated Gymnasium behind him, there was no obstacle to his enrolment at the university. His father spoke to friends with pride of the praise his *Matura* work in German had earned from his teachers.[2] Alfred as the elder brother was already installed in the family business, and for Stefan the next step was a doctorate—'any one would do'. There was as yet no thought, or indeed necessity, of a career, but his parents, though still somewhat reluctant, realized they would not be able to discourage his passion for literature. For him it was a new life that opened up. He could break free, not only from the discipline of school, but also from that of home: *universitas vitae*, a few years of complete freedom for his own life and for his endeavours in art. He read philosophy, with the history of literature as his second subject, but did little work in the accepted sense and was rarely to be seen at lectures. On the other hand, despite his modesty and uncertainty over his future, he worked very hard to establish a solid base for his interests: reading widely, writing continually, and above all developing literary contacts and friendships, many of which lasted for the rest of his life—Adolph Donath, Max and

[1] Letter to Franzos, 18 Feb. 1898 (StB).

[2] Letter to Friderike Zweig from Felix Frankl, 14 Mar. 1942.

Victor Fleischer, Franz Servaes, Erwin Guido Kolbenheyer, the artist E. M. Lilien, Jacques Hegner, Franz Evers, Richard Dehmel.

He changed rooms several times, but the addresses which are known were all in the VIIIth District of Vienna—its nearest approach to a Latin Quarter, the Josefstadt. One, probably during his first year, was at 2 Buchfeldgasse; another apparently at 9 Frankenbergasse.[1] In 1902 and 1903–4 he had rooms at 6 Tulpengasse. To those who knew him then his way of life was superficially of the most bohemian: rising late (though it was usually work rather than dissipation that determined his hours), cigarette and cigar ends and ash everywhere, unwashed coffee cups, unmade bed, books and manuscripts lying around. He was soon at the centre of a circle at the Café Beethoven, and a regular caller at the Café Rathaus in the Reichsrathstrasse and at the Café Reyl, which had by then taken the place, as a literary haunt, of the Griensteidl of the nineties.

I found him [writes Victor Fleischer describing their first meeting in the autumn of 1902] unshaven, although it must have been about eleven in the morning, and only half-dressed, in a simple student's room in which the bed was in disorder, as though he had just got up. I mention these details of our first encounter deliberately, because I was to learn later how characteristic they were for Zweig. I knew that he came from a very wealthy family, that he had been brought up in middle-class luxury, and that while still a young student he already disposed of not inconsiderable private means, thanks to a legacy from his grandparents. And yet he was living in a furnished room, scarcely better or more expensive than the one he helped me to find the same day—a typical *Bude* like those of many thousands of other Vienna University students. Why? He was on the best of terms with his family, and lunched every day at the Rathausstrasse—but for the rest he wanted to be master of his own time and to be completely free. And if the state of this room so late in the morning, and his own appearance, gave the impression that Zweig had only just got up, I was soon to learn that he already had several hours of serious work behind him, and that he did not shave or finish dressing only by way of compelling himself to stay in and not let himself be disturbed in his work by social contacts.—And, in the same way as he had withdrawn

[1] *Jugend* 421 and 446 ff.

himself from the unimportant duties of the parental home, without cutting himself off from his family, so he would live among a circle of those of his own age, spending hours talking in the cafés, to disappear suddenly for days or even weeks completely from our company if his University studies or some literary work of his own made any distraction or disturbance unwelcome to him.... A desire for economy, or a contempt for comfort, were not the reasons for his simple way of living. He knew how to value comfort, but more important than any comfort to him was unburdened liberty and personal freedom.[1]

An early project which occupied him a great deal during his first year was the publication of a volume of his verse. He had actually toyed with the idea while still at school, and had found a publisher, but on Donath's advice ('I am still grateful to him for this') had postponed it. In March 1900 he mentioned to Franzos that he had two volumes planned, and inquired about the possibilities with the Concordia Verlag in Berlin.[2] By the end of the year he had his first selection ready: 'I have published to date 150 or 200 poems, written double that number, and now have put together a volume under the title *Silberne Saiten* which contains—50: i.e. a most stringent selection. You will judge how stringent from the fact that only a minority are from those published in *Deutsche Dichtung*', he wrote to Franzos in November. 'But it is I believe a good volume and I am therefore in touch with one of the best publishers to produce it.'[3] Concordia, which Franzos apparently recommended, did not appeal to him, not only because he did not consider their productions impressive enough (he was fastidious over this, and wanted an original title-page, with the poems printed one to a page), but also because he was offering that firm a prose *Broschüre*, and did not feel he could approach a publisher to whom he was so far unknown with the two works at the same time. What he wanted was a production like Schuster & Loeffler's for Adolph Donath, or one of E. Diederichs's books.[3] In the end it was Schuster & Loeffler he approached—the precursors of the Insel-Verlag, and publishers

[1] Victor Fleischer, 'Erinnerung an Stefan Zweig' (*Sp* 36 ff.).
[2] Letter to Franzos, 17 Mar. 1900 (StB).
[3] Letter to Franzos, 2 Nov. 1900 (StB).

of Liliencron, Dehmel, Bierbaum, and Mombert—and the slim volume *Silberne Saiten* appeared under their imprint, with a title-page by Hugo Steiner and dedicated to his parents, in February 1901.

He had serious doubts himself of its success, but it was in fact very well received, making 'Freude und Freunde'. The publishers stipulated an option for subsequent works by him; Dehmel and Liliencron noticed it favourably; of forty reviews he had seen by the following October, only one ('a vulgarly witty five-line criticism by Sigmar Mehring' in the *Berliner Tageblatt*) was in any way adverse, the rest being full of praise and devoting whole essays and *feuilletons* to the book.[1] 'We have seldom had in our hands a first work which could so pride itself on its freedom from the faults by which one usually recognizes the beginner', wrote the *Norddeutsche Allgemeine*; and the *Revue Allemande*: 'a quiet, solemn beauty pervades the lines of this Young-Vienna poet, a translucence rarely to be found in first works. . . . Zweig is a virtuoso in technique, each single poem gives us fresh opportunity to enjoy the fineness of his diction, of immeasurable harmony and wealth of imagery.' Rilke sent him in gratitude a copy of a special edition of his latest poems, and two of the *Silberne Saiten* were later set to music by Max Reger (Op. 97 and 104).[2]

It was a success far greater than he had dared expect; but he realized full well that these verses of 'vague premonition and instinctive feeling' were created not out of his own experience but rather from a 'passion for language'.[3] He freely admitted later that they had no other origin than 'a playful urge, perhaps a vanity, to versify';[4] and he not only never permitted the volume to be reprinted but also excluded the whole of *Silberne Saiten* from his *Collected Poems* published in 1924. They are smooth, able verses, good examples of the type which found favour at the time; but there is nothing of the magical intuition of Hofmannsthal—at best, secondhand emotion refurbished in tranquillity. Erich Mühsam's severe judgement in 1911 is not altogether unjustified: 'a book that, with its obtrusive sickly-sweetness and insipid

[1] Letter to Franzos, 29 Apr. 1901 (StB).
[2] *WvG* 98.
[3] *WvG* 97.
[4] *Literarisches Echo*, vol. 17, no. 4, 15 Nov. 1914.

exaggeration, would hardly be worth mentioning, were it not typical of the pretentious manner which is spreading ever more widely through the Young-Vienna movement and which seeks to impress by mere playing with form.'[1]

At all events it set a seal upon his growing reputation as one of the more promising young poets of Vienna, and within three years he was considered worthy to join the eminent contributors to Donath's *Festschrift* on the occasion of Liliencron's sixtieth birthday.[2] He was not content, however, to remain classed only as a young talent in lyric poetry, and was more determined than ever to make his mark also as a prose writer. The fate of the *Broschüre* he had offered to Concordia (which he described in letters towards the end of 1900 as an article on Viennese lyric poets) is unknown; but he had a number of *Novellen* on the stocks in the following two years, and one was finally published, in 1902 or soon after, in Berthold Feivel's *Jüdischer Almanach* in Berlin. He had completed it by June 1900, and tried first to interest Franzos in it for *Deutsche Dichtung*, being unwilling, as he said, to offer it to a purely Jewish journal, because it lacked any form of nationalistic *Tendenz*.[3] The story, *Im Schnee*, describes the fate of a Jewish community in the Middle Ages, fleeing before the Flagellants and finally overwhelmed by a blizzard which brings them release from all earthly pain. It is a romantically conceived and romantically depicted episode, showing few signs of the craftsmanship which characterizes his later work, but none the less with strength and power in its narrative. It is noteworthy as treating one of the very few purely Jewish themes in Zweig's work; it is the forerunner of the dramatic poem *Jeremias*, and the legends *Rahel rechtet mit Gott* and *Der begrabene Leuchter*, of later years.[4]

[1] *Führer durch die moderne Literatur*, ed. Hanns Heinz Ewers; Globus Verlag, Berlin, 1911, 190.

[2] Poem 'Die Hände', in *Oesterreichische Dichter zum 60. Geburtstage Detlev von Liliencron*; Verlag Carl Konegen, Wien, 1904, 79.

[3] Letter to Franzos, 22 June 1900 (StB).

[4] *Im Schnee* was republished in 1963, edited by Erich Fitzbauer, with drawings by Fritz Fischer, in a limited edition of 500 signed by the artist, by the International Stefan Zweig Society, Vienna.

He had been thinking for some time of publishing a volume of *Novellen*. From the first summer vacation, in Marienbad in 1900, he sent Franzos a copy of one that had been published in the *Berliner Illustrierte*, and asked his opinion on a possible collection of eight or ten in book form, including the *Wiener Novelle* (*Die Liebe der Erika Ewald*) that Franzos had already rejected, and *Im Schnee*.[1] Again, from Ischl later the same month, he described yet another he had dashed off in a single day.[2] The project lingered, however, perhaps because of the criticism he received from the editor, and the volume *Erika Ewald*, with only four *Novellen*, did not appear until his last year at the university.

One of the early favourable reviews of *Silberne Saiten* appeared in the *Neue Freie Presse*, whose *feuilleton* was then under the editorship of Theodor Herzl. It had praised the 'soft blending of his forms, the gentle wash of his colours—not harsh gold but faint, tenderly glowing silver'. Zweig was encouraged later in 1901 to offer, not without some trepidation, an article on poetry for the paper, and has described the thrill with which he heard, when summoned for a personal interview with Herzl, that it had been accepted for the *feuilleton*.[3] To appear here, on the front page of the *NFP*, was the ambition of every writer of the day, and the competition for that honour was great. His acceptance was the beginning of an association which was to last twenty years, and of a life-long friendship with Franz Servaes, at that time art critic of the paper. Zweig achieved overnight a position of prominence in Viennese letters, and was particularly gratified to read Herzl's subsequent comment to the effect that Vienna need have no fears of a decadence in art, for besides Hofmannsthal there was a whole platoon of young talent in the city, with Stefan Zweig at its head.[4] A few months later the *NFP feuilleton* for 11 April 1902 carried his *Novelle*, *Die Wanderung* (to be collected in 1904 in the *Erika Ewald* volume), and on 12 October his essay on the

[1] Letter to Franzos, 1 Aug. 1900 (StB).

[2] Letter to Franzos, 29 Aug. 1900 (StB).

[3] *WvG* 104.

[4] Ibid. Otto Hauser, who thought he detected a striking similarity in character between Herzl and Zweig, wrote later that of all the young writers Herzl discussed with him Zweig was the only one on whom he set any real hopes (*Zeitgenossen über Herzl*, ed. Nussenblatt; Jüdischer Buch und Kunstverlag, Brünn, 1929, p. 51).

Belgian writer Camille Lemonnier. He had achieved a standing almost unheard of for a young man just twenty, and by the same stroke a somewhat unexpected security in relation to his parents. His father, impressed by this sudden rise to fame, readily agreed to his new proposition: that he should spend the second semester of the academic year 1901–2 at Berlin University.

5

'Verhaeren had attempted, the first among French poets, to give to Europe what Whitman had given to America: the creed of our age, the creed of the future.' *Die Welt von Gestern*

Despite these early successes, he was still uncertain of the direction in which he was going.

> My studies are in philosophy [he wrote to Franzos in December, 1901], and I am pursuing them with fair diligence and affection. Whether my future will lie in this field I do not yet know; at any rate I shall never be reduced to making money early. But I do not see much future in literature either. Journalism . . . I hate. . . . I can see at the moment no clear light for the future, but I am not really worrying too much about it: I still have two years of study, after that my year of military service (which I plan to spend abroad)—and by then something will have turned up. . . . The second semester I intend to pass in Berlin, somewhere hidden away and not in the literary world. . . . Hans Benzmann, S. Lublinski and the painter Lilien I know pretty well, and I should be well accredited in the *Neue Gemeinschaft*, not to mention the *Freie Literarische Vereinigung* and the *Kommenden* . . . but I doubt whether I have enough talent to dare to plunge into purely literary activity. I had a number of good notices of my book, but I don't trust that. And then—my eternal refrain—I have enough time to think about it. . . .[1]

What he sought in Berlin was a different sort of freedom, higher and more complete. Although he arrived armed with a number of letters of introduction, he made little use of them. He was after

[1] Letter to Franzos, 10 Dec. 1901 (StB).

'bad' society, in contrast to the proprieties of Vienna; feeling already that curiosity about men who live dangerously which accompanied him throughout his life, and the predilection for intense and unruly natures which marks so many of his stories—perhaps even himself exploring the dark abysses of perversion hinted at in his later *Novelle*, *Verwirrung der Gefühle*.

It seems more likely, however, that he was spectator rather than actor, and his experience of dangerous living vicarious rather than actual. His room, at least between April and June, was in the south-western suburbs at Klein-Zittau,[1] hardly at the centre of things; and his bohemianism, despite his protestations to Franzos, found its main expression in the literary and artistic world. Through Jacobowsky, who had published his first poem, he was introduced to the weekly meetings of the *Klub der Kommenden*, of which Jacobowsky was one of the founder members. In this heterogeneous circle, which met in a café on the Nollendorfer Platz, something after the fashion of the *Closerie des Lilas* in Paris, Germans from every social class (not only the bourgeois intellectuals who had been his associates in Vienna) mingled with exotic foreigners, Russians or Swedes; the old bohemian poet Peter Hille rubbed shoulders with the magnetic Rudolf Steiner. He found himself introduced into a society where every improbable character from naturalist fiction could be seen in the cafés, his table shared with heavy drinkers, homosexuals, or drug addicts. Here the idols were Ibsen and Zola, not, as in Vienna, Mallarmé and Baudelaire. He was in touch, at last, with real life, or so it seemed; and he found his self-confidence waning in this harsher light. He felt especially keenly the lack of reality in his *Novellen* and the soft outpourings of *Silberne Saiten*. A novel, almost finished (we have no record of its theme), was committed to the stove, and he resolved to follow the advice which Richard Dehmel had recently given him—'se faire la main' by undertaking translations from other languages.

He was fluent in French, rather less so in English, and while still at school had tried his hand at versions of French and Belgian poets. Before he went to Berlin he had collaborated with Camill

[1] Correspondence in ZE.

Hoffmann in the translation of a selection from Baudelaire,[1] which was published (Hermann Seemann Nachfolger, Leipzig) later in 1902 (interesting here that he deliberately omitted the more revolting realism of poems like 'La Charogne'). Now he threw himself into translation with a will, leaving aside almost all original work: a novel by Lemonnier, a short drama by Charles van Lerberghe, poems of Keats, William Morris, and W. B. Yeats, and in particular the works of Verlaine.[2] The French poet exercised an intense fascination, and he conceived the project of a small volume of selected poems in translation, undertaking the editing himself and writing a biographical introduction. The poets whose collaboration he sought displayed an impressive array of talent: among them Dehmel himself, Franz Evers,[3] Richard Schaukal, Otto Hauser, and Sigmar Mehring, together with the less well-known Klaus Klammer and Max Fleischer. Some of the translations had already been published elsewhere, but the selection was entirely his own, and many were done at his prompting specially for this collection, which Schuster & Loeffler put out towards the end of 1902.

The work of organizing and editing, stimulating others by his criticism and help, proved admirably suited to his temperament. Outstanding was the fifteen-page introduction, which showed Zweig's thorough mastery of his subject and a just appraisal of Verlaine's worth. The essay, which had to be omitted from the 1907 and 1911 enlarged editions for reasons of space, he early expanded to book form, and it appeared in 1905 as Volume 30 of Paul Remer's series of monographs, *Die Dichtung*, also under the Schuster & Loeffler imprint. But this shorter first version, in its finely chiselled prose, must rank high alongside his later work in the field of critical portraiture, the essays on Balzac, Dostoevsky, and Tolstoy.

With his usual modesty he included only three of his own translations in the anthology, most being from the pen of Dehmel and Evers. None of the longer translations he undertook during these

[1] Letters to Franzos, 4 July, 7 July, 29 Oct., and 5 Nov. 1901 (StB).

[2] *WvG* 116.

[3] Letters from Franz Evers, 11 Apr. 1902 and 11 July 1902 (ZE).

six months in Berlin seems to have been published, though some of the poems appeared in magazines, such as one of Elizabeth Barrett Browning's in *Deutsche Dichtung*.[1] There is no doubt, however, that Dehmel's advice was of immense value to him at this stage in his development, not merely in improving his own facility in both prose and verse, but in preparing him for the important role he was to play in European letters—that of the interpreter and introducer of foreign writers and their work to the German-speaking peoples. 'In this modest activity as go-between for outstanding treasures of art I experienced for the first time the assurance of doing something truly useful, a justification of my existence.'[2]

In this work much of his attention was drawn to the Belgians. While still at school he had discovered the poet Émile Verhaeren for himself, acquiring one of the first books, *Les Flamandes*, of a poet then unknown in Germany and Austria and often confused in the literature of the day with Verlaine. A chance introduction, it might be said, though he was sure later that it could not have been mere chance that led him to the man with whom he felt so strong an affinity. At school too he had attempted the translation of some of Verhaeren's poems, and had written to him in 1898 to ask permission for their publication. The vitality manifested in Belgian art and letters around the turn of the century,[3] of which Verhaeren, with his Whitmanesque approach to life, seemed to Zweig to be in the van, held a magical attraction for him, and he felt impelled to visit this 'little land between the languages' when he left Berlin for the summer vacation of 1902.

Lemonnier he found at once on arrival in Brussels, but to his great disappointment Verhaeren, to meet whom was his chief purpose, was away. His disappointment was happily short-lived, for it happened that the day he chose to take up Lemonnier's introduction to the sculptor Charles van der Stappen was the

[1] 'Blasse Liebe', in *Deutsche Dichtung*, xxxi (Oct. 1901/Mar. 1902) (Kl 1425).

[2] *WvG* 116.

[3] 'In general at the present time the greatest poetic power and deepest feeling for the world appears to manifest itself among the Belgian poets of Germanic origin: Rodenbach, . . . Verhaeren, Lerberghe' (Hofmannsthal to von Andrian, *Briefwechsel*, S. Fischer. Frankfurt am Main, 1967, p. 141).

very one which Verhaeren had appointed for his final sitting for a bust by his host.

For the first time I felt the firm clasp of his vigorous hand, for the first time met his clear kindly glance. He arrived, as he always did, brimming over with enthusiasm and the experiences of the day. As he fell to on his meal he began to talk. . . . He always came home like this, exalted with some chance happening, full of everything he had seen and done, and this enthusiasm had become a hallowed way of life for him; it sprang like a flame from his lips, incisive gestures illustrating his words, a wondrous ability to re-create, in rhythm and form, what he had seen. With the first word he went straight to the essence of people, because he was himself completely open, open to everything new, rejecting nothing, ready for every individual. It seemed as though he projected his whole being towards you. . . . He knew as yet nothing of me, yet already he was full of gratitude for my inclination, already he offered me his trust simply because he heard I was close to his work. And in spite of myself all shyness faded before the stormy onslaught of his being. I felt myself free, as never before, in the face of this unknown, open man. His gaze, strong, steely and clear, unlocked the heart.[1]

It was a religious, almost mystical experience for the young Zweig. He had met his first truly European poet, an apostle of a freer and more joyous humanity than he had yet encountered in Vienna or Berlin, the mainspring of whose productive force was a boundless enthusiasm for life. 'A decisive experience for me . . . like Dehmel and Rilke an example of deeper significance in the moral than in the literary sense.'[2] Hesitant till then, full of doubt whether a life devoted to 'nur Literatentum' could be worth while, he felt himself now suddenly fired by a determination to follow Verhaeren, to serve this man and his work.

Thereafter hardly a year passed without their meeting, either at Verhaeren's cottage 'Caillou-qui-bique' or in Paris, until the summer of 1914, when Zweig was compelled, before his usual visit, to take the last Orient Express for home from Ostende. Through these years he spent much of his time on the translation

[1] *Erinnerungen an Émile Verhaeren*; Privatdruck, Christian Reisser's Söhne, Wien, 1917, 16–17.
[2] Quoted H 26.

of Verhaeren's works. *Ausgewählte Gedichte* appeared with Schuster & Loeffler during his last year at University; in 1910, with the Insel-Verlag, the ambitious three-volume edition, comprising his monograph, the selected poems, and three dramas; and in 1912 a selection of the poems written since 1900, entitled *Hymnen an das Leben.*

6

'The examination was not made difficult for me.'
Die Welt von Gestern

The Berlin experience, brief though it was, and the meeting with Verhaeren, proved all-important to his future, saving him from what must have been a serious danger of lapsing into dilettantism. He recognized that the writer's profession, like any other, demands hard work, and that while an infinite capacity for taking pains does not necessarily make a genius, there can be no work of lasting value without it. The effort he devoted to the translation of Verhaeren over the years that followed, though it meant so much the less original work, was a labour of real love and his first schooling in the grind of steady application which was to lead him to the heights of success. He could so easily have coasted along on the laurels already won; lacking the spur of poverty, he might well have remained a mere littérateur. But the young man who returned to Vienna from Belgium in the autumn of 1902 would not now be content with that. Victor Fleischer, as has already been noted, remarked the independence and polite ruthlessness with which he sacrificed his social obligations to his work; Hans Müller-Einigen, also with him at the university, admired his self-control and wisdom beyond his years in advice to others. Now, his third year as a student over, there was a firm sense of direction in his life, a conscious plan of application to the serious profession of letters, and of dedication to the new spirit of Europe he had recognized in Verhaeren.

First, however, he must get his doctorate. The final year at Vienna saw him buckling down to his official studies, consuming a good deal of midnight oil, and working together with Erwin

Guido Kolbenheyer ('who may today', he wrote wryly in 1941, 'not care to be reminded of this, as he has become one of the public poets and academicians of Hitler's Germany').[1] On 7 April 1904 his thesis, on the philosophy of Hippolyte Taine, was presented, and he proceeded to the viva voce examination. Fortunately something of his reputation had preceded him into the examination room, and his inquisitors courteously desisted from probing his knowledge in the field of logic, preferring rather to dwell on the subjects in which they knew him to be better grounded.[1] Perhaps he took advantage of Otto Weininger's advice—'get Professor Müllner talking himself; stress the idealistic with Professor Jodl'.[2] His dissertation (a copy is extant in the University Library in Vienna) was competent and well reasoned. It may be, as Dumont has suggested, that his choice of Taine was due to the attraction of his theory of 'race, milieu and moment'.[3] The chief interest of the thesis for us now lies in his revealing quotation from Barzelotti's book on Taine published the previous year: 'history for him is simply applied psychology, and becomes what it ought to be, namely, the science of the causes and laws of human activities, and thus becoming a philosophy'—something of Zweig's own approach in his successful historical studies of later years.

In July he was able to circulate to friends and family the card[4] customary on these occasions:

> Stefan Zweig
> has the honour to inform you of his promotion
> to Doctor of Philosophy.

It was the first time, as he wrote in *Die Welt von Gestern*, that he had passed an examination with honours—and the last. 'Now I was outwardly free, and all the years since have been devoted to one struggle . . .: to remain equally free inwardly.'[1] For good measure, he was exempted on medical grounds from the *Freiwilligenjahr* of military service he had been expecting to have to

[1] *WvG* 121.

[2] Stefan Zweig, 'Vorbeigehen an einem unauffälligen Menschen—Otto Weininger', *Berliner Tageblatt*, 3 Oct. 1926; reprinted in *Europäisches Erbe*, ed. Friedenthal; S. Fischer, Frankfurt am Main, 1960, 225.

[3] Dum 28.

[4] *Ausst* 40.

undergo, which would have been distasteful to him, even though at this stage his pacifist views were not yet formed.

Meanwhile the *Erika Ewald* volume of *Novellen* was published by Egon Fleischel, Berlin: four stories, as he put it in a presentation copy,

> which date from four different years of my life and go back to the very beginning of my literary production. . . . In the last [*Die Wunder des Lebens*] I have consciously portrayed what the other three reveal only intuitively, namely that human life has currents running deeper than the external events which unite or divide us, and that a deep magic of life, perceptible only to the feelings and not to the senses, rules our fate even when we think to control it ourselves.[1]

A copy went to Ellen Key,[2] as a 'modest message of the great respect mutely awaiting in me its opportunity to reach you. You will make me proud, if you do not judge this hour lost.'[3]

[1] In a copy for the library of James Carleton Young (*Ausst* 40).

[2] Though he corresponded with the Swedish educationalist for some years after this, and may have heard her at one of her lectures in Germany, they did not, apparently, meet until 1907. He was clearly attracted by her liberal and radical opinions on love and marriage, no doubt also by her description of the vulnerability of youth in her *Century of the Child* (*WvG* 121).

[3] Letter to Ellen Key, undated (1904) (KB).

[1904]

Verehrtes Fräulein,

ich lege mein soeben erschienenes Novellenbuch „die Liebe der Erika Ewald' in Ihre Hände. Es soll Ihnen bescheidene Nachricht geben, von der grossen Verehrung, die stumm in mir die Gelegenheit erwartete, zu Ihnen zu gelangen. Sie machen mich stolz, wenn Sie es lesen; und Sie beglücken mich, wenn Sie diese Stunde dann nicht zu den verlorenen zählen.

Getreu und ergebenst

Stefan Zweig

Wien, I. Rathhausstrasse 17

LETTER TO ELLEN KEY, 1904, sending a copy of the Novellen volume *Die Liebe der Erika Ewald*

II. The World 1904–1914

'Up to the time of the first World War a feeling of temporariness dominated my life in mysterious fashion. Nothing I undertook, so I convinced myself, was the real, the actual thing—in my work . . . and not less with women I knew.'
Die Welt von Gestern

'I see the cities of the earth and make myself at random a part of them.' Walt Whitman

I

'That blessedly wingèd and swinging Paris of my youth is no more.' *Die Welt von Gestern*

When I try to think back to my years between eighteen and thirty-three and recall what I did then, it seems as though I spent the whole time travelling round, sitting in cafés or dallying with women. With the best will in the world I cannot remember having done any work or ever having learnt anything. The facts however contradict this: in those years I turned out a whole series of books, and a few plays which were produced on almost every stage in Germany and in other countries; I learned languages, and wrote and read endlessly. . . . This fact reinforces for me the feeling I had very early in my career that literature was not life itself but a form of expression of life. . . . I never sacrificed anything to literature: it was for me simply a higher form of existence, a way of making my experience intelligible and meaningful to myself.[1]

He had indeed spent a great part of these years in travel. Going abroad, beyond the confines of Austria, was not a new experience

[1] DDh 7–8.

for him, as one of so cosmopolitan a family. Although his parents do not seem themselves to have taken many holidays abroad, he had paid his first visit to France after leaving school, his father having given him a sum of money for passing his *Matura*. He had been to Italy during the summer vacation of 1903, and had also spent part of it on the Île de Bréhat off the Brittany coast, where he had written the *Novelle*, *Die Wunder des Lebens* (there is also a reflection of this visit in the poem *Stille Insel* (*Bretagne*), which appears in his second volume of verse). During his student days too—perhaps on the same vacation—he had seen Paris for the first time. Heading straight from the station to the Latin Quarter, he had gazed with awe at Verlaine's chair in the Café Vachette and the marble table on which the poet had been wont to beat angrily with his stick to command due deference. He had even—with some repugnance—paid homage to Verlaine's memory with an appropriate glass of absinthe.[1] And there had been the unforgettable stay in Belgium in 1902 and his first meeting with Verhaeren.

But as soon as his doctorate thesis had been presented he seems to have embarked on a deliberate programme of travel through the world, while pursuing with considerable diligence his chosen profession of letters. In the decade to 1914 he came to know intimately the greater part of Europe, and saw not a little of the rest of the world—'so gradually becoming a European'.[2] A comfortable allowance from his father, supplemented by a rapidly growing income from his writing, made these *Wanderjahre* easy.

Paris he had promised himself again, by way of celebration of his new freedom, and arrived there in May 1904. He was no longer a student, and the Quartier Latin was not, he felt, the right place to stay (and the shudder over that glass of absinthe had made him resolve to exploit his talents without the aid of alcohol). By chance ('it takes a foreigner to show us the most beautiful parts of our own city', André Gide told him later) he came across the Hotel Beaujolais at one end of the garden of the Palais Royal:[3] modest, quiet, near the Louvre, and within easy reach of the

[1] *WvG* 126–7. [2] DDh 8. [3] *WvG* 127–8.

Bibliothèque Nationale, where he worked in the mornings. It was small, somewhat primitive, a pale ghost of what had once been a fashionable palace among the uniform buildings erected by Philippe-Égalité in the eighteenth century; but it held memories of the past—of Balzac and Victor Hugo climbing the stairs to the *mansarde* of Marceline Desbordes-Valmore, whose work Zweig had already come to love; of Desmoulins rousing the rabble to storm the Bastille; of Lieutenant Bonaparte. It was an intimate part of Paris, in its very heart, yet well secluded; a peaceful oasis which the bustle of the city reached only as a faint murmur. He was to return to it often in future years.

Quiet hotel rooms like this, away from the fashionable quarters, often, indeed, in highly unfashionable resorts out of season, seem to have suited him best and served as the workshop for many of his first drafts. He showed even at this early stage a commendably professional, almost academic, approach to his craft, setting aside certain hours for work, and beginning each day with study in the Bibliothèque Nationale (whose Director, Julien Cain, and his wife Lucienne became his lifelong friends). From Paris he paid frequent visits to Verhaeren, who was then staying at Saint-Cloud, and through him met a kindred spirit in Léon Bazalgette, the indefatigable translator of Walt Whitman. These few weeks in France were memorable too for his first meeting with Duhamel; and he had the privilege of seeing Rodin at work in his *atelier*. Such contacts with artists 'fully conscious of their responsibilities to mankind'[1] led him to reject once and for all the sterile aestheticism of his first works.

2

'I want to get to know English culture and widen my spiritual horizon.'

Zweig to Ellen Key, 1906

After Paris, London—for how could one understand the world without knowing the country which had kept it 'rolling on its tracks for so many centuries'?[2] A contrast here, for he found

[1] Dum 93. [2] *WvG* 148.

London an esoteric, baffling world on which he could make no impression and into which he could not enter. In Paris, thanks largely to Verhaeren, he had had the entrée to a congenial circle; in London he found himself condemned for the greater part of his time to his room or to the British Museum.[1] He was, it is true, able to meet Arthur Symons, editor of *The Savoy*, the *fin de siècle* magazine perhaps nearest in character to the literary endeavours of his own Vienna (illustrated, we may note, by Aubrey Beardsley, whose drawings were to embellish *Volpone* twenty-two years later). Through Symons he secured an invitation to one of the ceremonious readings by W. B. Yeats, part of whose drama *The Shadowy Waters* he had already translated.[2] But he made no real friends in England, on either the literary or the social plane, and did not succeed in penetrating the surface of the Englishman or in understanding his 'private talk'. He reflected in later years that he would have done better to have taken a job while in England, on a paper or with some firm, for although he had, of course, no need of the money, he might in this way have discovered what lay beneath the British exterior.

About this time, probably in the autumn of 1904, he paid his first visit to Hermann Hesse's home in Gaienhofen on Lake Constance, breezing in with such youthful enthusiasm that he failed to notice the low beams of the old house, and gave himself a crack on the head that laid him out speechless for fifteen minutes.[3] But Paris remained his home from home, and he was back there, in rooms at 5 rue Victor Massé, by the middle of December for a stay of nearly six months, interrupted only by a trip to Spain and Algiers at the end of February 1905, from which resulted a series of three *feuilletons* for the *NFP*.[4] In Paris, through an introduction from Ellen Key, he met Johan Bojer, the Norwegian novelist, who was very taken with the qualities of the *Erika Ewald* stories and arranged for their review in Norway. The translation by Bojer's wife of the title story, and Bojer's own article on Zweig for

[1] *WvG* 149.

[2] *WvG* 150.

[3] Franz Baumer, *Hermann Hesse*; Colloquium Verlag, Berlin, 1959, 36.

[4] Correspondence Dec. 1904–May 1905 (ZE); letter to Franz Servaes, 4 Feb. 1905 (StB); letter to Ellen Key (? Feb.) 1905 (KB).

the Norwegian press later that year, with photograph contributed by the subject,[1] marked the beginning of his international fame.

In these years too we find the first signs of his reputation as a literary father-figure to whom younger aspirants could turn for helpful advice and criticism. In 1905 he met René Fülöp-Miller and devoted much time to a careful reading of the young poet's *Thaumaturgia*;[2] a few years later it was the turn of Franz Theodor Csokor to read to Zweig his first play.[3] Felix Braun has related how he too, four years younger than Zweig, and his hero-worshipper from afar in the lower forms of the Wasagymnasium, met with praise and encouragement for his own lyric efforts when they finally met in 1907.[4] Unpatronizing enthusiasm, wise guidance, and sound criticism flowed readily to these younger men from one who, though scarcely their senior, seemed already an Olympian.

In 1906 his second volume of verse, *Die frühen Kränze*, appeared: like *Silberne Saiten*, a stringent selection from his work, and with as little sign of true poetic originality. His purpose this time, as he wrote with the copy he sent to Ellen Key, was to create an organic whole rather than a haphazard collection of poems (he had thought of dedicating the sonnet sequence 'Die Nacht der Gnaden' to her, but had not had time to seek her permission first).[5] The main interest today of this rarely encountered volume is that it was the first of his to be published by the Insel-Verlag: the first in a long series of works bearing the famous ship imprint, until the shock of 1933 severed the fruitful partnership. Zweig was an Insel author for the greater part of his writing life, finding a kindred spirit in the Goethe-collector Anton Kippenberg, director of the firm, and doing a deal of work for the house in editing and advising on many of its projects. The Insel-Bücherei, one of the most successful publishing enterprises in Germany between the wars and since, was a series to which he contributed ideas and suggestions, and the magnificent, though regrettably

[1] Letters from Bojer, 27 Sept., Nov., and 4 Dec. 1905 (ZE).
[2] Fülöp-Miller (Arens[1] 167).
[3] Csokor (*Sp* 109).
[4] Felix Braun, *Licht* 457; *Mus Land* 193.
[5] Letter to Ellen Key, undated (KB).

unsuccessful, conception of the Bibliotheca Mundi, a series of the classics in their original languages, owed its origin entirely to him.

He paid a second visit to England in the spring of 1906. 'Paris with you and Rilke', he wrote to Ellen Key, 'would certainly have been wonderful, but this year my road takes me to London. I want to get to know English culture and widen my spiritual horizon.'[1] This time he spent nearly four months in the capital and, basing himself in rooms at 84 Kensington Gardens Square, travelled around a good deal more. He visited Scotland—an echo of this is evident, no doubt, in the *Novelle*, *Geschichte in der Dämmerung*—and Oxford. Several *feuilletons* were sent off to Servaes for the *NFP*, including the essay on Oxford and that on Hyde Park, extracts from which he was delighted to note in the *Daily Mail* and other English papers.[2] He saw Arthur Symons again, and Yeats. His real discovery, however, was William Blake, whose drawings in the Print Room of the British Museum filled him with enthusiasm. The whole personality of Blake, 'immature despite his extravagant proportions', was uncommonly gripping, and he seemed to Zweig, with Shakespeare, Keats, and Shelley, 'the greatest genius of the English'.[3] He reported for the *Frankfurter Zeitung* on a Blake exhibition: 'that most remarkable of all British artists', whose work was for him 'among the most significant of art'.[4] Moreover, through the good offices of Archibald G. B. Russell, whose book on Blake he now translated, he was able to acquire one of the Visionary Portraits, that of King John, the most beautiful he had ever seen, 'worthy of a Leonardo'.[3]

The climate was his worst enemy. 'I am living here in London somewhat unwillingly, because I love the sun and feel overcast skies like a ring of lead round the heart. And there are few people here who are close to me: too many cool and cautious, too few cordial. . . .[3] He had the same feeling of isolation as before. 'A pity you cannot accustom yourself to London', wrote Bojer

[1] Letter to Ellen Key, 15 Apr. 1906 (KB).
[2] Letter to Servaes, undated (StB).
[3] Letter to Ellen Key, undated (KB).
[4] Letter to Servaes, 1906 (StB).

from Paris.[1] But the essays show that he gained more understanding of the English: in particular, the Germanic illusion of the unpoetic Englishman was banished for him. The gardens at the centre of the 'greatest stone sea of the world'; the galleries, both private and national, filled with the finest works of art; schools in which the charm of history blends with green living fields—all were signs, he felt, of a people nearer to the ancient Greeks than any other of the modern world.[2] 'The indifference, the reserve, the conventionality, the hypocrisy, the literal belief, the fanaticism were unbearable for me, and only the physical beauty and inner purity of the people helped me over my antipathy.'[3] England was not then, and never became in his eyes, a part of Europe, the Europe whose intellectual unification was to be his highest aim and the connecting thread of his life's work. Poetic or not, and whatever their 'physical beauty and inner purity', the English remained for him a people apart, and he did not in fact recross the Channel until 1933, when England's relative isolation from Europe was a welcome refuge from the spread of the new barbarism.

3

'A bigger thing has taken hold of me, and I feel the true painful pleasure of creation.'

Zweig to Ellen Key, 1905

Meanwhile he had turned his thoughts to drama. In July 1905, sending Ellen Key a copy of his Verlaine study in the *Die Dichtung* series, he had told of his plan for a short, possibly privately printed, biography of the eighteenth-century Madame de Prie, mistress of the Regent and of the Duke of Bourbon, the story of whose suicide at the age of twenty-seven under curious circumstances had drawn his attention.[4] A month later, however, in Tirano, he had laid this aside in favour of something bigger:

a drama in verse, *Tersites*, the fate of the most ugly and most malignant of the Greeks before the walls of Troy. My play treats of the most

[1] Letter from Bojer, 20 (Apr. or May) 1906 (ZE).

[2] Stefan Zweig, 'Oxford'; *feuilleton* for the *NFP*, 1906. Reprinted in *Zeit und Welt*, ed. Friedenthal; S. Fischer, Frankfurt am Main, 1946, 200-1.

[3] Letter to Ellen Key, undated (?autumn 1906) (KB).

[4] Letter to Ellen Key, 1 July 1905 (KB).

malignant *because* ugliest, and seeks to express how great griefs can refine a soul while happiness merely hardens it. Tersites' opponent is Achilles, who has never been touched with sorrow; but just as Tersites, who has never known a woman, is in fact in closer harmony with the female soul than are the serene and shining ones, so his dark and repulsive life is actually worth the most. Dramatically the thing is, as far as I can see, uncommonly successful; it is undoubtedly the most beautiful I have written so far—as far as it is completed.[1]

A classical theme in iambic pentameters was perhaps inevitable; but his choice of the reviled, downtrodden, anti-hero Tersites was characteristic. Much of the drama was written during several months that autumn in northern Italy, and he had completed it by April 1906, just before leaving for England.[2]

His treatment was vigorous, though, apart from the choice of hero, not very original. The streak of pessimism in his own character found its reflection in such a personality, and it was certainly true that this three-act piece was the most beautiful he had written so far; but it strikes today's reader as contrived, conventional in expression, and convincing only in rare snatches. It was a *Talentprobe*, as certain critics pointed out after its publication by Insel in 1907;[3] but the reception in general was by no means cold. Sigmund Freud, in one of his earliest letters to Zweig,[4] praised it, as did Csokor.[5] For himself, he had seen no particular prospect of its success. 'I have absolutely no hope that it will be produced,' he had written in August 1905, 'and am not writing with this in mind.'[1] In February the following year he told Ellen Key he was not even sure whether he would publish it, for he did not know whether it had enough power to sustain the drama. 'Perhaps I will keep it by me: not from selfishness (for I have nothing left for my works as soon as they are finished) but from timidity.'[6] A blank-verse drama on a Greek theme could, after all, scarcely promise to be good box-office.

[1] Letter to Ellen Key, 12 Aug. 1905 (KB).
[2] Letter to Ellen Key, 15 Apr. 1906 (KB).
[3] *Führer durch die moderne Literatur*, 190.
[4] Letter from Freud, 3 May 1908 (Freud *Br* 273).
[5] Letter from Csokor, undated (1907) (ZE).
[6] Letter to Ellen Key, 9 Feb. 1906 (KB).

He was accordingly pleasantly surprised, after sending a few copies out to the leading theatres, to receive a warmly phrased letter from Ludwig Barnay, Director of the Königliches Schauspielhaus in Berlin, offering the première there with, in the role of Achilles, none other than Adalbert Matkowsky, one of the most renowned German actors of the day. He realized that it was an almost unique distinction that a first play should go direct to the German Hoftheater, but he still claimed a certain indifference about the production.

The cult of the theatre, as opposed to that of the book, is to my mind a sign of the spiritual passivity of our times. . . . The theatre can never, I think, be a fulfilment for artistic endeavour [he wrote in September 1907]; in spite of Matkowsky, the last of the heroes, who is to play Achilles, in spite of all possible success, the première will be a secret bitterness for me . . . however much there is in the play which needs the word and the stage, there is no less that requires silence and darkness.[1]

He could deny it, but his sense of anticipation was in fact keen; and in the event it took a hard knock. Billed for March 1908, the play became the subject of wranglings in Berlin, the exact nature of which is not now clear, but which left him bitter and tired; and when it was postponed to April he threw everything to one side and went off to Merano to enjoy three weeks' winter sunshine.[2] Meanwhile the Court theatres in Dresden and Kassel had also accepted the play. On his return from Merano he decided to withdraw it from Berlin, where in any case a serious illness attacking Matkowsky had made necessary a further postponement.[3] In August he wrote:

I have had an unpleasant summer because of all sorts of private dissensions . . . with Tersites it was certainly a bad business, but I think one should prefer to renounce a success if it is at the expense of personal pride. True, the management very well knows how much it was in

[1] Letters to Ellen Key, undated (? autumn 1906 and ? early Sept. 1907) (KB).

[2] Letter to Ellen Key, 2 Apr. 1908 (KB); R 58.

[3] Letter from Raoul Auernheimer, 8 May 1908 (ZE).

the wrong, and negotiations are in the offing to heal the breach. But it does not affect me, and never has.[1]

His spirits were raised temporarily when he learned that Joseph Kainz, the Austrian actor, whose fame was almost equal to Matkowsky's, was enthusiastic enough about the play to recommend it to the Vienna Burgtheater, with himself not as Achilles but as Tersites; but Schlenther, the Director, a determined realist from his time in Berlin, wrote to say he could not see any possibility of success beyond the première.[2] In the end, he was glad to go to Dresden in November, where Servaes had given him an introduction to Paul Wiecke, who was to play the title role. 'Wiecke is such a splendid fellow that, in spite of the certainty of failure, I count my stay in Dresden as a gain.'[3]

The première at the Court theatre there was on 26 November 1908, with a simultaneous performance in Kassel. Though his fears proved groundless, and the play's success was not inconsiderable, he could not conceal his disappointment at the Burgtheater's refusal (a few more years were to pass before he reached this height). The death of Matkowsky coming shortly afterwards served to increase his gloom over this first attempt at drama. He had not, however, neglected his work in other fields. The year 1906 saw the publication of his translation of Russell's book on Blake—*Die visionäre Kunstphilosophie des William Blake*—and the award of the Bauernfeld Prize for lyric poetry. In the following year he contributed a critical/biographical Foreword to Klaus Klammer's translations of Rimbaud, under the title *Rimbaud: Leben und Dichtung*; completed another *Novelle, Die Gouvernante*; and laid plans for a collection in which this and *Scharlach*, written about 1906, were to appear. The projected essay on Madame de Prie was forgotten, and nothing remains of his draft: Balzac had now seized his attention. 'I am all Balzac again,' he wrote to Servaes in 1907, 'and am also advising the Insel-Verlag with its new 15-volume edition, for which Hofmannsthal is writing the Introduction and which I am enormously looking forward to.'[4] His own introductory essay to volume ii of Brieger-Wasservogel's

[1] Letter to Ellen Key, 2 Aug. 1908 (KB).
[2] *WvG* 161.
[3] Letter to Servaes, Nov. 1908 (StB).
[4] Letter to Servaes, 1907 (StB).

series on the great masters, *Balzac: Sein Weltbild aus den Werken*, brought him warm congratulations from Hofmannsthal, who described it as 'hors pair'.[1]

None of his work so far could be classed in any way as realism, still less as naturalism; yet the realism of Balzac fascinated him—'the scientific method', as he had written in his dissertation on Taine, 'of first assembling the details which create man's dependence, and then deducing from them general laws illustrated by the individual'. (One should attempt a novel, he said to Felix Braun about this time, only when one has known life in its every detail, down to the prices in the shops.) Probably a greater fascination, however, was that of Balzac at work: the daimonic energy shown first in his fantastic production and then in the volcano-like eruptions on proof after proof of his corrections and re-writings. One of Zweig's most valued items in his autograph collection in these pre-war years was a proof, corrected (if that is the word) in the author's own hand, of *Une Ténébreuse Affaire*. (He reproduced part of this as an illustration to an essay entitled 'Die unterirdischen Bücher Balzacs' for Hans Feigl's *Deutsches Bibliophilenkalender* in 1917.) His project of a full critical biography of Balzac remained with him for the rest of his life, never to reach completion.

4

> *'The globe itself is still my homeland. . . . I feel I could not die before I have known the whole world.'*
> Zweig to Ellen Key, 1909

'Up to the time of the First World War a feeling of temporariness dominated my life in mysterious fashion.' It was thus with his move from Rathausstrasse to an apartment of his own, a *pied-à-terre* rather than a permanent residence, on 1 February 1907. It was at 8 Kochgasse, in Vienna's VIIIth District, not far from his rooms while a student, with a small balcony overlooking the Schönborn Park with its 'singing fountain'. Living in the same house was a very old lady on whose head as a baby Goethe's

1 Letter to Hans Feigl, undated (? 1908) (StB).

hand had once rested.[1] When in Vienna he continued to take most of his meals with his parents, but this flat—'at last my own home!'—set a final seal, if one were needed, on his complete independence. It was furnished with taste but was not luxurious. Apart from some red-leather armchairs and a rich red carpet, the only signs of affluence were the presence of an old manservant, Josef (who, lately in the service of a crippled General, continued to spoil the new master like the old), and the occasional calls of a secretary, Frau Mandl, a motherly body whose services he shared with Siegfried Trebitsch and for whom the unused kitchen was turned into an office. Bookshelves were, of course, plentiful, and the autograph collection, with its ancillary assembly of sale catalogues (in itself in later years a rarity), was at last properly housed and ordered. His best-loved prize, the manuscript of Goethe's *Mailied*, found a place under glass on the wall opposite Blake's King John.[2] All in all, it was a framework which absolved him from the slightest preoccupation with the practicalities of life; which he could, and did, leave at a moment's notice (in the nine months following his move he visited Prague, Berlin, northern Italy, Corsica, Sardinia, and Rome); but which formed his first firm base for books and autographs, and a post-box for his already enormous mail.

It is likely in fact that this feeling of temporariness, which he ascribed in *Die Welt von Gestern* only to his early years, had roots deeper in his character than he realized. He never lost, even in his permanent home in Salzburg between the wars, the urge to be untrammelled by fixed responsibilities, to be on the move, to free himself from wife and home at unpredictable intervals, dearly though he cared for both and sweet though every return seemed. But for the moment, nothing he undertook seemed the real, the actual, thing either in his work, which he regarded as merely preparatory sketches, or with the women he knew. He still looked upon himself as 'a beginner who faced immeasurable time', and he was hesitant about final decisions of any kind.[1] 'The Viennese avoids by instinct every area of decision', as Hans Müller-Einigen once aptly put it. There was more of the Viennese

[1] *WvG* 152. [2] *WvG* 152; Fr 70, 78; *Bildb* 36.

in Zweig the European than he would have cared to acknowledge.

'Sketches'—in fact a not inappropriate description of his work at this time. *Tersites* apart, it was high-grade literary journalism, and his life was that of a publicist rather than of an author. Poems continued to bombard the editors of papers and journals, and he turned out a constant stream of reviews. He made efforts to place his *Novellen*: he sent *Die Gouvernante* in manuscript to Servaes from a pension on the Via Emilia in October 1907, in the hope of its making a special *feuilleton* for the *NFP*, from whose pending-tray he withdrew the earlier *Scharlach* to send it to the *Oesterreichische Rundschau* for June 1908. The essays on Rimbaud and Balzac, however, had been more solid works, and he was, he wrote to Servaes in January 1908, at last beginning to learn what had earlier eluded him—the art of rewriting, and to resist the urge to get quickly into print.[1]

A few years before he had been struck by the appearance in Harden's *Zukunft*, to which he had become a regular contributor, of a series of aphorisms, under a pseudonym, which seemed a quite remarkable combination of good sense and concentration of expression. Inquiry of Harden produced a letter from their author, who turned out to be Walther Rathenau, son of the Director of the Allgemeine Elektrizitäts-Gesellschaft, and himself already an industrial magnate of some standing, on the board of over eighty companies. They entered into correspondence, and on a visit to Berlin in July 1907 Zweig telephoned him. It was characteristic of Rathenau that, though this was the eve of his departure for German East Africa with State Secretary Dernburg of the *Reichskolonialamt*, he none the less found time, from 11.15 that night until 2 in the morning, for a long discussion with this much younger man who had been one of the first to encourage him in his hesitant steps into the new world of literature (despite his success in business, Rathenau considered himself as first a writer and philosopher). Zweig was deeply impressed by the precision and rapidity of his thought, his command of every subject, and his clear-thinking objectivity: most of all, perhaps, by the deep

1 Letters to Servaes, 21 Oct. 1907 and 14 Jan. 1908 (StB).

unrest beneath the apparent superiority of this personality. One chance remark on this occasion struck him forcibly, and made him determine to extend his travels beyond Europe. 'You cannot understand England,' said Rathenau, 'as long as you just know the island, nor our continent of Europe unless you have been outside it at least once. You are a free man, make use of your freedom. Literature is a wonderful profession, because haste plays no part in it. A year more or less is of no importance for a real book. Why don't you go to India, and to America?'[1]

A year later he began to plan a journey to the East. 'In three months I start on my great Indian journey,' he wrote to Ellen Key on 2 August 1908, after describing his troubles over *Tersites*, 'and that is more important to me than anything else: it is an end, and I hope the beginning of something new. . . . When I return I shall think about my book on Verhaeren.'[2] His itinerary is not well documented, but we know that he saw Ceylon, Madras, Gwalior, Calcutta, Benares and the foothills of the Himalayas, Rangoon and the Irrawaddy, and Indo-China. Between Calcutta and Indo-China, and on a boat trip up the Irrawaddy, he had as companions one Karl Haushofer and his wife. Haushofer, then on his way to take up his post as German Military Attaché in Tokyo, gave Zweig his first insight into the qualities and discipline of the German General Staff officer: already familiar with the Japanese language and some of its literature, he worked unceasingly on the boat, keeping a diary, making notes or consulting his dictionary, and Zweig learned a great deal about the Orient and the world in general from their long conversations. For years afterwards, in fact, they maintained cordial relations; and it came as an unpleasant surprise twenty years later for Zweig to hear Haushofer described in Munich as 'Hitler's friend', and to find the half-formed geopolitical theories he had thought so interesting in 1908, as a means of drawing the nations together, adopted and travestied for quite the opposite purpose by the National-Socialists.[3]

[1] *WvG* 169–72. [2] KB.

[3] Haushofer, 'popularly, but erroneously, believed to have some knowledge of England', was the only person in whom Rudolph Hess confided before his startling

Ceylon and India depressed him, though to Ellen Key on his return he described India as 'a land of wonders, which would make even you look on Italy merely as a pleasant foretaste of a deeper beauty'. It was his first experience of the colour bar, and the elevation of the European to the status of a white god shamed and embarrassed him. He was appalled at the hunger and poverty to be seen on all sides. India was an admonition rather than a call to romance, and it was the people 'which a ship, a journey and loneliness bring together', rather than the temples and landscapes, that did most for his education in the sense Rathenau had intended.[1]

5

'Admire one another!' Emile Verhaeren

'Welcome back to Europe!' wrote Hermann Hesse on 7 April 1909.[2] Rathenau's advice had been sound, and the journey had indeed been a broadening experience; but Zweig remained a European, and was far from having fallen under the spell of the East. He published a poem on the Taj Mahal, *feuilletons* on Benares and Gwalior for the *Berliner Tageblatt* and *NFP* in March 1909, and an essay on 'Die indische Gefahr für England' in July. On landing at Marseille, however, he went straight on to Paris to meet Verhaeren and Rilke (and also met for the first time, in a café opposite the Bourse, Jules Romains, who later recalled the natural, man-of-the-world way in which the young Austrian spoke of his somewhat adventurous journey).[3] By May he had already started his book on the Belgian poet, 'with all love and admiration, with the earnest endeavour not to let it be too apparent how much I am his disciple, how much my own development has come from him'.[4]

flight to England on 10 May 1941 (Kirkpatrick, *The Inner Circle*, Macmillan, London, 1959). It was his son Albrecht who mentioned the Duke of Hamilton to Hess, and who for his contacts with the opposition movement was executed after the July plot of 1944.

[1] *WvG* 172–6; Fr 53–5; *Bildb* 43–4; *Ausst* 45; letter to Ellen Key, 4 May 1909 (KB).

[2] Card (ZE).

[3] Jules Romains: 'Stefan Zweig — ein grosser Europäer' (Arens[2] 323), and lecture given in Vienna in 1958 (quoted Dum 331).

[4] Letter to Ellen Key, 4 May 1909 (KB).

He had described to Ellen Key four years earlier his love for Verhaeren,

> which really knows no bounds. In my year in Paris he admitted me completely to his life, I can say with pride, as a friend and (despite the difference in our years) as man to man. . . . Friendship is Verhaeren's noblest art: he has a modest, beautiful way of winning people. The best men of our time are in his circle: Rodin, Maeterlinck, Carrière, Lemonnier, Van der Stappen. . . . He is not in any way intellectual (I mistrust intellectual people because they are too negative and are incapable of the warmth of love) but he is so full of the knowledge of experience that my life has been more enriched by him than by any other person.

He had thought then that a book on Verhaeren, before he was sufficiently known, might do more harm than good.[1] Now he felt it was time, and completed it before the end of the year: a sensitive tribute and a clear exposition of the poet's achievement and philosophy. At the same time he continued with his translations, turning now to the dramas *Hélène de Sparte*, *Le Cloître*, and *Philippe II*, all of which were finished in time to form volume iii of the Insel edition of 1910. In the summer of 1909 he visited Verhaeren again at 'Caillou-qui-bique' to put the finishing touches to *Helena*. (Paul Zech, who chanced also to be there, recalled that Verhaeren prophesied for them both a biblical lifespan —'he was wrong in the case of his "dear son" Stefan Zweig'— and for himself an early, tragic death.)[2]

Although, as he had said to Ellen Key, he had won for Verhaeren an élite in Germany through his translations of the poems —Dehmel, Hesse, Johannes Schlaf ('who at my instigation is writing a book on him'), and many others[1]—he felt now that still more must be done to gain for the poet in Germany and Austria the reputation he deserved. He began thinking of an organized *tournée* through these countries, which he hoped would bring him to his rightful place in European letters after the Insel edition was published; and in the succeeding years spent a lot of effort in private publicity work to this end. He undertook a further

[1] Letter to Ellen Key, 12 Aug. 1905 (KB).

[2] *Ged* 20.

translation, himself, of Verhaeren's *Rubens*, for the Cassirer Verlag's new magazine (later published in book form by Insel); urged Servaes to write an essay in the *NFP* after the very successful première of *Das Kloster* in Germany;[1] agreed to Jethro Bithell's proposed translation of his monograph for publication in England without fee for himself;[2] and pressed the Deutsches Volkstheater in Vienna to include *Das Kloster* in its repertoire.[3]

Not all his friends were so enthusiastic: 'I would rather read a single line by Stefan Zweig than all the Belgians and Americans together!' wrote Max Brod.[4] But Maeterlinck sent him warm appreciation of the monograph ('your intuitive study, which at moments has the penetration of a great visionary, will remain one of the highest models of the genre'),[5] and Kainz and Moissi gave public recitals of Verhaeren's verse in Zweig's rendering. It was an intensive effort over more than two years, which, despite a multitude of other interests and much original work of his own, he pursued by further translations (the verse selection *Hymnen an das Leben* in the Insel-Bücherei 1911, *Rembrandt* 1912, single poems in the *Insel-Almanach*), essays in various journals, lectures on the poet and his work, and a massive correspondence over the arrangements for the tour. The result was an outstanding success. He travelled to Germany at the end of February 1912 to meet Verhaeren, and was able to report to Arthur Kutscher of the Neuer Verein, Munich (where Verhaeren was later to appear), that his first lecture in Hamburg was a triumph: 'he gives a single talk, "La Culture de l'Enthousiasme", incorporating a number of his poems, which he reads splendidly'.[6] It seemed a symbol of Franco-German fraternity when Verhaeren and Dehmel embraced each other publicly. From Berlin, where Verhaeren met Rathenau and Reinhardt and his appearance went equally well,

[1] Letter to Servaes, 1910 (StB). It was Harry Graf Kessler and Hofmannsthal, however, who apparently first succeeded (in 1910) in interesting Reinhardt in *Helenas Heimkehr* (*Briefwechsel*; Insel, 1968, pp. 285, 539).

[2] Letter to Jethro Bithell, 16 Feb. 1910.

[3] Letter to Heinrich Glücksmann, 19 June 1911 (StB).

[4] Letter from Max Brod, 25 Nov. 1910 (ZE).

[5] Letter from Maeterlinck, 27 May 1910 (ZE).

[6] Letter to Kutscher, 2 Mar. 1912 (Sch).

they travelled to Vienna, the back room of Hugo Heller's bookshop on the Bauernmarkt having been engaged for 8 March. 'Great rolling waves of verse broke upon me', recalls Felix Braun: 'I see the short, rugged, broad-shouldered Belgian rhapsodist in the light of the room, and later in the darkness of the street standing next to Stefan Zweig, whose slim figure towers above him.'[1]

Zweig, with his customary modesty, kept well in the background at these appearances, and successfully resisted Kutscher's attempts to get him to give an introductory talk and reading of his own translations at the Munich lecture which concluded the tour on 15 March.

> Verhaeren reads and speaks so compellingly, with such immeasurable impressiveness, that beside him one appears like an unctuous priest. . . . As I saw in Berlin, any form of introduction merely holds things up. He talks for about 50 or 55 minutes, Herr von Jacobi about 15: every minute beyond this would be on the debit side. . . . Anyway, I am not a particularly outstanding reader and would rather have my translations interpreted by an expert, such as a well-known actor.[2]

Looking back later, he felt that Verhaeren's popularity in Germany reached its peak that year (in Berlin Verhaeren had been told that he was one of the crown princess's favourite poets, and that the Kaiser would have attended his lecture but for a prior engagement in Cuxhaven).[3] Austria remained less welcoming. Apart from fifty lines in *Die Zeit*, there had not been a word in the Vienna press about the Insel edition, Zweig complained to Servaes in 1910; but at least he had now been able to introduce personally the few there who recognized Verhaeren's genius.

This long devotion to another had not affected his own production. The essay on Dickens, later the second pillar of *Drei Meister*, appeared in 1910 as Introduction to the Insel edition of the works; and he started work on an essay on Dostoevsky. There was a steady series of reviews for a variety of German and Austrian journals, and in 1910 he completed the *Novelle*, *Angst* (not to be published, however, until about ten years later). The following

1 Felix Braun, *Licht* 474–6.

2 Letter to Kutscher, 2 Mar. 1912 (Sch).

3 Letter from Verhaeren to Marthe Verhaeren, 5 Mar. 1912 (quoted Dum 33–4).

year saw his Introduction to Lafcadio Hearn's *Das Japanbuch* and his second volume of *Novellen*, *Erstes Erlebnis*. Four stories 'from the land of childhood' (*Scharlach* was not, after all, included), they were dedicated to Ellen Key, with a reference to the 'clear autumn days of Bagni di Lucca' they had spent together in 1907, and were well received, with steady if unremarkable sales in the Insel list for the next twenty years. One, however—*Brennendes Geheimnis*—was published separately in 1913, and had touched the 200,000 mark by the time the Reichstag fire gave a satirical point to the posters advertising its film version in Berlin. 'I have not been so deeply gripped by any work on the mysterious and dangerous period that is adolescence since Heinrich Mann's *Stürmische Morgen*', wrote Csokor to Zweig in December 1911.[1] The tangled feelings and unrealized longings of youth seemed to most readers to be beautifully expressed here, despite the absence of realistic detail; and over the years there were few to agree with the scathing comments of Emanuel bin Gorion (*Ceterum Recenseo*, 1929) who condemned all Zweig's work—poems, essays, and particularly the *Novellen*—as false, impure, and poisoned, mere railway-carriage reading.[2]

The theatre too continued to draw him. Two projects for dramas, one on a biblical theme, had come to nothing during 1908 and 1909,[3] but the disappointment over the Burg's refusal of *Tersites* had had the compensation for him of attracting Kainz's attention to his work. At the actor's request he wrote in 1910 a play especially for him, *Der verwandelte Komödiant*, with a part 'to fit him like a glove'. 'A feather-weight rococo affair with two big lyrico-dramatic monologues', the first sketches delighted Kainz, and on its rapid completion it was accepted by the Burgtheater. But on his return from a German tour Kainz was struck down by cancer, and, after an operation, was dead within a few weeks, before rehearsals could begin. 'Do you think the Lord will grant that I act in that piece of ours? That could make me well', he said with a sad smile to Zweig visiting him on his

1 Letter from Csokor, 17 Dec. 1911 (ZE).
2 Emanuel bin Gorion, *Ceterum Recenseo*, 51, 100.
3 Letter to Ellen Key, 2 Aug. 1908 (KB).

sickbed. It was not to be, and this second stroke of fate, with now two of the greatest actors in the German language dying while on the point of appearing in Zweig's plays, could not fail to induce a deep superstition in the author.[1]

Nevertheless, he was not deterred from offering a tragedy, *Das Haus am Meer*, to the Burg. It was in blank verse, a melodramatic piece (perhaps inspired by Tennyson's *Enoch Arden*) about the German pressgangs of the time of the American War of Independence, vigorous and well constructed. After completing it in 1911 he had claimed indifference to its fate, and in fact an aversion to seeing his plays produced in Vienna: 'for me personally it spoils all pleasure if the audience is not something anonymous, composed of hostile strangers, but a conglomeration of faces I know'.[2] But actually the pull of the Burg could not be resisted. When the new manager, Baron Alfred Berger, accepted it, he was relieved, paradoxically enough, to see no famous names in the cast for its production: but he had not thought of Berger himself, who intended to direct it—and a fortnight before the first rehearsal Berger too died. This time, however, the play went on, and Zweig's première at the theatre that was the ambition of every Austrian playwright was on 26 October 1912.

In an interview with the journalist Paul Wilhelm immediately before the first night he discussed dispassionately his career as a dramatist, and the dark fate which seemed to have hung over it so far.

I was extraordinarily moved when I heard that Matkowsky, who had already read himself into the part [of Achilles], on a walk with the writer Georg Engel who was trying to talk him out of his forebodings of death, suddenly stopped and recited the verses from *Tersites*—

> Der Priester Künste wären mir ein Scherz
> Doch in mir raunt die unheilvolle Stimme
> Und Ahnung frißt an meinen heitern Stunden,
> Denn bin ich fröhlich, scheine ich es nur. . . .
> Ahnst Du dies Leid und jenes andre noch:
> Daß Feige, Schmutzige, vom Los Befleckte
> Noch Sonne trinken werden, warme Luft

[1] *WvG* 161–3. [2] Letter to Paul Zech, 23 Aug. 1911 (Sch).

An ihren Wangen fühlen, neue Dinge
Mit neuer Schönheit seh'n, indes ich schon
Hingleite schlafend in die Dunkelheiten?[1]

A few days later the artist's presentiments were fulfilled. . . . The play in its later production in Dresden . . . won for me a further personal importance in that I owed to it the interest of Joseph Kainz. . . . I discussed with him a plan for a one-act play *Der verwandelte Komödiant*, which has since been produced in Breslau[2] and has now been accepted by the Deutsches Volkstheater here, and which I wrote—I am not ashamed to confess it—expressly for Kainz. Just as I was ready to bring him the final manuscript, the papers carried the news of his grave illness which within a few months carried off this incomparable artist—a loss no less a blow for me than that of Matkowsky. And now—*Das Haus am Meer* is my third drama. It was placed as first première of the current season and I thought all was secure, when I heard of the sudden and shattering passing of Baron Berger. Fortunately Hugo Thimig has taken on the work with redoubled interest, and I hope I may now at last experience the joy of seeing my work produced on a Vienna stage.[3]

The play indeed achieved an instant success in Vienna, and did well shortly afterwards in Munich, Hamburg, and Berlin with Reinhardt. Zweig was never able, however, to rid himself of the feeling that the fates were hostile to his dramatic endeavours. 'Undoubtedly the closely succeeding deaths of Matkowsky and Kainz had a definite effect on the direction of my life at that time', he wrote in *Die Welt von Gestern*.

If they had acted in the first dramas of a twenty-six-year-old, then it is quite possible that, thanks to their great art, capable of making a success of even the weakest play, I would rapidly have become widely known, perhaps undeservedly so, and would thus have been deprived

[1] 'The priestly arts seem but a jest to me; but deep within I hear the whisper of the voice of doom, and foreboding eats away my hours of joy—for if I seem happy, it is but the outward semblance. . . . Canst thou conceive this suffering, and that other greater yet—the fact that cowards, base fellows, all those besmirched by fate, will still drink in the sun, feel the warm air on their cheeks, see new things in a new beauty, when I already glide sleeping into the depths of darkness?'

[2] In the Lobetheater, 5 May 1912.

[3] I have been unable to identify the Vienna paper in which this interview appeared on 27 Oct. 1912.

of years of slow learning and experience of the world. It was natural enough for me to think I was being persecuted by fate . . . but it is only early in life that one believes fate to be identical with chance. Later one realises that the actual course of one's life is determined from within.[1]

The interview with Wilhelm gave him another opportunity for a mention of Verhaeren. He said that he regarded as his most deserving literary achievement the establishment of the Belgian poet in Germany, and Wilhelm noted that among his autograph collection figured the manuscript of 'La Multiple Splendeur'. He also noted that, apart from the 'Mailied' in its frame on the wall, the collection was housed in a steel cabinet—necessary, he presumed, in view of the owner's frequent travels abroad. Zweig's hard work had in fact not kept him all the time at Kochgasse. In the spring of 1911, no doubt still with Rathenau's words in mind, he had been over to the New World—New York, Canada, the Panama Canal, the Caribbean. 'America, especially Spanish America . . . truly a grandiose picture, which we in Europe cannot for a moment imagine, a great rhythm which flows equally strongly through men and things. And the countryside of the tropics, Cuba, Jamaica, Porto Rico! A light never to be extinguished in oneself, the sun burns into one's blood!' he wrote to Paul Zech.[2] In the States he gained an insight into the 'divine freedom' of the country: no one asked about his nationality, his religion, his origins (and he had travelled there without a passport). With nothing to do in New York, he went through the motions of job-hunting as though he were a penniless immigrant, and found that there was limitless opportunity in this young country for anyone willing to work. And he was delighted to find in a bookshop in Philadelphia a copy of one of his own works displayed. He did not cross to the west coast, but fulfilled his longing to see the Pacific by taking a ship down to the Panama Canal, then under construction: 'I was one of the last of this day to see [the two oceans] still separate.'[3] His essay 'Die Stunde zwischen zwei Ozeanen', for the *NFP* of 6 July 1911, commemorates the visit. Aboard his ship returning to Europe was Gustav Mahler,

[1] *WvG* 167. [2] Letter to Zech, undated (Sch). [3] *WvG* 176–9.

mortally ill, for whom he had written the poem 'Der Dirigent' for a 1910 anthology of tributes to the great conductor,[1] and whose passing he was to mourn in an essay for the *NFP* in 1915.

Back in Vienna, he underwent a minor operation in the area of the ribs, in Dr. Anton Loew's sanatorium in the IXth District.[2] It was nothing serious—the cause is not known—but he seems to have kept his friends in ignorance until it was all over. His main trouble was the effect of the anaesthetic; and in fact it was six weeks before he fully recovered—'six silly, empty, lost weeks . . . which kept me away from all work', as he put it to Zech.[3]

6

'There was a sort of electric crackling in the joists, coming from unseen frictions, every now and then a spark flew out.' *Die Welt von Gestern*

Looking back on the first decade of the century and the years immediately preceding the First World War, Zweig described in his autobiography the optimism, unbelievable to present generations, which prevailed in Europe—the strength that each different country derived from the common upswing of the times, the jubilation in Strasbourg and Belgium at the first flight of the Zeppelin, the joy in Vienna at Blériot's crossing of the Channel, his own hopes for European unity; and then the growing unease at the infectious urge to expansion, the slight discomfort whenever a rattle of shots came from the Balkans. Among his friends in France, Belgium, Germany, were many who stood against war; but, as he later realized, this, like his own, was a passive stand. It was enough, they thought, to profess the ideal of peaceful understanding and intellectual brotherhood beyond language and frontier, to think as Europeans and fraternize internationally. Bazalgette in Paris was the centre of a group of young people who had renounced all narrow nationalism and aggressive imperialism; Romains, Duhamel, Charles Vildrac, Durtain,

[1] *Gustav Mahler: ein Bild seiner Persönlichkeit in Widmungen*, ed. Paul Stefan; Piper, München, 1910, 58–61.

[2] Letter to Servaes, undated (? Apr./May 1911) (StB); statement to the author by Friderike Zweig.

[3] Letter to Zech, undated (Sch).

René Arcos, Jean-Richard Bloch, were all 'passionate champions of the Europe to come and, as the fiery trial of war proved, steadfast in their hatred of all militarism'. In Austria, Franz Werfel; in Germany, the Alsatian René Schickele; in Italy, G. A. Borgese; encouragement came from Scandinavia and from the countries of the East. But the new dawning they thought to discern was in reality the glare of the approaching world conflagration.[1]

In the epilogue to his translation of Barbusse's *Les Suppliants* (*Die Schutzflehenden*), made during the war years but not published until 1932, he described the premonitory quality of this 'erster Versuch': 'the feeling of that pre-war generation which knew, more with its nerves than with its mind, that an evil tension, dangerous and inescapable, hovered over it; but it thought, we all thought, that this fate was approaching us from within ourselves, whereas it came in fact from without, from the anonymous constellation of world history, not from the horoscope of our own ego'.[2] And their idealism was ineffective, without practical links with reality. Above all it lacked an organizer, a man of perception and vision, who could canalize, catalyse, the energy latent within them.

Zweig found such a man for himself in the last moments. On an earlier visit to Florence (perhaps as far back as the autumn of 1907) he had come across by chance (or was this, too, determined 'from within'?) a copy of the *Cahiers de la Quinzaine* containing 'L'Aube', the first instalment of *Jean Christophe*, and saw for the first time the name of Romain Rolland. With eagerness he secured and read the rest of the novel as it appeared.

> Here was the man, the poet, who brought all the moral forces into play . . . a soaring faith in the unifying mission of art. . . . It was the first consciously European novel . . ., the first decisive appeal towards brotherhood, more effective because it reached broader masses than the hymns of Verhaeren, more penetrating than all the protests and pamphlets. . . . In Goethe's words, 'er hat gelernt, er kann uns lehren'.[3]

[1] *WvG* 180–7.

[2] Barbusse, *Die Schutzflehenden*, trans. Stefan Zweig; Rascher, Zürich, 1932, 246.

[3] *WvG* 188.

Inquiry later in Paris about the author proved for a time fruitless. Verhaeren thought he remembered a drama called 'The Wolves', Bazalgette had heard that Rolland was a musicologist who had written a little book about Beethoven; but no one seemed to know how to find him. Finally Zweig established contact by sending Rolland a copy of one of his books (probably *Die frühen Kränze*), and they entered into correspondence. In 1911 he asked Rolland for one of his manuscripts for the collection, promising it 'a place of honour between Flaubert and Balzac'.[1]

They met, at last, in February 1913, up five narrow winding flights in an unpretentious house near the Boulevard Montparnasse (so near *la foire sur la place* and yet so far from it). Rolland opened the door and led Zweig into his small study, filled to the ceiling with books. For the first time he saw Rolland's remarkable blue eyes,

> the clearest and kindest eyes I have ever seen in anyone, . . . singular pupils . . . that could glow with a wondrously communicative and beneficent light. . . . In this simple, almost monastic cell, the world was mirrored as in a camera obscura. . . . I sensed . . . a human, moral superiority, an inner freedom without pride, the freedom of an independent soul. At first glance I recognised in him—and time has proved me right—the man who was to be Europe's conscience in a crucial hour.

They spoke about *Jean Christophe*. Rolland told him that in it he had tried to fulfil a threefold duty—his gratitude to music, his profession of faith in European unity, his appeal to the nations to awaken to consciousness. The time had come to be alert: the powers of hatred, with unscrupulous material interests behind them, were more vehement than those of reconciliation: obscurantism was visibly at work, and the battle against it, he said, was even more important than their art. 'Art can bring us consolation as individuals, but it is powerless against reality.' It was the first time Zweig had had brought home to him the duty of facing the constant possibility of a European war with preparation and action. 'You are a European,' Rolland had written to him in May 1910, 'and I am one too.'[2] Their friendship, sealed at this

[1] Dum 343. [2] Dum 123.

meeting, Zweig described as, together with that of Freud and Verhaeren, 'the most fruitful and, at certain times, the most decisive for the future course of my life'.[1]

7

'It was a sort of turning-point then in my life.'
Friderike to Stefan Zweig, July 1912

In the summer of 1908 Alexander Girardi, one of the best-known and most original folk-singers of Vienna, who had become for the city almost what Bellman had been for Stockholm, gave before he left for Berlin a farewell evening at the *Heuriger* known as Stelzer's, in the suburb of Rodaun. It was a memorable occasion for Vienna, and the line of fiacres stretched from the baroque gate of the Kalksburg Jesuit hostel to the old foursquare house in which lived Hugo von Hofmannsthal himself. Stefan Zweig was there with a group of other young poets and writers, in relaxed mood, sharing the mixture of gaiety and melancholy which marked the evening. At a nearby table he caught the eye of, and smiled perhaps a little forwardly at, a young lady whose dark beauty and enigmatic smile in return held his attention for a while. One of her friends, a passionate lover of poetry, noticing the exchange, was only too pleased to be able to tell her who the distinguished stranger was, and to dilate on his achievements in the realm of letters, even quoting from his translation of Verlaine; and a young doctor who was one of her company praised the depth of feeling and psychological maturity which had characterized his Introduction to the Verlaine volume written at so early an age.[2]

Friderike Maria von Winternitz, *née* Burger, was then twenty-six. A Catholic, though her father was Jewish, she had been married two years before to Felix von Winternitz, a civil servant, and they had a one-year-old daughter, Alix Elisabeth. She was already beginning to drift apart from her husband, however, for despite their earlier community of interests she found him immature and weak. His mother having died when he was very young, he sought in his wife a substitute for her, and his father's

[1] *WvG* 188–91. [2] Fr 59–64.

over-strong ambitions for him tended also to weaken his character. The evening with her friends at Stelzer's had been a welcome relaxation for Friderike after visiting Felix, then in a sanatorium with stomach trouble, more especially as she had noticed his interest had been aroused by a female fellow patient. His carefree attitude towards money and her own family's financial difficulties (her sister's husband was a gambler, whose debts the family, herself included, was constrained to meet) had already made it necessary for her to turn her youthful literary talent to use, and she had followed up an early novel with stories and *feuilletons* for papers like the *Wiener Zeitung* and the Berlin *Vossische Zeitung*. She had therefore a feeling of sympathy with the poet and writer who had smiled upon her, and although the need to hurry back to her little daughter made any closer acquaintance then impossible, she was eager to read something of his work.

In the next four years she had in fact little time to do so. Life together with her husband became increasingly impossible, and her none-too-large dowry, much of which had been used for the obligatory caution money for his entry into the Civil Service, had now entirely disappeared. A sister for Alix was born in 1910, Susanne Benedictine. With the support and encouragement of her father-in-law, Hofrat von Winternitz, with whom she always got on well, she increased her journalistic activities, and, as a regular job when her housework was done, gave lessons in French literature and history, after passing the necessary qualifying examination. It was a struggle for existence, carried through with the great determination and strength of character she was to show throughout her long life. Every ounce of her strength proved necessary when Suse, not yet two, developed from an attack of dysentery an almost chronic failure of metabolism which baffled the doctors of the day and nearly proved fatal.[1]

In the summer of 1912 she moved with the children out of Vienna to Lower Austria for four months. Here, at Mannigfallmühle bei Gars, in the Kamptal, she hoped for a better chance of recovery for Suse, and for more time to devote to her literary work (though with typical kindness she had also undertaken to

[1] Fr 67.

look after the two children of Dr. Erich Stoerk, a close friend whose own marriage was on the rocks). She came only once to Vienna during this time, on 24 July, for a brief twenty-four-hour visit. At dinner with Felix in the garden of the Riedhof restaurant, not far from his town flat, they were joined by the same young poetry-lover of the Stelzer evening four years before, who brought her instead of flowers a copy of one of the earliest titles of the Insel-Bücherei—Zweig's translation from Verhaeren, *Hymnen an das Leben*. In the height of summer, the garden was empty, save for one table where two men sat: one was Stefan Zweig.

He did not recognize her, and she herself was not too sure if it was he. But he recognized his book, and once again smiled towards her, this time perhaps wondering who this new reader might be. She found him changed since Rodaun:

> no longer a callow Bohemian, but a *soigné*, good-looking man—accustomed, it seemed, to say things to a woman with a glance which made words superfluous. Nothing of melancholy or pain in this warmly open manner: no longer the poet of *Tersites*, but the gay author of *Der verwandelte Komödiant* . . . in which a young actor rescues a high-born lady from a painful predicament by his gift of words and self-confidence.[1]

It was a very different scene from the crowded Rodaun *Heuriger*: no Girardi, no music, no *Waldmeisterbowle*, just a slim volume in her hands bearing his name.

But the curtain did not yet fall. After overnighting at the old Hofrat's apartment in Kochgasse, only a few doors from Stefan's own, she returned the following morning to her mill-house, the three-hour train journey beguiled by the beautiful verses of the *Hymnen*, whose vehement 'yes' to life gave her strength and happiness. At this point her life, where the contrast between her own maturity and her husband's ineffectiveness was now so sharp, and her artistic powers were developing, these two encounters seemed a sign from destiny. On the evening of her return she sat down to write, not without some feeling of shame at such schoolgirl-like behaviour, a letter to Stefan Zweig, unsigned, yet

[1] Fr 68–9.

by no means in the style of many which reached him from female admirers (did he recall this when he wrote *Brief einer Unbekannten* a decade later?):

Dear Mr. Stefan Zweig,

Perhaps there is no need of explanation why I find it easy to do something which people call 'improper'. The reason why it does not seem to me monstrous does not belong here. Yesterday I was in Vienna for half a day and a night, away from my gentle countryside, my mill-house, where forest and water surround me and not the culture of the city.—And there such a welcome chance befell me.—I saw you a few years ago one summer evening at Stelzer's, at Girardi's farewell. Someone said: that's Stefan Zweig. I had just read one of your Novellen, and I read some sonnets whose sounds stayed with me (whether I had read them before, I cannot say). It was a nice evening then. You were sitting, I think, with friends, who were filled, or seemed to be filled, with an enthusiasm. It was a sort of turning-point then in my life. . . . —And yesterday you sat near me at the Riedhof, and a friend of mine brought me the *Hymnen an das Leben*. I read them today to the tune of the wheels as I rode back in the early morning to my summer home. Outside lay the fields in the happiest of sunshines. And so I thought it not unnatural to send you a greeting. The *Hymnen* are so beautiful! A few of them I knew. *Das Wort* I like very much. I had several times read it aloud to myself from the Insel-Almanach. And when I was near you yesterday, it occurred to me: it is not all one whether one spends one's life translating Peladan and Strindberg or Shaw—or Verhaeren. Tell me who you translate, and I will tell you what you are. And how you translate, probably, too. *Nachdichtungen*, a wonderful word!

I write also. Perhaps you may have seen something of mine in the last few days, or passed it over. I would like to send you something as a greeting from the world most dear to me.

Why are you in the city? One should almost never be in a city. It is so beautiful out here. It would be wonderful too for you.

I had your address from someone who told me once about your balcony when he saw my Christmas book-list on which *Tersites* stood. I imagine you will not want to mention this stupid letter to anyone. And I am not writing to get you to reply, although this would please me. If you should feel like doing so—write to Maria von W., Poste Restante, Rosenburg am Kamp. Many greetings![1]

[1] *BrW* 7–8.

The copy she enclosed of her *feuilleton*, 'Sommerbriefe', was from the *Wiener Fremdenblatt*, by-lined only 'F. M. v. W.'

8

'The joy you gave me still surges within me.'
Friderike to Stefan Zweig, October 1912

His reply came by return. She saw for the first time the violet ink he always used, the 'SZ' monogram letter-head, the firm but flowing round hand he had developed from the spiky *deutsche Schrift* of his early days. He answered her letter at once, he said, not so much because in her feuilleton (which he praised) she had described so well the impatience with which one awaits letters on holiday, as because of his gratitude that she had reminded him of that evening at Rodaun with its gaiety and magic. He was glad she had not taken amiss his smile at the Riedhof, which he confessed had held the hope of knowing her better. And there had been what he also thought a sign from destiny: a cousin of his had invited him for a car tour that weekend to the Kamptal, and although the trip had been called off at the last moment, it seemed that there was indeed a mysterious force impelling them to meet. Now, much to his regret, he was off very soon for his annual visit to Verhaeren and would be spending a few further days in Ostende, but the hope of seeing her on his return would be joy to him on his journey. Could she perhaps telephone him before he left? He would so like to hear her voice and to know who she was.[1]

With her joy at receiving this prompt reply was mingled the fear that he would not in the event remember her—he must after all get letters like hers every day—but the finger of fate could not be ignored, for at the weekend when Stoerk came to see her he said that he had nearly brought two other visitors with him, one of whom he was sure she would have welcomed as a colleague in literature. A certain consul, husband of one of his patients, had invited him to join him and a cousin of his in a tour in his new automobile: the cousin was none other than Stefan Zweig. Unfortunately the consul had been obliged at the last minute to defer the jaunt.

[1] Fr 72–3.

She replied at once, on 30 July, promising to ring him the following morning, and dropping her anonymity, adding a postscript: 'You will certainly wish to know whether "Mrs." stands before my name. It does.'[1] From the telephone cabinet of the tiny local post-office next day she heard his voice for the first time, and a letter from him followed, suggesting a meeting in Vienna, as his departure was now a little delayed; though he did not say so, and she could scarcely believe it, she had the impression that he had stayed longer in order to see her. It could not be arranged, in the event, but during his three weeks in Belgium their correspondence continued, on his side as though they were already old friends, with long descriptions of his experiences and impressions.

Before leaving he had sent her some books. Now on his return she sent him, with some misgivings, some of her own work, old and new, published and unpublished. She was due back in Vienna in the early days of September, to the house in Döbling which Felix now left entirely to her, and where she would be free to receive Stefan, though she did not wish to appear too forward in inviting him. They spoke often on the telephone, and she accepted his invitation to visit his apartment in Kochgasse on 7 September:

> You will be mistaken in the self-confidence you attribute to me. But it is this way: I am often turned in on myself, and cannot foresee whether confidence will come to me, remain, or disappear. And even though I have the gentle hope that it will weaken before you, it is mingled with the fear that this and all kinds of other inadequacies on my part might cause you to regret the loss of an hour which seems shining to me. I will gladly come to you, because this is pleasure for me and need disturb you only to the extent you yourself wish—certain as I am that you will not think it strange that I do not do a bit of play-acting and refuse to come because it is 'improper'.[2]

A sudden relapse in Suse's condition, however, made this visit impossible, and it was not until 15 October that they met for the first time, he coming to Döbling, and bringing for her an inscribed copy of *Erstes Erlebnis*.

Her daring in approaching, as a literary novice, so established a

[1] *BrW* 9. [2] *BrW* 11.

writer (the rehearsals for his *Haus am Meer* had already begun at the Burgtheater) made her ill at ease. For him it was no new experience to lend his ear to young authors whom he thought had talent. Perhaps for both, therefore, this first meeting was in fact a little of play-acting, a flirtation with literary overtones. She told him of her plans for a visit to Berlin to see publishers and editors; he spoke of Nietzsche, Hölderlin, Lenau (who had once lived in Döbling), and of the many treasures he would like to show her at his home, in particular the portrait of Verhaeren by his wife and the 'Mailied' manuscript.[1] Shortly afterwards (though only after a false alarm about Suse had put the date off once again) she had this privilege. Despite the contrast between his life and hers—the one carefree and without material worries, the other a daily round of serious duties and responsibilities—she felt a deepening understanding between them.

She made no attempt to conceal these meetings from her husband, whose indifference was undisturbed; but she unburdened her deeper feelings to his father. President of Austria's Union of Writers and Journalists and senior official in the Foreign Ministry's Press Bureau, Hofrat von Winternitz was typical of the wide ranging culture of pre-war Vienna. He had been one of the committee which had awarded Zweig the Bauernfeld Prize in 1906 and had taken a genuine pride in the young man's early achievements. Now he suggested to his daughter-in-law, knowing how it would please her, that she should take on for him the notice he had been asked to do for the *Hamburger Fremdenblatt* of the first night of *Das Haus am Meer*. She remarked, as Zweig took several curtain calls for the author, his embarrassment at public appearances of this kind; and indeed he told her afterwards that for that reason he would probably not attend the première in Hamburg scheduled for 23 November. But the play's success was undoubted, and she wrote an enthusiastic notice for the Hamburg paper.[2]

Before her departure for Berlin they were unable to meet, and she was the more pleasantly surprised to find word from him awaiting her on arrival. He was in fact himself in Berlin;

[1] Fr 75–6. [2] Fr 79–81.

planned, contrary to previous intentions, to go on to Hamburg, where he was delighted to hear how well the play's production was going; and invited her to join him there. In the hope that she could, he had already taken the liberty of reserving a room at the Vier Jahreszeiten, his own favourite hotel, and although he would be too busy to see her before the first night, the thought that she would be there would help him over the hurdle of publicity. Reassuring news about her children (one of her brothers, a doctor, was seeing them almost every day) eased her conscience in yielding to this temptation, and she arrived in Hamburg on 21 November. There were flowers in her room, and he had arranged not only for an old friend to act as her guide round the city but also for Wlach, Director of the Schauspielhaus where his play was to be performed, to take her to the theatre the preceding evening to see *Gabriel Schillings Flucht*. Her interviews with editors in Hamburg went well, as they had also in Berlin—this was the start for her of a long collaboration with the *Hamburger Fremdenblatt*—and she felt for the first time for many years lightness of heart and release from her daily cares. Then, on the morning of 23 November came another letter from Stefan. It had not been easy for him, he wrote, to know her near and not to see her, but he was saving their meeting as a reward for his work. Would she come with him the next day to Lübeck to celebrate his birthday? He would like her to go ahead there, and meet him from the train in the evening after he had shaken off all his responsibilities. No answer would mean she accepted. She did not reply.[1]

9

> *'New warmth, a new look at life . . . had come upon him, and he acknowledged the miracle of two made one, even if he neither would nor could entirely bridge the gulf between man and woman.'*
>
> Friderike Zweig

Das Haus am Meer was if anything a greater success in Hamburg than it had been in Vienna—the prophet away from his own country, she thought—and he seemed to her, though tired, more at

[1] Fr 82–4.

ease in responding to the calls for 'Author!' The following day she set off for Lübeck, went on to Travemünde, where she saw the sea for the first time in her life, and then returned to meet him at the station. It was only much later that she discovered his gentle deception over his birthday and that this gay evening, their first together, was actually a few days in advance of the true date. He told her of his mounting pleasure as the hours had gone by without a reply from her, and of how much this acceptance had meant to him as an earnest of their friendship. From now on they were on 'Du' terms.[1]

How much of real love was there on his side? Until now there had been no rival in his life for his work, and an involvement like this gave him pause, despite its attraction. When they met again in Vienna he warned her that she did not know his world, a darker one than hers, and that she did not know him—thinking of the periods of black depression to which he was prone. He had had many affairs, but had never been tied. This promised to be more. They were neither of them any longer young, and their relationship at its present stage could not be shrugged off as a mere episode without effect on their lives. She was not afraid to entrust herself to him, but the demands of reality could not be blinked. For both it seemed best to try to break the link before it became too strong.[2]

The fluctuations in Suse's condition—a spell earlier in a sanatorium in Munich had done no good, and there was a succession of alarming crises—gave Friderike the excuse she needed to remove for a while from Vienna. A well-known paediatrician in Ritten, near Bolzano, was recommended to her as successful in the cure of weakly children, and thither, on a bitter cold night of January 1913, she repaired with both the girls and a nurse who had joined her from Munich. Stefan, who had meanwhile been in Germany again for the Munich performance of *Das Haus*, was planning to visit Paris in March. But his letters, the books he sent her, showed that her flight had been in vain: the geographical separation, her loneliness in the beautiful Dolomites (she moved on to Merano), served merely to deepen her affection and admiration for him.

[1] Fr 84–6. [2] Fr 86–7.

From Paris, where he was staying at the Hotel Beaujolais and reported his delight at meeting Rilke, and his first encounter with Rolland (he had sent her *Jean Christophe*), he wrote that he had met an attractive person who seemed to personify the city for him, and that he had his distant friend to thank for the greater freedom of perception he was now experiencing.[1] The slight pang of jealousy she felt at this news aroused in her no feeling of bitterness (she was to learn later that it was precisely this calm acceptance on her part which was the strongest bond to hold him to her). To know that he was happy and free was all the joy she needed, she wrote, and she was touched by the sympathy in his letters when she told him of the latest and very grave turn in Suse's illness in the early days of March. The thought of him had given her strength through the nights of crisis, and now the good sense of a young Merano doctor seemed to have brought the little one through.

Greeting cards—one in particular, signed by Rilke, Rolland, Verhaeren, Bazalgette, and Stefan[2]—and poems came to her from Paris: 'Wie die Schwalbe'—

Ach, so neigen und nahen sich
In meine einsam dunkelnden Stunden
Stille Gedanken, du Ferne, an dich'[3]—

and 'Ein paar Verse zum Erwachen',[4] both of Goethean simplicity and feeling, incomparably more mature than the dim outpourings of *Silberne Saiten*. They left no doubt in her mind of his feelings for her, which neither their separation nor his new-found girl friend in Paris could weaken.

She could not see clearly how their future would work out, but one thing was sure: she could not return to her home in Döbling. On the way back from Merano at the end of April she sent the children on to their grandfather and stopped herself for two days at Semmering, as it were to regain her breath before this new phase in her life. She could not in fairness to Felix, towards whom

[1] Fr 88. [2] *BrW* 35.

[3] 'Ah thus, in my darkling hours of loneliness, swoop down and approach quiet thoughts of a loved one afar.' In Fr 91–2 and *Gesammelte Gedichte*; Insel, 1924, 67.

[4] In *Gesammelte Gedichte*, 68.

she retained affection, to his father, or to the children themselves, think in terms of a permanent separation, but equally she could not bring herself to go back to the Döbling home, though Felix had by now quite accustomed himself to a bachelor existence with his father. Divorce, and remarriage to Stefan, would anyway be quite impossible in Catholic Austria. She had to find some sort of compromise. A temporary home at Baden, not far from Vienna, was her solution. Here Felix could feel free to see her as often as he wished; here the Hofrat himself often came on visits; and the little spa had in the past been a frequent refuge for Stefan when he wanted peace and quiet away from the city. It would be the best arrangement for this period of transition, though she could not yet perceive what it was a transition to. She could achieve a discreet independence, continue her writing (she had completed a novel while in the South Tyrol), and leave Stefan the freedom she knew he wanted, while yet being admitted, as far as he would allow her, to his life. It all made sense, but it was none the less an equivocal situation, which surprisingly enough Stefan (the free, the hater of all convention) was the first to want to see ended. At the end of the year he asked her formally whether she would be prepared to go further and seek an annulment of her marriage.[1]

10

> *'Dostoevsky is nothing, if not experienced from within.'* — *Drei Meister*

These years 1912 and 1913 had seen a series of Zweig essays in various periodicals. 'Balzacs Codices vom eleganten Leben' (Berlin, *Das Literarische Echo*) and 'Karl Loewe, der Dichter' (*NFP*), both in February 1912, were followed by a fine piece on Jakob Wassermann in the *Neue Rundschau* in July, on which Martin Buber wrote him his congratulations. In January 1913, after the visit to Lübeck, he wrote for the *Berliner Tageblatt* an essay on Gustav Falke, the poet and novelist from that city 'with the golden towers', on the occasion of his sixtieth birthday. From Paris in the spring of that year he agreed to contribute to Feigl's *Deutsches Bibliophilenkalender*

[1] Fr 92–3.

for 1914 an article on autograph-collecting: 'Das Autographensammeln als Kunstwerk' ('the fee is of no consequence', he wrote to the editor, 'I fully realize you have not the resources of a great newspaper').[1] With Feigl's permission he published the article in the *Vossische Zeitung* on 14 September—better there, he thought, than in the *NFP*, for he did not want an army of visitors clamouring to see his collection, nor to reveal in Austria how much money he was devoting to the 'collector's bug'.[2] But his main preoccupation in 1913 was with the study on Dostoevsky. He had not yet conceived the idea of *Drei Meister*, in which the previous essays on Dickens and Balzac would be joined by that on the Russian, and the essay he now planned was on a considerably larger scale. His research work for it was enormous, and he found his refuge in Friderike's house in Baden of great benefit when he needed quiet, not least because she herself, familiar with Dostoevsky's novels, was able to discuss and make suggestions as the work progressed. He continued on this work through the war years, and the final product, a bare 109 pages, is perhaps the finest example of his ability to condense, chisel, and polish, when we compare it with the original manuscript preserved in the Schiller Nationalmuseum, Marbach. The poem 'Der Märtyrer (Dostoiewski, 22. Dez. 1849)', later collected with *Sternstunden der Menschheit* in a slightly different version, appeared in the Insel-Almanach for 1913, and at the end of the year the essays *Der Rhythmus von New-York* and *Rückkehr zum Märchen*. During a short summer stay at Puchberg in Lower Austria he also completed the *Novelle*, *Die Mondscheingasse*.[3]

[1] Letter to Feigl, undated (Mar. 1913) (StB).
[2] Letters to Feigl, 19 and 22 Aug. 1913 (StB).
[3] *BrW* 44.

III. The First World War and Friderike 1914–1918

But beware, Polyphemus!
There burn in secret
The fires of revenge
In our souls . . .
And out of the cavern of blood and horror
We are striding,
We, brothers of the peoples, brothers of the ages,
Over your stinking corpse
Into the eternal heavens of the world.

'Polyphem', 1917

Europe! I will not tolerate
That you die in this delirium.
Europe, I shout who you are
In the ears of your assassins.

Europe! They stop our mouth;
But our voice will carry up through all,
Like a plant forcing up through stone.

Jules Romains

I

'Never believe that, even in thought, I could shake the foundations of your "partly" tied existence.'

Friderike to Stefan Zweig, April 1914

The following year promised little change for Zweig. He was still working on the Dostoevsky, not yet in its final form, and on a biographical study of Marceline Desbordes-Valmore. Lectures were to be given in Berlin in January, in Mannheim, and in Hamburg; and he was being asked to talk again in Berlin at the end of February, this time on Dostoevsky.[1] A major project with the Insel-Verlag, first conceived in 1912 and only now taking shape, was an edition of the complete poems of Verlaine in German, himself as usual undertaking to select and organize the contributors. He also had plans for collaboration with the composer Oskar Fried, presumably on a libretto, and they were to meet in Berlin during his visit (nothing in fact came of this).[2] His bust by Gustinus Ambrosi, finished the previous year, was to appear in the deaf sculptor's Graz exhibition that summer, alongside those of Ginzkey, Strindberg, Gerhart Hauptmann, and Schönherr.[3] There would be his usual summer visit to Verhaeren at 'Caillou-qui-bique', and later perhaps a long-planned visit to Japan and China, returning through Russia.[4] The political rumblings of the last few years—Agadir, Fashoda, the Balkan War, the treason of the Austrian Captain Redl—had been only momentarily disturbing, and there was no feeling, as there was in the similar situation twenty-five years later, of the inevitability of war.

If Stefan Zweig felt a sense of crisis that year, it was in his personal life. Friderike had said that she would fall in with his wish and arrange a formal separation from her husband. Both knew that the possibility of their marriage remained remote. Nevertheless, the step could not fail to bind him to her, and he felt himself obliged to terminate his affair with the French woman he had met in Paris the previous year. He discussed this liaison (of which we know next to nothing) fully with Friderike, and resolved to bring it to an end when he revisited Paris in the spring.[5] Staying with her father-in-law for a day or two, she wrote to Stefan on the eve of his departure in March:

Forgive me for taking up your time, but I fear I shall not be able to see you alone, and I want, I must, tell you something before you go. To tell you that you must not think I am sad: if I am at times, it is my nerves, not I. I am always your lamb, that wants to be joyful with you.

[1] *Bildb* 130; letters to Zech, Feb. 1914 (Sch).
[2] Letter from Fried, 4 Feb. 1914 (ZE).
[2] Letter from Ambrosi, 1 Mar. 1914 (ZE).
[4] Letter to Ellen Key, 4 May 1909 (KB). [5] Fr² 41–2.

And do not feel worried that you are leaving me behind engaged in a battle. I hurried up with my affairs to get them in order before you left. All is now in order, and the money side too is fixed.—I do not want you ever to feel this as a kind of warning, just stay free and cool, as you think best for yourself. I believe in you—but I want nothing from you. I have made myself free now, because I want to be purer before you and before myself, and because it was your wish. It was the first wish you have ever uttered, and I have waited a long time for one. But do not think that it did not lie in the nature of things. You merely made the struggle and the decision easier for me. And for that I thank you, whatever may happen.[1]

For her it was clearly more of a crisis than she would admit to him. Though to go back to Felix was now unthinkable for her, and she was also firm in her resolve not to make demands on Stefan, it was all the same an extremely serious step she was contemplating. The settlement would leave her very little money, and as she was retaining custody of the two girls, still very young, she would have to develop her literary and journalistic work to support herself. She wanted to be near Stefan, to help him, as she knew she could, in his work, but she really did want him to stay free, and was prepared to suit her life to his in whatever way he decided. The legal negotiations took several weeks and cost her many sleepless nights. Though she was overjoyed when a letter came at the end of March inviting her to join him in Paris, she was not sure whether she would in fact be well enough to make the journey. It was both a nervous and a physical crisis, in which her own determination was strengthened by many sympathetic letters from him. Felix, in agreeing to the separation, had made only one condition: that it should be concealed from his father. The notarial side was therefore conducted in St. Pölten, well away from Vienna. When the final papers were signed there in April she was able to board the express direct for Paris with a sense of great relief. With her she brought for Stefan a Brazilian butterfly under glass, which he used for many years thereafter as an ash-tray.[2]

Despite her request to book her at another hotel nearby, to

[1] *BrW* 53–4. [2] *BrW* 60; Fr[2] 39–40.

avoid any awkward meeting with his Paris girl-friend ('the slightest sideways glance would cause me pain'),[1] he had insisted on getting her a room at the Beaujolais, where he as usual had been staying. Did her freedom really mean much to him? As she herself wrote later, had the separation not happened to have been carried through before the war, it would surely have been prevented by its outbreak, and the lives of all of them would have been very different.[2] One might have expected that he would at least have touched upon this in his autobiography, when treating of that critical year: but his deliberate exclusion of all mention of Friderike is maintained even here, and we can only guess at his feelings, more especially as his letters to her of this time have not been preserved. That he had a deep affection for her there is no doubt, and their lives in the two years since their first meeting had become closely woven together. She was prepared to discount his warnings about his periods of depression, confident, as the event proved, that she was strong enough to survive these and could help him over them. For his part, her attachment to him—a mature woman whose tastes coincided with his own and whose literary ability was itself considerable—seemed to bring many advantages, without his having to compromise on that most precious possession, his personal freedom. 'A few good people, very few, are around my life,' he had written to Benno Geiger before Friderike's arrival, 'a woman who means much to me; for that very reason however I enjoy at the same time many hot experiences (it is the body alone that can truly *experience*).' Breaking now with this woman, as he had promised Friderike, seemed like putting an end to an epoch, cutting out of his heart a piece of the Paris and the France he loved (though neither he nor she could foresee the permanent separation the war was to bring); and when he and Friderike left for home together at the end of April she saw for the first time tears in his eyes.[3] But this seems to have been the only sacrifice, the only compromise, he made in their twenty-five years together.

[1] *BrW* 58. [2] Fr[2] 44. [3] Fr[2] 41–2; Geiger 430.

2

'Each individual experienced an intensification of his personality.' *Die Welt von Gestern*

Meanwhile there was much to be done during his six weeks' stay in Paris. 'We thought of war occasionally, but no more than we thought of death—as a possibility, but probably a distant one. Paris was too beautiful in those days, and we were too happy.'[1] He worked hard on the Dostoevsky essay: 'finished for two years, and yet never finished: it troubles me and rejoices me unendingly'. He completed the biographical part of his planned book on Marceline Desbordes-Valmore. There was a heavy correspondence with other poets over the Verlaine translations: Hans Carossa (who promised to try a few of the lyrical poems), Rudolf Binding, Paul Zech, Hasenclever, Herbert Eulenberg (who completed three of the sonnets in three days), and Ernst Hardt were all in touch with him, and Insel had drafted a publicity leaflet.[2] Friderike had the pleasure of meeting Rolland for the first time when he called at the Hotel Beaujolais. During his last few days in France Stefan accompanied Verhaeren to Rouen, where he was to lecture, and leaving him at the station—the very place where two years later one of the machines whose praises Verhaeren had sung was to tear him to pieces—promised to see him again as usual on the first of August at 'Caillou-qui-bique'. His departure with Friderike, though in one sense the start of a new life, was unclouded by any premonition of the tragedy to come for Europe: 'a simple, unsentimental leavetaking, as if going from one's home for a few weeks'. His plan for the next few months was clear: finish off the Dostoevsky somewhere in the country in Austria; then rejoin Verhaeren in Belgium, and perhaps in the autumn undertake the trip to the Far East and Russia. 'All lay clear and plain before me in this, my thirty-third year. The world offered itself like a fruit, beautiful and rich with promise, in that radiant summer.'[3]

It was indeed a summer to remember, as an old vineyard

[1] *WvG* 197.

[2] Letter to Benno Geiger, 21 Mar. 1914 (Geiger 430). Carossa, *Führung und Geleit*; Insel, 1933, 81. Letters from Zech (Sch), Carossa, Binding, and Eulenberg (ZE).

[3] *WvG* 198.

worker in Baden bei Wien remarked to Stefan just before he left for Belgium, a summer the like of which had not been seen for many a year and which promised an exceptional wine-harvest.[1] While he was in Belgium Friderike planned to stay for a while at the *Kuranstalt* Tobelbad bei Graz, where Erich Stoerk and his second wife were now doctors, and try to recover her strength, which had been sorely tried in the last months. Then, leaving the children with the Stoerks, she was to meet Stefan in Zürich and go together with him to Italy. At this time he felt that if their two lives were to be joined it was essential for her to devote her spare time from the children to her own literary interests, begin new work: a woman without children or any activity of her own would make demands on his time, and on him, which he could not fulfil.[2]

In *Die Welt von Gestern* he has described how the assassination at Sarajevo brought these plans to nought, when on 28 June 1914 the shot was fired 'which in a single second shattered the world of security and creative reason in which we had been educated, had grown up and been at home—shattered it like a hollow vessel of clay'. He and Friderike, Benno Geiger with them, heard the news in Baden, where a crowd gathered round the bandstand to hear the announcement of Franz Ferdinand's death.[3] But there seemed no need to put off his visit to Belgium. From Ostende and Le Coq, the little seaside resort nearby where he planned a few weeks' stay before going on to Verhaeren's, he watched the mounting tension in Europe—Austria's ultimatum to Serbia, the evasive reply, the exchange of telegrams between the monarchs, the barely hidden mobilizations—and the preparations in Belgium itself, which, rumour had it, was to be invaded by the Germans in spite of the treaty. Though he had ridiculed these fears expressed to him by James Ensor and Crommelynck ('you may hang me from that lamp-post if ever the Germans march into Belgium'), the critical last days of July rapidly dispelled any lingering optimism in the holiday-makers' minds, and as if by magic the beaches cleared.[4] He knew it was time to return home.

[1] *WvG* 203.
[2] Fr 100, Fr[2] 43.
[3] *WvG* 198–201.
[4] *WvG* 203–5; DDh 8.

Booking his tickets for the Orient Express (as it turned out, the last), Stefan positively pleaded with Siegfried Trebitsch and his wife, who were also in Le Coq, to follow his example, offering them his own *wagon-lit* reservation if only they would agree to go. When they refused to be shaken in their false optimism, he said: 'You will regret it, my dear fellow . . . we are at the beginning of the end of the time that was our life.'[1] To Anton Kippenberg he wrote on his last day in Belgium:

> I am travelling direct to Vienna: although I am not a soldier of the first line I do not want to be missing in these days. Perhaps I may be able to get over to Leipzig—but of course books must now be the last thing for any decent citizen to be thinking of and I do not propose to burden so uneasy a time with mine. . . . I regret missing my days with Verhaeren, but this regret too I must lose in the more important feelings of this hour.[2]

Just outside Herbesthal the train was halted for a while, and he saw unmistakable signs that the rumoured German invasion of Belgium was a fact. Slowly past ran an unending stream of freight wagons, loaded with tarpaulin-covered shapes that could not conceal their military purpose. When they finally pulled into Herbesthal, the station was closed, and behind the locked waiting-room doors could be heard the rattle of sabres and the thud of grounded rifles. As the train moved on, there remained no doubt in his mind: he was riding back into war. In Austria the next morning the general mobilization placards, the flying banners, were the final confirmation. Vienna was in tumult, and he himself was swept along, as he confessed later, by the majesty, rapture, and seduction of this popular enthusiasm. 'In spite of all my hatred and aversion for war, I should not like to have missed the memory of those first days. As never before, thousands and hundreds of thousands felt what they should have felt in peacetime, that they belonged together', acknowledging the 'unknown power which had lifted them out of their everyday existence', giving a 'wild and almost rapturous impetus to the greatest crime of our time';[3] impelled like Rolland's Clérambault to 'run with

[1] Treb 221–2.

[2] Letter to Kippenberg, July 1914 (Sch).

[3] *WvG* 205–8.

the herd, rub against the human animals his brothers, feel like them, act like them'.[1] 'The whole people is as though transformed, poured into a new mould', as Harry Graf Kessler wrote to Hofmannsthal early in August; 'to have experienced this will probably be the greatest event of our lives.'[2]

3

'Farewell, dear friends, companions of so many fraternal hours over there in France, Belgium, England, we must say goodbye for many a long day.' 'An die Freunde im Fremdland'

His claim, in *Die Welt von Gestern*, not to have himself succumbed to this sudden outburst of patriotism—to have lived too internationally to be able overnight to hate a world that was as much his own as Austria—is scarcely borne out by the facts.[3] 'He wanted to be in it', as Friderike said,[4] and a letter to Kippenberg of 4 August shows clearly enough how in fact he felt:

> I shall be called up in the next few days, and in all probability in a few weeks shall be at the front; at all events I am making my dispositions today. There will be a request to you among them, in the event of anything happening to me, namely to make a selected cheap uniform edition of my works published with you and of various works not yet published, editor to be proposed by me, timing to be decided by you. I believe I may count today on the fulfilling of this wish, having in mind our long and always friendly relationship. . . . We are sending our last man into the field. Most of our poets, from Hofmannsthal on, are already in national service. If England stays neutral, I am hopeful: we all know that this time everything is at stake. May God protect Germany![5]

He would be leaving very soon, he wrote to Friderike, as a private soldier for the Polish front.[6] But the military machine ground slowly, and nearly two months later he was still in Vienna: the *Landstürmer* who had not seen service, to whom he was to belong, had still not been called up. In a letter to Kippenberg

[1] Romain Rolland, *Clérambault*, Ch. 1 (Dum 142).

[2] Hofmannsthal/Kessler, *Briefwechsel*; Insel, Frankfurt am Main, 1968, 384.

[3] *WvG* 211. [4] Fr 103. [5] Sch. [6] Fr 102.

he described the horrors of the Eastern Front, where a close friend of his, before the very eyes of his helpless company, had been sucked under with his horse in a swamp.

Not purgatory, but Hell itself! I am writing you this so that you do not, like so many in Germany, underrate the efforts of Austria. My greatest happiness would be to ride as an officer against a civilised enemy—but if I get out there, it will be to fight as private soldier against filth, cold, hunger, and a rabble. This may explain for you why not a single intellectual from Austria has so far volunteered for the front, and those who have had to go have actually got themselves transferred back again (Hofmannsthal, Werfel). And we lack cohesion, as you no doubt well understand. Brody did not mean so much to me as Insterburg: the news of the first left me calm, but I trembled to learn of the second and its devastation. There is only one final, highest form of cohesion: in the last analysis our language alone is our country! —I am of course doing nothing in the way of literature, but have helped with two others, by dint of ten hours work a day, to set up an organisation which has brought in several hundred thousand in a few days.[1]

My great ambition, however, is to be an officer over with you in *that* army, to conquer in France—in France particularly, the France that one must chastise because one loves her. It is strange to think that against no-one would I have more *élan* than against those who stand highest in my estimation, for it was their presumption that was the beginning of all misfortune. Perhaps our regiments will be so intermingled that some will get over there—on that day I would do my utmost to come too. I have no hatred for Russia, for she like Germany is fighting for *ein erweitertes Volkstum* ('an enlarged nationhood'); but France fights for her image, her frivolity, and England for her moneybags. . . .[2]

Both Friderike and the army, however, had other ideas. For her it was inconceivable that this slight figure, wholly unfit for the rigours of the trenches, should not be found some task more suited to his genius. The army, despite itself, agreed, for his first medical inspection pronounced him unfit for front-line service (perhaps the history of his operation two years before, the scar

[1] There is no record of what this organization was.

[2] Letter to Kippenberg, undated (? autumn 1914) (Sch).

standing out against the white skin, helped here), and he was reserved 'for other duties'.[1] And as the days passed, the elation he had felt began to give way to a pessimistic defeatism, lacking the cynical humour of Karl Kraus or Robert Neumann, horrified only at the slaughter to which an early end now seemed increasingly impossible. He had grown a beard soon after his return to Vienna, as a sort of mourning sign for the times;[2] and Felix Braun recalls how, in their circle of friends at the Café Beethoven, their views began now to take opposing turns: 'I was for the preservation of Austria, but he wanted only the victory of peace.'[3]

Despite his disclaimer to Kippenberg, his pen had not been idle. Three essays in particular are significant for his state of mind at the time. 'Ein Wort von Deutschland' and 'Die schlaflose Welt', which appeared in the *NFP* on 6 and 18 August respectively (the first probably drafted on the journey from Ostende) celebrate the *Schwertbrüderschaft* of Austria/Hungary and Germany, but the unequivocal patriotism of the first is moderated in the second. This is total war, no one can remain outside it, and a terrible price must be paid for the new order to come. 'An die Freunde im Fremdland', in the *Berliner Tageblatt* of 19 September, is an almost despairingly sad farewell to his friends in the enemy countries. 'This hatred against you—although I do not feel it myself—I will not try to moderate, for it brings forth victories and heroic strength. . . . Do not expect me to be your advocate, however much I may feel this my duty! Respect my silence, as I respect yours! . . .' 'No matter who may be the victor' was the only phrase struck out by the censor.[4]

At the end of September the army was to review his case, he wrote to Kippenberg, and he should then be directed to some kind of service—'at last! this position of waiting was unbearable'.[5] Just at this moment he received a letter from Rolland in Geneva, enclosing for him (it seems almost unbelievable to our generation how benign was the censorship of those days) a copy of his *Au-dessus de la mêlée*, with the encouraging words: 'I am truer to our Europe than you, my dear Stefan Zweig, and say farewell

[1] Fr. 105–8. [2] Fr 103; *Mus Land* 200. [3] *Mus Land* 199.
[4] *WvG* 220; H. [5] Letter to Kippenberg, 28 Sept 1914 (Sch).

to none of my friends.'[1] This resumption of their correspondence (which lasted up to the Second World War) did much to strengthen Zweig's faith in the future of Europe. The letter also told him something of Verhaeren. The Belgian, not surprisingly, had been swept along by the wave of hatred against Germany which had followed the invasion, and unlike Zweig was bitterly polemical in his patriotism. Rolland had been able to discover his address:

> he is living at 18 Matheson Road, Kensington, London [Zweig wrote to Kippenberg on 18 September], and is breathing there the terrible atmosphere of lies in the French and English papers. I have asked him through Rolland to be just in his anger, but what must I fear when Rolland writes: 'Hélas, il connaît aussi maintenant la haine.' I will not of course beg him to 'spare' Germany, but I find it frightful for his sake that in his book on the destruction of Belgium he should transform reports into poems. . . . I should much like to know whether my book on him, with its current topicality, has appeared: it had finished printing at the end of July and was to have been published in August.[2]

(In fact, it appeared in Constable's list at Christmas, showing, as he said to Kippenberg, the English mentality when it came to a conflict between patriotism and business.[3] In a first-class translation by Jethro Bithell it was a considerable success.)

To Rolland later he wrote of the gulf separating him now for ever from Verhaeren, whose attacks on Germany he saw reprinted in the German press.

> You know how much I have loved him—like a father, a master—and yet I cannot now grieve . . . to be hated in person for one's race is a destiny which my Jewish blood has learned over the years to bear with a smile . . . and, strangely enough, precisely in the vehemence of his utterances I detect a profound sadness, a despair which I honour and respect.[4]

'In a war, the word is powerless: you either join in, or you keep silent', Carl Zuckmayer once said.[5] Zweig felt miserable now in his own powerlessness to influence events. Rolland's idea of an

[1] *WvG* 220; *ZwV* i. 46.
[2] Sch.
[3] Letter to Kippenberg, 23 Dec. 1914 (Sch).
[4] Letter to Rolland, 23 Mar. 1915 (Dum 49).
[5] Arens[1] 121.

international group in Switzerland to fight all forms of hatred and to campaign actively against the war he took up with enthusiasm, elaborating it to the form of an international moral parliament, in which Germany might be represented by Gerhart Hauptmann, Austria by Herman Bahr; Holland, Frederik van Eeden; Sweden, Ellen Key; Russia, Gorki; Italy, Benedetto Croce; Belgium, Verhaeren; Switzerland, Spitteler; Poland, Sienkiewicz; England, Shaw or Wells. Such an assembly could show, he thought, that idealism as well as nationalism existed in the world.[1] But his own patriotism was still very much engaged (in December we find him writing to Rolland to defend the German bombardment of Rheims),[2] and he was as anxious as ever to join the battle in some way, even if not at the front. Finally Ginzkey, who was a regular army officer and indebted to him,[3] was able to arrange an assignment in November to the *Kriegsarchiv* in the Stiftskaserne in Vienna, on what would nowadays be termed Information work. 'A very responsible position', he called it in a letter to Kippenberg: 'I have had no military service, and shall in this way be able to serve the common good with my strongest asset, my brain. My desire to get into hospital work was not fulfilled, but the job I am to have is in fact far more interesting and more suited to me.'[4] It meant putting on uniform and undergoing basic training, and there might be some possibility of field employment in this line. One Bohemian paper reported him in fact as already 'in the field', and he had to write a correction.[5]

4

'The world renews itself, as always, through suffering.' Rolland to Friderike, Easter 1915

Friderike had meanwhile regained her health almost completely at Tobelbad, and had been busy helping the Stoerks with their many difficulties.

[1] Letter to Rolland, Oct. 1914 (*ZwV* i. 77–8).

[2] Letter to Rolland, 11 Dec. 1914 (Dum 146).

[3] Statement to the author by Friderike Zweig.

[4] Letter to Kippenberg, Nov. 1914 (Sch).

[5] Letter to Kippenberg, undated (Sch); card to Servaes, 10 Dec. 1914 (StB).

Do not fear [she had written to Stefan at the end of June] that I will not be able to stand your little outbreaks of nerves, and do not compare *anything* with Paris. We will neither of us think any more about that. But, my love, do not expect me to change again. . . . I am not worried that with me you will feel that longing to be alone so much, for I myself am often absent and taciturn. Dearest, I talk like this, and still secretly tremble whether everything will be all right. I shall pray to God daily to give me the chance to be exposed to your 'depressions'. —One thing I *expect* from you, however, my little brother. You must work with *me*. . . . The hours when I sat with you as your pen flew like the wind over the pages are just as unforgettable for me as our nights.[1]

The events of July brought her much worry, almost desperation, at being pinned helpless so far from Vienna. Felix was called up immediately in the rank of captain, and with Alix she was able to meet him in Graz on his way south from Vienna. She was relieved to hear that Stefan was back from Belgium and to know that he was near, but even in the first days of August had not fully grasped the implications of the hour.[2]

It was only when she received his letter early in August saying that he expected soon to be off as a private to Galicia that she was shaken out of her feeling of helplessness, and telegraphed to say she would meet him in the Café Eiles in Vienna on the evening of 4 August. Whether she was able to pull any strings over his military call-up is not certain—though she had some sort of contact with the War Press Bureau which she was putting to use for another friend[3]—but she was, anyway, relieved to find that the call-up of the *Landstürmer* was proceeding for the moment very slowly. Back in Baden, she felt almost ashamedly happy to be near him, even starting a novel and feeling strong enough to look after, in her turn, the Stoerks' two children as well as her own for a while in September. Stefan often came to Baden to see her, as did the 'old gentleman', her father-in-law, with much unpublished news from his work at the Foreign Office. It was he and Friderike who between them put things in motion to get Stefan into the medical corps, in vain as it turned out. Friderike

[1] *BrW* 61–2. [2] Fr 101; Fr² 43–4; *BrW* 63–4. [3] *BrW* 65.

herself began part-time work as a kind of V.A.D. in one of the Baden hospitals.[1]

By the end of 1914, however, it was becoming more and more difficult for her to remain in Baden, which in addition to emergency hospitals now housed the Imperial Court, a military headquarters, and that of the war correspondents, and train travel to and from Vienna for the ordinary citizen was not easy. She wanted to be nearer Stefan, and to have the children nearer their grandfather and her own mother. She settled, therefore, in yet another temporary home, at 49 Lange Gasse, not far from Stefan's and the Hofrat's apartments. It was here that, stimulated by a message from a friend of Rolland's, a Frenchwoman temporarily in Switzerland, asking what Austrian women were doing to end the war, she approached the President of the Austrian Women's Union, and was the main driving force in setting up the International Committee for a Lasting Peace, which carried out much good work in its efforts to clear away the atmosphere of hatred and substitute one of humanity.[2]

She was not able to see Stefan every day, but in her letters during the early months of 1915 did her best to encourage him to return to his own work. 'The day, despite the War Archives, is still long, if you will but remember that it is a sin—the only true sin—to work without a will.' And again:

If only I could arrange peace and quiet for you to work. This wonderful work you are planning [*Jeremias*], if only you would begin it . . . perhaps in the words of the beginning the fire within you will break out. . . . Please, please, do not think I would not sacrifice seeing you, if you will only take the decision. . . . You, the free one, must not be petrified with words like 'It's no good', 'I can't work away from the sea', etc. Stay three or four days at home after a weekend . . . and report sick. Don't you seek how the gain of these few days would justify a thousandfold the deception? Try a trip out somewhere after the office, say to Rodaun, set yourself down between two good pubs—Stelzer and the Roter Stadel—and try to work, use the evening, spend the night out there, then you would have many good hours.—If it just succeeds once, it will succeed many times.[3]

[1] Fr 109. [2] Fr 109–10. [3] *BrW* 70–2.

Her efforts, and those of Rolland, to whom she wrote describing Stefan's inability to concentrate on his own work, were probably decisive in restoring a purpose to his life and in crystallizing his positive pacifism. 'The hour is hard, but great,' wrote Rolland to her on Easter Monday 1915, 'and our task is beautiful. Our sufferings will be envied us later. There are moments for humanity when tears themselves are fertile.'[1]

5

'"I have a hatred for hatred", said Olivier. "If only you had!" said Christophe.'

Rolland, *Jean Christophe*

'Stefan Zweig, Recruit, Poet (retired)', as he signed himself in a letter to Servaes in December 1914,[2] found himself in congenial company in the Stiftskaserne. Ginzkey, Csokor, Paul Stefan, and Alfred Polgar; Bartsch, Albert Ehrenstein, and Hermann Bahr; Strobl, Erwin Rainalter, and Siegfried Trebitsch were all employed by the War Archive. Werfel came later, after a spell on the Eastern Front, and even Rilke joined them for a few months, until a benevolent medical examination released him from the misery of uniform.[3] They worked on the styling and improving of publicity releases, ran the official journal *Oesterreich-Ungarn in Waffen* (which an anonymous wit among their number—was it Ehrenstein?—retitled 'Oesterreich-Ungern in Waffen'),[4] a literary periodical *Das Donauland*, and the war library. In his first month Zweig found himself very hard worked, with basic military training in addition to his office duties;[5] but thereafter settled down to a modest six-hour day which left him ample leisure. This he used at first to good advantage for his own work, and he was able to report to Zech at the end of the year the near-completion of the Dostoevsky essay and two *Novellen*.[6] For a time he deserted his flat in Kochgasse and lived in a small hotel

1 *BrW* 72–3.

2 To Servaes, 10 Dec. 1914 (Sch).

3 *WvG* 218–19; Brod 41; *Mus Land* 199; Treb 226; correspondence in ZE.

4 'Austria-Hungary in Arms' became 'Austria Reluctantly in Arms'.

5 Letter to Servaes, 10 Dec. 1914 (Sch).

6 Letter to Zech, undated (Sch).

FRIDERIKE MARIA VON WINTERNITZ, about 1912

PLATE 5

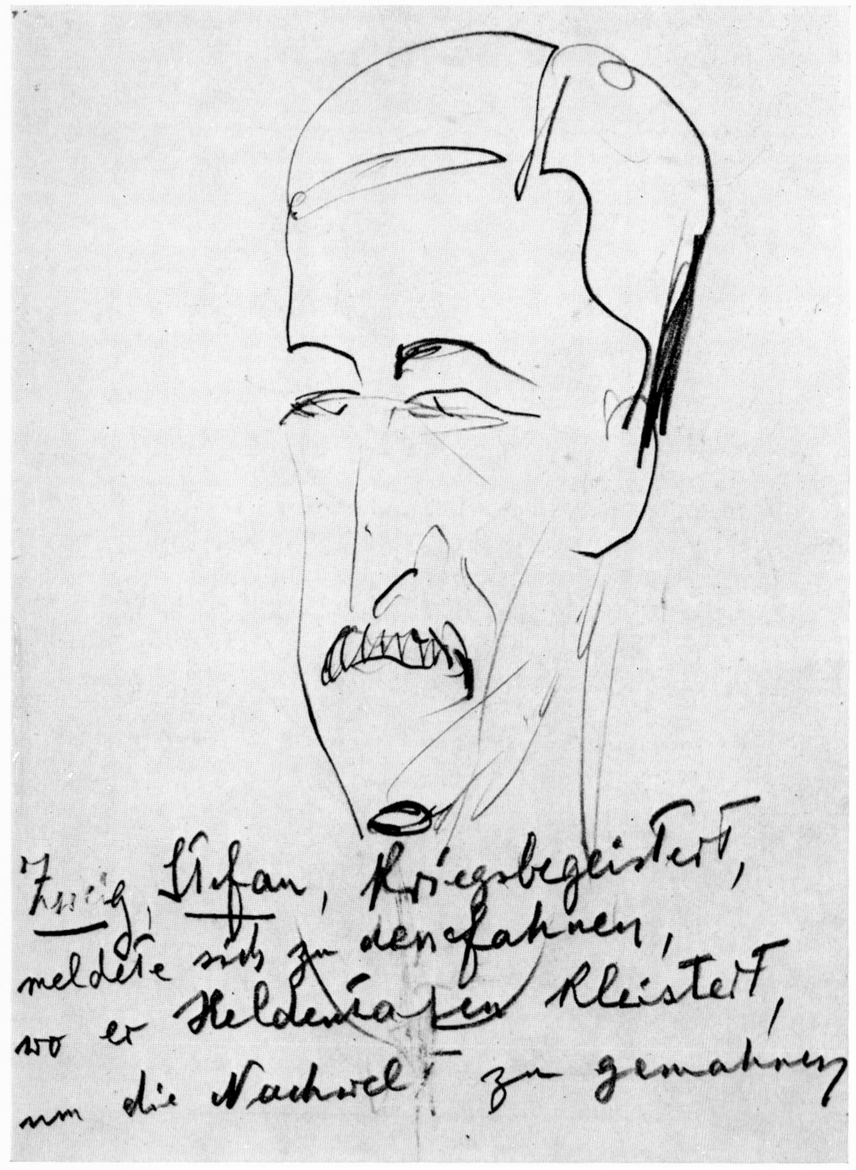

CARICATURE AND VERSE BY BENNO GEIGER, about 1915–16, in a friend's album (Zweig's 'enthusiasm' for the war sees him 'pasting together heroic deeds for the edification of posterity'—a reference to his service with the War Archive in Vienna)

at the Hietzingerplatz, walking daily to Mödling and taking the tram in to the office.[1] 'My military duties give me plenty to do,' ran a letter to Kippenberg on 23 December, 'and I have today been promoted to corporal. The only thing which troubles me is that I cannot get over to Germany, but there is no leave at the moment. How I should have loved to have seen Germany in this year: not to have experienced this will be something lacking for the rest of my life.'[2]

When did his feelings towards the war really change? From the beginning he had never felt hatred for the opposing side, and had been revolted by the patriotic dithyrambs which so many of his friends on both sides had felt urged to intone. Lissauer's 'Hymn of Hate' was to his mind as disastrous as Verhaeren's 'Belgique Sanglante'; and Hermann Hesse's call in September 1914 to the poets of the world not to lend their voices to the war's chorus of hate was as welcome to him as it was to Rolland.[3] Nevertheless, in the early months, as we have seen, he was committed to his country's side, and described his work in the War Archives with some pride as 'important and secret'.[4] It would be quite wrong to describe him as a pacifist from the start. When he himself looked back in 1922 he had forgotten this early period:

> For me, perhaps more than for any other German writer, the war was a moment of decision, cutting straight through the middle of my life. . . . I do not reckon it any particular merit (attributed kindly to me by others) to have recognised from the first moment the ruinous senselessness of Europe's suicide and to have set myself against war with all my moral power: for me the community, the unity of Europe was as self-evident as my own breathing.[5]

And by the time he came to write *Die Welt von Gestern* he had convinced himself that his pacifism (or, more accurately, his opposition to the war) had dated from its very outbreak: although he admitted that, disinclined to the heroism demanded of a conscientious objector in Austria, he had to accept, perhaps justly, the reproach of indecision that was so often made to 'my revered master of an earlier century, Erasmus of Rotterdam'. 'I looked

[1] Treb 241. [2] Sch. [3] *WvG* 215; Baumer, op. cit. 42.
[4] Letter to Kippenberg, undated (Sch). [5] DDh. 9.

around for some activity in which I could serve without being militarily active . . . my appointment [in the War Archives] was certainly not a glorious occupation, . . . but one at least that seemed to suit me better than pushing a bayonet into the entrails of a Russian peasant.' The deciding factor, however, was that he had sufficient time to devote to what he believed was the most important service in the war: the preparation for the understanding to come.[1]

The evidence of the sparse correspondence preserved from this time indicates that in fact his ideas did not crystallize until Easter 1915, when he began *Jeremias*. In January of that year, in a letter to Rolland, he described his revulsion against England's treacherous and profiteering *Schadenpolitik*, quite beyond the bounds of morality, whereas he felt no iota of hatred for France; he added that he was also working in the letter censorship department of the Foreign Office.[2] To Paul Zech, in the early months of 1915, he wrote:

> I too will be moving out . . . but at least I am now an N.C.O. and no longer completely subordinate. I might . . . be posted to the Italian front, but it will be two months yet (I am for the moment still indispensible in the office, and am anyway very badly trained). . . . Germany . . . will come out of this war improved. She will be the last European state to have comprehended the meaning and essence of democracy and to work her way towards it.[3] [Then to Joseph Leftwich:] I am a military person—a *Zugführer*. I work seven to eight hours every day at my war service. My nerves are torn. I feel very much diminished in my whole sense of life. For those who believe in Europe, these days have become a catastrophe. I have much on my heart, but the words all stay within and wound my soul.[4]

By March he was already writing to Rolland about 'our convictions' (for which he said Hofmannsthal showed no sympathy),[5] and published in the *NFP* a translation of Rolland's essay 'Our Neighbour, the Enemy'.[6] Although, as he said himself, *Jeremias* is not a specifically pacifist play—rather, the apotheosis of defeat[7]

[1] *WvG* 212. [2] *ZwV* i. 244. [3] Letter to Zech, undated (Sch).
[4] Leftwich, 82. [5] Letter to Rolland, 17 Mar. 1915 (*ZwV* i. 303).
[6] 'Notre prochain l'ennemi'; the translation appeared, very slightly censored, in the *NFP* for 25 Mar. 1915. [7] *WvG* 233.

—it is clear that from now on he saw himself as a pacifist. Rolland's own words to Friderike that Easter Monday, positive and optimistic, could well have been Zweig's: 'This fearful crisis forces every soul to examine its conscience, to look deep into itself and to be involved. I am convinced that from this conflict of the nations of Europe will spring the conscience of Europe, like the rainbow of the Rheingold from the thunder-clouds.'[1] In May Rolland wrote to him: 'You are indeed the many-sided and noble European spirit our times need and whose appearance I have been awaiting these twenty years.'[2]

6

'One cannot conquer the unseen! Men may be killed, but not the God who dwells in them. A people may be subjugated, but never its spirit.'

Jeremias

It seemed he had now found himself. With *Jeremias* he had the feeling, for the first time, that when he spoke it came from himself and from his time.[3] His first leave from the *Archiv*, in the early summer of 1915, he spent with Friderike at Gstettenhof near Mariazell,[4] and it was a time of great happiness for them both. She found the children, once again left in the Stoerks' care, in good form when she returned, and was most of all relieved that Stefan was now able to write again.

Feigl, who had published Zweig's essay on autograph-collecting in the 1914 *Bibliophilenkalender*, was now pressing him for another for the 1916 edition, and on his return from Mariazell he promised it within the next few weeks. The calls of duty prevented this, however, and on 12 July he had to write asking for more time: 'I am off to darkest Galicia tomorrow.'[5] *Einjahrs-freiwilliger Feldwebel* Dr. Stefan Zweig[6] (the date of his promotion to the exalted rank of sergeant-major is not known) was being sent on special duty by the *Archiv* to the area which had initially

[1] *BrW* 73. [2] *ZwV* i. 346; Arens[1] 171. [3] *WvG* 234. [4] *BrW* 74.

[5] Letters to Feigl, 7 June and 12 July 1915 (StB).

[6] Card from Ehrenstein, 24 July 1915 (ZE); card to Kippenberg from Lemberg, undated (? end July 1915) (Sch).

been occupied by the Russians, but had now been recaptured by the Austro-German offensive of spring 1915. His task was to secure for the files copies of all the proclamations and placards from the Russian occupation before they were torn down and destroyed (the colonel in charge happened to be aware of his collector's mania and thought him therefore a highly suitable man for the job). He was equipped with a special pass, entitling him to travel on any military train, move entirely freely, and use civilian accommodation (it earned respect and awe, for with his sergeant-major's uniform without special insignia all thought he must be a General Staff officer in disguise or engaged on some mysterious mission). It was an unusual opportunity to see something of the war outside the military machine; and he made good use of it. The collection of the material required was easy—simply a matter of finding the right contact in each town and recruiting him for the leg-work—and in Przemysl and Lwow, Tarnow and Drohobycz, on troop trains and hospital transports, he saw much: not the heroism of war, but its ghastly aftermath.

The terrible misery of the civilian population and of the Jews in the ghettos, eight or twelve to a room below ground level; the extraordinary likeness between captor and captured and their natural fraternization; the suffering and squalor of the hospital trains, with their almost total lack of drugs and bandages; the shelled cities and looted shops, 'whose contents lay about in the middle of the street like broken limbs or torn-out entrails'; the contrast between all this and the official phrases he had himself helped to churn out on the 'inflexible will to conquer', our own troops' 'trifling casualties' as against the 'gigantic losses' of the enemy—all made an indelible impression. More, it kindled in him the urge actually to fight against the war. He had recognized the adversary:

> false heroism that prefers to send others to suffering and death, the cheap optimism of the conscienceless prophets, both political and military, who boldly promising victory prolong the war; and behind them, the hired chorus, the 'word-makers of war'. . . . It had always been the same, the eternal pack through the ages, calling the prudent cowardly, the humane weak . . . the same who derided Cassandra

in Troy, Jeremiah in Jerusalem; never had I sensed the greatness and tragedy of those figures as in these all too similar hours.[1]

The well-tilled fields he saw between the war areas gave him hope for the eventual recovery of Europe. Best hope of all, however, awaited his return to Vienna in the middle of August, where he found greetings—transmitted no doubt by Rolland—from Verhaeren. 'A sign', he wrote to Zech, 'of awakening, a greeting of newly-kindled reflection, [which] has warmed the very depths of my heart. At such small signs rejoices the enslaved soul, the stifled being!'[2] He re-read *Jean Christophe*, greatly moved again by its prophetic quality, and was encouraged not only by Rolland's letters but also by a message of friendship from Henri Guilbeaux, the translator of his poems into French, now also in Geneva.[2] His efforts to interest other writers in Germany and Austria in some form of intellectual manifestation—Rolland's idea of an international conference in Switzerland to draw up a united appeal for world conciliation—met with no response. He felt that he could not approach Gerhart Hauptmann directly (had not Rolland's own appeal to the author of *Die Weber* anyway failed?), and found that Rathenau refused to do so on his behalf, saying the time was not ripe. Thomas Mann was firmly in the patriotic camp; Dehmel proudly signed his letters 'Leutnant'; and Zweig knew from his own conversations that neither Hofmannsthal nor Jakob Wassermann could be counted on.[3] As early as October 1914 Rathenau had refused for himself, pleading pressure of work.[4] But Zweig felt none the less that he was not alone. He had access, which he used as far as he could, to the more important journals of Austria and Germany. He noted the technique, used by one of his friends in France, of favourable publicity by apparent attack—an article in the *Mercure de France*, feigning to take issue with his 'An die Freunde im Fremdland', succeeded in republishing almost every word of it in translation—and later used similar devious methods himself to oppose war and encourage

[1] *WvG* 227–32.

[2] Letter to Zech, undated (Sch).

[3] *WvG* 224–5.

[4] Walther Rathenau, *Tagebuch, 1907–1922*; Droste Verlag, Düsseldorf, 1967, 189, Note 29.

international conciliation (notably in a review in 1917 of Barbusse's *Le Feu*, and in the 1918 essay 'Alessandrio Poerio: ein Italiener bei Goethe',[1] in which he expressed his admiration for Benedetto Croce).

Though by no means lacking in physical courage (Friderike recalls his swift intervention once in a street brawl, where a woman was being threatened with a knife),[2] he was not a fighter by nature, and it would have been surprising to find him more directly active than this. 'Let others draw the consequences of action, for my part I am only a man of moral action. I can bring together and soothe, but I do not know how to fight.'[3] Withdrawing into oneself and keeping silent while the others ranted and raved, was how he later described these war years.[4] But when early in 1916 Rolland suggested to Charles Baudouin that Zweig might collaborate in the pacifist journal *Le Carmel* which Baudouin was starting in Geneva in March, he agreed readily, and sent him for the April/May issue the essay 'Der Turm zu Babel', with its strong message of hope for the future of Europe.[5] (Again we can only marvel at the broad meshes of the censor's sieve which passed this for republication in the *Vossische Zeitung* in May 1916.)

The new Tower of Babel, that great monument to Europe's spiritual unity, is decayed; the workmen have dispersed. Its battlements are still standing, its invisible masonry still rises over a confused world; but without the common toil, the conserving, continuing labour, it will fall into oblivion, like that other tower of mythical times. Today there are many among all nations who desire this. . . . But there are others still, those who believe that no people, no nation could ever succeed alone in attaining that which the united strength of Europe could hardly achieve in centuries of common effort. . . . The time is not yet ripe for joint activity; the confusion which God instilled into our souls is still too great, and it may be years before the brethren of former times work together again in peaceful competition with eternity. But we must return to the edifice, each to the place he left in the moment of confusion. Perhaps we shall not see one another for years at the work, perhaps we shall rarely hear from one another. But if

[1] *WvG* 225–6.
[2] Fr 105–6.
[3] Letter to Arcos (Dum 322).
[4] *WvG* 218.
[5] Letters from Charles Baudouin, 8 and 27 Feb. 1916 (ZE).

we toil away now, each at his post, with the old ardour, the tower will rise again, and on the summit the nations will be reunited.[1]

He was gratified to hear from Baudouin in August that the London *Socialist Review* wanted to translate the essay, and especially to hear through him of Verhaeren's admiration of it.[2]

That summer he also wrote 'Die Legende der dritten Taube', with its similar burden: Noah's third messenger, which failed to return to the ark, having found haven on dry land, but now, disturbed by the second Flood of world war, is condemned to fly unceasingly until peace returns.

On its wings hang all our dark thoughts, its fear carries all our desires, and the wandering dove, hovering in trepidation between heaven and earth, carries the message of our fate to the Father of all mankind. And again, as it did thousands of years before, a world waits for someone to stretch out a hand and acknowledge that its trial has been long enough.[3]

This too appeared in *Le Carmel*, in Baudouin's translation, early in 1917; it also attracted Hauptmann's attention in December 1916,[4] and found a place in the Artur Wolf Verlag's *Legenden und Märchen unserer Zeit*, Vienna, in 1917.[5]

7

'Now, in the peaceful Kalksburg garden, surrounded by loving care, with children's voices near, affirmation of life conquered over despair.'

Friderike Zweig

I am caught up in all kinds of vexations [he wrote to Feigl during the summer of 1916], have to keep reporting time and again to military hospitals to have my medical category checked and rechecked . . . this

[1] *Europäisches Erbe*, 278–9.

[2] Letter from Baudouin, 17 Aug. 1916 (ZE).

[3] Stefan Zweig, *Legenden*; S. Fischer, n.d., 217.

[4] Letter from Hauptmann on reverse of offprint of the *Legende* as published in *Bildermann*, 1. Jahrg., Nr. 17 (ZE).

[5] Ed. Emil Kläger. The *Legende* (128–33) has an illustration in colour by Franz Christophe. It was also published in *Der Wunderkelch: ein Sammelbuch neuer Deutscher Legenden*, ed. Theodor Etzel and Karl Lerbs; Walter Seifert, Stuttgart/Heilbronn, 1920, 291–4.

'I' belongs less and less to me, it—for in truth I am become an 'it', a foreign being belonging to the state—can no longer dispose of itself and of its time. . . . I am very tired, I have given up $1\frac{1}{2}$ years of my life to work for others and to the eternal unrest . . . my strength is really at an end.[1]

The demands and vexations of his military work, and the 'lost $1\frac{1}{2}$ years', were one of the main burdens of his letters at this time. Yet he had found a certain equilibrium. In the spring, some time during April, he had settled with Friderike in an ideal haven outside Vienna, at Kalksburg bei Rodaun, a place where he could commence his 'personal war in the midst of war, the struggle against the betrayal of reason'.[2] Here, just a few steps from Stelzer's, the scene of their first meeting, were two small houses, rococo pavilions, part of a one-time country seat, close together in the same garden and separated only by a little group of trees. It was the solution to their living together in propriety. In the one Friderike settled with the children, their nurse Lisi ('the hop-pole'), and a cook; the other made a home for Stefan when he returned in the afternoons from the office, close enough to be managed and kept clean for him without difficulty.

In the garden was a fountain with a moss-covered statue, and enough grass to sustain a goat whose milk eked out the already dwindling cow's-milk supplies. Their rations were also greatly improved by the good-quality bread still on issue to the military, which Stefan faithfully brought back each day in a packet under his arm; and they were able to dine most evenings at Stelzer's, which now also housed the *Kriegspressequartier*. Anton Wildgans and Alfons Petzold, living in Mödling, were frequent visitors, as were Csokor, Victor Fleischer, Felix Braun and his sister Käthe, and Ginzkey, now employed at the Press Section. Rilke too, who like Hofmannsthal lived quite close, often came over to enjoy the peace of their garden and the comfort of a particular deck-chair which Friderike later lent him for his own. Both he and Stefan found a special well-being there. 'Light out of the darkness is dawning in me', wrote Stefan. It was here that he brought *Jeremias* to completion.[3]

[1] Letter to Feigl, undated (StB). [2] *WvG* 219. [3] Fr 114–19; *Bildb* 50.

I am living now in Kalksburg [ran a letter to Servaes in Berlin], and travel in and out daily to save a few hours for my own work. I am working on something very big, a tragedy which is to justify the faith my friends have had in me for years: at last the great, decisive matter before which I have been hesitating for years. I am writing without regard to practical theatre, purely for the idea and the characterisation. But perhaps all the same it will break a way through. But when, oh when? . . . The crucified world, this outlook for eternity, can only comfort if we think that we have loaded on our shoulders the suffering and torment of coming nations, that we are atoning for the sins of our fathers and [ensuring] the peace of our children and grandchildren. Only this thought—that we are the sacrifice for others—can make us firm. There will be no decision in our cause, we shall not reap the harvest from this sowing of blood.[1]

In *Jeremias* he poured out in symbolic form all the feelings that were agitating his being: dread of the future, hatred for war and warmongers, the fate of Jaurès and of the other voices of warning, 'many of whom stood near to me in brotherhood'.[2] Jeremiah sees salvation for the spirit, not in the useless struggle for victory, but in defeat. He is the man who in times of enthusiasm is despised as a weakling, but 'in the hour of defeat proves himself to be the only one able not only to endure it but also to master it'. As in *Tersites*, Zweig shows the energizing power of defeat, the spiritual power of the vanquished.[3]

Friderike felt, with justification, no little pride in having made possible the completion of this work, which represented Stefan's own ascent from despair to hope. Through the summer and autumn days of 1916, back from the daily grind of the *Archiv*, he found the solace of the Kalksburg garden, the loving care with which he was surrounded, both encouragement and spur to finish this 'hymn of peace in the midst of war',[4] 'a tragedy of another time but the strongest and most penetrating symbol of ours'.[5] He bound up in red leather a fair copy of the manuscript in his own hand, prefaced it with a sonnet of Dedication to Friderike, and laid it in her hands. The volume remained one of her most precious possessions until it was sequestered by the

[1] Letter to Servaes, 1916 (StB.) [2] DDh 9. [3] *WvG* 233.
[4] Fr 117. [5] Letter to Rolland, early July 1915 (Dum 210).

Gestapo twenty years later. The sonnet, of which unhappily there is no full copy extant, began:

Als rings im Land die Waffen starrten
Und Feuer unsere Welt verheerte,
Was war da mein, ein kleiner Garten
Und du darin, Geliebte und Gefährte;

acknowledged her protection and encouragement, under which the work had flourished—'Wie war ich müd, wie oft wollt' ich erlahmen!'—and closed

Zum Eingang schreib ich dankbar deinen Namen.[1]

This very real debt to Friderike goes unrecognized in *Die Welt von Gestern*, where he attributes the main stimulus for the work to his visit to Galicia and passes by in silence her contribution. His choice of a biblical theme was, as he says there, an unconscious reversion to something 'which had remained unused in me up to that time: my community, either in my blood or darkly founded in tradition, with the Jewish destiny'.[2] Martin Buber, formerly with the publishers Ruetten & Loening and now editor of *Der Jude*, had commented, in a letter to him of May 1916, on his attitude to Jewry: 'it has a beneficial effect on me to find that it is possible for one to feel Jewry, Jewishness, in such a vegetatingly matter-of-course way.'[3] Yet here, in *Jeremias*, he discovered his people, who had been conquered time and again by others, and yet had outlasted them all by their secret power of 'transforming defeat through will'; who, eternally tried through suffering, had eternally affirmed submission to the adversary's might as a way to God.[4]

For him it was a work of exorcism, of catharsis. 'A confession in symbolic form', he called it to Rolland: 'I know that you will recognize my own experience in this historical tragedy.'[5] Publica-

[1] 'When the land all round bristled with weapons, and fire laid waste our world, yet was there mine a small garden, and in it you, my loved one and companion . . .

How tired I was, how often would have flagged! . . .
Its threshold bears in gratitude your name.'

BrW 82; *Bildb* 51; Fr 117–18. The versions given by Friderike Zweig vary slightly.

[2] *WvG* 232–3.

[3] Letter from Buber, 17 May 1916 (ZE).

[4] *WvG* 233–4.

[5] Letter to Rolland, 18 Feb. 1917 (Dum 211).

tion alone would be a miracle for a work that not only foreshadowed defeat but even praised it; a stage presentation seemed out of the question, both because of the theme and of the poem's inordinate length. Yet, when it appeared with the Insel at Easter 1917, 20,000 copies were sold at once, an incredible figure for such a work at such a time; and it met with an enthusiastic reception not only from those friends like Rolland to whom it could be expected to appeal but also from those such as Rathenau and Dehmel who had stood rather on the other side.[1] Thomas Mann called it 'the most significant poetic fruit of this war I have yet seen'.[2] Rilke wrote to Zweig of his pleasure that 'in spite of everything a new work of yours has succeeded'.[3] Zweig had the feeling that here at last he had given himself absolutely completely, and was happy that this had been recognized by those who were important to him.

> May it also have its effect on the times—not only poetically, but through the intensity of its thought! [he wrote to Servaes]. The theatres are for the moment closed to it, and if as you say the papers also stay closed . . . then this work (in which the sacrifice of two years and my best powers lie hidden) will have been done in vain. . . . Without being overweening, I ask myself: where are the works of recent years which have *more* claim to be heard and to be evaluated?[4]

8

'A real jumping-off point for Europe.'
Die Welt von Gestern

Jeremias did not owe its completion entirely to Kalksburg. For some weeks from the end of September 1916 Zweig had been able to get even further away from it all with Friderike—to Salzburg. In letters he had complained bitterly of his 'imprisonment' and the lack of leave: even for an excursion to Baden he needed written permission, and the border with Germany was for him an 'uncrossable wall';[5] 'it would be my dearest wish, after three years of prison, for once to see, to feel the world, but

[1] *WvG* 235. [2] Letter from Thomas Mann, 9 Sept. 1917 (TMArch).
[3] Letter from Rilke, 5 Sept. 1917 (Arens[1] 146).
[4] Letter to Servaes, undated (StB). [5] Letter to Servaes, 1916 (StB).

between us and Germany lies an iron curtain!'[1] At the end of August, however, he told Feigl that he was about to make a 'partly official, partly private visit' to Germany.[2] Friderike must have joined him in Salzburg on his return at the end of September. She noted in her diary: 'The tortures of uniform have fallen away from him like a bad dream. He needs nothing but rest, his enjoyment is so light and cordial, he experiences his existence as pure delight.'[3] There was no thought in their minds then that Salzburg would one day be their permanent home; but they were casting around already for a place where the ideal conditions of Kalksburg could be prolonged, for, although Stefan had assured her that he would not delay a moment in legalizing their relationship as soon as it was possible, years might have to pass before this. The South Tyrol, which both knew and loved, had been one possibility. Now in Salzburg, on a walk up to the Kapuzinerberg, they came across a long, rather dilapidated house, simple, but with its small tower and dominating position showing the character of an old country seat of some noble family. Leafing through the advertisements some months after their return, they remarked a notice for a Salzburg property, at a reasonable price, which seemed from the description to be very much like the house they had seen: and so it proved, after a telephone call to the number given.[4]

Originally a seventeenth-century archbishop's hunting-lodge, it rested against the ancient ivy-clad fortress wall of the town. Late in the eighteenth century it had been enlarged by a room at either side. A splendid old tapestry, and one of a decorated pair of bowls which the emperor himself, on a visit to Salzburg in 1807, had rolled down the corridor, bore witness to a distinguished past. Before the war the so-called 'Paschinger-Schlössl' had been owned by Frau Marie von Ziegler, a colonel's lady, who had sold it in 1916 to Dr. Joseph Kranz, a prominent industrialist. With his war profits (it seems he dealt in methylated and other spirits) Dr. Kranz had bought it in haste, as a home for his 'adopted

[1] Letter to Servaes, undated (StB).

[2] Letter to Feigl, 31 Aug. 1916 (StB).

[3] Fr² 49. [4] Fr² 74; Fr 125–6.

daughter', a young war-widow named Gina Kaus; but she did not like the house, and he was now as hastily selling. Stefan surprised Friderike by his proposal that she should proceed at once to look at it, and even more by giving her full powers to negotiate the purchase if she thought it suitable.[1]

His trust in her, as she wrote later, gave her over the years not a few hard nuts to crack. The house was in miserable shape. There was no electricity, no adequate heating, and only rudimentary plumbing; the road to it was impassable for any vehicles but heavy lorries, and was lit only by a few lanterns placed by the monks of the nearby cloister, for this was a Hill of Calvary at whose stations pilgrims stopped on their way to the church. But once within, once she had seen the main reception room with its five windows, its charming rococo stove, its Dufour tapestry commissioned by the original Herr Paschinger in 1806, she knew that this was what they sought, and worth every effort, every risk.

There would clearly be a deal of both. While on this first visit she set to with characteristic energy to ensure that, although they would obviously not be able to settle here for some time to come, the minimum living comforts could be attained when they did. It was wartime, and labour and materials were lacking. But she organized the few neighbours into a successful petitioning of the local authority for lighting the approach road; made a provisional agreement with a contractor for the necessary repairs; and was able to return to Vienna with all the required assurances from the municipality, and detailed estimates for Stefan of the cost of putting the place into a livable condition. Without having seen it again himself he agreed at once to the purchase, and in August 1917 it was completed.[2]

It was perhaps unfortunate that he left the business entirely to her. It was his way, of course, to avoid entanglement in the day-to-day affairs of practical life, and she was glad, now as always, to devote her energies to settling these for him. He also disliked having to admit how rich he was, and here, although the price

[1] *WvG* 264–5; Fr 126–7; for the details of Frau von Ziegler and Dr. Kranz, a clipping from an unidentified Salzburg paper, 1937 (at the time of Zweig's sale of the house); statements to the author by Friderike Zweig.

[2] Fr 127–8.

was extremely advantageous, the purchase of such a property betrayed substantial means. The decision was naturally his: but always afterwards, when it suited his mood, he would refer to Kapuzinerberg as 'your house', and in the dark days of the thirties it became for him a 'nightmare' that was one of the heaviest weights in the scales deciding their estrangement. At this point, however, it was in every way a good buy. In spite of the success of *Jeremias* it had become clear to him that after the war his work would depend on living away from the big cities: Salzburg, not yet the Mecca of the Festival crowds, centrally placed but quiet, would be the right spring-board, the essential base from which he could travel. It was a 'villa in Europe' which had the additional advantage of remoteness, making easier their settling down as man and wife, until the day, not yet foreseeable, when they would be able to marry.

Friderike wondered later what led him to say just now, for the first time, that he intended to marry her when it was possible. He had just finished reading her novel *Vögelchen*, which she had completed during the summer and autumn of 1916 at Kalksburg, and she learned afterwards from friends that it had made a deep impression on him. But she felt that the main reasons were first his desire to reassure her, to give her a certain sense of security, since they were in effect already a family, and second, the need he felt for a more permanent relationship before they left together on a somewhat venturesome journey.[1] For, greatly to his surprise, he had received shortly after the publication of *Jeremias* an offer from the Director of the Zürich Stadttheater to produce the drama forthwith, and an invitation to attend the première.

9

> *'There, amid 120 million men locked in battle, we were a handful, a small round table of European comrades.'* *Autobiographische Skizze*, 1922

His colleague of the *Archiv* Albert Ehrenstein had been in Switzerland since the end of 1916, sending a card from the frontier on

[1] Fr 125.

30 December: 'To you and all longer-serving NCOs of the *Archiv*, heartiest Buchs-greetings!', and had been bombarding him ever since with letters in lightly veiled language suggesting various devices by which Zweig could join him there. One of his ideas had been to get Moissi to ask to produce *Der verwandelte Komödiant*, so that 'Ast' the author could come to Zürich; another, which looked more promising, that one or other of the literary circles there should ask Zweig to give readings from his works. 'When will the translator of Verhaeren come? Leave period up!' ran a letter of 28 August.[1] Neither had dreamed that *Jeremias* would provide the means; and Stefan at first did not dare to hope that he would receive official approval to accept the Stadtheater invitation, and relied rather on the possible reading engagements.

> I am played out [he wrote to Zech in August], *Jeremias* was everything I had in me. . . . I am to have two months' leave to give readings in Switzerland . . . and what this will mean to me! . . . to feel the air of Europe, to be free for two months! And what could I not do there, as against here, where I rot away. My *Jeremias* freed me from torment; but I feel now that I loved the suffering. . . . Here in Austria all are of one mind for peace, we are Europe again in spirit.[2]

His chief in the *Archiv* had not hesitated to give his official blessing, and was indeed enthusiastic: 'You, thank Heaven, were never one of the warmongers: do your best out there to bring this thing finally to an end.'[3]

There was in fact in Austria, in high places, no aversion to letting the neutrals know she no longer shared Germany's war ideology, and that she was worthy of their helpful and humane understanding; and this, as Friderike thought later, was probably the main reason why no obstacle was put in either Stefan's or her way when they applied to make the journey. She herself went as a delegate of the Austrian Women's Union to give talks on the aid given to evacuated Polish women and children. For Stefan the main object, apart of course from the opportunity of

[1] Card and letters from Ehrenstein, 30 Dec. 1916, 14 Jan., 11 Apr., 28 Aug., and 12 Sept. 1917 (ZE). [2] Letter to Zech, Aug. 1917 (Sch). [3] *WvG* 237.

seeing Rolland, was to have the chance on neutral ground of a wider field of action for his convictions. For them both it meant being able to come closer together than conditions in Austria would allow, where consideration for their families had enjoined great discretion (and where Friderike had already become the target of criticism on the part of some of her relations).[1] 'Have a good journey, my dear Zweig,' wrote Rilke at the end of September, 'and let your own life become cherished and carefree again, in free movement and with new impressions.'[2]

It was towards the middle of November when they set off, leaving Alix and Suse in the care of their grandfather. On the way they spent two days in Salzburg to look at their future home, and here happened to stumble on one of the great political secrets of the time. Stefan had been surprised to hear such frank words from his chief in Vienna: he had not suspected that since the death of Franz-Josef a year earlier there had been under way a discreet but determined movement against Germany's wild expansionism and towards a separate peace. In Salzburg there was a group of Catholics, pronounced pacifists and fanatical 'old-Austrians', all firmly opposed to Prussian, German, Protestant militarism, and led by the international lawyer, ex-Hague Court President and Privy Councillor Heinrich Lammasch and the priest Ignaz Seipel (both destined to play important roles as Chancellors in the post-war history of Austria). Lammasch had been very impressed by *Jeremias*, which had struck a sympathetic chord, and he asked Zweig to visit him while in Salzburg. After complimenting him on the drama, which he said fulfilled the Austrian ideal of conciliation and, he hoped, would 'operate beyond its literary purpose', he confided his aim of a separate peace.

The October Revolution in Russia, eliminating her as a serious military force, had produced a moment of decision for Austria, he considered: there was no real obstacle to peace if Germany would give up her aggressive ambitions. If she did not, and the pan-German clique in Berlin continued to resist negotiations, Austria would have to act independently. And he revealed, to this virtual stranger, that the young Emperor Karl had promised

[1] Fr 129–30; Fr[2] 75. [2] Letter from Rilke, 20 Sept. 1917 (Arens[1] 148).

his support in this purpose, even to the length of renouncing the alliance while there was still time to prevent Austria being dragged down to catastrophe. 'No-one can accuse us of a breach of faith: more than a million of our men are dead. We have sacrificed enough!' He spoke with such calm and determination as to convince Zweig that an Austrian separatist movement was no longer in the stage of preparation but actually in train. Karl's weakness, or more probably Germany's early intelligence of his secret letter to Clémenceau, prevented the public renunciation of the alliance by which alone Austria could have succeeded; but with no foreknowledge of the outcome Zweig was greatly encouraged by what he heard from Lammasch to hope for an early end to the war, and to see his own journey into Switzerland as a positive contribution.[1]

To any traveller across the frontier at Buchs, from starved and walled-in Austria to the luxury of unrationed, free Switzerland, the contrast was astounding. For Zweig, whose real torment in Austria had been the lack of personal freedom rather than *Ersatz* coffee or the shortages of ham or chocolate, to breathe the free air of a neutral country was an almost cataleptic experience. 'Au milieu de l'Europe avide, l'îlot des vingt-quatre cantons' seemed to him, as it had to Rolland in *Jean Christophe*, a miniature of the Europe, indeed the world, of the future. 'Refuge of the persecuted, the centuries-old abode of peace and freedom . . . how momentous the existence of this single supra-national state for our world!'[2] On 14 November, from the Hotel Rhätia at Buchs, he wrote at once to Rolland to announce his arrival;[3] and from Zürich, before calling on the Stadttheater, proceeded immediately to Villeneuve to see him. As 'enemies', subjects of belligerent governments, their meeting on 20 November presented a problem to which the only possible answer was complete openness, and Zweig had no hesitation in giving his name to the porter at the Hotel Byron and asking for Rolland ('we felt no obligation to participate in an absurdity merely because the world behaved absurdly'). It was the first French hand he had touched, the first words he had spoken to a Frenchman, for three years; and he was

[1] *WvG* 238–40; Fr[2] 75, 77–8. [2] *WvG* 242. [3] *ZwV* ii. 476.

conscious too that the friend with whom he now stood face to face was the most important man of the hour, that in him 'the moral conscience of Europe found words'. It was deeply stirring for him to see this physically ailing but morally steadfast man working night and day on his Red Cross task, his vast correspondence, his diary, his novel *Clérambault*, 'preserving the conscience of a Europe fallen into madness'.[1] (There was, it must be admitted, a good deal of *naïveté* in his veneration of Rolland as an ascetic: René Arcos noted that Zweig was the only friend in Switzerland ignorant of the relationship between the author of *Au-dessus de la mêlée* and a charming American woman.)[2]

Rolland's diary of the war years (published only very much later, and never seen by Zweig) contains a perceptive impression of Zweig as he appeared that November. He remarks first on his youthful aspect (but puts his age almost correctly at thirty-five), and on the touch of Semitic cunning in the face, with its long nose, at first sight almost antipathetic.

> There is nothing attractive in his speech, which is heavy, severe, monotonous when he speaks French. But the longer one converses with him the more clearly does his honesty and magnanimity emerge. . . . I had the feeling that strength of will was for the greater part in this nobility of soul, as is often the case with distinguished Jews. . . . For him in this war the most important thing is to keep his soul pure, to preserve an absolute inner independence from the monstrous machine of the State which grips us all, and although his situation is less favourable than mine he has succeeded in this. He pursues this scrupulous independence to the utmost. Although his intention was to give a lecture in Switzerland, he insisted on paying for the journey himself; . . . he sends an article[3] to Guilbeaux' journal, has no fear of thus compromising himself, and intends nevertheless to return to Austria without deigning to seek from Count Kessler a pretext on which he could remain in safety in Switzerland. He is very human, yet of a noble sternness against everything which does not respect humanity. Thus he cares as little as I for those who sacrifice men to ideas, be those ideas never so fine; he cannot understand theorizing over future organisation when every effort should be devoted to bringing the

[1] Fr[2] 78; *ZwV* ii. 480–2; *WvG* 243–5. [2] Dum 124.
[3] 'A mes frères français' (*Demain*, ii. 125–8).

present sufferings to a rapid end. . . . He will never forget the behaviour of the Austrian intellectuals in this war. He is not personally angry with them; but he declares he will never form part of a group to which such men (in particular Hofmannsthal and Bahr) belong. For him the monstrous events of the war have divided the sheep from the goats.[1]

To Rolland Zweig said then that apart from himself and Werfel not a single Austrian intellectual had been able to preserve complete independence.[2]

True enough, perhaps, but surely too harsh a judgement if Austrians and Germans be counted together in this context, for among those in Switzerland were Fritz von Unruh, Leonhard Frank, and Wilhelm Friedmann, as well as the lively Ehrenstein. Zweig could, however, hardly be blamed for noting the sparse representation from the Central nations at this 'small round table of European comrades amid the millions of combatants'. Here were Rolland, Pierre-Jean Jouve, René Arcos ('mon cher petit père'), the young Belgian artist Frans Masereel ('the natural son of Walt Whitman'), and Annette Kolb; Busoni, René Schickele, and Chapiro; James Joyce, Andreas Latzko, and Henri Guilbeaux; Baudouin, the Swiss Robert Faesi, Leonhard Ragaz, Oskar Fried, and Hermann Hesse. 'Never in my riper years did I respond to friendship with such enthusiasm as in those hours, . . . and the bond has survived the years.'[3] 'Zweig was one of the most noble and most courageous of our little Europe', said Jouve in 1920.[4]

He met men of all nations in the old Hotel Schwerdt at Zürich, where Goethe, Fichte, and Casanova had in their time been guests and where he now settled for a while. As he put it in his autobiographical sketch in 1922, 'we played no politics (which I still despise today)—we simply prepared for peace . . . and proclaimed by our bearing Rolland's *Au-dessus de la mêlée* and the neutrality of art'.[5] He had seen Lenin's telegram to Rolland, asking him to travel in the famous sealed train with him to lend his moral authority to the Bolshevik cause, and had thoroughly endorsed Rolland's refusal, his firm determination to remain unaligned and

[1] *ZwV* ii. 490–1. [2] *ZwV* ii, 482.
[3] *WvG* 248. [4] Jouve 228. [5] DDh 9.

to serve independently the common cause. For this was exactly his own innermost desire. Patriotic delusions had severed old associations: these new friends joined him in the fight against the common enemy, 'in a common intellectual trench'. The little papers *Demain* and *La Feuille*—the former founded by the mercurial Guilbeaux, the latter appearing daily with Masereel's mordant woodcuts against the horror of war—carried their banner. They realized full well that what they printed here was confined to Switzerland—and, of course, the files of the German and French intelligence services (papers stolen by the French from the room of a German agent in Berne, showing subscriptions to *Demain*, were sufficient for Guilbeaux to be accused of being in German pay). But their very sense of isolation drew them closer together.[1]

Sadly missed was Verhaeren, who had been in Switzerland shortly before his tragic death at Rouen on 28 November the previous year. Arcos, who had also seen him in London before that, wrote to Zweig in December 1917: 'I can tell you that I found him much changed when I met him here in Switzerland again: he was beginning to see clearly. Was not hatred in the heart of such a man anyway an anomaly? and the sure sign of an irremediable disorder in the world?'[2] Zweig had telegraphed to Rolland from Vienna when he heard the news: 'Please tell Mrs. Verhaeren that the death of her husband, my beloved fatherly friend and master, signifies the greatest loss for me and that I share her pain with my whole heart. . . .'[3] A month before the tragedy Verhaeren had assured Zweig, through a Swiss friend, of his unshakable regard. 'He was cured,' Zweig wrote to Zech, 'and would have been the first to recognize his error had not fate dragged him off, beyond recall. Dear friend, this man was a part of my life; everything good in me I owe to him, he taught me that one must be simple as a man to be great as a poet; such simplicity went out from him, such cordiality. What have we lost in him!'[4] His moving memoir of Verhaeren was published in a private printing before he left Vienna in 1917.[5]

[1] *WvG* 246–51. [2] Letter from Arcos, 21 Dec. 1917 (ZE).
[3] *ZwV* ii. 141. [4] Letter to Zech, 6 Dec. 1916 (Sch). [5] See p. 23, n. 1.

Zürich, to which he now returned to discuss putting his drama into rehearsal, was at the time the most international city of Europe. Though Geneva, which had been the home of Lenin and the other exiled Russian revolutionaries, was probably the busier nest of intrigue, Zürich ran it a close second. Every language and every trend of thought seemed to be represented. Alfred Fried, Nobel Peace Prize winner, published his *Friedenswarte* here; von Unruh gave readings of his dramas; Latzko's *Menschen in Kriege* was a sensation on its publication in Zürich. There were those without a country: Joyce writing in English, but harshly rejecting all association with England; Feruccio Busoni, born and educated in Italy, by choice a German; the Alsatian Schickele, his inclinations with France, but writing in German. There were spies, *provocateurs*, speculators, propagandists of every hue; English women married to German officers, French wives of Austrian diplomats; countless individuals whose international associations had been disrupted by the war, all depending for their future in one way or another on its outcome. The Café Bellevue and the Odéon were the centres of lively debate, a zealous motley of opinion and controversy, where the war was seen from a European rather than from a national-political standpoint, as a 'horrible and mighty happening which was to change not merely a few boundaries on the map but the form and future of our whole world'.[1]

The production of *Jeremias* took time to arrange, and Zweig was meanwhile plunged into this hurly-burly, where the war was experienced more intensively than in the belligerent countries because of the greater detachment. He quickly sensed that not all the 'pacifists' and 'anti-militarists' he met were genuine, that among apparent refugees and martyrs in heroic causes there were many dubious characters in the pay of the warring intelligence services. One of his earliest public appearances had been a joint reading from their works with Jouve at Bodmer's *Lesezirkel* in Hottingen, at which the Austrian consul-general had been present and had shaken the hand of both speakers; later an alleged 'socialist' offered him a suspiciously large fee for a lecture to a

[1] *WvG* 251–5.

working-men's club in Chaux-de-Fonds, which, as it proved, knew nothing of the proposal. It meant being continually on one's guard. He found also that even among the few whom he could regard as absolutely reliable there were still fewer who really shared his own ethical convictions. His bourgeois 'capitalist' origins made him naturally suspect to the extremists of the Left, for whom his name was turned to 'Erwerbszweig' (branch of industry). For his part, he regarded most of these people as professional revolutionaries or café-conspirators, whose whole existence depended on opposition, and who lacked the moral resources for a truly positive contribution to the reconstruction that would be necessary after the war.[1]

10

'Now or never we shall experience a new generation.'

Zweig to Kippenberg, November 1918

Meanwhile his prescribed leave from the *Archiv* was fast running out. It would, no doubt, have been possible to write to obtain a prolongation; but he felt increasingly unable to return to any form of military service, and had decided now to try for a release, so that he could remain in Switzerland. The best chance for this would be if the *NFP*, for which he had worked for so many years, requested it: and this was scarcely a matter for correspondence. Friderike therefore returned alone to Vienna in December on this delicate mission, her doubts over the outcome more than outweighed by the anticipation of spending Christmas with her family. On the way she tried, without success, to see Felix, last heard of as a supplies officer near Innsbruck, but posted away just before her arrival, for she wanted to get his advice on whether she should bring one or both of the children back with her to Switzerland.

After a Christmas made happier by the gifts and food she had brought with her (Vienna was on short rations indeed that winter, although the children's were supplemented by supplies

[1] *WvG* 255–8; Robert Faesi, 'Erinnerungen an Stefan Zweig', 1302.

from Holland), she obtained, through the good offices of the music critic Paul Stefan, then a captain in the *Kriegsarchiv*, an interview with the owner of the *NFP*, Ernst Benedikt, and put her proposition to him. He demurred at first, for he had just obtained the release from military service of another member of his staff and was not keen to intervene again; but she finally secured his agreement, mainly by the gentle hint that she would ask a rival journal if he refused. On Stefan's undertaking to contribute a monthly *feuilleton*, his military service was formally ended, and he was authorized to remain in Switzerland. Friderike decided to bring Suse back with her (although now quite healthy, the child was still considerably under-weight), leaving Alix still with the Hofrat. Early in January 1918 she was able to meet Stefan at Buchs with the good news.[1] (To the French, as Chapiro reported to Stefan after his interrogation on his associations with such 'enemies', this release was clear proof that Zweig—'Lui! un soldat de l'armée active!'—was in Switzerland on a 'pacifist propaganda mission' for the Austrian Government.)[2]

They spent first a few days in the Engadin, for Suse's sake. Here Zweig wrote his first *feuilleton* under the agreement, 'Bei den Sorglosen': pointing up the sharp contrast between these carefree holiday-makers in the fashionable winter-sports centres and the misery of war-torn Europe surrounding them—the schizophrenia of the human heart, which longs for happiness for the whole world, yet is ashamed of that of any individual, the heart which 'hates freedom from care and also hates its own bitterness, its purposeless sadness, which helps no-one'. (These were thoughts which Friderike rightly considered characteristic of Zweig all through his life: never fully enjoying his worldly goods or his pleasures, save only the lonely pleasures of the mind, so that he sought constant refuge in work; knowing himself rich, yet with a dark antipathy towards the wealthy; too often prey to 'purposeless sadness' and unreasoned pessimism.)[3]

Back in the Hotel Schwerdt, with Suse placed in a children's home nearby, Zweig felt he could stand the babel no longer.

[1] *BrW* 82–3; Fr 142–8; Fr[2] 79.
[2] Letter from Chapiro, 26 July 1919 (ZE). [3] Fr 148–9.

Friderike had brought with her his draft of the Dostoevsky essay: he needed quiet to finish it and to start other projects. The chatter and the uneasy atmosphere of espionage in Zürich grew insupportable. With Friderike he withdrew to the little Hotel Belvoir ('das Nidelbad') in neighbouring Rüschlikon, where he would be under no obligation to see any but such real friends as Faesi, who lived just across the lake, and Masereel, and could make good use of the short time which, it was now possible to hope, remained till the end of the war.[1] Here he completed the Dostoevsky—'not much altered, only concentrated'[2]—and began the play *Legende eines Lebens*. Its theme—the problems of the son of a famous father—was suggested to him partly by visible Wagner and Wesendonck family associations in Zürich, partly by Duhamel's *Dans l'ombre des statues*, which he had seen at the Odéon in 1912 (he considered at one time as title 'The Great Shadow', but rejected it as too similar to Duhamel's). Friedrich Marius (the names chosen after Friderike's), imprisoned in the cult of the dead poet who was his father, finds a way to the realization of his own personality when the idealized picture of his father, sedulously fostered by mother and publisher/biographer, is shattered by the reappearance of the other woman. He achieves the harmony and balance that Zweig, in this peaceful corner of Europe, had himself now found.[3]

Over the months the regular *feuilletons* he had undertaken became something of a burden—slavery, he called it once to Friderike[4]—but nevertheless made a vehicle, though mostly indirect, for his ideas of brotherhood and peace. One he had written earlier, at the end of 1917, after a visit to Rolland's Red Cross centre—'Das Herz Europas'—was republished separately by Rascher in Zürich in 1918, and also appeared in translation in *Le Carmel*. His most outspoken article for the Vienna paper was a review of Berta von Suttner's eloquent advocacy for peace, *Die Waffen Nieder!*, on 21 June 1918, based on a speech he had made the previous April in Berne at the Women's Congress for International Understanding. But for the most part his work in

[1] Fr 153–4; *Bildb* 62; Faesi, op. cit. 1303; *WvG* 257.
[2] *BrW* 93. [3] *BrW* 88; Dum 330. [4] *BrW* 96.

this sense was confined to Switzerland, notably in an article for *Friedenswarte*—'Bekenntnis zum Defaitismus'—in July. 'We want neither victory nor defeat for anyone, we are enemies of victory and friends of renunciation; Europe must be released from her torment, at any price.'[1] Arguing for humanism against national patriotism, he groups all opponents of the war under the title of 'defeatists'—'a title', as he wrote to Rolland, 'that will one day be one of honour'.[2] The article earned him the warm support of Prince Hohenlohe, then in Zürich, who wrote on 3 August: 'I too am a defeatist in your sense, that is, I consider it all-important that this revolting, senseless, mad slaughter must cease; everything else is mere empty talk.'[3]

To Rolland, however, it seemed an unfortunate turn: defeatism to him was on the same plane as the fury of hatred and greed he wished to be free of. 'I am no Buddhist or Tolstoyan non-resister, I do not see myself in the role of the conquered', he noted in his diary: 'I say to the power that hurls me to the ground: "You will not conquer the spirit, it will conquer you." '[4] For Zweig, on the other hand, it seemed necessary to go beyond mere peace at any price—to seek the renewal of the spirit in defeat itself. This was indeed the theme of *Jeremias*, which had finally been presented in a shortened version at the Stadttheater on 27 February, and which had achieved a notable success, with even the American ambassador among the audience (though Werfel and Ehrenstein thought there was too much 'Reinhardt ballet' in it).[5] There were naturally political attacks (notably later in the Vienna *Reichspost*), but Zweig wrote to Rolland on 7 April his joy that 'at last our hour has struck . . . almost against my will I feel I am nearer to those who like Guilbeaux preach the social Flood'.[6]

In fact, however, it was not in him to follow to their conclusion the political implications of his stand. Although he occasionally expressed sympathy with the republicans among the Germans and Austrians in Switzerland, he could not bring

[1] R 100.
[2] *ZwV* ii. 657.
[3] Letter from Prince Hohenlohe, Hotel Baur au Lac, Zürich (ZE).
[4] *ZwV* ii. 658.
[5] *Ausst* 53; letter from Ehrenstein, 2 Mar. 1918 (ZE); photograph R 64.
[6] *ZwV* ii. 569.

himself to sign manifestos such as that sent him by Otto Flake in June or the republican-democratic declaration conceived by Alfred Fried in October.[1] He was not a little irked to find himself placed, unasked, on the Comité Directeur of the communistic *Clarté* group founded by Barbusse and Magdeleine Marx in September.[2] 'Loneliness, or the printed word: for the moment these are for us the only possible forms of existence', he had written to Rolland in April: 'discussions are the greatest danger for spirit and soul';[3] and to Emil Ludwig the same month:

> That you so carefully avoid Zürich and Berne, those snake-pits of intrigue, where propaganda, ideas of revolution and espionage mingle like brothers, shows a clear appreciation of our times. I have fled here, quite away from it all, go down to Zürich once a week to get books, otherwise live completely cut off and for the first time feel myself free, now that I do not see these people who, themselves confused, seek to create confusion in others.[4]

In Rüschlikon he found expression for his hatred of the war in the *Novellen*, *Der Zwang* and *Episode vom Genfer See*. The first, modelled on his own and Friderike's experience of opposition to the State machine and of finding liberty in a neutral land, is a powerful plea for freedom of conscience; the second a moving episode of the plight of the prisoners of war. Masereel, who often came to see them, undertook the illustrations for *Der Zwang* (originally entitled *Der Refraktär*), and rightly took Stefan and Friderike as his models for the artist and his wife. Younger than Stefan, he infected him with a schoolboy-like gaiety, and together they took delight to *épater le bourgeois*: during the Swiss general strike they took a walk down the train-less railway lines, calling each other by Russian names and generally behaving like *Lausbuben*.[5]

Rolland came to stay at Rüschlikon for a few days in May, and they had long talks on the wistaria-covered terrace, with its

[1] Letters from Flake, 26 June 1918, and Alfred H. Fried, 23 July and 5 Oct. 1918 (ZE).

[2] Letters from Magdeleine Marx, 4 and 12 Sept. 1918 (ZE).

[3] *ZwV* ii. 574.

[4] Letter to Ludwig, 28 Apr. 1918 (Sch).

[5] Letter from Masereel, 25 Oct. 1918 (ZE); Fr[2] 83, 84–5; Fr. 141.

wonderful view of the Zürich Lake, and on walks in the woods around. He read them extracts from *Liluli*; and Zweig, who had already translated his *Aux peuples assassinés* for publication by Rascher in January, the proceeds going to the Red Cross, and had started on *Clérambault*, agreed to revise the existing poor translation of *Colas Breugnon* and to start on *Le Temps viendra*.[1]

During the summer Friderike, after a long struggle with the Austrian authorities, succeeded in getting permission for Alix to join them, though not for her factotum Lisi. She installed both girls in Amden bei Weesen, on the Walensee, where she spent a good deal of time away from Stefan.[2] August and September were busy months for him. Over and above his *feuilleton* commitment, he was putting the finishing touches to *Dostoevsky* (Kippenberg was expected in Zürich, and he hoped to be able to give him the manuscript for eventual publication as the third essay of *Drei Meister*); Paul Stefan was also due from Vienna, and pressing for an essay[3] for the *Archiv*'s journal *Donauland*; *Legende eines Lebens* was nearing completion. Apart from a few friends like Faesi, Ehrenstein, Wilhelm Friedmann, and Hesse, and their hotel neighbour the Danish nobleman d'Obry, he saw no one; but his correspondence was the greater, in particular with Rössler, of the Avalun-Verlag, over publication of *Zwang*, for which Masereel's woodcuts were delayed by the artist's influenza. In addition there was the revision of a translation of Rousseau's *Émile*, which Friderike had undertaken to help pay her own way in Switzerland ('your money mania', Stefan called it), and which he now took over to give her more time with the children. He was working 'like a convict', he wrote to her at Amden.[4] Apart from the occasional pieces, publication had to wait till after the war; but *Legende eines Lebens* had its première at the Deutsches Schauspielhaus, Hamburg, on Christmas Day 1918.

He had also started his book on Rolland. 'I doubt whether you yourself can conceive how felicitously and with what conspicuous purpose Fate has shaped your life', he had written to him

[1] *ZwV* ii. 599 ff.

[2] *BrW* 86.

[3] 'Die Schweiz als Hilfsland Europas' (*Donauland*, II. Jahrg., 7 (Sept. 1918)).

[4] *BrW* 86–98, 101.

in May; 'with what joy shall I show that not chance, but necessity, made you what you have become . . . your life belongs to the few that show the sudden turns of a work of art . . . without this war one would never have comprehended the unity of your work'.[1] That Rolland was the target for attack from all quarters, even more intense after the war ended, made him only the more eager to complete this work of piety: 'we have more to thank him for in these times than any other person'.[2]

As the last months of the war dragged out, he could on occasions be optimistic. The situation during the summer, with the Germans giving way more, he welcomed: 'soon now the military party there will have sung its last song'.[3] But later:

> I am filled with a nameless bitterness against the times: never as now was it so senseless that the slaughter should continue. The German defeat was good, in order that the power of Ludendorff should be broken, but now there reigns in America a boundless jubilation. They have tasted blood. And now *they* want the victory, which the Germans two weeks ago wanted, the great decisive victory with the enemy on his knees. Truly, we are all criminals, we who remain silent, and perhaps it will be necessary to speak out.[4]

His mistrust of big words like 'freedom' or 'justice' was becoming an *idée fixe*, he wrote to Rolland in October,

> I cannot bear to hear them any more. . . . I think I have expunged all trace of nationalism from my heart; and yet I suffer, because Austria accepts everything, because she no longer defends herself, . . . because she is thwarted in her desire to lay down her arms. . . . I hold fast to life, but not from a love of life, simply from terror of the Flood. . . . I am often sad, but I feel the tremendous drama, the great tragedy of this collapsing world, and my whole being trembles. Perhaps in years to come we shall look back with a vague sadness to these days of the year 1918, when a monstrous force filled our soul.[5]

This pessimism was tempered, however, by an increasing clarity of purpose in his own life, and by a realization of the work that would have to be done when the conflict was finally ended. Asking himself what nationality he would choose in the Europe

[1] *ZwV* ii. 604–5. [2] *BrW* 100. [3] *BrW* 90.
[4] *BrW* 94. [5] *ZwV* ii. 757–9.

of the future, he inclined towards the Jewish, although he was no Zionist, for there there would be 'a sense of inter-nationality, of fatherland in the spirit'.[1] After the Armistice, on 15 November, he wrote to Kippenberg:

> For three years, with a prophetic pessimism, I have seen everything coming as in fact it came. And today I am literally the only person, among the subdued people around me, who is without worry about the future. . . . I believe the hard years that are to come will be beautiful in a high moral sense. . . . Organically everything had to happen as it did; it is too late for regrets, now is the time for work. . . . I see much work for the Insel-Verlag. . . . It is a time for a new idealism: the patriotic kind I have never shared. . . . Now we need the other kind, that which the early Verhaeren showed, Walt Whitman, and—always he!—Goethe.[2]

He knew well, from letters and visitors, what fearful conditions obtained in Austria, but it was time now to prepare for his return there.

What was lost, and what remained? he asked himself as he drew up his personal balance-sheet for these four years.

> Lost: the light touch of the past, the *brio*, the playing at creativity, the easy wandering over the globe; and then some external things like money and freedom from material care. Remaining, on the other hand: some treasured friendships, good knowledge of the world, the old passionate love of knowledge—joined suddenly by a new, tough courage and a feeling of responsibility after so many lost years.[3]

The responsibility: that of 'helping to surmount the defeat by means of my art . . . precisely because my opposition to the prolongation of the conflict had given me a certain moral position, especially with young people'.[4] 'My aim would be one day', he had written to Rolland in January 1918, 'to become not a great critic or a literary celebrity but a moral authority.'[5]

[1] Letter to Rolland, 10 Dec. 1918 (Dum 166).
[2] Sch; *IAusst* 229.
[3] Quoted R 124.
[4] *WvG* 260.
[5] Letter to Rolland, 21 Jan. 1918 (Dum. 199).

IV. Salzburg and Success 1919–1925

. . . one's own house, that is
At first a cloak to hide one's nakedness,
But slowly grows upon you like a skin,
And holds you fast, seems as with living roots
To bind you firm to earth.

Das Haus am Meer, I. iv

'So I build on, slowly and at the same time passionately, with hands still eager, raising this structure begun by chance ever further towards the barely glimpsed cerulean of time which hangs uncertain over our life.'

Der Kampf mit dem Dämon

I

'These last years have . . . brought him out of balance. But there is absolutely no doubt that once in the peace and comfort of an orderly household his balance will be restored.'

Ida Zweig to Friderike, February 1919

Zweig had kept secret from his parents his purchase of the Kapuzinerberg house, and had also never spoken to them of Friderike, though it was to be assumed that they would have heard something of the liaison. For some time Friderike had urged him to bring it into the open with his family. Now, with their return to Austria imminent, he agreed, and wrote to his mother, at the flat she and her husband had now taken at 10 Garnisonsgasse, enclosing some chocolate and breaking the news about Friderike, but for the time being keeping quiet about his intention of withdrawing altogether from Vienna and settling in Salzburg.

The contents of your letter surprised me [she replied on 23 January 1919], although I had already heard from a trustworthy quarter that you had an intimate relationship of the kind. Now I am faced with the fact. I hope that you, as a mature, serious man, have carefully considered this important step and made a choice worthy of yourself. As far as we have heard, the lady in question is highly intelligent, and also of a gentle disposition, which can only be of advantage to your character. You know, my dear child, how I depend with my whole soul on you, my children, and that your future was my constant care, so you will understand how nearly your decision affects me, so many questions come to mind for which there is no space in a letter. We must save them until we meet. My deepest wish—to have a daughter—has now been fulfilled, and we therefore greet as such your chosen one in advance, and I look forward with great joy to draw her to my motherly breast. May the future bring you, my dear son, the happiness that we pray will be yours.

Stefan sent this off to Friderike, who was in Nyon at the time, telling her he had now, in reply, sent his mother 'the bitter Salzburg pill—enough of secrets now'—and suggesting Friderike might herself write to his mother, as she had always wanted. 'The preliminary peace treaty is to be signed in March, and that for me will be the signal to return home. Then, I hope, will come that other peace, inner peace.'[1]

To Friderike, in February, Stefan's mother replied:

Your welcome letter moved me greatly, all the more since your feelings expressed in it agree with mine. . . . I can say, without hesitation, that Stefan's decision to found a home made me immeasurably happy. . . . Stefan needs uncommonly gentle treatment, the necessity for which you, as a sensible woman, will no doubt have recognized. His heart is good, his ways of thought noble. These last years have dealt more or less hardly with him, as with all of us, and brought him out of balance. But there is absolutely no doubt that once in the peace and comfort of an orderly household his balance will be restored.

[1] *BrW* 99–101.

Her reaction to Salzburg is not recorded, but it was doubtless a 'bitter pill' indeed. As Alfred said in a letter to Stefan, their parents had in fact planned a separate flat for the couple at Garnisonsgasse. 'But Vienna is quite impossible for me. I hope that too can be overcome', he wrote to Friderike in Nyon.[1]

In January he had thought of a flying visit to Vienna, but, as he wrote to Victor Fleischer,

> I must have a definite possibility of return here, since I plan a final return home with Friderike only in the spring. My longing for cafés with raspberry juice and the chatter about war experiences that goes with it is not exactly inordinate. . . . I have no desire to see patriots and idiots, and do not wish to take commissions back with me to Switzerland.[2]

In the event he did not go.

Reform of the marriage laws in Austria, to give the possibility of dispensation for divorced Catholics to remarry, was now under heated debate, pressed by the Social-Democrats, resisted by the Christian Socialists. Stefan and Friderike followed developments closely from Switzerland. Despite his moods of depression, when he would say he was willing to release her, they felt they belonged together, and she had learned in these years how to handle him, by keeping the children away, leaving him to himself for a time, or encouraging him to go off on his own. 'You realise that I do not want to bind you at this moment to me,' he had written to her at Amden, 'so bad a companion am I, impossible to assuage, full of evil humour, while your children take such pleasure in your presence and are so happy with you near. I am in a crisis at the moment—it will pass, but I do not want to infect others, I do not seek solitude for my own pleasure (for I have no pleasure now) but out of respect for the peace of others.'[3] But he was committed, and, when such moods passed, had no thought of evading his commitment.

With them now at Rüschlikon was Erwin Rieger. Zweig had known him slightly in Vienna, for he was the stepson of the outspoken colonel in charge of the War Archives. Like Rilke, a

[1] *BrW* 102–3.

[2] Letters to Fleischer, undated and 14 Jan. 1919. (Sch).

[3] *BrW* 87.

former cadet turned anti-militarist, the young poet and lover of French literature had managed to reach Switzerland early in 1918, and at first earned his living as a chemist's assistant in Zürich during the disastrous epidemic of 'Spanish influenza' then reaching its peak. He became attached to Stefan and Friderike, and began now, in a small way, the work of assistance in research and translation which was to be so valuable to Zweig over the next ten years. A loyal friend and disciple, he was to write the first biography of Zweig in 1928. Early in 1919 he accompanied Friderike on a visit to Lugano; and on his return, leaving her to go on to a Congress in Berne, and to Nyon, where she had temporarily installed the children to learn some French, began to help Stefan plan their return to Austria.

Though at first he was happy to know she was in Nyon, Stefan's impatience to get home now grew. He had plenty of work on hand, in particular his book on Rolland and the translation of Barbusse's *Les Suppliants* he had now begun, and (as always) needed Friderike to take charge of the practical arrangements for their transfer.

> Twelve hours distance apart is too much [he wrote to her]; we shall have a lot of running around over getting passports, permit for the nanny, moving, packing. I should like to get my work more forward. . . . Just because nothing can be decided in advance, and one has to be ready for sudden changes, and every day's delay in correspondence can be significant, so my purpose must be right to keep ourselves . . . together in or near Zürich, with our heavy luggage ready to move at any moment, so that we can take quick decisions when required. If we cannot do otherwise then you and Rieger will have to go on in advance. . . . I cannot possibly reckon everything to the day and hour. This terrible cold cannot last, the winter must be over in a few days; don't take this decision too hard, everything will soon be all right. We are fighting now the great fight for the great peace, each in his way, but in the last resort one for the other.[1]

Friderike returned to Rüschlikon with the children and bringing with her Loni, their Swiss nanny, whom it was her intention to take with them when the time came to leave for Salzburg, so

[1] *BrW* 104.

that Lisi could deal with the Vienna end of their move. Towards the end of March, equipped as for an Arctic expedition, with as much food as they could carry (baby-food, a forbidden export, replacing the sawdust stuffing of Suse's doll), the little group took train for Salzburg.[1]

2

'I knew it was a different Austria, a different world, to which I was returning.'

Die Welt von Gestern

Zweig confessed later that he hesitated at Buchs, the frontier station which had brought him such an exciting moment sixteen months before. This would be a turning-point in his life—would it not be wiser to think again? He concluded in favour of the difficult way, and boarded the train again. When they stopped at Feldkirch, on the other side, there awaited them a symbolic experience. The special train drew in carrying Emperor Karl and Empress Zita of Bourbon-Parma into exile. As Karl took his last look at Austria,

> all those who stood there sensed history, world history, in the tragic sight. . . . The locomotive started with a violent jerk as if it too had to overcome a disinclination to move, and slowly the train passed on. The officials followed it with a respectful gaze, after which, with that air of embarrassment to be seen at funerals, they returned to their duties. It was the moment in which the monarchy, almost a thousand years old, really ended. I knew it was a different Austria, a different world, to which I was returning.[2]

Their journey was a nightmare after they had changed from the trim Swiss carriages into the windowless, pillaged Austrian coaches, smelling still of the iodoform from the countless sick and wounded they had carried during the war. Jammed tight, with more crowding on at every stop, holding on desperately to their luggage in the darkness, they finally reached Salzburg after a run several times longer than normal. Leaving Rieger to continue on to Vienna, they descended more or less intact (but forgetting in the flurry to off-load Loni's two rucksacks), and found

[1] Fr 161–2; *WvG* 260. [2] *WvG* 260–2.

temporary quarters in the Hotel Nelböck, where he and Friderike had stayed on his leave in 1916.

Kapuzinerberg was out of the question for the moment: the roof leaked badly, there was no coal for miles around for heating, and in any case residence permits had first to be obtained—no easy matter for those who were still officially resident in Vienna. Stefan could claim his house-ownership, but for Friderike and the children, not yet bearing his name, the outlook was not good, as each *Kronland* barred immigrants because of the grave food shortage. To crown all, Loni, already in despair over the presumed loss of her baggage, fell prey almost at once to an apparently acute appendicitis; and Friderike, who had hurried off to beg a hospital bed from a local doctor friend, was horrified to find on her return that the girl had been whisked off to his apartment by the hotel doctor (who smelt hard currency) with a view to immediate operation. Friderike was able to retrieve her, but it was clear, when the condition subsided in a few days, that Loni would have to return to her family in Zürich.[1]

Stefan, who had prudently left his bags at the station, could stand this for only a few days, and had no compunction at leaving for Vienna without much warning to Friderike. In a letter posted to her from the train at Wels on 29 March he wrote:

> I went because there is no train on Sundays and I should not have got to my affairs until Tuesday and meantime exploded with impatience. It will be much easier for me to come back to Salzburg as soon as I have dealt with the *most* urgent things in Vienna, perhaps next week already when there will be more trains.—On our affairs, only this: 1) Don't economise on food. 2) Get someone to help, if L. remains out of commission. 3) Get a lawyer, if things look as if they are going wrong. 4) Deposit the luggage, insured, with a forwarding agent. 5) Order everything we agreed. The house must at least be in good order and occupiable at any time. Either we enjoy it ourselves, or we had better sell it or rent it. Please telephone at once if you need me. The worst case, that you are not allowed to stay, I simply will not envisage: we will be able to defend ourselves, if necessary I will do it publicly. But if you *have* to leave, then there is

[1] *WvG* 262–4; Fr 163–4; Fr[2] 87–8.

no alternative to Vienna. We will do everything there to win back the Salzburg house.—All goes well on the journey. Attnang was a terrible sight, with the people bellowing like a herd of bulls as they stormed the restaurant and literally choked themselves over a few scraps of sausage. A terrible sight, which promises much for Vienna.—My dear, do not be angry with me for going off to Vienna. You know I have been on the move for a week and am at the end of my tether with impatience and that I really have an *incredible* amount to do here which *cannot be put off*. I know how strong you are, you will get through all right; don't economise; above all arrange things so that you do not have to worry about the children. If they can eat, that is the only important thing—education, psychological handling, learning are only minor matters. The only important thing is to *get into some sort of order*, whether better or worse does not matter. But order there must be.[1]

Much as Friderike too longed to go to Vienna, not only to see her own family, but also, after their exchange of letters, Stefan's parents, there was nothing for it but to grit her teeth and do what was necessary in Salzburg. She sent for Lisi from Vienna, and, on the assumption that the residence permits would be forthcoming (which they eventually were, after many days of wrangling and badgering the authorities), settled in with her and the children in one of the few rooms at Kapuzinerberg which did not let water. Apart from finding builders, plumbers, plasterers for the necessary work, her most immediate and most daunting task was to clear the property of unwanted guests. The widow of the gardener of the previous owners, a witch-like old creature, still occupied part of the house with her grown-up son and daughter, and while it was not difficult to move her down to a room in the town, goats and all, the rest of the family presented something of a problem. Boy and girl looked upon Kapuzinerberg as their home, and the nineteen-year-old lad, who had grown up in the turmoil of war and come home with shell-shock after a short period in the army, was now one of a number of wild communistically inclined youngsters who had declared their own private war on property-owners and subsisted by theft and poaching. For Friderike, not even the titular owner of the house,

[1] *BrW* 105–6.

the situation was not without its danger, more especially as the boy had been joined by several of his cronies. She succeeded in moving him into a garden house, where he stayed until picked up by the police, and in ejecting the others. The girl she kept on as a maid for a while, until tuberculosis took her off. As spring approached, however, the fruit trees blossomed, and workmen began as best they could in the current shortage of materials, the situation took a turn for the better, and within a month she was able to assure Stefan that the 'order' he wanted was, more or less, established.[1] His 'lamb' was a great deal tougher than he realized.

Stefan had meanwhile reached Vienna on 30 March and moved back into Kochgasse and the care of old Josef. He sent her word by hand of Lisi:

> The post is awful, and so is the telephone. To date not a line done on Rolland. Written letters, sold books for 1200 crowns, errands and cares, phone ringing from morning till night. But I am happy and calm. . . . At home I am fed and spoiled. My parents are preparing the most cordial welcome for you, you will be getting a whole lot of furniture, curtains, linen, crockery, my good mother is really touching, my father very old and much gone back mentally. . . . *Jeremias* is to be given in May, I have little inclination for it, nor for the lecture.—Tell me when you are coming, whether you want to stay with me, whether I should send money. . . . Don't worry too much about the children, they will be all right without you. . . . Good Frau Mandl wants a holiday (not at my expense) and would like to come to us, it would be invaluable for me if this diligent woman could set up my archives and get the Rolland-Dostoevsky thing finished. Think, my love, how wonderful that would be for Stefan Pasha. Only these first months are important, to load up the cart, after that it will run by itself. And she is a wonderful housewife. I think you may be somewhat against the idea.—For packing up here I shall harness the old work-horse Josef and Frau Mandl, so that you have none of the burden. . . . So everything is going in orderly and passable fashion, provided communism does not appear the day after tomorrow. So come as soon as possible. . . .[2]

The lecture he mentioned was one on Rolland. They had been in correspondence about Rolland's projected 'Déclaration de

[1] Fr 165–7. [2] *BrW* 106–7.

l'indépendence de l'esprit', for which he was collecting signatories from all nations, and on which Zweig was to represent Austria. Bertrand Russell, Upton Sinclair, van Eeden, Barbusse, Selma Lagerlöf, Einstein, were all being canvassed.[1] Zweig's lecture, given at the Wiener Konzerthaussaal on 11 April, was devoted mainly to this 'call to brotherhood of comrades in work of the mind', 'We do not recognise the peoples,' Rolland had written in it, 'we recognise the People—one, universal . . . we work for Humanity in its entirety.' But the lecture was also a Testament of Friendship and witness to Rolland's work during the war. 'I know of no-one who has a deeper and more pious cult of friendship than Zweig,' wrote Rolland in his diary after receiving a copy of the talk, 'friendship is his religion.'[2]

The contrasts of misery and frivolity in Vienna made Zweig firmer than ever in his resolve to quit the capital for Salzburg as soon as he could. He found that his former friends there spoke a different language now: they no longer understood one another. The city he regarded as doomed: 'next autumn there will be an emigration such as has never been seen before, first of those elements with capital out to the former provinces, then of those willing to work to other parts of the globe, and there will remain only the soft, inactive slime of this great city.'[3] He had long feared the disintegration of Austria, and had earlier in the year expressed to Kippenberg his disgust at 'the new intellectuals, eager for power, without discipline, caught up in ideologies and without ideals—I count it an honour, although I am one who never wrote a line for the war, to stand now to one side. As an intellectual, I am ashamed of these intellectuals, as a Jew of these too forward Jews, as a democrat of these revolutionaries.'[4] With the exception of Amann he found the writers of Vienna too far removed from himself.[5]

In Europe the brave promises of a new world were fading: Wilson's vision clouded at Versailles, Barbusse's *Clarté* channelling

[1] *ZwV* ii. 919. This is the only manifesto Zweig is known ever to have signed (*ZwV* ii. 929).

[2] *ZwV* ii. 934; *Bildb* 70; Arens[2] 31.

[3] Letter to Rössler, 19 May 1919 (StB).

[4] Sch; *IAusst* 189.

[5] Letter to Rolland, 4 Apr. 1919 (*ZwV* ii. 929).

its intellectual internationalism down the single track of the class struggle, Rolland's 'Déclaration' ineffectual and lost. Zweig was lucky that, unlike friends such as Victor Fleischer, he did not have to earn a living[1] to support his writing, and was free to make the decision to 'stand to one side'; he was lucky, too, to have Friderike to smooth the path of practical application of his plans. But to have decided on Salzburg as his retreat as far back as 1916 showed quite remarkable foresight, a perception that was the other side of the coin of his pessimism. As he had felt when he crossed the frontier at Buchs, this was a turning-point in his life: 'gone was the time when I could pretend to myself that whatever I essayed was purely temporary. The middle of life had been reached, the age of mere promises had gone by; the time had come to confirm promises, to stand the test, or to give up for good.'[2]

3

'How often there stands—unseen by contemporaries —a woman protective and active within a work, so quietly and self-evidently interwoven with it that its own creator may himself be oblivious.'
Friderike Zweig, *Pasteur*

His own residence permit for Salzburg was finally issued on 26 April. During that month Friderike had at last been able to pay a short visit to Vienna, and had been touched by the warm reception shown her by his parents. She did not feel as closely drawn to them as she had to her first father-in-law, the Hofrat, but from this first meeting felt a deeper understanding for their weaknesses than had either of their sons. Then, at last, on 29 April, the moment came to enter into their first home together. As a welcoming gift he hung the Blake drawing of King John on the wall of her room. She had prepared a library for him on the ground floor, with a Sandringham carpet in the deep red he

[1] His brother, struggling to maintain the family business in what was now Czechoslovakia, was greatly irked by his reluctance to be consulted over it (although he visited the factory in July 1921).

[2] *WvG* 278.

loved, and large enough to house his books and the ever-growing autograph collection and archives (he had brought back in triumph from his parents' home an ancient iron travelling-chest, which had once belonged to his grandfather and was just what he wanted to store his manuscript treasures). On the first floor he had a study and bedroom, next to the great drawing-room with its tapestry, from which on the other side opened her own room with balcony, her bedroom, and the children's rooms and bathroom. Above was the little tower with an attic; on the ground floor an old-fashioned panelled garden room opening on to a conservatory; and in a semi-basement servants' quarters and an enormous kitchen. The garden contained a charming little pavilion, and the fruit trees were in full bloom. Everywhere doors led into the garden and gates to the nearby woods.[1]

For the moment it was not all theirs. They felt compelled by the acute shortage of accommodation (although there was as yet no official requisitioning) to release two rooms for the use of another family, which Friderike wisely chose from among the police officers of the town. When, two years later, an all-party commission charged with the requisitioning of all spare accommodation paid a visit, they could hardly credit this voluntary compliance; and although they nevertheless proposed dividing up the historic drawing-room into four, to house four more families, Friderike appealed successfully to the Ancient Monuments Commission to preserve it, against a payment by Stefan to municipal funds amounting almost to the original purchase price of the house itself. The police lodgers in fact stayed many years.[2]

But they were almost alone, and for Stefan it was an ideal workshop. He wrote to a friend on 19 May:

> With the narrowing of life we have all experienced in these last five years I have also made a decisive reduction in my circle of friends. . . . My decision to leave Vienna was unshakable. . . . A year or more ago, before this was clear to the others, I bought a house here, which you will find delightful, and I hope to be able to live out a small

[1] Fr[2] 89; Fr 53, 170–1, 180–1; *BrW* 107.

[2] *WvG* 266; Fr 171–3; *BrW* 139.

quiet existence here.— . . . You probably know that I am living with Frau von Winternitz (who has a very important novel[1] appearing with S. Fischer shortly), and that we are still unable to marry, because, in our free Republic, Catholic divorcées like my wife are condemned to such forms of existence. I am doing a lot of work, above all a long book about Rolland, which I am taking great pleasure in myself, should be ready by the autumn, and I have other work in hand.[2]

For their marriage there was nothing for it but to wait.[3] They had considered trying in Hungary, and had even got as far as arranging for Friderike's adoption there as a first step, but the chaos after the Bela Kun rising made it impossible. This apart, there was no real cloud over their happiness. As his mother had said, he needed 'uncommonly gentle treatment', and the security of home as an anchor, a counterweight to the unrest always latent in him: Friderike found her happiness in providing this for him. 'It was the happiest thought of my life', he wrote to Fleischer in July, 'to leave Vienna in good time and to choose a quieter form of life, which suits me exceptionally well.'[4]

His work flourished accordingly. Steady progress on the *Rolland* was accompanied by essays, like that on Walt Whitman for the *NFP*, and a correspondence even more intensive than he had conducted from Switzerland: with Rössler, harrying him over the publication of *Der Zwang*, which was still delayed; with Masereel, who was keen to illustrate *Die Mondscheingasse*; with the Director of the Deutsches Volkstheater in Vienna, who was to produce *Jeremias* in its Austrian première in the autumn, and whom he was pressing to accept his translation of Rolland's *Le Temps viendra*.[5] There were flying visits to Vienna, where (despite his 'reduced circle of friends') he seemed never to have a spare moment between publishers, Bertha Zuckerkandl, Benno Geiger, the antiquarian Hugo Heller, and particularly the Civil Servants who persisted in inaction over their application to marry.

[1] *Vögelchen*; S. Fischer, Frankfurt am Main, 1919.

[2] Letter to Rössler, 19 May 1919 (StB).

[3] According to Friderike, there were 30,000 couples in this plight in Austria at the time. Fr 131, 173–4.

[4] Letter to Fleischer, 20 July 1919 (Sch).

[5] ZE; StB; Sch; *Ausst* 53.

His 'dark moods' sometimes returned, however, not always provoked by the notorious Salzburger *Schnürlregen* or the *Föhn*. A revealing letter of August 1919 is extant from them both to Fleischer.

> Stefan is often in a rage of despair [wrote Friderike], and whatever I can fend off, divert or postpone, I do—but where then, what with the housekeeping, district education authorities, bringing up the children, the garden, to find time for the letters one would like to write. . . . With 'the boy', as you call him, it is often hard, for he is on occasion violent, even in front of others, and this I do not always bear with the equanimity the circumstances demand. . . . It is beautiful here, like paradise. But I would prefer any small corner with less disturbance in my own home.

Stefan's part of the letter (it is not clear whether he had read the foregoing) ran:

> There is not a single Jew who is not in Salzburg, and since Reinhardt arrived these people swarm here like black flies, Aussee has vomited itself empty,[1] we have sometimes a hard job to defend ourselves. My work is quite ruined by it all. . . . Fritzi is very jealous, although my peccadilloes can be counted on the fingers of one hand and were anyway reckoned with from the beginning. But that is her weak point, and unfortunately also mine. [There followed a P.S.:] Fritzi has opened this again *in secret*, to see what I have written, hence the delay.[2]

There is no doubt that Friderike had a heavy cross to bear on such occasions.

That there were to be no children of their union must have been long her secret disappointment ('what a joy, to bear three sons for the man one loves!' she wrote once).[3] But she realized that her whole care must be to try to give him security in everyday life to counterbalance his deep strain of unrest, to foresee and forestall all outside disturbance. 'The circle was widely drawn for me, but I had to stay within it.' Her own literary work suffered, but over the years she managed to complete a number

[1] Was this a sour reference to Hofmannsthal? Cf. *Hofmannsthal/von Andrian Briefwechsel*; S. Fischer, 1968, 304.

[2] Letter to Fleischer, date uncertain (?15 Aug. 1919) (Sch).

[3] *BrW* 200.

of translations which ensured her a modest separate income to devote to the children (Stefan after their marriage refused to accept the due allowance for Suse and Alix from von Winternitz, and where her own ideas differed from his on their bringing-up she felt impelled to a measure of independence in their regard.)[1] Somehow she learned to maintain her equanimity, to forget the dark clouds which passed so quickly, and to be ready with new encouragement when his good humour returned.

A short absence from Salzburg was usually enough for this. His deeper feelings, of friendship for his fellow men and of love for Friderike, seemed actually to flourish at a distance and to dwindle with proximity. His natural shyness and abhorrence of 'discussions', coupled with the gentleness which made it hard to say no, risked stultifying each and every relationship if it continued too long at a stretch, and the most minor of irritations often served to induce his 'black liver'. To escape, sometimes on the moment's spur, was the only way to preserve the relationships he really valued. It was thus with Victor Fleischer, with Rieger, later with Felix Braun, and thus above all with Friderike, who perhaps was the only one really to understand.

In September he had sent off, at last, to Kippenberg the manuscript of *Drei Meister*, with the final version of *Dostoevsky* distilled to a third of its former bulk. 'Now everything is finished which I had on hand from my old work: I can think more freely of new.'[2] The Insel-Verlag was not yet his sole publisher—André Suarès's *Cressida*, which he was translating with Rieger, was to appear in Carl Seelig's Die Zwölf Bücher with E. P. Tal, like *Die Zeit wird kommen*, and *Rolland* was to go to Ruetten & Loening in Frankfurt—but there were nevertheless many projects to be discussed with Kippenberg, and he badly wanted to get over to Leipzig. He paid a further visit to Vienna at the end of September, where disappointments awaited him, both over the *Ehedispens*, on which the Civil Servants appeared to have lost the file, and over *Jeremias*, which, despite postponement to 9 October and a complete sell-out of tickets half an hour after the box-office opened, was to be limited to one performance only ('ah, how

[1] Fr 177–9. [2] Letter to Kippenberg, undated (? Sept. 1919) (Sch).

disgust for business chokes me, and yet one must plunge head-first into it in these ghastly times').[1] On 19 October, however, he was able to leave on his first visit to Germany since the war.

'My travel literature is the German railway timetable', he wrote Friderike gaily from Munich, '. . . I would have made a good hotel-porter.' On arrival in Leipzig the following day he called immediately on the Director of the Insel-Verlag. The house was flourishing, with a full list of new books and reprints, and he found immediate agreement to his own proposal that they should take on *Der Zwang* (Rössler having finally given up), run a further 7,000 copies of *Jeremias* (totalling 20,000 to date), and reprint *Die frühen Kränze*, as well as undertake to bring out the *Verlaine* in two volumes. His book on Marceline Desbordes-Valmore was also agreed upon. All this was properly prepared in contract form, to be signed on his return from north Germany, and was highly satisfactory. But he was most pleased by success in what he called, after Goethe, the *Hauptgeschäft*—the Bibliotheca Mundi project, into which Kippenberg enthusiastically entered, and for which they were able to decide the first fifteen volumes, to start at Christmas 1920. The galley-proofs for *Drei Meister* were already waiting for him, and he experienced not a little difficulty in trying to correct them on this busy journey.[2]

He had undertaken lectures on Rolland in Berlin, Hamburg, and Kiel. On arrival at the Westend Hotel in Berlin on 23 October he found that all seats for the lecture, to be given in the Tribune Theatre, had already been sold, and it proved a sensational success, although, as he wrote to Friderike later, it was impossible not to notice a certain resistance to the ideas. He did not yield to the popular demand for a second performance ('too much like a concert-singer'), but confessed his regret not to have given his talk in a larger theatre, and thus earned 1,500 or 2,000 marks instead of the 200 from the Tribune. It brought him much to the public eye, and he felt that despite the laggardly post from his Salzburg base he was achieving more by this trip than by a hundred letters. *Jeremias* was under consideration for the Staatstheater, in a shortened version, and the Lessing-Theater had in

[1] *BrW* 111–12. [2] *BrW* 112–18.

mind a production of *Legende eines Lebens*. After the second talk in Hamburg, which also went well, and a third in Kiel, he returned to Berlin to pursue both these projects. It was tiring, but stimulating: 'am I so much the provincial, or is it a sign of age, or a proletarianisation of our circumstances? at all events, in the evenings I am thoroughly tired with all this driving around, telephoning, waiting, discussing.' From Hamburg he wrote to Friderike on 29 October:

From all this I see that I must base my life on more mobility, on conservation of energy, and not on money. I can certainly achieve more than hitherto if I do not remain for ever the slave of my correspondence and of my disorder. . . . You are in fact (forgive me) still not experienced enough in handling the mail. It seems I must travel more to train you up by experience to a perfect forwarder and administrator of my correspondence.[1] Otherwise everything seems to be in good order. I am curious to see Salzburg, inwardly I have quite forgotten it: when I am on a journey all ties suddenly fall away, I feel myself quite unburdened, disconnected, free. You cannot feel this, for when you are alone you feel yourself abandoned or incomplete. How powerful, pure and without any spiritual disloyalty is this feeling in me: you perhaps do not envy me it (it is not a woman's feeling) but there is something in it marvellously uplifting and invigorating. Whole past epochs suddenly return: nothing is lost, everything still full of inception, enticement.[2]

Back in Salzburg, in November, 'breathing European air', he could follow his 'untroubled way over the ruins of our *Kaiserreiche* into our good Europe'.[3] In fact, the visit to Germany, and what he had seen of Austria since coming back from Switzerland, combined to cloud this optimism, to show him that the regeneration he had hoped defeat would bring was being thwarted by a facile opportunism.

One thing I cannot forgive Germany [he had written earlier to Kippenberg], that, scarcely free, she has given herself to small minds, an Erzberger, a Scheidemann; that her misfortune was only a misery and not a tragedy! Why is there no leader now in Germany, why

[1] Friderike was indeed afforded ample opportunity for training in this, and learned to calm what they called his *Postnervosität*.

[2] *BrW* 120–6; Fr 239.

[3] Letter to Zech, date uncertain (?Nov. 1919) (Sch).

does she always call on the trimmers and the clever ones. . . . We here in Austria were small, and have remained small, with no will to greatness. In Germany there was such a will—and what have the politicians made of it![1]

In Leipzig he had noted the depth of contempt in which the Germans held the current *Regiererei*. There was hardly a soul he met who did not openly long for a return of the monarchy or a dictatorship. Anti-Semitism was rampant, anti-French feeling almost as strong; with it all, the shops overflowing with goods, at fantastic prices, and in the air the smell of impending bankruptcy.[2]

In an 'Appeal for Patience', written now for Stephan Grossmann's Berlin *Tagebuch* and published in January 1920, he argued strongly against what he called this opportunism in defeat, the parrot-cry of 'united Europe' from a purely herd instinct, and urged patience to bring the victory of convictions over mere opinions. But his pessimism often gained the upper hand: 'we are a lost generation, we shall never see a united Europe'.[3] 'One must admit that Barbusse has recently conducted himself with courage', said Jouve in a letter to him early in December; '. . . We cannot refuse him our sympathy, despite the presence of Anatole France, that prudent mandarin, who plays the role of lightning-conductor for *Clarté*. The best and most just attitude to take, I think, is one of individualism towards every kind of group.'[4] Zweig had a great admiration for Magdeleine Marx, whose *Femme* he planned to translate with Friderike; but he turned a deaf ear to her pleas for contributions to the weekly *Clarté*.[5] He felt his publication of the *Verlaine* was a real contribution to international understanding, 'doubly important now . . . as a sign that lyrical Germany is not entirely behind the ridiculous attempt to split art into the hostile divisions of nations and languages';[6] but he was increasingly repelled (as also was Rolland for a time) by the misdirected and politically committed internationalism

[1] Letter to Kippenberg, undated (? Sept. 1919) (Sch). [2] *BrW* 113–18.
[3] *Tagebuch*, ed. Stephan Grossmann, Berlin, i. 1, 10 Jan. 1920, 7–10.
[4] Letter from Jouve, 9 Dec. 1919 (ZE). [5] Correspondence ZE.
[6] Quoted Zohn, *German Life & Letters*, v. 3 (April 1952), 208.

to which groups like *Clarté*, despite the idealism of Barbusse, were tending. His instinct, like Jouve's, was to take an individualist line—'we are the enemies equally of the men of power and of the men of communism, of the intellectuals of the *NRF* as of those of *Clarté*'; and he showed this in an open letter to Barbusse published in Grossmann's *Tagebuch* in the summer of 1920.[1]

It was rare, however, for him thus to expose his views in public, for a compelling cause of his highly individualist approach was precisely his intense reserve and natural shyness. As Dumont has pointed out, the frankness and self-revelation of his letters to Rolland were due to his conviction that they would never be published, and when in November 1919 Rolland sought his permission to quote extracts from them in his *Journal des années de guerre* he was very reluctant to agree. 'My reserve in all personal matters is very great. You saw that I published the Verhaeren book[2] only in a private edition, and—to speak frankly—my book about you is taking so long to complete because I wish as far as possible to avoid speaking as an intimate and betraying what I have learned solely through your goodness to me.'[3] *Die Welt von Gestern* is the final proof of his sincerity in this: of all his biographies, it is the most lifeless and most impersonal. Jouve, in his own book on Rolland, records Zweig's view that 'there exists in every true man a certain modesty which prevents him from expressing how much he loves another'.[4]

4

'Dostoevsky, Rolland, bibliotheca mundi, three translations in 3–4 years, this may well be counted enough!'

Zweig to Fleischer, May 1920

In December 1919 the slow-moving wheels of the Austrian Civil Service finally ground out the dispensation for his marriage to

[1] *ZwV* ii. 968–9; letter from Magdeleine Marx (incomplete), 3 Oct. 1919 (ZE); letter from Masereel, 30 June 1920 (ZE); *WvG* 277–8; R 112; letter from Jouve, 13 Feb. 1922 (ZE).

[2] The 1917 *Erinnerungen*, of course, not the 1910 monograph.

[3] Dum 196.

[4] Jouve 9.

Friderike. It was one of the advantages of that *Proporz* system of administration, which seemed to suit Austria so well and to which she returned after the State Treaty in 1955, that where one official was politically hostile to a given course of action his immediate superior or inferior, as a member of the other coalition party, could generally be reckoned favourable. So it was in Zweig's case. The Landeshauptmann, a Christian-Socialist named Rehrl, refused to grant the *Dispens*, but when he was on leave the file reached his deputy, the Social Democrat Preussler, for whose party's programme this was an important plank, and there was then no doubt about the decision.[1] 'I shall probably have to go in January to Vienna with Friderike for the completion of that well-known matter,' Stefan wrote to Fleischer on 9 December, 'for which indeed we may need your personal presence for an hour.'[2] He had apparently agreed with Friderike that she should not be present when the registry marriage was solemnized in the Rathaus; but when the day came at the end of January 1920 it was Felix Braun and not Fleischer who stood proxy for her. Stefan's mother was present, and she and he telephoned Friderike in Salzburg immediately after the ceremony.

The first letter from Friderike *Zweig*, on 30 January, ran:

My dear, How did you spend our wedding night? Steffi, it occurs to me that I should have written a bride's letter to your parents. But I cannot, you must see that. I really feel there has been no change. That is because you have rid me of my sentimentality. If that were involved, I should write you a letter that could be framed. I have a dim idea of what I would say in it—but as I say, it cannot be, and my prayers, my dear one, I shall say also when you are back with me.

She continued (as though to show how well she was learning the proper administration of his correspondence) to give a situation report on the mail—Thomas Mann sending for his collection the manuscript of his *Novelle*, *Die Hungernden* (from *Der kleine Herr Friedemann*), 'as a sign of my most cordial esteem'; the successful outcome of a lawsuit against the Lessing-Theater in Berlin and their undertaking to produce *Legende eines Lebens* the following

[1] Fr² 121–2. [2] Sch.

autumn; Kippenberg asking if Rolland's *Liluli* was available;[1] the Berlin publisher Kiepenheuer wanting him to edit a collection of *Novellen.*

The train stoppage is annoying. As little as I grudge you to your mother, I would be happy if you were back here.—I have done a lot on your letters, gutted whole heaps. It is hard work dividing those from friends on publishers' stationery from those purely of business. Everything has to be read, otherwise they pile up and order is lost again. A glance would be enough for you. Particularly troublesome for me as I try to classify are the letters from women at the time when I thought there was not much time over for anyone but me; and in addition there are some which would make you look like a Don Juan in the eyes of the worthy Frau M. So it is out of the question for you to give her these letters to look through. You have forgotten yourself what impossible ones, and how many, there are among them. But with time all will be in good order, and your library too. . . .—I hope, my darling, that all has gone well with your affairs, and you are not too tired but have also had a little time for relaxation. From your correspondence I learn you are going to Berlin. That was news to me. Now I have written you everything the day has brought with it. Kisses from your Mumu.[2]

It must have been a grievous disappointment for her to find that the regularization of their union made in fact so little difference. Though she be never so emancipated, for a woman the outward tokens of affection remain all important; and although Friderike doubtless agreed with Stefan that it would be more decorous for her to be represented by proxy at the actual ceremony, and was overjoyed by his telephone call, the fact remains that she did not hear from him again for several days. The calm tone of her letter must have cost her a lot. But she had gained what she had longed for. The marriage lines from the Vienna Rathaus would, she realized, build no cage for this free spirit, nor would she want it so. They were, however, the spiritual rock on which she could build their life together, durable and firm as the Kapuzinerberg itself.

[1] Zweig never succeeded in the translation of this fantasy—perhaps the only time he had to acknowledge the insurmountable barrier of language (cf. Dum 235–6).

[2] *BrW* 126–8.

The imposing well-furnished house was no doubt the envy of those who did not suspect how Spartan was his life. Who in fact detected the hermit in the man who spent the whole day writing and reading—his correspondence alone was almost beyond managing—dictating to his secretary, walking up and down to develop his thought, and only in the evening hurried down the ancient path into the town, to eat in an inn, smoke his cigar in a café and play a game of chess with a friend?

So Felix Braun remembered, many years later, the Salzburg routine of these post-war years.[1] The Café Bazar was a favourite haunt after dinner, or, for an undisturbed game of chess with his young friend Emil Fuchs ('Schachfuchs'), a café in the Getreidegasse; and there were often late-night walks through the town or up to the Mönchsberg. He sought relaxation too in long mountain climbs in the company of Hermann Bahr, taking some pride in the physical achievement these represented.[2] The Vienna bookseller Heinrich Hinterberger, on a visit about 1920 to see the manuscript collection, noted how Friderike could smooth over difficulties with a few well-chosen words and act as a foil for her husband's impatience and unrest. He also heard Stefan, in the midst of this well-ordered life, describe his recurring feeling of insecurity and his need then to go off on his own.[3]

Financially he had few worries. The creeping inflation in Austria, soon to gallop, was for the time being more than compensated by his success in other countries. 'My book on Rolland', he wrote to Fleischer in March, 'is coming along quickly, has already been sold sight unseen to England. In fact other countries are my only support, Czechoslovakia with our factory, Germany with royalties—in Austria I simply pay out, sums that are already terrifying. But I am not worried. The Bibliotheca Mundi alone will keep my head above water in a few years.'[4] He had also arranged for *Rolland* to appear simultaneously in Sweden as well as in England, and hoped thereby not only for hard currency but

[1] *Mus Land* 201.

[2] Felix Braun, 'Persönliches über Stefan Zweig zum 80. Geburtstag', 28 Nov. 1961; Fr. 178–9, 188–9.

[3] Heinrich Hinterberger, *Liber Amic* 46–7.

[4] Letter to Fleischer, 30 Mar. 1920 (Sch).

also for international success: 'it may become a sort of standard work for the essay, in the spirit of Georg Brandes'.[1]

The *Rolland*, he said, was to be the book of a life, unlike his *Verhaeren*, which had been a book of literature. In it he showed his gratitude for the privilege of having experienced the miracle of so pure an existence, whose ideas and dreams, apparently overcome and destroyed by the powers of darkness, would yet conquer. In Rolland's 'Déclaration de l'indépendence de l'esprit' he saw the raising of the standard of the invisible republic of Europe; in the author the man who had ensured that 'the holy light of brotherhood was not extinguished in history's most violent storm'. He dedicated it to the few who, 'in the hour of the trial by fire, remained true to Romain Rolland and our holy fatherland of Europe'. Published by Ruetten & Loening in 1921, at a time when most authors, Zweig included, complained of their poor sales, it made a remarkable impact. The first edition was followed two years later by a second, and by 1925 a third, enlarged, edition had brought the total sales to 18,000. As Dumont has noted, Rolland's literary fortunes east of the Rhine depended entirely on Zweig's efforts: almost ignored in France, his works in German translation made money and his plays appeared in a wide range of German theatres.[2]

In October Zweig made a second business trip to Germany, for further lectures and to see Ruetten & Loening about the publication of *Rolland*. It was also a chance to see Victor Fleischer, who, disregarding Stefan's Cassandra-like views on the future of German publishing, had now joined the Neuer Frankfurter Verlag (later to become the Frankfurter Verlagsanstalt, and to receive over the years much help, both with advice and money, from Zweig). But his pleasure over the favourable terms of the *Rolland* contract, and well-attended lectures in Wiesbaden, Stuttgart, and Heidelberg, was marred by bad news from Vienna: Alfred wrote that their father had had a slight stroke, and although it passed without serious effects and there proved to be no need for his presence, he felt uneasy, and longed to be back near at hand in Salzburg.[3]

[1] Letter to Fleischer, 24 May 1920 (Sch). [2] Dum 239 [3] *BrW* 130–6.

Drei Meister was meanwhile extremely well received. Thomas Mann, to whom he had sent an inscribed copy, found it a 'brilliant critical work of art', and thought the Dostoevsky 'the boldest and most knowledgeable since Mereschkowski yet "essayed" on this great son of the 19th century'. Unlike Tolstoy, Dostoevsky seemed to Mann a great sinner rather than a great artist: 'but at all events he was something great, terrifyingly, shatteringly great, and that your essay has permitted me to feel this greatness again—so strongly as seldom before—leads me to send you my gratitude in genuine admiration'.[1] For Freud, on the other hand, his treatment of the 'confounded Russian' was not so satisfying: 'there are gaps, riddles unsolved . . . it seems to me highly unlikely that he was in fact an epileptic', but rather (like so many great men accused of this) 'a pure hysteric'. His praise for the book as a whole, however, was unstinted, in particular for Zweig's trick of intensification by repetition, 'by which your sentence approaches nearer and nearer to the heart of its subject', and which he compared to the piling up of symbols in the dream which allows the hidden meaning to filter through ever more clearly.[2] The essay formed the Introduction to a twenty-five-volume edition of Dostoevsky's works published the following year by the Insel.

5

> *'The* Steffzweig *is an artificial product, created on the occasion of a Vienna poets' congress from the feathers, skin, hair, etc. of every possible European animal. It is so to speak a Volapük animal. Nowadays belief in its organic existence is confined to distant lands and certain Geneva circles.'*
>
> 'Dr. Peregrin Steinhövel', *Bestiarium Literaricum*, 1920

'More than ever let us remember Candide and "cultivate our garden". But I preach to the converted', wrote Arcos from Geneva in August 1920.[3] It was true that Zweig was to some extent withdrawn from the world in these early years in Salzburg.

[1] Mann *Br* i. 180. [2] Freud *Br* 330–2. [3] Letter of 17 Aug. 1920 (ZE).

'You will no doubt sit in resignation in your Salzburg castle,' Faesi had forecast in 1919, 'and if you have the guard you once planned of "Capitoline geese" their cackling will be a symbol of the general lack of understanding in our contemporaries.'[1] Politically he was certainly resigned, seeing politics in France and Germany just as mad as in wartime. There seemed only one way to salvation: 'on the one hand to withdraw completely into ourselves and on the other to grasp with all our passion the ultimate community, that of pure humanity'.[2] Yet he was constantly active in the cause of internationalism as he saw it. 'We younger people, who have lived once as Europeans in the spirit, are I hope once and for all secure from any relapse into nationalism', he said in a letter to the Germanist Jethro Bithell in England, explaining how even during the war he had not allowed himself to be led astray by Verhaeren's aberration.[3] But it was as an individual, and not, if he could help it, as a member of a group, that he liked to work.

In 1921 the English section of the International Women's League for Peace and Freedom planned a summer school in Salzburg. Friderike, as a prominent member, was much involved in the organization and preparations: Stefan's immediate reaction had been to flee, despite the fact that many of his old wartime friends were to attend. Rolland was somewhat surprised at his decision to be absent, wrote Jouve in June; although he himself, having listened to Stefan's discussions with Friderike on the subject of the League, was less surprised, he urged him all the same not to let down old friends like Bazalgette and Vildrac who were thinking of coming. Zweig allowed himself to be persuaded ('one must pretend to believe in all these actions and stifle one's secret pessimism'), and returned earlier than he had planned from a visit with his mother to Marienbad and with Alfred to the family factory in Reichenberg. Jouve stayed at Kapuzinerberg during the school.[4]

[1] Letter of 14 May 1919 (ZE).

[2] Letter to Servaes, 8 Feb. 1921 (StB).

[3] Letter of 20 Aug. 1921.

[4] Fr[2] 90–1; *BrW* 137–8; letters from Jouve, 1 June 1921 and undated (ZE); letter to Rolland, 27 Nov. 1920 (Dum 171).

Baudouin, who also came, outlined in his diary an interesting and significant picture of Zweig at a reception given for the party at Kapuzinerberg on 11 August:

> Amid this distinguished throng, [he] is in his element. He deploys his whole talent as an intermediary. . . . He is cosmopolitan in the best sense of the word. . . . He would have the self-satisfaction of a spoilt child, if it were not for his eagerness for human contact. . . . A cordial warmth emanates from this person with so moderated an ardour, as he darts from one group to another, with a light and easy step in which there is something of the dancer, of the Mercury . . . and, I would add, of the feline, if this word could evoke only a picture of a certain native elegance of movement without any implication of cruelty or cunning. This image is strengthened as I regard the prominent well-coloured cheekbones, the quivering nostril, and the eyes, somewhat elongated but well opened. In him, beneath the being of intelligence, there is a being of instinct and of flair, a taste for the hunt converted and turned towards the seeking out of human contacts. And in the glance sparkling from these smiling, caressing eyes, the image of the feline seems no longer true: it is a warm, velvet-like glance whence emanates more intensely this virtue sensible in the whole person . . . which I would describe as of a warm and sensual vapour, the same which envelops one at the reading of certain pages of his Novellen. . . . Yes, this intermediary, this being of communication and of communion is in his element among these groups of human beings, these little planetary systems between which he darts like a free comet. . . . And then, all at once, he is no longer in his element. It is like a slight nervous fault: the sociable man of a moment ago would seem almost shy. He seeks out those to whom he feels himself closest; he confesses to us that these people tire him quickly, bore him, and that he longs for nothing so much as the *tête-à-tête* of friendship.[1]

This was exactly it. 'Being of communication and of communion', he preferred to bring his talent as intermediary to bear through individual friendships rather than in the extended social exposure of the *salon* or the cocktail-party. He had been glad, at the request of the publisher Kurt Wolff, to look after Rabindranath Tagore when the sage passed through Salzburg in June,

[1] Baudouin 23–5.

deeply hurt by many acts of tactlessness in Germany;[1] but the purposeful, almost professional internationalism of Jane Addams, Emily Green-Balch, and the numerous Asian satellites who attended the August school was evidently too much for him. It is significant that it was almost twenty years before he is known to have given such a reception again—for his German and Austrian friends in the Hotel Wyndham, New York; and indeed he resolved that this intolerably crowded summer of 1921 would be the last to see him in Salzburg during the *Festspiele*.

'A spring tide of people, 5 to 10 every day . . . I've not written a line since the 20th of July', he wrote peevishly to Fleischer at the end of August; 'I have taken care that it will not happen again that my own time is denied me to such an extent by others.'[2] He could enthuse over the intellectual diversity of Salzburg—'now Schmidtbonn and Latzko were here, yesterday Alfred Wolfenstein and Hans von Hülsen, today Kurt Martens,' he wrote to Servaes in January, 'we have become a sort of suburb of Munich, . . . and so one escapes the danger of growing into a Kotzebue-ish provincial'.[3] But during the Festival the city seemed too much like the cross-roads of the world: 'a literary bourse, a dramatic fair', resulting for him in a quite unparalleled weariness of people.[4]

At the end of March he had made his first post-war visit to Italy—'a belated honeymoon' with Friderike. His misgivings whether Austrians, as the late arch-enemies of the Italians, would be welcome were quickly dispelled. 'Lei e Austriaco? Ah! che piacere! Finalmente!' said the friendly receptionist when they arrived at a Verona hotel. In Milan on the following day, remembering that his old friend G. A. Borgese was on the editorial staff of the *Corriere della Sera*, he somewhat diffidently sent in his card: much as he longed to see Borgese again, with whom he had spent many a stimulating evening in Berlin and Vienna before the war, he remembered how strongly his friend had aligned himself against the Central Powers, even supporting Mussolini,

1 Correspondence Wolff 413–14.

2 Letter of 27 Aug. 1921 (Sch).

3 Letter of 29 Jan. 1921 (StB).

4 Letter to Katharina Kippenberg, 6 Sept. 1921 (Sch).

and did not wish to chance being turned away. It was therefore a real delight when, hardly down the steps from the *Corriere* offices, he was overtaken by Borgese, his animated face glowing with pleasure. In a few minutes they were talking as cordially as always: indeed, returning from opposite sides, they became closer than before. Again, in Florence, the painter Alberto Stringa, also an old friend, rushed up to him in the street, and embraced him so vehemently that Friderike, who did not know him, thought the curious bearded stranger intended to attack him.[1] The war certainly seemed buried and done with.

But the strike in Venice on the day of their arrival there, the threats to their lone blackleg gondolier, their first sight of young Blackshirts, singing the *Giovanezza* in the Piazza San Marco, were a grim warning to Zweig that Europe's troubles were by no means over.

> Visual impressions always have something convincing about them. Now, for the first time, I knew that this hazy Fascism, until then almost unknown to me, was something real, something well directed, and that it made fanatics of decided, bold young people. . . . Out of curiosity I bought a few copies of the *Popolo d'Italia* and perceived in the sharp, concise, plastic style of Mussolini the same resoluteness as in the quick march of these young men across the Piazza San Marco. Naturally I could not dream of the dimensions which this struggle would acquire in less than a year. But from that hour I was conscious that a struggle was imminent here and everywhere, and that *our* peace was not yet *the* peace.[2]

To Servaes he wrote, in January 1923: 'I often shudder at the thought of the raging madness of this world fascism, of the brutal triumph of force: it will be the ideal of the next generation, and football enthusiasm will soon give way to a more evil fury.'[3] 'No-one wants to liquidate the war, neither France nor Germany', he said to Rolland in 1921.[4]

[1] Stringa visited Kapuzinerberg soon after this chance meeting and did several pictures of the house and garden (Fr 308).

[2] Letter to Fleischer, (?21) Mar. 1921 (Sch); *WvG* 279–82.

[3] Letter of 22 Jan. 1923 (StB).

[4] Letter to Rolland, 4 Sept. 1921 (Dum 172).

6

'Stefan Zweig, of all those who in Germany today master the art of the word, is one of the most intensive. Not only in his gifts, but in his will and in his vitality.' Richard Specht

My garden replaces for me those lands further afield through which I have so often travelled and to which I only seldom find the way now. Work, once merely consequential, the radius as it were of the circle of my life, has now become its centre, and my only hope is that it may have gained in value to the extent that I have devoted to it greater intensity from my life.[1]

Written in 1922, this was not strictly accurate in describing renunciation of travel, for he remained restless and continually on the move: in 1921, as well as going to Italy and Czechoslovakia, he paid two visits to Germany and one to Switzerland, not to mention a stay in Bad Gastein, and the following years showed much the same mobility. It was true, however, that he was now developing a new attitude towards his work. 'It is a good discipline for art', Jean Christophe had said, 'to restrict its efforts within implacable limits.' From *Drei Meister*, distilling the essence of the novelist to depict him as a type, there grew now in Zweig's mind the concept of a 'typology of the spirit', of further trilogies in similar form to portray the *Baumeister der Welt*, the master builders of the world of the mind. His *Novellen* he envisaged as a chain, to the first ring of which—the dark longings of childhood and adolescence in *Erstes Erlebnis*—he planned now to link a second, a series of adult and exotic passion: here too a typology, a striving after architectural form from the most diverse of materials. *Die Mondscheingasse*, so far published only in an obscure magazine, was joined by *Der Amokläufer*, *Phantastische Nacht*, *Die Frau und die Landschaft*, and *Brief einer Unbekannten*, all written at Salzburg. *Amok: Novellen einer Leidenschaft*, as the volume was entitled, proved his first popular success, with editions of 150,000 in eight years.

These stories gripped like those of Somerset Maugham, though by no means written in Maugham's flat, spare style, and lacking

[1] DDh 9.

his realism (the protagonists are never named, sometimes not even rating an initial, and we learn almost nothing of their background). They are convincing in their depiction of the dark passions lying just beneath the surface of our daily life: either because they are first-person narrations—a tale told to the author on board ship from the Far East, his observation of tell-tale hands over the baize of the Monte Carlo tables—or because, when the third person is employed (as in *Brief einer Unbekannten*) there is an apparent identification of author with hero. They called forth an enormous number of letters from his readers, who, because they recognized the validity of his portrayal of the frontiers of the unconscious, proceeded to treat him as confessor and psychiatrist, for they could not but believe that his personal experience was here revealed—a powerful but, to him, most unwelcome and embarrassing tribute, for there was in fact almost nothing directly autobiographical in the *Novellen*.

The architectural concept of his work, the edifice of grand design to be completed brick by brick, owed perhaps something to his admiration for the daimonic energy of Balzac. But his restless mind lacked the steady patience needed for a *Comédie Humaine*. His activity in these Salzburg years was, as Richard Specht noted, a 'radio-activity', loaded with tensions: 'in his presence one seems to see fine wires vibrating, stretching out to all corners of the world'.[1] He was no Hofmannsthal, withdrawn from the world. He was capable of sustained and concentrated effort, and welcomed for this the isolation of Kapuzinerberg or an out-of-the-way seaside resort or lakeside village; but after a few weeks of solitude would feel his life becoming too automatic, like the perpetual motion of a waterwheel under a mill-house, and the need would come over him, as he put it once to Friderike, of 'new supplies of life and passion'—as a cigarette meant nothing to a real smoker, so 'little episodes and literary successes' meant nothing to one 'greedy for life'.[2] And he would be off again on one of his innumerable journeys, sometimes organized in advance, such as a lecture tour, sometimes without plan into the blue, enjoying the admiration of young girls, exploring the backwaters

[1] S 8. [2] Letter to Friderike Zweig, Oct. 1922.

of small towns in France, living dangerously. As his fame grew (and he did not look his forty years) there was no lack of young women admirers with whom to play the Don Juan; and there was a touch of sadism in the way he spared Friderike none of the details of his affairs, on his return, or even in the almost daily letters he wrote her while away. Yet he kept himself well under control, and there was nothing of the 'lost week-end' about these diversions: few days, no matter where he might find himself, passed without work, and he always returned refreshed to Salzburg. 'I feel I can think over things so much more freely when away from home', as he wrote once from Berlin.[1] Far from being dissipation, such excursions actually aided concentration. Friderike knew better than to complain, for she realized they were psychologically and even physically necessary for the full flowering of the work she so much admired.

His highly mobile spirit had an incredible diversity of application. Original work was paralleled by the intensely seminal role he played during the twenties in the literary and publishing world of Germany, Austria, indeed of Europe. The year 1922 was typical. With the Insel, in addition to *Amok*, appeared the legend *Die Augen des ewigen Bruders*, the *Episode vom Genfer See*, and the two-volume *Verlaine: Gesammelte Werke*; with Ruetten & Loening his translation of Rolland's *Clérambault*; with Axel Juncker an Introduction to a Frans Hellens novel; and with Lehmann & Schulze, Dresden, his contribution to the Deutsche Dichterhandschriften series—a facsimile of his manuscript for *Brief einer Unbekannten*, accompanied by an autobiographical sketch and an appreciation of his work by the editor, Hanns Martin Elster. In addition to a number of book reviews he published the essays 'Ist Die Geschichte gerecht?', 'Arthur Schnitzler zu seinem 60. Geburtstag', and 'Walther Rathenau' (after his assassination in June), and that on Rudolf Pannwitz, whose work he was keen to encourage. To Frans Masereel, whom he had met in Munich during his third German lecture tour the previous October, and was able to welcome with his family for a stay in Austria in April, he proposed a volume of the artist's woodcuts, with essays

[1] Letter to Friderike Zweig, 24 Nov. 1922.

by himself and Arthur Holitscher, and persuaded the Axel Juncker Verlag to start with it a series Graphiker unserer Zeit. The collaboration with Holitscher, a communist and *Gesinnungsgenosse* of Barbusse, went well, despite their divergent political views, and the book was published in 1923. (Masereel, typically, was completely happy to fall in with all Zweig's suggestions: 'I leave you complete liberty for French, English, Chinese, Negro, etc. editions as well as for the rights . . . I await *my* book. I am delighted that it is you writing this monograph.')[1]

He contributed a poem 'Aufschrei des Schweigens' to a Nansen volume for Russian famine relief, and sent one, as we have already noted, to his old school for its fiftieth anniversary. With Victor Fleischer he embarked on the preparation for publication by the Frankfurter Verlagsanstalt of a two-volume edition of a selection in translation of Sainte-Beuve's essays, again with an introductory essay by himself; and his correspondence[2] shows how extraordinary was the effort required for this—badgering Fleischer, organizing the translators and their fees, dealing with Joseph Gregor at the Vienna Hofbibliothek over suitable portraits for the illustrations, and enlisting the aid of the ever ready Rieger. Early in August he sat for his portrait by Le Fauconnier.[3]

There was time with all this to dream again (a dream he was never to realize) of a 'great drama or novel' 'which I have long had in draft', as he wrote to Rolland, sending him a copy of *Amok*.[4] Time too for more journeys abroad: to Berlin in November, to the North Sea coast with Friderike in August,[5] in March to Paris, meeting Rolland again ('splendid as ever') and Bazalgette ('mon plus vieil ami, dont je suis le plus fier'). A reluctant guest of honour with Galsworthy at the founding meeting of the *Cercle Littéraire* on 24 March, he entered with enthusiasm into a proposal to form a group in Paris to foster links between French

[1] Correspondence ZE, in particular letter from Masereel, 13 Oct. 1922 and letter from Holitscher, 26 Apr. 1923.

[2] Sch.

[3] The portrait is reproduced in R 96. Cf. letter from Jouve, 14 Nov. 1922 (ZE): 'J'ai vu l'admirable portrait de Fauconnier: grande chose, et par l'art, et par le sujet.'

[4] Letter to Rolland, 12 Oct. 1922 (Dum 213).

[5] Correspondence with Fleischer (Sch). They stayed about three weeks, first at Bad Kampen, Sylt, and for the last week in better rooms at Westerland.

and German literature, and on his return home started a lengthy correspondence with Kurt Wolff outlining the plan for a new European review in French, bringing translations of new poets and authors and poems in the original language: 'a great European forum, like a combination of the *Nouvelle Revue Francaise*, *Weisse Blätter*, the *Neue Rundschau* and the best of Italy, England, Spain, etc.'. Publishers would be required in each country to complement the capital promised by the French house so far engaged, and he turned to Wolff rather than to 'his own' Insel, since the latter would have little interest in such a project, whereas Wolff's authors (such as Werfel, Unruh, Schickele) would figure largely in it. To the hard-headed publisher's many detailed questions on the practicalities (in particular the franc/mark exchange rate) no reply is extant; but, as Zweig wrote to Pannwitz in May, he gave up many weeks to 'these—in the general sense—thankless efforts'.[1]

He is reported once to have joked, in reference to a busy acquaintance, that 'he must have someone who does his sleeping for him'. Specht thought this might well have been applied to Zweig himself[2]—though in fact he slept well, and showed a remarkable concentration and economy of effort in activities which in another might have degenerated to mere dilettantism. Rieger went so far as to compare his powers with those of Rathenau,[3] whose 'unprecedented intensity of knowledge and activity' Zweig described in his memorial essay that year.[4] A hardy parallel, to which we would not today subscribe; but we can certainly agree with the importance Rieger gave to Zweig's 'unseen work'—the infinite trouble he took, not merely in the presentation of foreign authors and artists in Germany (in addition to Verhaeren, Rolland, and Verlaine, he had written on Chateaubriand, Rousseau, Jens Peter Jacobsen, Masereel, and Latzko), but also in seeking out and encouraging young talent. Even in that busy year of 1922 he found time for long letters to Pannwitz,

[1] *BrW* 151–5; letter to Rolland, 12 Apr. 1922 (Dum 96); Wolff 414–18; letter to Rudolf Pannwitz, 15 May 1922 (Sch). The journal, *Europe*, began publication in 1923, with René Arcos as one of its editors.

[2] S 9. [3] R 204. [4] *Europäisches Erbe*, 234.

and to the Insel in an attempt to persuade them to publish a volume of Faesi's verse.[1] Erich Maria Remarque, sending poems for his judgement in 1921 with a letter of near-despair—'remember that this is a matter of life and death for me!'—received a most cordial reply, and was to thank Zweig later for arranging the translation into French of *All Quiet* and ensuring its fantastic success in the former enemy country.[2] Just before his birthday in 1922 he received from Hans Carossa, sensible of his debt to one of the first to strengthen him in his hesitant beginnings as a writer, a poem of tribute:

Wer einem Wink folgt im Sein,
Vieles zu Einem erbaut,
Stündlich prägt ihn der Stern.
Und nach glühenden Jahren,
Wenn wir irdisch erblinden,
Reift eine große Natur. . . .[3]

Ernst Fischer, Erwin Rainalter, Walter Bauer, Klaus Mann, Joseph Roth, Erich Ebermayer—the list is endless of the younger men he helped on, not only by friendly words but also by finding publishers or jobs, writing forewords to their work, offering constructive criticism and writing enthusiastic reviews. 'I always open your letters with the anticipation of a joyful message,' wrote Ernst Fischer once, 'and always find my expectations exceeded.'[4]

The murder of Rathenau on 24 June 1922—modern Germany's first step along the road to Auschwitz—served to bring out once more Zweig's political pessimism. It was further proof for him that the peace could not last. To Fleischer, with whom he had been discussing plans for his summer holiday in Germany, he wrote on 29 June:

I do not think I shall come to Langen: I cannot bear now to get within two leagues of any Pan-German youths. Rather Frankfurt

[1] Sch; ZE.
[2] ZE.
[3] Letter from Carossa, 20 Nov. 1922 (ZE), enclosing a holograph copy of the poem. 'Who follows a sign in his being and builds the manifold into one, receives hourly the impress of the star. And after the glow of the years, as we earthlings grow blind, there ripens a nature of greatness.'

For a later version, see Carossa, *Führung und Geleit*; Insel, 1933, 190.

[4] Letter from Fischer, 5 Aug. 1924 (ZE).

Jews, rather Norderney, than these intellectuals who have murdered a Rathenau. . . . Saddest of all: they will achieve everything: just as they achieved U-boat warfare and the consequent prolongation of the war, so now they will rush into a new war. They will sit again in the rear areas while the youngsters are mown down. In France all stand ready to arms. One does not mistake these symptoms. . . . I'd rather go to a spa with 700,000 Galician Jews![1]

To Rolland the same day:

I cannot see these people at close quarters if I am to continue to love the idea of the German people. The nearer one gets to them the more difficult it becomes to remain impartial and to preserve the image of the true intellectual greatness of Germany.[2]

He had had the chance of talking to Rathenau only a few months before, during his visit to Berlin at the end of 1921, when once again the busy minister found time for his friend. His dramatic account of their meeting and the shock wave of panic and inflation after Rathenau's death, in *Die Welt von Gestern*, is not chronologically accurate—his holiday in Westerland, on the island of Sylt, was not in fact until August—and the artist takes over from the historian in his memories of this undoubted *Sternstunde* in Europe's story: 'it was mere chance that I did not witness the historically fateful scene . . . the tragic episode with which the disaster of Germany, the disaster of Europe, began'.[3]

At the time, however, his optimism was not so easily stifled as in later years. Indifferent in money matters, he maintained a remarkable gaiety through the inflation period. 'The most sensible thing one can do with money now,' he writes to Fleischer, about to welcome Friderike on a visit to Frankfurt in October, 'is to spend it', and asks him to make available for her whatever she needs from his mark income. Again, in the following year, as the inflation galloped on, 'I shall have at the end of August 12 or 13 million marks available if you would like another issue . . .

1 Letter of 29 June 1922 (Sch).

2 Letter to Rolland, 29 June 1922 (Dum 173).

3 *WvG* 283–5; *BrW* 144 shows that he in fact met Rathenau on about 17 Nov. 1921, and there is no record of another meeting before the assassination on 24 June 1922.

but one should not always be counting and reckoning, but enjoying life'. To avoid depreciation in the time taken to transfer funds to Austria from Germany, he made a practice during 1923 of making over all his mark income to Fleischer, urging him to spend as he liked and they would settle up in better times. (One of his letters is on the reverse of a notification from the Berlin *Börsen-Courier* that his fee for an article 'Der richtige Goethe' is 10 billion marks: he says he has told them to credit Fleischer.)[1]

Looking back later, he felt that this time of the utmost instability was that in which he worked and lived with the greatest zest: 'never have I experienced in a people and in myself so powerful a surge of life as at that period when our very existence and survival were at stake'.[2] His addiction to tobacco provides a useful barometer for his morale: as with Mark Twain, constant practice made it easy for him to give it up, and the numerous occasions when he did so were almost always—as now at the end of 1922—those when the needle was set at 'Fair' ('for the increased respect of my person I inform you that I have given up smoking of my own free will, have been holding out for a week, and feel extremely well . . .').[3]

Though he hated the publicity which his success now brought, and professed no head for business, he was far from spurning the success itself, and could be sharp in his criticism if his publishers seemed to be neglecting opportunities. During the Christmas period in 1922, on a visit to Vienna, he was annoyed to find that *Amok* was missing from most of the bookshops, and complained disgustedly to Fleischer that the Insel's *Schlamperei* over stocking the distributors had cost him at least a thousand copies: 'the Insel is choked by its own noblesse, which is not very favourable for us'.[4] From time to time he would claim weariness of fame. During the early summer of 1923, once again in Westerland but this time without Friderike, as he worked on the Masereel essay and on tributes to Bahr and Kippenberg for their forthcoming

[1] Letters to Fleischer, 21 Oct., 9 Dec. 1922, (? 17 Jan.), 20 July, 19 Sept., 3 Nov., and Dec. 1923 (Sch).

[2] *WvG* 272.

[3] Letter to Fleischer, 13 Dec. 1922 (Sch).

[4] Letter to Fleischer, 29 Dec. 1922 (Sch).

anniversaries, he expressed his fear of becoming a 'writing automaton': 'my successes weary me inexpressibly and I should like nothing better than for once to have a fortnight as a private person, careless and free, in some remote corner . . . '.[1] But this was, at least for the present, something of a pose (it would be different before another decade had passed); and there is no mistaking the satisfaction he found now in his work and his life, notwithstanding the fantastic difficulties of the inflation in both Germany and Austria.

Friderike was able to take a holiday that summer too. Lix was boarding at the convent of the *Englische Fräulein* near Reichenhall, but Suse could go with her, and they decided on Warnemünde. Though doing a great deal to help her, both in the choice of resort and, of course, with money (again the income from his sales in Germany could relieve her housewife's anxiety in such an unprecedented landslide of values), Stefan had no thought of staying with her, even for a short time, and they merely met between trains at Munich.[2] She did not have more than a couple of weeks for this her first holiday by the sea, for Rolland was expected at Kapuzinerberg at the end of June—the first time it had been possible to arrange a visit since the war, and naturally a great occasion for Stefan, who fussed endlessly over the arrangements for his room, his diet, his comfort, and rest. Indisposition after a trip to England in fact made it necessary for Rolland to put off his arrival until August; and Friderike felt it was a miracle that this frail body could survive the journey at all to be there with them.

Stefan had gone as far as Bischofshofen to meet him on his way via Zürich. Their train was an hour and a half late arriving in Salzburg, and Friderike, at the station, had to telephone to delay the lighting of the little lanterns which Suse had placed with such joy along the garden path. Rolland, though paler than they remembered him in Switzerland, seemed not unduly delicate; but they were glad that they had been able to plead his health to restrict visitors, for during his twelve days' stay they saw clearly what the vigour of his letters had always concealed—

[1] Letter to Fleischer (?29 May 1923) (Sch). [2] *BrW* 169–72.

the slender thread on which his bodily life depended. Friderike's worries were fortunately needless, for the weather remained fine, indeed more than usually hot on some days, and there was small risk of his catching cold on his walks to and from Kapuzinerberg. But he remained firmly wrapped up in his 'gilet breton'.

Zweig had given up for him his own bedroom and study, so that he had virtually a separate apartment, with the balcony and adjoining the drawing-room with the piano. The mornings he would spend here, resting, and most evenings at the concerts arranged by the International Union of Modern Musicians and a group of Austrian musicians (according to Friderike, he took but moderate pleasure in the atonal compositions of the moderns). Of the callers in the afternoons, whom the Zweigs carefully spaced out, Schnitzler (whose attitude to the war he had admired), Paul Amann (an old pen-friend, engaged now on translating a novel of his), and Hermann Bahr were those who meant most to him. To Friderike there seemed something Olympian in his talks with Bahr, who, a complete contrast in nature and physique (there is a photograph of them together on a garden seat in Rieger's biography), had immense respect for the Frenchman and was at once on terms of trust with him. Rolland liked Rieger very much, and spoke of asking him to act as his secretary for a while. He was also glad to have the opportunity of meeting Paul Stefan, who was in charge of the International Music Festival.[1]

It is regrettable that Zweig's own feelings about this visit—the only time when Rolland was his guest at home—are nowhere recorded. From Friderike's diary one has the impression that Rolland, though never malicious, saw through the *poseur* who was very much a part of Stefan. 'I shall never forget the smiling, understanding glances he exchanged with me over Stefan's minor male stupidities, he had a delightful, benevolent, roguish superiority over all this "maleness", a sort of "que voulez-vous, c'est un homme, auquel il faut un cigare".' To Suse, when she complained to him that Stefan did not like her cats, he exclaimed: 'Un poète qui n'aime pas les chats!'—for they ran to him, and he would pick them up to show Suse that someone loved them.

[1] Fr[2] 104–8; R 80; Fr 184.

(There was actually little of the true animal-lover in Zweig, although he was fond enough of Rolf, the Schaefer they had at this time, whose affection was undemanding, and who would be content to sit quiet when his master had not the time or the inclination to throw *Apportel* for him.) A devoted disciple, he was perhaps at times too serious for Rolland: after the visit, in a letter of 12 August, Zweig wrote: 'I think I have the gift of being able to serve (our "Dienen")—you know from what I told you that I pay for this gift with a complete inability to dominate, to be the boss, to take responsibilities.' Rolland always had difficulty in dissuading him from calling him 'Maître': 'we are all apprentices', he would tell him.[1]

7

'In my personal life the most remarkable thing was that in those years there arrived in my house a guest who settled down benevolently—a guest I had never expected: success.'

Die Welt von Gestern

The end of 1923 brought a *memento mori* for both Stefan and Friderike. After Rolland's departure Stefan had paid a short visit to Vienna, but had to return there at short notice at the end of August when his father, now seventy-eight, underwent an emergency operation for hernia: it was successful, but left the old man very weak, and he was to survive only two more years. Shortly before Christmas Friderike too was summoned to Vienna, where her mother, just over eighty, lay dying. She was able to stay with her until the end. Her affection for her mother had always been great, and although the rest of the family had been near and she had not been lonely in these last years, Friderike regretted that the direction her own life had taken had caused them to miss many hours together. The death about the same time of Hofrat von Winternitz, whom she had continued to hold in great affection, was also a blow to her.

To distract her from her grief Stefan arranged that they should embark in January on a project which they had had under

[1] Fr² 109–12; Dum 127, 195; Fr. 190.

consideration for some time: the installation of central heating in the still somewhat comfortless house on Kapuzinerberg. Originally they had not thought of it as a year-round residence—and in fact it was not, at least for Stefan. The development of the Salzburg Festival and his need to escape its disturbance each summer, however, meant more emphasis on winter residence than they had previously thought likely. So proper heating was essential. The installation was no easy matter in such a rambling old house, and Friderike was kept too busy to mourn. Stefan meanwhile evaded the disorder by taking ten days in Paris at the end of January. He sent her a teasing letter from the train, describing the beautiful girls who might join him in the compartment, and sympathizing rather callously over her 'uneasy heart' and the noise he was missing in the house.[1]

Back in his beloved Hotel Beaujolais (his stay two years before, while it was being remodelled, had been in the Hotel des Colonies, rue Paul Lelong), he found Paris more delightful than ever before. In 1922, despite his sympathetic understanding for France's war-time suffering and the warmth of his friends Bazalgette and Deprès, the impression he gained of hatred still stored up there had made him feel somehow distant, unaffected, uninterested. Now Paris was once more the city of his youth. 'God, how beautiful this city is. In the evenings an unparalleled lustre in the darkness—with the smell of the sweet, mild air I breathe in my whole youth, lean out of the window with my whole being'; and again to Friderike: 'you cannot know what the time here meant in my life—liberation from Vienna, simply becoming a human being'. There were friends in dozens: 'I've seen enough people to last me for eight months!' 'Paris is splendid, full of life, brimming over with men more dynamic than ever', he wrote to Rolland. Sitting out with René Arcos in a café, he felt this was a place which had no winter.

He darted out and around on a multitude of errands: seeing publishers (Grasset, Stock), preparing a radio talk for 15 January, trying to avoid having to act as guide for a friend speaking only

[1] Letter to Fleischer, 31 Aug. 1923 (Sch); *BrW* 174; letter to Friderike Zweig, 24 Jan. 1924; Fr[2] 127–8.

German ('God give me brutality'), sitting for his portrait by Masereel, looking in on the Belgian painter's exhibition at the Galerie Billier, visiting Verhaeren's widow at Saint-Cloud. There scarcely seemed time for his favourite pursuit in Paris—strolling through the streets and looking at the bookstalls on the Quais. There were invitations from Salvador Dali ('a chapter for itself'), Hanna Orloff, Le Fauconnier, James Joyce, and Magdeleine Paz (formerly Marx). Small wonder, amid such a whirl, that he felt a twinge of conscience towards Friderike:

> My dear Fritzi, I am *honest* when I say to you that I regret every hour that you are not here—it is a contrast to Salzburg as though created by God, and I promise you that next year (if I still have money, which is to be hoped) we will come here for two weeks.—So, next year, my dear, my good one, who has to live amid the hammering, while your Stefzi breathes and enjoys the mild sea air (with shrimps).[1]

The Masereel portrait stirred his admiration. 'It is quite different from what you expected,' he wrote to Friderike, 'un-modern in the most daring way, without any colour experiments, clear and open, and like all his portraits a work of genius in the likeness.' 'I hope tomorrow to make those few purchases for you, otherwise I shall be bringing you only my portrait, which is to be yours.' It was actually sent later to Vienna, where there was to be an exhibition of Masereel's work. 'I have enlarged the eyes slightly, very slightly,' wrote the artist in April 1924, 'for despite your protests I have observed that the eyes have something Asiatic or Indian about them. . . . I have not yet started your portrait in woodcut.' The fate of the work in the upheavals of the thirties is unfortunately unknown, as is that of the woodcut (completed in 1926).[2]

It was all wonderful: 'now staying at home and working will be doubly so'. He was ready now to complete the second volume of the Baumeister series, with the essays on Kleist, Hölderlin, and Nietzsche, under the title of *Der Kampf mit dem Dämon*. In

[1] *BrW* 174–7; letter to Friderike Zweig, 30 Jan. 1924

[2] *BrW* 177–8; letter from Masereel, 8 Apr. 1924 (ZE). For a reproduction of the woodcut see *Blätter der Internationalen Stefan-Zweig-Gesellschaft*, Nr. 4/5 (Apr. 1959), 9.

contrast to the years of work on Dostoevsky, the 'Kleist' virtually wrote itself in a few weeks, the manuscript first version being completed by March 1924. The whole volume was in proof twelve months later and—such was its author's reputation now—3,500 copies were sold before publication date. By August 1925 the first printing of 10,000 was almost exhausted. Dedicating it to Freud, Zweig described in his Introduction how he proposed to develop his 'Typology of the Spirit': not its reduction to a formula, but the distillation of its essence from comparative studies like Plutarch's *Lives*, not the creation of a rigid system but a necessarily fragmented and limited study of the limitless world of the mind. 'So I build on, slowly and at the same time passionately, with hands still eager, raising this structure begun by chance ever further towards the barely-glimpsed cerulean of time which hangs uncertain over our life.'[1] The struggle with the daimon, which no creative personality can escape, results either in victory, as with Goethe, or in submission and apparent defeat, as with Hölderlin, Kleist, and Nietzsche—all three the very type of the poet transported, possessed by the daimon. 'They do not obey their own will (with terror they recognize this in their ego's wakeful moments) but are vassals, possessed (in the double sense of the word) by a higher power, the daimonic.'[2]

For Zweig this was the easiest of his Baumeister studies to write[3]—neither the long gestation of the *Drei Meister* nor the 'burden' which *Drei Dichter ihres Lebens* became two years later. He thought that he himself, like Goethe, could remain master of the daimon. 'You know,' he remarked once to Jules Romains, 'I am a creature of terrible passion, full of violence of all kinds. It is only by dint of self-control that I can contrive conduct that is more or less reasonable.'[4] But, like Goethe, he knew the fatal attraction of the daimon, over which his mastery could be asserted only by writing it out of his system. This form of catharsis, as

[1] Stefan Zweig, *Der Kampf mit dem Dämon*; Insel, 1925, 8. [2] Ibid. 9.

[3] It was not as easy as he had expected, however, 'because in the composition a certain innate monotony must be avoided. I must be careful not to fall into a set form of essay, but to write with individuality determined by the rhythm of the subjects' (letter to Fleischer, 31 May 1924 (Sch)).

[4] Arens[2] 343.

with *Novellen einer Leidenschaft*, acted as his best inspiration, and in few of his works is his style freer and more flowing, less repetitive and contrived, than in *Der Kampf mit dem Dämon*. Goethe *was* Werther, but stayed alive by writing the story of Werther's death; Zweig, we might say, was Kleist—but in the end could not escape his own fate by writing of Kleist's suicide, the end of 'that tragic nature whose whole existence was a tragedy', 'the hunted one' who 'knew better how to die than how to live'.[1] 'The man who knew Hölderlin, Kleist, and Nietzsche so well', as the poet Ivan Heilbut observed after Zweig's death, 'must have been a brother of theirs.'[2] Freud's comments on the book, regrettably not recorded, would have been of immense interest.

Of Nietzsche, Zweig took an original view. He quotes with approval Nietzsche's prophecy: 'After the next European war I shall be understood', for in the aftermath of war he sees him as Europe's guide to freedom, the man whose books, in Jakob Burckhardt's words, 'increased independence in the world'.[3] 'The last four pages are written for you and in your teaching,' he wrote to Rolland, 'to celebrate the truly free and independent man as the highest form of humanity. My whole essay is a hidden polemic against the attempt . . . to claim Nietzsche for Germany, for war, for the "good cause of Germany", he who was the first European, our ancestor . . . le superbe "sans-patrie".'[4] How differently were others to look back on Nietzsche only a few years later!

The ease with which this volume had been completed made him look forward the more readily to the next, and, as the same letter to Rolland shows, he had already settled on its theme: those characters who spent their lives in self-scrutiny—Stendhal, Rousseau, Tolstoy, 'who have left us three autobiographies whose truth and falsehood I want to try to determine'.[5] He transmitted his optimism to the house magazine of the Insel-Verlag, the *Inselschiff*, which went as far in its issue for autumn 1925 as to

[1] *Der Kampf mit dem Dämon*, 228.
[2] Letter to Friderike Zweig, 26 Feb. 1942.
[3] *Der Kampf mit dem Dämon*, 319–21.
[4] Letter to Rolland, 4 May 1925 (Dum 128).
[5] Ibid. (Dum 292).

describe the author as not only working on this new volume but also planning a successor on Shelley, Novalis, and Leopardi as 'elemental poets'.[1] There is evidence also that at this time he was returning to an earlier notion of a trilogy on women of the empire and Restoration period: to the essay published in 1920 on Marceline Desbordes-Valmore, and another unnamed, he was preparing to add, he told Fleischer, one on Rahel Varnhagen (the unnamed one may have been on Marie Walewska). Why this plan came to naught we do not know, but it may, as Dumont suggests, have been because of the inherent difficulty of valid comparison between Marceline and Rahel, and because the frame of his existing essay tended to place Marceline rather in French-language company such as that of Rimbaud or Verhaeren.[2] In the letter to Rolland already quoted he spread his wings still further ('I have a world to build, will my poor life be enough for this task?'), and sketched the further subjects he had in mind: more on the 'possessed' of the nineteenth century (Van Gogh, Strindberg, Poe, Blake); Michael-Angelo, Villon, and the pre-Shakespearians; victory over the forces of evil (Keller and Conrad Ferdinand Meyer); the clear-thinking 'architectonic' minds (Spinoza, Schiller, Voltaire); the great visionaries (Plato, Dante, Goethe, Shakespeare).[3] A Balzacian concept, indeed, but, as we have already noted, Zweig's temperament lacked the steadiness and patience required.

Meanwhile, in a 'certain monotony of life, which has the regulated character of that of an official',[4] he turned out shorter pieces in a minor flood, either new, or (as with the essay on Busoni contributed to the *Inselschiff* in 1924) dug out of his unpublished-material drawer. There were essays on Byron, Chartres Cathedral, Gotthelf and Jean Paul, Hermann Hesse, Musset and Baudelaire in German versions, Salzburg (*Die Stadt als Rahmen*), Caesar and Napoleon, Proust, *Die Monotisierung der Welt*; occasional pieces—tributes to Kippenberg, R. H. Francé, Oskar A. H. Schmitz, Thomas Mann the 'genius of responsibility', all reaching their

[1] *Inselschiff*, vi. 4, 317.
[2] Letter to Fleischer, 30 June 1925 (Sch); Dum 106–7; Fr. 197.
[3] Dum 212–13.
[4] Letter to Fleischer, 10 June 1924 (Sch).

fiftieth birthdays, and a memoir of Leo Feld; introductions or epilogues to the works of others—Chateaubriand's *Romantische Erzählungen*, Otto Heuschele's *Briefe aus Einsamkeiten*, stories by Ginzkey and Bahr, Renan's *Jugenderinnerungen*, Hans Prager's book on the philosophy of Dostoevsky; articles on autograph-collecting and sales; a steady stream of reviews. He saw through the press his *Collected Poems* at the end of 1923 (never much of a daimon here, but such as it was now decently buried). With all this and *Der Kampf* he found time not only for two of his best short prose works—*Die unsichtbare Sammlung*, a beautifully told story of the German inflation, and *Denkwürdiger Tag*, a miniature on the centenary of Goethe's *Marienbad Elegy*—but also to start on the next *Novellen* 'ring' of his 'chain', *Verwirrung der Gefühle* (in June 1925 he was working on three).

His restless energy still kept him very much on the move. Hardly back from Paris, in February 1924 he was off to Vienna because of the death of an aunt, his mother's only sister, and was there again in May to meet Rolland, who was over to attend some Richard Strauss performances. On 13 May Zweig gave a lunch at the Hotel Meissl und Schadn, in the Neuer Markt, for Strauss and Schnitzler to meet Rolland, and the following day they visited Freud at his home in Berggasse. Freud had always wanted to meet Rolland and was grateful when Zweig suggested the call. He accompanied his friend as far as Innsbruck on the return journey.[1] In July he was in Zürich ('the order here is indescribable . . . one forgets what chaos we are living in'), moving on afterwards to Boulogne.

> I have a well-schooled instinct: no luxury . . . a room on the fourth floor, looking out over the harbour with its departing ships. . . . Then into the bargain a quite wonderfully lively French provincial town with market and cafés and all the unique savour of France, which one feels much more strongly than in Paris. . . . I love, as in Ostende, to feel a town at my back—Westerland is just a holiday resort built in isolation.

Masereel joined him there for a few days, and they got on, as always, extraordinarily well together: 'it seems as though I am

[1] Letters to Fleischer, 28 Feb. and 6 May 1924 (Sch); Freud *Br* 348; *BrW* 180–1; letter to Fleischer, 31 May 1924 (Sch).

one of the few who can bring out again his gaiety and good spirits. We bathed together, ate meals worthy of Pantagruel, ran around together: it was quite splendid.' Though he did not get much work done, he read a great deal, mainly Proust, and returned, via Amiens and Rheims, much refreshed at the end of the month.[1] In November came the promised escorting of Friderike to Paris, at last able to share with him the delights of the city again, and they celebrated his forty-third birthday in the congenial company of Arcos, Rieger, and Masereel.[2]

As his success grew, he was in demand for lectures and readings. In October he received an invitation to address—'as the first enemy alien'—students in Brussels in December (it is not clear whether he accepted),[3] and early in 1925 he was booked on an intensive series of lectures in southern Germany. Carnival time there was not exactly apposite, but his first performance in Freiburg im Breisgau had a good attendance, audience attentive with not even a cough to be heard; then it was Heidelberg, Frankfurt, Stuttgart, Baden-Baden, and Wiesbaden (where his lecture had to be postponed because of Ebert's death). 'I am reading my way slowly back home through the cities, no stage fright (it comes easy to me, like a game).' The intellectual appetite of these provincial towns surprised him, and his letters to Friderike showed an unusually complaisant attitude to the recognition attendant on his fame.

I have wonderful accommodation here [he wrote from Wiesbaden], in the old feudal Hotel Vier Jahreszeiten. The proprietor regards all the club's lecturers as his guests, knows all my books. In these matters of education the people here in Germany are incredible, one is known right down to the hall porter. And my books are going especially well, as all the booksellers tell me—I am afraid of being idolised and becoming the darling of the German schoolgirls' world. Two ladies have already reported themselves and are in readiness, one an old girl friend of my youth. But I am no lover of warmed-up dishes.

[1] *BrW* 179–80 (the letter to Friderike from Zürich should be dated 17 July); letter to Fleischer, July 1924 (Sch).

[2] Card to Kippenberg, 30 Nov. 1924 (Sch).

[3] Letter to Fleischer, 18 Oct. 1924 (Sch).

He had worries over the proofs of *Der Kampf*, which he had left to Friderike, and felt obliged to check by telephone with the Insel in Leipzig, to make sure there would be no misprints, before he could rest easy: 'I live for my books, as you for your children', he wrote to her.[1]

His attitude towards Suse and Alix was a strange mixture of affection, impatience, and stepfatherly domination. He liked them to be seen and not heard, but would never relinquish entirely the desire to have his say over their schooling and their outside interests, which to him seemed puerile and lacking the intellectual curiosity he thought essential. Robust and full of life, their character was completely different from his; but on the whole they got on well with him, regarding him with an amused tolerance as an inhabitant of another world. Friderike wisely recognized how essential it was to keep those worlds apart and to maintain in her own hands the direction of the girls' lives. She contrived often to take them with her on holiday alone; and in July 1925 went off to Paris and the Normandy coast with Suse, leaving Alix for a short time with Stefan at Salzburg until she was able to visit her father, who had been seriously ill. His work going well, Stefan was able to write her with an unexpected gaiety, inquiring anxiously after Suse's health (measles had been suspected) and urging her to get the utmost out of the holiday. 'I have plenty of inspiration, and plans for far ahead: if I am left in peace, the weak old brain-box still functions passably. Love to Suse, bathe as much as you can, there is only one sea.'[2]

A month earlier it had been Rolland again. A Händel festival in Leipzig had drawn the music-lover once more to Germany, and together the friends listened to *Belshazzar* at the Opera (where Zweig, knowing Rolland's horror of crowds and the demands of society, had reserved him a discreet box), and to Bach motets in the Thomaskirche. Rolland had brought him a copy of *Jean Christophe* illustrated by Masereel. He saw Kippenberg, of course, and the young Richard Friedenthal ('unbelievably gifted') was also in Leipzig. With Rolland and his sister Madeleine

[1] Letter to Fleischer, 16 Feb. 1925; *BrW* 181–4.

[2] Statement to the author by Friderike Zweig; *BrW* 187–9.

he went on to Weimar to see Goethe's house and the Nietzsche archives in the charge of the aged Frau Förster-Nietzsche, delighted like a child to see Rolland, and touchingly (and to Zweig unexpectedly) grateful for the essay in *Der Kampf*. It was all wonderful: he had never heard such choirs and organs in his life. He even felt that a youth corps parade of 25,000 which Rolland chanced to witness in Leipzig was good for him: 'men of goodwill should appreciate the dangers; he was absolutely horrified by their faces as they marched past, so fixed were they in grim determination and powerful military bearing'.[1]

In August it was time again to escape the turmoil of the Salzburg Festival. From the Grand Hotel, Zell am See, where, completely unknown and knowing no one, he hoped for quiet to complete his *Novellen*, came news for Friderike of yet another recurrence of his latent depressive mood.

> There is no real reason for it, either in my work (which is not going so badly) or in smoking (which I am anyway stopping for a couple of days as a trial). It is a crisis of age, linked with an all-too-great clarity of vision, quite out of proportion to my age—I do not deceive myself with visions of immortality, know how relative is all the literature I create, do not believe in humanity, take pleasure in so few things. Often something comes out of such crises, but often they drive one further into oneself. . . . One should resign oneself, through these ten years, war and postwar, one lacked the right measure of joy and youth. And our war nerves cannot indeed ever be completely restored, pessimism reaches deep down under the skin. I expect nothing more from myself—for whether I sell 10,000 or 150,000 copies is after all immaterial. The important thing would be to start something new, another kind of life, other ambitions, a different relationship to existence—to emigrate, not only in the outward sense. The lecture tour was really not a good thing. I did it from weakness, from being unable to say no, to compel myself to be a little on the move. I should like in the coming years to force myself to be more mobile—frequent short journeys, that is best for us.[2]

Such depressions recurred now more frequently, and events were to substantiate his 'all-too-great clarity of vision', though

[1] Letter to Emil Ludwig, 10 May 1925 (Sch); *BrW* 185–6.

[2] *BrW* 189–90.

nine years were to pass before he began to seek that other way of life, to emigrate not only in the outward sense. His pessimism was indeed deeply ingrained, but by no means yet all-pervading. 'Next March', he wrote to Fleischer that October, 'it will be a quarter of a century since *Silberne Saiten* appeared: one ought to be thinking of retiring, yet is absorbed in ever renewed effort.'[1]

[1] Letter to Fleischer, 26 Oct. 1925 (Sch).

V. Sunset 1925–1929

'The work still won't go right, in all my things something has been tangled up in the last eighteen months.' Zweig to Friderike, December 1928

'Thought destroys happiness. The pleasures it grants are rare and problematical.' Klaus Mann

I

'At Locarno we spoke European. It is a new language which must at all costs be learned.'
Briand, February 1926

There were yet many pleasures in life. In his studies for *Verwirrung der Gefühle*, in particular for the teacher's seminar on the Elizabethans, he had been captivated by Ben Jonson's *Volpone*, 'an amusing farce about money', as he described it to Rolland.[1] In November 1925 he was off again to France, and settled for a short time in Marseille, in the Hotel Beauvau, an old establishment, recently remodelled, once visited by Chopin and Lamartine. Here—once more, as at Boulogne and Ostende, with a 'living town' at his back, a view over the harbour that reminded him of Hamburg's Alster, but with the sun and colour that only the Mediterranean could offer—he loosely sketched out in a few days a free adaptation in prose of *Volpone*, intending later to write it in verse. Returning through Avignon and Dijon, and Villeneuve, to see Rolland again, he found an inquiry from the Dresden Court Theatre about his plans for new works, and sent them the prose

[1] Letter to Rolland, 26 Sept. 1925 (Dum 331).

version, explaining that it was merely a first sketch of an eventual comedy in verse. The theatre telegraphed immediately, asking him for the love of heaven not to change a thing: and it was in prose that the play took its final form, to be produced almost world-wide and to be one of his greatest dramatic successes. It was published the following year by Kiepenheuer, with illustrations by Aubrey Beardsley, and Jules Romains quickly produced a French translation. Zweig was intensely proud of it, as his letters to Rolland and Fleischer show, and retailed to Rolland his amusement at the hesitations of the Burgtheater over producing it: 'You, a serious man, a play like this!' 'Exactly, when one is serious,' he had replied, 'one does not stop at half-measures, even in farce.'

It was indeed a *tour de force*, nine days' work, of which one and a half were in Villeneuve, with almost no correction or polishing required afterwards. And the stay in Marseille had quickly restored his good spirits: the cheap living, the remoteness from Austria, and—most beautiful of all—the dirt in the harbour streets. 'This stink is the Orient: not for nothing was smoking invented there.' He was glad he had not gone to somewhere like Rapallo, or even Paris. 'The only cloud is to watch the beautiful white ships sail off and not be able to sail with them: I often feel as though the East is my home.'[1]

His relationship with Rolland was at its closest during these years. He had been much moved (to the point of confusion, almost of shame) to read the Dedication of *Le Jeu de l'amour et de la mort* in August 1924: 'To the faithful spirit whose patriotism is for Europe and whose religion is friendship, to Stefan Zweig, I dedicate in affection this drama which owes its writing to him'; and in the Preface:

> the good European Stefan Zweig, who has been for fifteen years my most faithful friend and best counsellor, has not ceased to remind me . . . of my task of quarrying in the bloody mountain of the Revolution. And so I have set my pick once more against the rock; here is the first block which this spring I have detached. I inscribe on it the name

[1] Letter to Friderike Zweig, 7 Nov. 1925; *BrW* 190–5; letters to Rolland, 2 and 14 Dec. 1925 (Dum 331–2).

of Zweig. Without him, it would have continued to sleep beneath the earth.

'You may indeed be proud of this dedication', wrote Arcos. In Rieger's translation the play was produced in Vienna, and there followed successes in Hamburg and Munich, where his own *Verwandelter Komödiant* made a curtain-raiser: 'what a victory, to get a French author acclaimed in the very bastion of nationalism!' he wrote to Rolland.[1]

He had no hesitation in accepting a further lecture tour in Germany in the New Year of 1926, for 29 January was Rolland's sixtieth birthday and the opportunity for him to bear witness to his brother European. He had collaborated with Duhamel and Gorki in the elegant volume of tribute *Liber Amicorum Romain Rolland*, published for the occasion in Zürich,[2] and the German tour was preceded by a visit there to appear as *Festredner* at a Rolland evening. He went on to Frankfurt, Wiesbaden again (where the house was sold out), Lübeck (city of memories, he wrote to Friderike), and Hamburg; finally, Berlin, where he held forth no fewer than nine times, including a lecture on Rolland in the Meistersaal. No afterthoughts this time that the tour was a mistake, though the ceaseless and, to his mind, senseless whirl of Berlin troubled him, and between lectures he took refuge in the library with Beethoven's *Conversationshefte*, to seize a few hours 'in a peaceful beyond'.[3]

Looking back at sixty on the post-war years of travel, he noted how different they were from those of his youth. Now he was no longer a stranger in the world; he had friends everywhere, publishers, a public. 'In every city of more than 5,000 inhabitants', wrote Robert Neumann, 'this unobtrusive, smooth character had a friend—bookseller, member of the local literary society, editor of the local paper, who would be waiting on the platform

[1] Rolland: *Le Jeu de l'amour et de la mort*; Albin Michel, Paris, 1925, Preface and 18; *BrW* 181; card from Arcos, 20 Sept. 1924 (ZE); letter to Rolland, 17 Aug. 1924 (Dum 230).

[2] Rotapfel Verlag, Zürich, 1926; in French, Albin Michel, Paris, n.d.

[3] *BrW* 195–6; letter to Fleischer, 13 Jan., and card 27 Jan. 1926 (Sch); letter to Bethge, 9 Feb. 1926 (Sch). The Meistersaal Lecture on Rolland is reprinted in *Europäisches Erbe*, 102–21.

when Zweig arrived, introduce his lecture, and write the dithyrambic feuilleton for the next day's local journal.' 'I was able to agitate with greater sweep and better effect for the idea which over the years had become central to my life: the intellectual unification of Europe.'[1] But, as we have before noted, his 'agitation' tended to remain on the personal plane rather than in that of organizations. In 1924 he had corresponded with Count Richard Coudenhove-Kalergi, whose concept of *Paneuropa* held, as might be expected, considerable attraction for Zweig: the red cross on the golden sun as symbol of humanity and reason. He held himself aloof, however, from the organization which such a concept demanded.[2]

Baudouin, in Salzburg in October 1926 and Zweig's guest again for the first time since 1921, discussed with him an invitation he (Baudouin) had received to attend the congress of a *Kulturbund* (designated less happily in French *Fédération des Unions Intellectuelles*) in Vienna later that month, at which Hofmannsthal was to preside. 'A laudable concept, born in the aftermath of war, to give a concrete reality and a rudiment of organization to the "international of the mind"', Baudouin noted, with, as usual, many personal rivalries and doctrinal frictions already making their appearance, and a particular interest attaching to Coudenhove-Kalergi's *Paneuropa*, originally a sort of branch of the *Kulturbund*, but already with a force of its own, both political and economic.

> The idea is to create Europe, but without England and without Russia . . . in particular a *Mittel-Europa* . . . which makes one think of a Germanic Holy Roman Empire. The idea seems to attract the peoples who are the successors to the former Habsburg monarchy, who suffer from their fragmentation. . . . As a first step a limited European federation has the merit of not being too ambitious; but on the other hand, is it not without danger to form a central European bloc in opposition to the two others constituted by the British community on the one hand and the Soviets on the other? At all events, these movements . . . possess here a harder, more concrete reality than one would be tempted to believe.[3]

Baudouin did not record Zweig's views, but there is little doubt

[1] *WvG* 298; Neumann, 115–16.

[2] Letters from Coudenhove-Kalergi, in particular 9 July 1924 (ZE).

[3] Baudouin 186–8 (17 Oct. 1926).

that the latter's whole instinct was against participation in such an organization, not so much from a political point of view (though he would no doubt have felt repelled by the idea of such a partial Europe) as from the feeling that any political solution must be preceded by a conscious desire of the peoples and, above all, of the individuals, of Europe for unity. In March 1929, it is true, he accepted an invitation from Lee van Dovski to lecture (in the spirit of Coudenhove) in The Hague and Utrecht on 'The European Idea in Literature', and gave the same talk also in Brussels: 'somewhat unwillingly,' as he wrote to Kippenberg, 'but . . . the attitude of the press had so far made it impossible for a German to take part in this international symposium, and the choice of the authorities fell on me, as I am legitimized through Verhaeren and, because I am an Austrian, the right man to break the ice—so I felt it was my duty'.[1] But, in the last resort, nothing could for him be a substitute for personal contacts and individual persuasion, through which alone could a true union of minds be achieved.

To this feeling must also be added his aversion to the kind of public contact demanded by the congress hall: lecturing, casting his own words before an anonymous audience, was one thing, but he could never feel at ease in the close quarters of the conference room, where the publicity called forth by his fame was an acute embarrassment. (It is ironic that Hofmannsthal, the unworldly poet *par excellence*, whose distaste for Zweig's commercialism was barely concealed, should occupy the chair in Vienna that Zweig would never have dreamed of accepting.) 'Nothing indeed concentrates more the inner powers of a man than withdrawal from the world; nothing on the other hand is more perilous, for a moral stand that seeks to endure, than public life and its dangerous fire, fame', he wrote about this time in a memoir of his Hamburg friend, Dr. Ami Kaemmerer.[2]

Such an attitude was endemic in his character. The urge to

[1] Lee van Dovski, 'Stefan Zweig zu seinem 25. Todestag am 22. Februar 1967', *Der Bund*, Berne, 118. Jg. 67, 17 February 1967; letter to Kippenberg 8 Mar. 1929 (Sch).

[2] Stefan Zweig, 'Gedächtnis eines deutschen Menschen', in *Die Ausfahrt, ein Buch neuer deutscher Dichtung, 1. Reihe*, ed. Otto Heuschele; Verlag Silberburg, Stuttgart, 1927, 5. Cf. also *BrW* 153–4, letters of 21 and 23 Mar. 1922.

withdraw, the dread of getting involved, showed itself even in those personal relationships through which he hoped to build a unified Europe; and in his moments of pessimism he realized all too clearly how little he was in fact achieving. Such a crisis was occasioned in 1926, after the death of his father on 2 March, when only two weeks after the funeral he came into sharp conflict with his mother. She showed, as he wrote to Fleischer, a dangerous mixture of two quite distinct tendencies:

complete helplessness combined with selfishness, incredible lack of independence with ungovernable obstinacy—neither my brother nor I can think of having her stay with us, because with her inner unrest she simply creates unrest. . . . In myself I am tired and played out. We are a beaten generation, we lack the *élan* of a country on the up-grade, of a time that will raise us up ourselves; we have been fed with hatred, purged again with terror, attacked by stupidity, our spirit distracted by the senseless fireworks of money games. How can we create something complete, strongly-tempered, based on peace, when our powers are so obsessed by externals! To collect oneself, of course that is the key, but then comes, like now, some blow striking straight into one's work, turning everything upside-down, for the sixth, the seventh time already, so that even while building up one comes almost to expect disturbance. Well—I'll try once again the healing powers of French wine and the blue of the southern sea.[1]

With Friderike—'burdened by a wife'—he toured southern France: Languedoc, Aigues-Mortes, Sète, Montpellier, Narbonne, and Toulouse; and was able to write much more cheerfully to Rolland after his return in April ('the church of the Albade collapsed the day after my departure: it was nice of it to wait until I had seen it').[2]

Like the young Klaus Mann, to whom he had given so much encouragement, he could not escape the feeling of living in an interval between two catastrophes;[3] yet the peace he sought, the inner freedom, was ever harder to find, no matter how much he travelled. To Rieger, who after all knew him intimately, and to Specht, both of whom wrote about him at this time, he seemed to

[1] Letter to Fleischer, 23 or 24 Mar. 1926 (Sch).

[2] Letters to Fleischer, 23 or 24 Mar. 1926 (Sch) and Rolland, 25 Apr. 1926 (Dum 253).

[3] *Suche*, 33; *Wendepunkt* 160.

combine a restless psychological curiosity, 'the daimonic urge to see,' as Rolland had put it, 'to know and to live every life, which has made him a "Flying Dutchman", a passionate pilgrim', with a thoughtful economy of powers and an admirable capacity for concentration. Noting the almost infinite variety of his activities and the inexhaustible stream of essays, reviews, *Novellen*, legends that poured from his pen, Specht saw no breathlessness, nothing of business in this busy nature.[1] His pessimism and recurring sense of ineffectiveness were well concealed, and only Friderike and Fleischer were witnesses to the crises in his spirit.

To the stream of visitors to Kapuzinerberg, distinguished or obscure, he appeared the epitome of the cultivated European man of letters, and none detected the latent despair beneath the urbane exterior. 'Zweig has the cult, the genius of friendship. The hospitality one enjoys in his house is generous and easy', noted Baudouin.

> It envelops without embarrassing. . . . Our breakfast is prolonged into one of those moments of leisure he loves: a conversation tête-a-tête, now in French which he speaks quite well, now in German in which he assures me politely I ought to exercise myself more. . . . He leads me into his library, a long room, with sliding glass doors and grills, where nothing has been neglected to make his books, in their dark and light dress, feel at home. . . . Zweig takes a voluptuous pleasure in things of beauty; he knows how to caress the spine of a book. The glass cases are also adorned with autographs, of which he is a great collector, and the most precious of which he has framed. . . .[2]

(He was in fact devoting all the revenues from *Volpone* to his beloved collection, and in addition to a number of musical scores, including one of Debussy's, had recently been able to acquire thirty-two pages of Montesquieu's *Esprit des Lois*, a Robespierre speech—these two cost him 5,500 Swiss francs—an unpublished portion of Louvet's memoirs, two poems from *Les Fleurs du Mal*, and the *Pensées* of Madame Roland.)[3] 'At times the duties of host must have tired him', wrote Felix Braun ten years after his death; 'when I think back on him, I see now how lonely

[1] R 34; S 8–9; Rolland, Preface to *Amok*; Stock, Paris 1927.
[2] Baudouin 189–90 (18 Oct. 1926). [3] Dum 205.

he must often have felt. Many of his readers sent him thanks, and this seems to have been his only unclouded pleasure. For the power to take pleasure withered early in his spirit.'[1]

But we should not let such hindsight, influenced by a desire to explain his tragic end, distort our picture of him now, at forty-five undoubtedly at the height of his powers. The success of *Volpone* was followed by that of the third 'ring' of the *Novellen* chain, *Verwirrung der Gefühle*, 30,000 copies of which were sold within three months of its publication in the autumn of 1926. His five historical miniatures, *Sternstunden der Menschheit*, including the *Marienbader Elegie*, were finished—'between report and Novelle, an entirely new epic-dramatic genre' as they seemed to Csokor[2]—and he was already deep in preliminary studies for the next trilogy on 'the inward-turning autobiographical natures'[3] of Tolstoy, Stendhal, and Rousseau, as well as for the totally different character of Joseph Fouché.[4]

In June 1926 appeared his essay inveighing against the obscurantism of the Brockhaus family in locking up the priceless manuscript of the Casanova memoirs, which so incensed him as an expert that he determined now to make Casanova rather than Rousseau the third in his trilogy.[5] His essay on Freud's seventieth birthday earlier that year the old man thought one of the best of the many public tributes he received,[6] and Zweig was delighted to hear from Baudouin in Vienna, who had spent some hours with Freud and Adler, that the savants had discussed *Verwirrung der Gefühle* 'in terms which would not have displeased you. Adler finds you have done some "psychoanalysis"; so there you have the fraternal foes reconciled on your back! Indeed the miracle of poetic art!'[7] His letters to Fleischer of 1926 are full of ideas for the future activity of the Frankfurter Verlagsanstalt.[8]

1 *Mus Land* 201–2.
2 Letter from Csokor, 2 Dec. 1927 (ZE).
3 Letter to Pannwitz, 26 May 1926 (Sch).
4 *BrW* 198.
5 Stefan Zweig, 'F. A. Brockhaus — Beschwerde gegen einen Verleger (Casanova betreffend)', *Berliner Tageblatt*, 29 June 1926. Cf. *Drei Dichter ihres Lebens*; Insel, 1928, 30, footnote.
6 Stefan Zweig, 'Zum 70. Geburtstag von Sigmund Freud', *Münchner Neueste Nachrichten*, 5 May 1926 (also in *NFP*); Freud *Br* 365.
7 Letter from Baudouin, 27 Dec. 1926 (ZE).
8 Sch.

And the flood of articles and essays was unabated: Beatrice Cenci, Philippe Daudet, Emil Lucka, Schmidtbonn, Otto Weininger, Ben Jonson, Verhaeren on the tenth anniversary of his death, were all subjects for the untiring energy which so impressed Specht.

He still travelled unceasingly, a few days at a time in one place. In Switzerland in August he found that he could preserve the anonymity he craved for a week at most, and drove himself on through Berne, Zermatt, and Riffelalp to Villeneuve. Later there were some days in Munich; in the autumn to Vienna for the rehearsals and première of *Volpone* at the Burg, with Raoul Aslan in the role of Mosca; then yet another lecture tour in Germany—Mainz, Cologne, Aachen, Düsseldorf, and Berlin. 'Oh la gloire quelle saleté, quelle ordure!' he wrote to Friderike from Berlin, where he was nearly overwhelmed with hospitality: dinner with the publisher Fischer, guest of honour at a banquet at the Bristol 'with all the bigwigs—frightful but unavoidable'. Friderike meanwhile reported a piling up of further invitations for lectures and appearances, but he was glad to take her advice to put on the brake a little: 'one must keep a little private life'.[1]

2

'Hofmannsthal has just died. With him and Rilke the old Austria is at an end.'

Zweig to Rolland, July 1929

'My life becomes ever more complicated', Zweig wrote to Pannwitz in January 1927; 'today I am off to Vienna for three days, in February I have to be in Munich to give the Memorial oration for Rilke in the Staatstheater—his death has shaken me beyond all measure.' He had noted with disgust how the papers had passed over this shattering event in a few lines, 'forty, fifty, sometimes a hundred were enough to close the "Rilke case" for the public. Time takes a fearful revenge on all those who do not completely descend to the public level, and punishes all self-isolation.'[2] His oration on 20 February was a most moving tribute, in an effort to correct this criminal neglect of a poet—'reverent stone-mason

[1] *BrW* 196–207. [2] Letter to Pannwitz, 27 Jan. 1927 (Sch).

ZWEIG'S STUDY AT KAPUZINERBERG

PLATE 7

FAMILY GROUP, KAPUZINERBERG

Stefan, Suse, Alix, and Friderike, with Kaspar at her feet

at work on the never-to-be-completed cathedral of language'—whom he himself held in higher esteem even than Hofmannsthal. He had refused to speak at the Requiem for Rilke in Vienna, for he felt that there the only possible candidate could be Hofmannsthal.[1] Two years later it was to be the latter's own turn.

Zweig's early admiration for Hofmannsthal had never weakened; and though their paths had diverged, and they met only rarely, he never lost his feeling of reverence and respect for the other. They had come a long way since Hofmannsthal had been able to congratulate him on his early Balzac essay. To Hofmannsthal a writer like Zweig, who let himself be influenced by the world and its events, and by popular taste, was nothing more than a journalist; and he felt extreme distaste for (as his friend Leopold von Andrian put it) 'the littérateurs of this world from whom no true poet can divorce himself but must live and write for a public they have corrupted'.[2] That Hofmannsthal could not abide Zweig is attested by Benno Geiger. He regarded him as a living plagiarism of his own existence as writer and poet: 'did he publish a Novelle, there was Zweig a month later publishing another; when a play of his was produced, Zweig was ready at the Burg with one of his own'. Geiger also thought that Zweig's all-too-evident Jewishness contributed to the older man's antipathy: Hofmannsthal preferred to forget his own semi-Jewish ancestry. A letter written about Zweig to Katharina Kippenberg two years before his death is damning in its faint praise:

I do not know Zweig's Novellen; I would guess they rank below Carossa's prose in both human content and in purity of presentation; but they must have something in them that really stills the hunger of the reader, something in them, the rhythm perhaps if not the subject, the half-truth of the accent, the debatable perhaps in the values (for there are values behind every poetic work) must exert that true instantaneous attraction which cannot be accorded the work . . . of Carossa or Taube.[3]

[1] *Abschied von Rilke*, Staatstheater, München, 20 Feb. 1927 (published Rainer Wunderlich Verlag, Tübingen, n.d. (1927), and reprinted 1946, 25.–32. Tausend, 1952); letter to Katharina Kippenberg, 8 Jan. 1927 (Sch).

[2] Hofmannsthal/von Andrian, *Briefwechsel*; S. Fischer, Frankfurt am Main, 1968, 405.

[3] Geiger 427–8; letter of 28 Apr. 1927 (*IAusst* 219).

Friderike too thought, later, that there was an element of jealousy in his attitude to Stefan, and that he might have been able to forgive the latter's greater worldliness, his pacifism and anti-fanaticism, if he had not been so vastly successful in his work. 'Hofmannsthal had a family to support and was often in financial straits, and it would therefore have been humanly understandable had he regarded the materially carefree Stefan as a rival.'[1]

To Zweig the sudden death of the poet he continued to revere, though he was well aware that his feelings were not reciprocated, represented, coming as it did so soon after the passing of Rilke, the end of the old Austria. Only just before, Robert Braun, visiting him at Kapuzinerberg, found him overjoyed to have rediscovered the early *Loris* poems, but heard him recite them with something of the sadness of a farewell. The signs were multiplying that Europe was at the end of her mission, said Zweig: creative powers were in catastrophic decline, and they were plunging into a trough of poverty in art, into barbarism. On 18 July 1929 he wrote to Kippenberg: 'I have been away for two days, enjoyed the luxury of not reading the papers, and have just heard now on my return: Hofmannsthal! First Rilke, now he—it is no mere accident, but a symbol, and not a good one.' To Rolland he mourned the passing of an era: 'his life was a long tragedy—perfection at twenty, and then the gods withdrew their voice from him. I liked him little personally, but I was his pupil and his death has moved me greatly.'[2] He felt honoured to accept the invitation to give the memorial address in the Burgtheater; and his just appreciation of the poet and his work gave no sign of his hurt at the absence from the ceremony of his widow.[3] Only some time afterwards did he learn through Richard Strauss that Hofmannsthal had from the first made it a condition with Reinhardt for his collaboration in the Salzburg Festival that Zweig should never be invited to join them; now, with Hofmannsthal in his grave, came Reinhardt with a formal request for his collaboration in the

[1] Fr² 95.

[2] Letter to Rolland, 22 July 1929 (Dum 208); letter to Kippenberg, 18 July 1929 (Sch); Robert Braun, *Sp* 79.

[3] Letters from Heinrich Eduard Jacob, 4 and 11 Nov. 1929 (ZE).

Festival's dramatic programme and permission to produce his plays at Salzburg. It was an unkind cut, and Zweig, with his 'often quite naïve trust in his fellow-men', as Friderike wrote, could hardly credit such ruthless rivalry in the poet he had so unstintingly admired. He had little taste from then on for working with Reinhardt.[1]

3

'To Moscow? Go with God!'
Thomas Mann to Zweig

Meanwhile *Drei Dichter ihres Lebens* (Casanova, Stendhal, Tolstoy) had been completed by the end of 1927. The essay on Casanova, doubtless spurred by his indignation against Brockhaus, had come easily to him during yet another jaunt to Switzerland that August (out of the way, while gas was being installed at Kapuzinerberg, and Moissi studied his parts for the Festival in the garden pavilion). Taking the cure at Zuoz, in the Engadine, with no smoking (his mental barometer once again at Fair), no coffee, deep breathing, and cold showers, he met untroubled the inevitable loss of anonymity: 'I have here the most wonderful invitations to tours in Rolls-Royces, very funny and amusing offers, you will be amused', he wrote, partly in English, to Friderike: 'but I would prefer to write my Casanova than to live it.'[2] The other essays, however, became a burden. In the course of the preparation for that on Tolstoy he wrote an epilogue to Tolstoy's unfinished drama *The Light Shineth in the Darkness*, called *Die Flucht zu Gott*. With Stendhal the subject aroused once more his feelings of insufficiency: alone in Salzburg, he wrote to Friderike (who had in her turn gone to Switzerland to board Suse in a Quaker School near Nyon):

> I am working, but still not with the right speed of thought, it seems as if screws are loose in the machine: the best thing would be to stop the motor completely in one's fiftieth year and try once more to experience the world instead of describing it. I am full of mistrust

[1] Fr 296–7; Fr² 95. [2] *BrW* 208–11.

against this eternal literature, it is an unnatural condition if one completely lacks ambition. The less I hear of the mirror image St. Z. the more I am myself: for once I should like to be absolutely completely myself.[1]

For a long time he was uncertain of the title for the trilogy, and settled on *Drei Dichter* only just before the book went to press. He dedicated it to Gorki, 'one of the mightiest stormy petrels of the new realism towards which we are all moving', in his words to Willi Fehse two years later.[2] (Shortly before publication he wrote an article in honour of Gorki for the *NFP*.)[3] The book was well received, Thomas Mann in particular finding the Tolstoy essay 'the most critically profound of any of your writings . . . it is a joy to follow the unfolding of your life's work, your development'.[4] Felix Braun noted once again his friend's tendency to over-emphasis and repetition, but felt that this very fault could show the attentive reader how much knowledge of life and men, of outward and inward reality, lay behind such a book, which embodied the two strongest qualities of his art as a writer: *die erklärende und die verklärende* ('exposition and transfiguration').[5]

In 1927 the Russian edition of his complete works had appeared with the Wremya publishing house in Leningrad, prefaced by Specht's brief but penetrating monograph on the author, to which reference has already been made, and with an Introduction by Gorki ('it seems to me that no-one before him has written about love with such depth, such immeasurable sympathy for mankind'). Now, a year later, perhaps as a result of the Tolstoy essay, came an invitation which flattered and excited: to represent the writers of Austria at the Tolstoy centenary celebrations to be held in Moscow in September 1928. He was eager to go, not only because it would be a pilgrimage to the ultimate source of Rolland's and his own philosophy, but also because he felt that to have seen Russia, to gain some direct impression of the effects of the gigantic

[1] *BrW* 215–16. [2] Fehse, *Sp* 64.

[3] Stefan Zweig, 'Rede zu Ehren Maxim Gorkis', *NFP*, 25 Mar. 1928. Reprinted in *Begegnungen*, 1937; a slightly revised version appeared as the Introduction to the Insel edition of Gorki's *Erzählungen*, 1931. Cf. *BrW* 219, *Ausst* 67.

[4] Letter of 7 May 1928 (Mann *Br* i. 279).

[5] Braun, review in *Die Literatur*, quoted *Inselschiff*, ix. 4 (Autumn 1928), 323.

upheaval of 1917, was essential to his education as a European. The 1914 war had cut off, with its 'bloody sickle', his plan to go there when he was working on the *Dostoevsky*: now the Revolution had made Russia the most fascinating land of the post-war world, as enthusiastically admired by some as it was fanatically hated by others. He knew that his works were widely disseminated there in vast cheap editions, and that so popular an author would be assured of a welcome;[1] but he had so far hesitated to make the journey, which seemed to bring with it the obligation to take a public stand, for or against, and his deep detestation of the political and the dogmatic left him no desire to be forced into print with judgements, after only a brief survey of the limitless land and its still unsolved problems. On this occasion, however, far removed from the political, there could be no such objection. Tolstoy could scarcely be called a Bolshevik, and Zweig's essay on him qualified him to speak about the apostle of non-violence. 'It seemed to me too a significant demonstration in the European sense for the writers of all countries to unite in homage to the greatest of them all.'[2] 'Go with God!' Thomas Mann had written: 'I have not been invited . . . since the imprimatur was refused my *Zauberberg* because of its bourgeois tendencies, I know that I am not persona grata back there.'[3]

When he set off on 8 September (three days after the première of *Die Flucht zu Gott* in Kiel), he found the journey itself an experience. The ruined cities of Polish Galicia that he had seen in 1915 had risen anew: 'once again I realized that a decade, so large a slice of the individual's existence, is but the flicker of an eyelid in the life of a people'. In Warsaw, where he spent a night, there was no sign remaining of the ebb and flow of the military tide. Along the flatter, sandy approaches to the Russian frontier the whole population of each village turned out to see the passage of the train which was the only link between the West and the forbidden East. At the frontier station a blood-red banner across the tracks, with Cyrillic characters he could not read but which were

[1] Although *Drei Meister* had not passed the censor in the U.S.S.R., 'because the conception of Dostoevsky was not on Bolshevist lines' (*BrW* 188).

[2] *WvG* 299–300; *BrW* 188. [3] Letter of 1 Sept. 1928 (Mann *Br* i. 283).

translated for him—'Workers of All Lands, Unite!'—signalled his entry into the Soviet Republic, the Empire of the Proletariat.

The train to which he changed, true, was hardly proletarian: a luxurious *wagon-lit* of the Tsarist era, vastly more comfortable than those to which he was accustomed in the West, and better suited to these great distances, broader because of the gauge and much slower. As they ambled on through the steppes, he had a feeling of familiarity with this country he was seeing for the first time: 'the melancholy landscape, the little huts and villages with their onion domes, the long-bearded men, half peasant, half prophet, greeting us with their broad good-humoured laugh, the women with their gay kerchiefs and white aprons, selling *kwass*, eggs and cucumbers'. Though he had not a word of Russian he seemed to understand these touchingly simple people in their baggy blouses, the young workers in the train with their endless chess games or animated discussions; and he realized that he owed this to the masterly realism of the great Russian authors he had read, Dostoevsky, Tolstoy, Gorki.[1]

His two weeks in Russia were a bewildering mixture of great haste and irritating delays, of enthusiasm and repulsion, of alternating hot and cold. He had scarcely set foot in Moscow before he was informed that he was to speak at the opening ceremonies that very night at the Bolshoi, on 'Tolstoy and Foreign Countries'. There was a characteristically late start (he soon learned that Western punctuality was out of place here), and he eventually came to the podium at eleven o'clock. Unprepared, he had decided to speak extempore: 'the great opera house (the most splendid I have ever seen, with its 4000 seats), the flashlights, klieg lights of the cine-cameras are something to give one pause, but in the end it went off pretty well for a speech given after a 54-hour train journey'. The speeches were still continuing when he left, dog-tired, at one in the morning. From then on it was an intensely packed round: from the Grand Hotel he was led in rapid succession to the Dostoevsky Museum, the historical museum, the ceremonial opening of the Tolstoy House, the Tolstoy Museum ('my book on him is being sold at every street corner for 25

[1] *WvG* 300–1; *BrW* 221.

kopeks, called out by the vendors like a newspaper'), *Eugen Onegin* at the Opera. The next day came the train journey to Tula and in cars to Yasnaya Polyana, Tolstoy's grave under the trees he had planted as a young man, 'the most beautiful grave in the world'. On his return, four more museums, ten calls (including his first meeting face to face with Gorki), the theatre again.

And so it went on, culminating in an 'excursion' at the invitation of the Wremya (twelve hours in a sleeper) to Leningrad. Touring the treasures of the Hermitage, he marvelled at the troops of workers, soldiers, and peasants being lectured by art commissars on Rembrandt and Titian; at this absurd but none the less impressive impatience to lift these illiterates at one stroke to an understanding of Beethoven and Vermeer. There was an unmistakable pride in the man in the street in his new 'ownership', in the technical achievements of the new Russia, which his child-like faith ascribed entirely to the Revolution and the 'little fathers' Lenin and Trotsky. But it made Zweig wonder whether the nation could ever prove capable of learning, whether the Great Plan could ever be realized, or would instead be lost in the boundless limbo of Mother Russia. 'Now one was confident, now distrustful. The more I saw, the less was clear to me.'[1]

This dichotomy lay, he felt, deep in the Russian soul itself, deep in the soul of the very man they had come to honour.

> What was Tolstoy, in fact? [said Lunacharsky to him on the train journey to Yasnaya Polyana], a revolutionary or a reactionary? Did he know himself? As a true Russian he wanted everything too quickly, after thousands of years to change the whole world with one flick of the wrist.—Just like us [he added with a smile], and, like us, with a single formula. It is quite wrong to regard us Russians as patient. We are patient with our bodies, even with our soul. But in our thought we are more impatient than any other people, we want to know all truths, 'the' truth immediately and at once.

The warmth and cordiality of all those he met—the drivers, students, Tartars and Mongols, writers—their incredible generosity, boundless and genuine confidence in their Western visitors, simple faith that they had now found 'the' truth—'this is *ours*, *we*

[1] *WvG* 302–4; *BrW* 222–3.

have built that'—above all, the feeling, strange and exhilarating to a Western writer, that books really meant something to the 'people', made a deep impression on Zweig. He could understand how it was that foreign authors, seeing themselves celebrated as never before, and apparently beloved of the great masses, succumbed to the temptation on their return 'to render praise for praise, exaggeration for exaggeration'.[1]

That he himself was not among their number was due, he wrote later, not so much to any strength of character as to the action of a young Russian whose name he never learned. Returning from an evening with students, still glowing from their lively enthusiasm, he found in his pocket a letter, unsigned, written in French, which one of them must have thrust there unobtrusively at some point in the evening. It was in wise, human terms, not a letter of some 'White' counter-revolutionary, but nevertheless full of bitterness against the ever-increasing curtailment of liberty in recent years. 'Do not believe everything you hear,' wrote this unknown, 'do not forget that with all you see there is much not shown to you. Remember that those who speak with you mostly cannot say what they would like, but only what they are allowed. We are all watched, you no less than us. Your interpreter reports every word. Your telephone is tapped, your every move checked.' He gave examples and details, which of course Zweig was not in a position to verify; but he was sufficiently impressed to follow the writer's instructions to burn the letter ('do not just tear it up, for they will collect the pieces from your waste-basket and put it together again'), and to think deeply over his experiences of the last days. It was true that, despite all the warmth and comradeship, he had had no single opportunity to speak with anyone alone; with his ignorance of the language, how could he feel with justice that he had a true impression of these people? And how tiny a part of this vast domain had he been able to see! 'If I was to be honest with myself and with others, I had to admit that my impressions, however exciting and stimulating they might be in details, could have no objective validity.' So, unlike most travellers of his kind, he wrote no book after his return, with

[1] *WvG* 304–7.

either praise or condemnation: merely a series of three articles at the end of October for the *NFP*,[1] which he carefully restricted to the non-political, and of which the *pièce de résistance* was his description of the grave at Yasnaya Polyana. 'I was wise to be so reserved, for only three months later there were great changes in what I had seen and after a year the rapid transformations would have made nonsense of every word. All the same, I have seldom in my life felt the current of our time so strongly as in Russia.'[2]

Although he maintained some of the personal and literary contacts established on this visit (Konstantin Fedin, Tolstoy's niece, Vladimir Lidin—whose wife he financed in 1930 during her medical treatment in Wiesbaden),[3] he retained a healthy scepticism, and in the following years was much more reserved than Rolland with regard to the U.S.S.R., condemning in letters to his friend in 1936 and 1937 the personality cult of Stalin, and approving Gide's *Retour de l'URSS*.[4] He remembered his unknown correspondent's bitterness over the lack of freedom for the individual in Russia, which for him overrode any possible attractions of communism; and he saw, with a prophetic insight, the danger, as he wrote to Rolland in October 1929, of 'a development of a Russian nationalism, a social nationalism, if I may venture the expression'.[5]

4

'The more daring his metamorphoses, the more interesting appeared to me the character, or rather non-character, of this most thoroughgoing Machiavellian of modern times.'

Zweig, *Joseph Fouché*

Their diverging views on the Soviet Union may well have contributed to the relative estrangement which his relationship with Rolland was to suffer in the next ten years. As early as December

[1] In reprint form in a brochure, these articles were of no little interest later to the Nazis: 'In Salzburg, after his emigration, I had several enquiries . . . about [its] availability, unmistakably from Nazi-inspired sources' (Fr 312).

[2] *WvG* 307–8.

[3] Letters ZE, in particular from Vladimir Lidin, 13 Oct. 1930.

[4] Dum 132–3.

[5] Letter of 3 Oct. 1929 (Dum 177).

1928 Zweig detected, both from letters and when he saw Rolland again at Villeneuve, a certain coldness in the older man's manner, and wondered what, or who, could have induced it.[1] For himself, however, his studies on Fouché, whose biography he had already embarked on, led him still to press Rolland to continue his great drama of the French Revolution with a *Robespierre*. 'He fascinates me more and more,' he had written in June, 1928, 'and working on my *Fouché* I have been struck at each encounter. . . . I see the dramatic moment of his life when he leans towards terror (which is not at all in his nature), when his idealism and humanitarianism are broken against reality.'[2] (His *Fouché* might in fact have been a *Robespierre*, had he not felt that the latter subject should rightly be tackled by Rolland. Though he continued to prod, however, it was ten years before Rolland finally quarried this block from the 'bloody mountain' of the Revolution.)

Though he claimed later that he had written it for his 'own private pleasure',[3] *Fouché* had a deeper purpose, as is clear from a letter to Emil Ludwig in 1928:

> to give a picture of the pure politician, who serves every ideology, accepts every post, sits in every saddle, never has an idea of his own, and yet through this very flexibility outlasts the most powerful men of his time. It is to be a sign and a warning for the politicians of this and every age and to show in graphic form the danger the 'usable', the practised politician represents for all nations and for Europe.[4]

'Stresemann and all the others are lesser editions of him', he put it to Rolland: '. . . a book against politics which have no faith or ideas, in other words the politics of Europe today'.[5] He did not, however, expect it to sell, and argued strongly with Kippenberg against venturing a first printing of even 10,000 for a book with an unsympathetic character and no feminine appeal.

Its reception came as all the greater surprise, and he confessed to Fleischer at the end of 1929, when the second printing of 20,000 was already in hand, that his hopelessly wrong forecast made him feel pretty stupid. Reviews verged on the lyrical: 'the

[1] Letter to Friderike Zweig, 23 Dec. 1928 (*BrW* 224).

[2] Letter to Rolland, 20 June 1928 (Dum 231–2).

[3] *WvG* 291.

[4] Letter of 2 May 1928 (Sch).

[5] Dum 302–3.

best German prose . . . one of the most mature works yet from Stefan Zweig's pen' (Joachim Maass); 'one of the psychologically most competent biographies of the great Napoleonic age' (Friedrich Kircheisen); 'an unparalleled picture of the time, the whole gamut of politics—origin, scope, abuse, advantages, critique and end—which no contemporary of such an age could possibly have unravelled; . . . one must admire the greatness which can contrive to turn the life of so repulsive a man into a great work of the writer's art' (Joseph Gregor). In Hans Hellwig's words, Zweig showed 'strangely penetrating vision to write, a few years before the Nazis came to power, a book about a man who personified amorality in politics . . . a warning to contemporary readers'[1]—a warning which had for Germans the same fascination, but as little effect, as for the English the fashionable denigrations of Britain in the sixties. When his spaniel Kaspar sired a litter in April (the faithful Rolf had had to be put down eighteen months before), the pick was named 'Fouché' and sent to Erich Ebermayer in Leipzig: oddly enough, he was to become ungovernable in the first months of Hitler's rule in 1933—'clearly affected by the atmosphere of the times', Zweig wrote then, 'and, following the example of so many intellectuals, quite losing his character'.[2]

Almost at the same time he had finished a drama on an incident in Napoleon's Egyptian campaign (in which Fouché also appeared), *Das Lamm des Armen*. Here again, he did not expect much success for this piece, which he described as 'very hard, very bitter'; but it was much sought after, and became the subject of a tug-of-war between the Deutsches Volkstheater (who proposed Moissi as Napoleon, and Dagny, the successful actress daughter of Franz Servaes, as Bellilotte) and the Burg (who proposed to star Werner Krauss).[3] It is doubtful whether Zweig remembered at the time his earlier superstitions over the deaths of Matkowsky and Kainz (according to a letter to Ebermayer, he had actually promised the lead to Moissi); at all events he contracted with the

[1] *WvG* 291; *Inselschiff*, xi. 1; Gregor manuscript review (ZE); H 81–2.

[2] ZE; letter to Ebermayer, 10 June 1933 (*BdFr* 54, *Heute* 104).

[3] Letter to Rolland, 28 May 1929 (Dum 216); letter to Fleischer, 11 Sept. 1929 (Sch).

Burgtheater for the Vienna première, which would have to be delayed till the following year because of Krauss's engagements with Reinhardt.[1] Once again Fate stepped in, however: no illnesses or sudden deaths, it was true, but a 'palace revolution' at the Burg, which caused the producer to pursue Zweig all the way to Rome at the end of January 1930, to persuade him to release them from the contract to employ Krauss.

At the première on 12 April it was Raoul Aslan who appeared as Napoleon. From the author of *Volpone*, still making its triumphant way across the stages of Europe and America, the tragicomedy was assured of success; and even before it went on at the Burg there were simultaneous performances on 15 March 1930 at Breslau, Hannover (where Zweig was in attendance), Lübeck, and Prague.[2] Felix Braun found it masterly in its action, characterization, and motivation; though he criticized the over-precision and too great directness 'which in medical terms is an over-treatment', and urged Zweig to remember that 'that which is unsaid is an essential to the mastery of style'.[3] Gerhart Hauptmann, thanking him for an inscribed copy, wrote: 'for a long time I have been enriched by your fine, warm and at the same time sharply penetrating mind, whose unique quality is your secret. . . . *Bildung macht frei*. You are the best example for me of the truth of this today somewhat neglected maxim. . . . *Bildung* has not only freed your soul, but also your mind, and what is more your poetic genius.'[4]

The manifold themes of Revolutionary and Napoleonic France held a fascination for him at this time. He had been attracted by the unusual personality of Adam Lux, the German revolutionary idealist who entered the service of France, and—inspired no doubt by Rolland's juxtaposition of Jean Christophe and Olivier—essayed several sketches between 1926 and 1928 of the story of this encounter between German and French idealism, with its eventual foundering on the 'implacable rock of reality'.

[1] Letters to Ebermayer (*BdFr* 49) and Fleischer (Sch), 21 Sept. 1929; letter to Servaes, 28 Sept. 1929 (StB).

[2] Letter to Ebermayer, 15 Feb. 1930 (*BdFr* 49); Fr 295–6; *BrW* 230–1.

[3] Letter of 6 May 1930 (ZE).

[4] Letter of 9 Nov. 1929 (ZE).

But he never succeeded in completing it.[1] To Ludwig in May 1928 he expatiated on the theme of a 'history of the great social revolutionaries': 'The more I read, the more I am clear that Jean-Jacques Rousseau and Marx are *one* type, and that all the variants from Thomas Münzer to Marat are but . . . repetitions of the same.' He saw the need for a monograph on the revolutionary and social spirit as expressed in personalities, but felt he had too heavy a hand for such a task.[2] By the spring of 1930 he had Rieger working in Paris on some basic research for a study of Marie Antoinette, while he was completing on his behalf the revision of Hella's translation of *Fouché* and Olivier Bernac's of *Casanova*.[3]

5

'I consider Stefan Zweig as the German writer with the best *command of German.'*
Erzherzog von Habsburg-Lothringen
to Gustinus Ambrosi, about 1930

The closing years of the twenties were Zweig's most fecund. No writer of his stature (and very few journalists) approached his fantastic output at this time, a mass-production of the highest quality which excited the admiration of the literary world, and, too often, the envy of colleagues not gifted with this speed. Its very diversity and the manifold outlets it sought make the bibliographer's task almost impossible, but the record of his work for the years 1925 to 1929—it is to be hoped, virtually complete—will give the reader an idea of its scope and volume.[4] Small wonder that in his presence Specht thought to detect the 'quiet but explosive whirring of a high-speed engine':

he plunges into the world of the present with newspaper articles, builds a cycle of grandiose essays into a world picture, founds a *Bibliotheca Mundi* and edits it himself, bombards a great publishing house with ideas, goes on lecture tours, is in constant and productive

[1] Dum 175; Fr. 300.
[2] Letter to Ludwig, 2 May 1928 (Sch).
[3] Letters from Gregor, 19 Feb. 1930, and Rieger in Paris, 28 Feb. and 27 Mar. 1930 (ZE).
[4] See p. 359.

contact with all the intellectuals of Europe, maintains and augments one of the most valuable autograph collections, works over old comedies and has them produced, discovers new writers, drums them out and gets publishers for them, supervises the translations of his works, broadcasts ideas and suggestions in all directions, always has time for his friends and is the most ready to help of any of them, creates 'by the way' the splendid Novellen chain *Die Kette*, of which three volumes are so far to hand . . . and still finds the inner peace required for lyrical recollection and flight from the day into the distant world of legend.[1]

He lived only for his work; and there were many occasions when it brought him unalloyed pleasure. In 1928 he collaborated with Alexander Lernet-Holenia (under the pseudonym of 'Clemens Neydisser') to write the comedy *Quiproquo*, later entitled *Gelegenheit Macht Liebe*, and enjoyed for the first time anonymity in its moderate success—though it is true that the veil was thin, and indeed dissolved altogether when the critic Liebstöckl wrote '*Lernet*, Autoren, auf einen grünen *Zweig* zu kommen'. (The comedy was the first noteworthy vehicle for the young Paula Wessely on her rise to stardom.)[2] Yet, paradoxically, as he approached fifty, he was assailed increasingly by doubt. Most men at this age experience dissatisfaction and a sense of failure, and there are few who do not feel, as Zweig repeatedly did at this time, the urge to start anew, to break with the past.

Often this was for him a feeling almost of gaiety. 'My books sell excessively well,' he wrote to Arcos, 'but unfortunately I am neither ambitious nor proud, and I would prefer to be twenty, have three women a day and have my copy rejected by all the reviews. I have no talent for "dignity".'[3] He could still relax with pleasure in the company of young girls and bask in their admiration. But on occasion the dissatisfaction was more serious: to Rolland in June 1928 he expressed his nostalgia for 'pure science with its splendid abnegation', and said he felt a great urge to 'stop making literature for a few years, following the example of the great, Goethe, Schiller, who buried themselves in history or

[1] S 8.
[2] Lernet-Holenia, Arens[1] 149; *Ausst* 67.
[3] Undated letter, possibly early 1928 (Dum 323).

biology, to return with their strength entirely renewed'.[1] And at the end of the year he wrote from Montreux to Friderike that his work was still not going right, there had been something wrong in everything he had attempted in the last eighteen months.

I need someone who can tell me where the fault lies. . . . How wise are those Englishmen between 50 and 70 who hand over their house and business to their children and sit quietly here or on the Riviera, slowly reading their books and newspapers, playing a little sport, without ambition to win, and bridge in the evenings! I would like to be one of them—to get out of the 'business', which does not attract me because I have left all outward ambition behind me. With effect from the 1st of January I give up the whole game of doing and living for others—for a quarter of a century I've served all possible (and mostly impossible) people, and now I'm giving notice![2]

Meanwhile his work became more and more a series of unfinished fragments—'three whole drawers full' he complained to Lissauer in December 1929[3]—and while the machine, to all outward appearance, ground on as never before, his recurring wish was only to stop it.

This was not, however, just a reflection of the climacteric. Though at this age his natural tendency to pessimism was bound to be reinforced and to manifest itself ever more frequently in outbursts of discontent with the 'business', the *Betrieb*, the mainspring of his malaise was undoubtedly his almost uncanny perception of the agony which was to come to Europe in a few years. In retrospect, in his autobiography, he could deal with the decade before Hitler under the title 'Sunset'; the remarkable thing is that *at the time*, as can be observed from his letters and his discussions with others, he knew instinctively that the sun, apparently still at its zenith, had already begun to sink. Robert Braun, hearing him talk of 'Europe at the end of its mission', of the barbarism into which he saw it descending, was struck by the incurable pessimism in Zweig's dark glance, despite the pipe which lent such a comforting air to their meeting.[4] By 1931 he was already prophesying to Kesten a third world war (admittedly only 'by the turn of

[1] Letter of 20 June 1928 (Dum 215).
[2] *BrW* 226.
[3] Letter of 18 Dec. 1929 (StB).
[4] Robert Braun, *Sp* 79–80.

the century') in which they would 'once again with horror witness a new general betrayal by the writers and poets of all countries', a new *trahison des clercs*.

Another factor, as Friderike recognized, was that fame itself brought him increasing disturbance. He had refused from the start to have anything to do with Rieger's biography, and the luckless author was shaken in February 1928 to read between the lines of a letter from Friderike that the manuscript had disappointed him ('on your expressed wish I have refrained from every kind of exaggerated enthusiasm and striven for impartiality from the first line to the last'). When Fleischer tried to intervene, he received a sharp rejoinder from Zweig in Paris: 'You do me an injustice in the Rieger affair. . . . I was astounded to hear that Spaeth [the publishers] had reached an agreement with him, and I read the manuscript only *one day* before my departure (and toned it down here and there, I cannot bear praise, for I am not satisfied with myself).'[1] He sympathized with Rolland when Kra, the Paris dealer in autographs and rare books, put some of his letters up for sale: 'one pays for so-called fame with the surrender of one's private life . . . nothing belongs to us any longer'.[2] But it was not just that he felt deeply any intrusion into his private life or curtailment of his personal freedom: rather the fact that, having reached the heights, he felt less spur to extend himself, and at the same time a greater sense of responsibility in his art, so that spontaneity was bound to suffer. The paradox sharpened: his mounting discontent was matched and surpassed by the welcome accorded each new work by both public and publishers.

It is extraordinary [he had written to Pannwitz a few years earlier] how our profession, which should be the freest of all, in fact tends more and more to restrict our freedom: the past, what we have already achieved, puts more and more questions to us, makes ever increased demands, and the point we have reached, instead of becoming a foundation for the future, must itself be continually stepped up. Somehow the headlong tempo of the times has taken possession of us.[3]

[1] Letter from Rieger, 18 Feb. 1928 (ZE); card to Fleischer, 2 Apr. 1928 (Sch).
[2] Letter to Rolland, 20 May 1927 (Dum 132).
[3] Letter of 4 Oct. 1926 (Sch).

He remained trapped by the *Betrieb*, and only Friderike and his most intimate friends knew how he really felt. Lee van Dovski, meeting him for the first time at his Utrecht Lecture in March 1929, thought him a well-cared-for aristocrat, most un-Jewish;[1] to Specht his 'smooth, bourgeois-patrician manner and appearance, though not his vehement tempo', was that of the 'generation of Austrian poets of the eighties'.[2] Arnold Zweig, forty years later, thought the portrait of Stefan in the 1930 Reclam edition of *Angst* looked for all the world like an illustration of the title: 'eyes full of fear, in a hunted countenance'.[3] But no one remarked this at the time.

[1] Lee van Dovski, *Liber Amic* 27–8.

[2] S 7–8.

[3] Arnold Zweig, *Über Schriftsteller*; Aufbau Verlag, East Berlin, 1967.

VI. *Incipit* Hitler 1930–1933

'These flames not only illuminate the final end of the old era: they also light up the new.'
Goebbels, at the Burning of the Books, 10 May 1933

'Humanism is humiliated or dead. Conclusion: we must found it anew.'
Thomas Mann to Walter Rehm, June 1930

I

'Nothing occupies me more than this attempt to transform my mode of life.'
Zweig to Fleischer, July 1930

In the New Year of 1930 Zweig spent almost a month in Italy with Friderike. In more cheerful mood than usual, he treated this as a holiday rather than merely a change of workshop (it was the first holiday they had spent together since Paris six years earlier), though he was not entirely idle, and was already sketching out the first lines of *Die Heilung durch den Geist*. In Naples he saw Benedetto Croce; but the highlight of the visit was their stay for three days with Gorki, who had recently been allowed to settle, for health reasons, in a villa in Sorrento. Zweig was astounded at the Russian's vitality, and especially at the ease with which he found he could understand him: for Gorki was not only a great story-teller, 'narration was a functional emanation of his whole being', and Zweig had no need of the mediation of Baroness Budberg, Gorki's secretary, to follow his descriptions, so vividly could he convey by gesture, voice, and self-transformation the characters of his tale. The old revolutionary and friend of Lenin was not in fact in exile here (not, indeed, as much as Croce, the staunch opponent of Mussolini, was in his own country), and although he was then by no means fully committed to the Party, he made no secret of his home-sickness, his longing to be back with his own people in these years of decision. To be with him meant for Zweig to experience the true Russia, 'not the Bolshevist, not the Russia of old times or of today, but the broad, strong and dark soul of the eternal Russian people'.[1]

It was a memorable stay, capped with a leisurely car drive to Amalfi and along the coast—one which he and Friderike were to look back on as their happiest before the clouds began to drift over their Europe. But even now their planned stay in Rome was cut short by the call of the 'business', and early in February Stefan was 'chased home' by the tedious affair of the Burgtheater and Werner Krauss. In the following months he was in Salzburg, except for a short trip in March to Breslau and Hannover for the productions of *Das Lamm des Armen*, and to Berlin, where he saw Einstein, 'a devoted reader of mine'.[2]

Now, as though following his previous longing to lose himself in science 'with its splendid abnegation', he set to work seriously on the first drafts of a new trilogy of essays, *Die Heilung durch den Geist*; the 'mind-healers and healers through the mind'—Mesmer, Mary Baker-Eddy, and Freud. The subject, and the fact that his treatment was quite distinct from the grand design of the *Master Builders*, seem a gesture—albeit not a strong one—in the direction of the 'new way of life' he was seeking, 'a bold excursion into the secret land of the medicine of the soul'. 'It is my passion always to turn an unexpected corner and to learn more of life by spreading my net of subjects as widely as possible', in his words to Servaes in December 1930.[3] He abandoned the 'seventy fragments' which cluttered his desk, and plunged into the extraordinary and fascinating stories of Mesmer and the founder of Christian Science, completing these essays in a very short time. (Both appear to have been published in extract, or at least announced

[1] *WvG* 309–12; Fr 312–18; *Bildb* 132; Fr[2] 118–20.

[2] *BrW* 230–1. [3] Letter of 11 Dec. 1930 (StB).

in detail, during the summer, for in July he was angered to read in a bookseller's prospectus that the Christian Scientists were exploiting his piece on their founder as a puff for a book by Sybil Wilbur which he had ridiculed: 'business and faith go well together'.)[1] The study on Freud, 'to whom I owe so much', was much harder: for he felt, as he had with Rolland, a great diffidence in writing about a living person, and all the drama of this 'anti-poetic, purely scientific and bourgeois existence' lay in the world of ideas, difficult to make into a living picture.[2]

As the 'hunter of souls', in Rolland's words, 'who has made his own the perilous key of Freud',[3] it was inevitable that he should at some time devote himself to such a study. Freud was an eager reader of Zweig's works, and his letters were always those to which the author most looked forward from the shoal which followed each new publication. But he was not, as Friderike says, an unreserved Freudian; and he endeavoured in his essay, inspired by the objective style of the subject himself, to give a clear and simple account of the development of this important doctrine and the reactions to it.[4] According to Arnold Bauer, he had visited Freud on occasion at his consulting-rooms in Vienna, and their talks may in fact have taken on the character of a *Lehranalyse*.[5] The old man's collection of popular art was also of great interest to Zweig on his visits.[6] Freud, for his part, though admiring Zweig's work, was not, it seems, entirely enamoured of his amateur approach to psychology, and did not conceal criticism in his letters when he felt the occasion demanded. His correspondence with Arnold Zweig in September 1930 is revealing in this regard. Taken to task for having addressed Arnold as 'Doktor', he replied:

I had it is true an uncertain feeling as I wrote the appellation, but as unknown powers were clearly involved here it is not surprising that I disregarded it. The analysis I immediately instituted into this *Fehlleistung* led of course on to dangerous ground, and revealed as the

[1] *BrW* 235.
[2] Letter to Ernst Lissauer, 2 Apr. 1931 (StB).
[3] Quoted R 35.
[4] Fr 207.
[5] Bauer, 56. According to Geiger (423), Zweig carried at one time a certificate that he was a patient of Freud's, in order to avoid any difficulties with the law over his exhibitionist tendencies.
[6] Statement to the author by Friderike Zweig.

disturbance the other Zweig, of whom I know that he is at present engaged in working me into an essay which is to bring me to the public eye in the company of Mesmer and Mary Eddy Baker [sic]. He has in the last six months given me strong grounds for dissatisfaction, my originally strong urge to revenge has been banished into the subconscious, and so it is quite possible that I felt the desire to set up a comparison and effect a substitution.[1]

Beneath this banter there may well have lain a real dissatisfaction with Stefan's work.

The trilogy, and in particular the essay on Freud, seems to have been for Zweig something of a self-analysis. He recognized a complex in himself, in the need he felt to 'transform his way of life', but could not see how he could rid himself of it. 'Somewhere in my disposition I lack a necessary dose of brutality and self-assurance.'[2] In July Friderike took a trip alone to Switzerland (Suse was now working for a few months in a nursery in Geneva); prompted by her reading of Balzac's *Louis Lambert*, with its reference to Mesmer, and by news of their young friend Joseph Roth's despair over his mounting debts in Vienna, she wrote to Stefan her heavy feeling that

no-one, apart from me, really knows you, and one day the emptiest, silliest things will be written about you. For you allow few to get close enough to you, and your real *persona* is closed in on itself. Your written works are only a third of yourself, and no-one has grasped from them what is essential for the interpretation of the other two-thirds. Poor Roth, who would be clever and clairvoyant enough, and indeed has revealed to me something of your character, is too caught up in the web of the daimon world in which he has trapped himself and his wife.—I myself need concentration, solitude, absence of constraint, to formulate what I would like to say. And if I succeeded I would really not know whether I could overcome certain obstacles or whether once again, as with so many other things, it would have to be destroyed.[3]

She was hardly back home before he left for Hamburg. He paused for a day in Augsburg, where one of his youthful female

[1] Letter of 10 Sept. 1930 (Freud/Zw *BrW* 25–6).
[2] Letter to Fleischer, 7 July 1930 (Sch). [3] *BrW* 231–7.

admirers chanced to be passing through, and took delight in showing her the medieval beauties of the town, which he knew well, speaking with admiration of the 'united Europe' which the Fuggers' operations from here had for a time made a reality. Arrived in Hamburg, he plunged once more into anonymity, renting rooms in the house once occupied by Hans von Bülow on the Alsterglacis. As always, the change restored his gaiety for a short time.

> The rain it raineth every day, but with intervals between I can always go for walks, into all kinds of very clean, very dark cafés, read the papers, enjoy this dead quiet, sovereign flat, a splendid, thoroughly educated, attractive secretary. . . . I note that you have become a radio enthusiast on loan: there's one in the house here too which at the press of a button gurgles out operettas and similar muck.[1] God protect us from all this horror! I have not been for a moment nervous here, and the world appears as though it is no concern of mine, which God knows is right, whereas in Salzburg I feel it like a load pressing on my breast.

Now the *Freud* took shape. During the day he would work lying in bed, scribbling in pencil, the curtains drawn, by the light of a table-lamp. Loth to interrupt this good progress, he got out of a pressing invitation from Barbara Ring, his Norwegian translator, to attend the *Volpone* première in Oslo by pleading a non-existent lecture engagement; and only towards the end of his stay did he emerge from his shell to see Sigmund Warburg and Richard Friedenthal, in Hamburg for a lecture.[2]

Though *Die Heilung durch den Geist*, published by the Insel in 1931, indeed turned an 'unexpected corner', and the quite different, *undichterisches*, subject necessitated for him an unusually objective treatment, its form was closely aligned on the previous trilogies. Friderike found, reading the *Freud*, that in the rare cases where he gave his personal judgements, an excess of superlatives struck a jarring note in the otherwise 'noble objectivity' of the essay, which she praised for its 'just measure and calm

[1] He had steadfastly set his face against installing a radio at Kapuzinerberg.

[2] Statement to the author by Helene Freifrau von Ledebur; *BrW* 239–45; Vladimir Lidin, 'People I Have Met', *Writers and Artists Forum* (? date).

survey'. 'To the Freudians you will of course appear too cool, but you will in fact do them a greater service by your decisive and less passionate approach.'[1] Peter Flamm, reviewing for the *Berliner Tageblatt*, admired the selflessness of the presentation 'which almost puritanically avoids all temptation to adornment'.[2]

Freud himself went at some length into his reactions, which proved on the whole not unfavourable.

> The *Mesmer* seems to me the most harmonious, just and distinguished [of the three]. I think, with you, that the actual essence of his discovery, namely suggestion, has not to this day been really established, and that there is room here for something new.—On M. B. Eddy I was somewhat put out by the extent to which you developed the intensity. . . . Your presentation does not sufficiently stress the crazy and criminal aspects of the Eddy affair, nor the inexpressible darkness of the American background. . . . [I hasten] to express my satisfaction that you should have recognised the most important aspect of my own case. Namely, that if there is achievement to be considered, it was not so much a question of intellect as of character.

He presumed psychoanalysis was new to Zweig: 'the fact that you have been able to make so much of it your own is all the more worthy of recognition'. He criticized the scant reference to the technique of free association, and the historically inaccurate crediting to himself of interpretation of dreams by the *Kindertraum*; and he considered that Zweig's final doubt whether analysis could ever be used by the ordinary man rested on his ignorance of the technique, drawing a parallel with the early years of the microscope. 'There is no help for the fact that, in any field, not all are equally adept.'[3]

If Zweig had hoped, by the choice of this subject, and the escape to Hamburg, to exorcise his daimon of unrest, the attempt was not a success. Friderike's letters from Salzburg were a constant reminder of how the machine was racing on, and his commitments seemed still inescapable. To Fleischer, who had reproached him for such a brief and cool handshake when they had last met

[1] *BrW* 245. [2] Quoted *Inselschiff*, xii. 2 (Spring 1931), 138.

[3] Letter of 7 Feb. 1931 (Freud *Br* 398–9).

in Berlin (where, disregarding Stefan's warnings, he had set up his own publishing firm), he had written in July:

> Lack of inner self-confidence does not give me the hardness to defend myself as I should, there remains only flight, and up to now family difficulties have *never* made it possible for me, for the last twelve years, to stay away for more than three weeks at a time. . . . What you call 'success' I feel . . . as merely a burden. . . . I seem to myself like a hunter who is actually a vegetarian and can take no pleasure in the game he must shoot.[1]

This inner weakness, the inability to say no or to disappoint his friends (he had the greatest difficulty in screwing up his courage for the white lie to Barbara Ring) fought constantly with his urge to be free and uninvolved.

Often the result was only greater unhappiness. While he was in Hamburg the unfortunate Friderike was bombarded with letters from Henri Guilbeaux, their revolutionary friend from the war-time days in Switzerland, now in Berlin, who wanted advances of money to enable him to put on plays by Zweig and Rolland; unknown to her Stefan had in fact already sent him a total of 600 marks, but had, she thought, made some vague promises to Guilbeaux which he clearly was not going to keep. 'For God's sake', she wrote, 'be more reserved. You only irritate people with such kindnesses, which then are a constant source for you of a bad conscience. . . . Rolland is a wonderful example, but he seems to lay on your shoulders moral burdens which you can bear only if you space them out more.'[2]

So often now, for the 'apostle of friendship', did the warm glow of giving turn to ashes. 'I have a good conscience,' he had written to Rolland in the Guilbeaux connection, 'I have given more than 10,000 marks during the last year to friends in distress, the Jewish law requires only 10%.'[3] The Russian Vladimir Lidin had been to see him in Hamburg—a tragic figure, with his wife going blind and the German doctors unable to help, yet, coming from the prison-house of the Soviet Union, unbelievably grateful to be

[1] Letter of 7 July 1930 (Sch).

[2] *BrW* 242–4; letter to Rolland, 9 July 1930 (Dum 132).

[3] Letter to Rolland, 9 July 1930 (Dum 132).

in the Western paradise of freedom; and this was a reminder for Zweig—alas, temporary—of what true freedom he was himself enjoying. He was glad to help Lidin with a loan of 1,000 marks, just as he had been ready to keep Rieger (in the agonies of an unhappy love-affair and wanting to dash off to bury himself in Tunis) employed on research for him in Paris and proof-reading in Vienna.[1] Yet these personal involvements, piled on top of those of his own affairs, which seemed increasingly pointless and unproductive, made him seek refuge ever more often in flight.

Returning from Hamburg, he took Friderike off with him for a few days in Zell am See, and six weeks later was in Germany again for lectures in Frankfurt. A day was spent in Kassel in the company of two admirers, young German girls—a relaxation from intensive work that he always enjoyed. They joked and laughed together, and he took pleasure in showing them the treasures of Rembrandt and Frans Hals in Kassel. Over Christmas (avoiding this festivity was always a special joy) he stayed on in Frankfurt, 'to sleep in an unknown German hotel and, for once, in peace . . . to read a book'. Trying now to concentrate on *Marie Antoinette*, for which Rieger had assembled a good deal of material and prepared a chronological table, he set off with Friderike in the New Year, first to Paris for further research and then to the Balearics; but, driven away by the crowds and the frantic noise of building operations in Majorca, settled for nearly two months in Cap d'Antibes, where he persuaded Joseph Roth to join them. The company proved productive, and both he and Roth worked well, on *Marie Antoinette* and the *Radetzkymarsch* respectively. They visited cheap *bistros* instead of fashionable cafés, and he succeeded in getting Roth to eat more and drink less. It was a rare concatenation of work, friendship, and peace.[2]

[1] *BrW* 243–4; letter from Lidin, 13 Oct. 1930 (ZE); letter from Gregor, 19 Feb. 1930 (ZE); letter from Rieger, 14 Oct. 1930 (ZE).

[2] *BrW* 244; information from Helene Freifrau von Ledebur; letter to Fleischer, 29 Dec. 1930 (Sch); Fr 319–22; *BrW* 191, footnote to letter of 4 Nov. 1925; Fr[2] 132–4; Friderike Zweig, 'Reise mit Marie Antoinette und gelungene Flucht' (unpublished memoir).

2

> *'Equally tragedy develops when a mediocre or weakly nature is plunged into a monstrous destiny, into personal responsibilities which oppress and crush it; and this form of the tragic seems to me the more humanly stirring.'*
>
> Zweig, *Marie Antoinette*

These were years in which—again perhaps a premonition of what was to come—he felt more strongly in himself his Jewish inheritance.

> Although I do not come from a rigorously Jewish family [he said in an interview with David Ewen in 1931] (my mother and father were Jewish only through accident of birth), I have been vitally interested in Jewish problems all my life, vitally aware of the Jewish blood that is in me ever since I have been conscious of it. . . . There was another influence in my life that made me a Jew in heart and soul, as well as through birth . . . Theodor Herzl. He showed me the greatness of our race. From that friendship really stems my immense interest in Jewish matters.[1]

There is, of course, some exaggeration here; nevertheless, the role of the Jewish people in European culture had always been a theme of importance to him, witness the entire chapter of his *Rolland* devoted to this. 'The Jews have obeyed their sacred mission,' Jean Christophe had said, 'which is to remain the foreigners among the other peoples, the people which weaves, from one end of the earth to the other, the web of human unity'; and Olivier: 'they carry at random the pollen of thought'.

In 1927 the *Neue Rundschau* had published his stately legend 'Rahel rechtet mit Gott'; two years later had appeared his memoir of Herzl. Now too, through his friendship with Schalom Asch, who visited Kapuzinerberg for the first time in the summer of 1929, he became aware that there was a Yiddish literature which must be taken seriously, in a language that was not merely a jargon corrupted from German,[2] and he wrote a warm 'Geburtstagsgruß an Schalom Asch' for the Berlin *Literarische Welt* in 1930.

[1] Leftwich, 91. [2] Ibid. 96.

He was cautious, as might be expected, in responding to the frequent requests which reached him from Jewish organizations or journals to take as it were a public stand on his Jewishness. (For the *Zeitung des Centralvereins deutscher Staatsbürger jüdischen Glaubens*, however, he wrote an article in 1932 on Ernst Lissauer's persecution by the Nazis—'the man who was first outlawed because he was too German was cast out a second time because he was not German enough').[1] His apparent aloofness was to earn him criticism from the more zealous in the years to come, despite his occasional contributions to Jewish papers in more general terms, like the one recorded by Joseph Leftwich in 1929: 'Ever since the giving of the Decalogue the Jewish people has assumed service in the vanguard of humanity. Naturally, such an exposed position entails great danger, but this danger is an integral part of our task, because it is only in spiritual struggle that the individual becomes really alive and the community persists.'[2] The intense nationalism of the Zionist movement never appealed to him, but there is evidence that in 1932 he toyed with the idea of including Jerusalem in a visit to the Middle East.[3] A few years later, when it became necessary to disperse some of his papers, he found a home for the letters from those already dead (Rathenau, Verhaeren, Rilke, Hofmannsthal) with the library of the Hebrew University in Jerusalem.[4]

Germany in 1930 saw the beginnings of the rise of the National-Socialists. In the Reichstag elections on 14 September they gained the huge total of 6,409,000 votes, and with 107 seats were the second largest party (as compared with their 12 seats in 1928). At the time Zweig seems to have missed the significance of this, and he did not immediately link his darker forebodings with it.

> Many made a point [wrote Klaus Mann of this time] of remaining 'objective', 'understanding' and 'just' towards the deadly enemy. Stefan Zweig was one of this type. I liked him, admired him as a writer and friend, and was grateful for the encouraging sympathy he brought towards my work. . . . But it is possible to err dangerously from a

[1] Quoted, Leftwich, 82. [2] Ibid. 92.

[3] Letters from Rieger, 10 Feb. 1932, and Latzko, 27 July 1932 (ZE).

[4] Letter to Kesten, 12 June 1939 (*Exil* 103).

desire for conciliation and a love of justice, as Zweig did when he strove to interpret the catastrophe of the September elections as a 'laudable revolt of youth'.

In an article entitled 'Revolte gegen die Langsamkeit', in fact, Zweig had gone so far as to describe the election result as just such a revolt, 'perhaps not clever, but in its inmost being natural and entirely to be approved, against the dilatoriness and indecisiveness of "high" politics . . . the tempo of a new generation revolts against that of the past'. Mann was quick to publish a reply, in an article 'Jugend und Radikalismus':

> If anyone has the right to address himself to 'youth' in general, it is you, honoured Stefan Zweig. . . . You deplore the snail's pace of Geneva . . . but how can one feel sympathy for a radicalism that is trying to nullify the little that the older generation is bringing to fruition there? . . . Geneva will perhaps not bring us peace: but the others will bring us certain catastrophe. . . . With psychology one can understand everything, even rubber truncheons. But I am determined not to use such a psychology; [and he forecast the shame he would feel to have been one of a generation] whose whole drive to activity, whose radicalism, could have reversed itself in so horrifying a way and turned to a negative.[1]

The turn had not escaped the Russians, however. In December Zweig received a letter from Konstantin Fedin (a ploy behind which, with the knowledge of our day, we may reasonably assume the hand of the MVD) expressing the suspicions in Moscow that a 'new imperialist war' was being plotted against the U.S.S.R. He said he had written an open letter to Zweig in the Moscow *Literary Gazette* on the subject, and asked him to send a reply, which would be 'of great significance to his readers in Russia'. Zweig evidently complied, though no copy is extant in the West of the terms of his article, for in March 1931 Fedin thanked him for his 'open letter', which he had translated for the *Gazette* together with one from Rolland.[2]

Zweig's political ideas were generally immature and ill thought-out, and where he appeared to possess political insight this was

[1] *Wendepunkt* 249; *Suche* 114–18.

[2] Letters from Konstantin Fedin, 13 Dec. 1930 and 1 Mar. 1931 (ZE).

often more from instinct than from clear or logical perception. In these early stages of the Nazi rise, even his instinct seemed at first to have abandoned him. Rolland was writing contemptuously—of course from the extreme left-wing point of view—of 'the sinister buffooneries of the League of Nations', referring to Briand as 'an old clown'; and Zweig in his reactions seemed equally extreme, either to left or right, in his condemnation of the League as a nest of intrigue, the last refuge of secret diplomacy playing with the destiny of the peoples, 'ruining our European movement'.[1] In the summer of 1931 he wrote to Kippenberg:

> I cannot share the general optimism over the Hoover operation. Either the customs barriers within Europe are removed in the *immediate* future, or Europe is finished. Against two such gigantic monolithic organisations as America and Russia, a divided, unorganised Europe cannot compete economically: what crimes against all the nations have the miserable League of Nations, internecine politics and the idiotic Peace Treaty committed! When will trust, the only fertilizer of achievement, be once again in all our minds?[2]

As in 1914, however, he was not slow to realize the actual trend of events. In retreat during the summer of 1931 at Tummersbach, near Zell am See, his first card to Friderike described his satisfaction with the hotel, then continued (in French!) 'only rather more Nat. Soc. among the people than is agreeable—young people *sympathique* and polite enough, it is true, but wearing their cross—which shows how this movement has expanded among the solid middle classes'. But this was swiftly followed by a letter in which he described the visitors as 'ghastly people, sub-Germans . . . the swastika nonsense has seized hold of the middle class, with whom everything—socialism, religiosity, education—now becomes a caricature: these people who would be tolerable only if they were modest, are being harnessed into a stupid ruling class, or would-be ruling class. Still, it is interesting to see at close quarters.'[3]

For a short time the dynamic character of the Hitlerite movement clearly impressed him: he thought it a transient phenomenon

[1] Letter from Rolland, 5 Oct. 1930, and letter to Rolland, 8 June 1931 (Dum 175). [2] Letter of 7 July 1931 (Sch). [3] *BrW* 247.

which might even be desirable if it restored to Germany her taste for liberty. This feeling was strengthened in him when he considered the apparently sterile materialism of France, whose people, 'crouching over their treasure', he compared to Fafner: 'rather the stupid frenzy of the Hitlerites (which seduces the best idealists) than this great snoring of Fafner', against whom he saw embattled Siegfried in the shape of Germany. In Paris over Christmas and in January 1932, where he was assembling his material for *Marie Antoinette*, he 'descended into Hell', as he put it to Rolland, to the vaults of the Bank of France, so that he would thus have seen 'the two poles of our world, the Red Flag on the Kremlin and the Bank of France'.[1] But it was not long before his eyes were opened, and he was by no means the relatively easy prey to the seduction of the 'new Germany' that his friends Anton and Katharina Kippenberg proved to be ('people who although they collect Goethe and . . . are virtually citizens of the world', as Walter Bauer wrote bitterly in 1932, 'nevertheless seem to have fallen victims to chaos in the shape of the Third Reich and Hitler'.[2])

Now, as later, he was not to be drawn into anything approaching a public declaration, or indeed any form of public involvement. In 1931 there had been Nazi-inspired attacks on Moissi. The actor was writing a novel in which childbirth figured, and it was arranged through Suse, then working in a hospital, that he should attend a delivery as an observer. His wife sent a layette afterwards as a present for the mother: but as the latter was unmarried, the story when it leaked made a choice morsel for the anti-Semitic press. Zweig, reading the endless to and fro on the affair in the Austrian papers, congratulated himself on his prudence in guarding his own private life so jealously.[3] In March 1932 Ernst Fischer (another young writer who had received both encouragement and financial help from Zweig) pleaded in vain for an article from his pen against Fascism, 'to throw into the balance against all these

[1] Dum 177–8; see his essay 'Besuch bei den Milliarden', 1932 (reprinted in *Begegnungen*, 1937).

[2] Letter to Stefan Zweig, 17 June 1932 (ZE).

[3] Statement to the author by Friderike Zweig; *BrW* 248.

Werfels who luxuriate in the smell of Fascism and in these days can think of nothing better to do than preach religiosity, turning inward or whatever they call their muck'.[1] On the contrary, Zweig felt that the duty of a writer in such times was to publish only 'something that could bring inward hope, something inspiring and satisfying', and thought that in concentrating on an historical work like *Marie Antoinette* he was following that duty. In Tummersbach he had been working on what was to be his first novel, the *Postfräuleingeschichte*; but, partly from impatience; partly from the feeling that, as he said to Adalbert Muhr, he lacked the necessary 'artistic and human maturity' for a novel; mainly, however, because he thought that the historical rather than the epic was the right work for the time, he abandoned it in favour of *Marie Antoinette*.[2]

In reality this was self-deception, and we may search in vain for any sort of message for the times, however indirect, in a work which, paradoxically, was to be one of his most popular. The considerable research which the diligent Rieger had done, in particular among the heroine's unpublished letters in the Vienna *Staatsarchiv*, coupled with the recent acquisition for his collection of one of her minister's letters, had sharpened his interest in her story.[3] To write it was none the less an escape, and there is no comparison with the *Erasmus* of two years later. Critics were not lacking to complain of its escapism, but they had little effect on its success, which was literally world-wide (by the end of 1932, just after its publication, the *Inselschiff* recorded translations in progress in no fewer than fourteen countries, and the English version was selected the following February by the Book of the Month Club in the U.S.A.).[4] The story was brilliantly and

[1] Letter to Stefan Zweig, 15 Mar. 1932 (ZE).

[2] Letter to Ebermayer, 5 Feb. 1932 (*BdFr* 51); Adalbert Muhr, *Sp* 58; Willi Fehse, *Sp* 65; *BrW* 234; letter to Kippenberg, 7 July 1931 (Sch); letter to Fleischer, 6 Oct. 1931 (Sch).

The *Postfräuleingeschichte* was never completed, but eight years later, in July 1940, he collaborated with Berthold Viertel on a film-script adaptation of the story under the title *Das gestohlene Jahr*, eventually made by Ring-Film (Wien) and Kammerspielfilm (Hamburg) in 1950.

[3] *BrW* 249; Fr[2] 97.

[4] *Inselschiff*, xiv. 1 (Christmas 1932), 64; letter from B.W. Huebsch, 3 Feb. 1933 (ZE).

dramatically told: a well-known actor and film producer told Friderike that, reading the prison and trial scenes, he found himself hoping against hope that the unhappy queen might still be saved.[1] Yet there was a remarkably thorough background of research, as Albert Schweitzer (whom Zweig greatly admired as a humanist) noted: 'as an historian I took pleasure in the so solid, independent study of the sources which one detects behind your presentation, as a reader in your so simple and lively narration'.[2]

Rieger for some reason had expressly asked Stefan not to acknowledge his assistance with the book, and even in *Die Welt von Gestern* he does not get a mention when Zweig discusses his distillation of the basic research: 'I literally examined every bill to establish her personal expenses, studied every contemporary newspaper and pamphlet, ploughed through all the trial documents to the last line. But in the printed book there is no trace of this to be found . . . [it is] my ambition always to know more than appears on the surface.'[3] The resulting 640 pages, he said to Lissauer, were what was left from almost twice as many in the original draft. Both Felix Braun and Fleischer, however, found his style over-intense and repetitive still ('when one has once learned of the unhappy development of her marriage, why stress it again and again?' wrote Braun); and to Benno Geiger his emphasis on matters sexual was distasteful.[4]

To Hans Deissinger, who had sent him a copy of his book of verse, *Erde, wir lassen dich nicht!* at the end of 1932, he wrote: 'Remarkable, that there are still people who nourish in themselves this inner music! It is not granted to me.'[5] In fact the closing months of 1931 had afforded him an opportunity for such an escape into the world of pure art, indeed of music. Since the death of Hofmannsthal, Richard Strauss had searched in vain for a worthy successor as his librettist, and in October 1931 he asked, through Kippenberg, whether Zweig had any possible works for

[1] Fr 223–4. [2] Letter, undated (? end 1932) (ZE).

[3] Letter from Rieger, 7 Sept. 1932 (ZE); *WvG* 293.

[4] Letter to Lissauer, 25 Oct. 1932 (StB); letters from Braun and Fleischer, 10 Nov. 1932 (ZE); Geiger 426–7.

[5] Letter to Deissinger, 12 Dec. 1932 (*Blätter der Internationalen Stefan-Zweig-Gesellschaft*, 13/14 (Apr. 1962), 2).

him. With some diffidence Zweig sent him a couple of suggestions, for a *Tanzpantomime* and a 'gay, joyous, and lively *Spieloper*'; Strauss for his part suggested a theme not so far to be found in his works, that of 'the woman as rogue, or the *grande dame* as spy'. When they met in Munich towards the end of November they agreed on Zweig's second suggestion of an operatic comedy, for which he proposed to adapt Ben Jonson's *Silent Woman*: and in June 1932, even before *Marie Antoinette* had been finally completed, he sent Strauss a first draft of *Sir Morosus*, as it was provisionally entitled.

The composer found it delightful, 'the born comic opera, a comic idea worthy to be set alongside the best of the genre, more suited to music than either *Figaro* or the *Barber of Seville*'; and he was impatient for his new librettist to get on with it as soon as possible. His enthusiasm infected Zweig, and he was able to send him the text of the first act, completed during a short stay at Gardone, only two months after *Marie Antoinette* had gone to press. Working on *Die schweigsame Frau*, the title they had now decided on, had not seemed like work but a real pleasure, he told Strauss, who rejoiced: 'Bravi, bravi, ganz ausgezeichnet', and expressed his deep thanks to Kippenberg for the 'priceless service' in leading him to Zweig. 'I had not dared to hope that after the departure of my unforgettable Hugo I would ever again find a true poet who can discover and form such a good libretto.' Zweig's unclouded pleasure in the work is evident from his letters to Strauss.[1] It was a strange twist that he should now be filling the shoes of the poet who had treated him with such indifference and jealousy (in addition to the new libretto he also put the finishing touches to Hofmannsthal's *Arabella*).[2] He could not, then, foresee the difficulties the opera was to experience under the heavy hand of the Third Reich, or feel, as Friderike did later, that Hofmannsthal's posthumous blessing by no means lay on this collaboration with Strauss. One may wonder, however, whether some inkling of what lay in store for *Die schweigsame Frau* did not reach him from Felix Braun's letter describing a remarkable dream

[1] *Str* 7–31, 155–6; *BrW* 250; *IAusst* 255; Grasberger 340.
[2] Zohn and Barricelli, *Juilliard Review*, iii. 2 (1956), 7.

he had had on Christmas Eve 1932: 'we spoke of Hofmannsthal and were both in despair over his death . . . you uttered the strange words: "This death is a failure for us all." '[1]

3

'Was it always to continue thus, to sixty, seventy, along this straight, smooth path?'

Die Welt von Gestern

The approach of his fiftieth birthday in November 1931 had sharpened once again his sense of a crisis in his life, that 'typical crisis of the fifties . . . in which one feels one has lived one's life wrongly', as he put it to the actor Ewald Balser after seeing his *Faust* at Salzburg.[2] His fame, financial success, the admiration of his friends and public, had never been greater: but they seemed only a burden, and worthless in the face of the intense dissatisfaction he felt with himself and his work. A few days before his birthday he wrote to Fleischer (who had evidently, embittered by the struggle he was having in Berlin to keep his head above water, let slip some words of envy):

> My life is actually very peculiar, hardly comparable with that of other writers, and on the whole, I may say, has not been egotistic. Then the secret burdens, many cares with the family in Vienna, the difficulties at home, where I feel I am building and collecting only into emptiness—no, I have the *right* sometimes to be tired, sometimes to say no, once or twice in the month, and then this hits everyone who comes on that black day. I have had no material cares, certainly, but I have taken the cares of dozens on myself. I could have lived quite free for my work, but have taken service on myself—no, Victor, it was not and is not as light and easy as you think, then too the circumstance that I look on my work with mistrustful clairvoyance, take no pleasure in 'success' which as you have seen I have been side-stepping for years. . . . I fear nothing, neither failure nor being forgotten nor death—all I fear is being ill, growing old or growing bitter. . . .

He had spoken in similar vein to Lidin earlier in the year, expressing

[1] Letter from Felix Braun, 25 Dec. 1932 (ZE).

[2] Letter of 30 Aug. 1933 (*Ausst* 72).

his fear of old age and the fading of his strength. Even at forty-one, when Friderike's birthday wishes reached him a few days early (perhaps she remembered his deception that time at Lübeck), he had reacted half in jest, half in earnest: 'You want to see me older', and added in the margin of the letter 'Still two days to go.'[1]

The fiftieth birthday, traditionally a landmark of special note in the German lands, and for men of letters the occasion of a flood of celebratory articles (how many had he not himself written on such occasions, the latest for Emil Ludwig that very year),[2] was clearly going to be an inordinate trial for him in such a mood: and his one thought, as so often in his life, was to get away. From Zuckmayer, living in nearby Henndorf and now a close friend, he asked a 'favour of friendship'—to go with him to Munich, where he could avoid all the congratulations and celebrations, and they could dine alone on the day at Schwarz's, a small Jewish restaurant known only to a few connoisseurs, where blue carp, goose, and all the trimmings were prepared in a perfection to be found nowhere else. The waiters knew him, but maintained a perfect discretion. Over the schnaps, the necessary end to such a meal, he suddenly remarked to Zuckmayer: 'Actually I feel I have had enough of life. The only direction the future can hold is down.' Overnighting at the Hotel Leinfelder, he wrote to Ebermayer: 'Fleeing my birthday, I stick my head under the blanket in order not to view the world through fifty-year-old eyes.'[3]

His secret wish, as he described it in *Die Welt von Gestern*, was that something would happen, there would be some outside pressure that would tear him away from all this security and comfort and compel him, 'not just to continue, but to begin anew'.[4] He knew that of himself he could not find the courage for such a complete break, to launch out as Gauguin had done on a completely new track (and when the outside pressures indeed came,

[1] Letter to Fleischer, 22 Nov. 1931 (Sch); Lidin, op. cit.; letter to Friderike Zweig, 24 Nov. 1922. Cf. also *BrW* 149–50.

[2] Stefan Zweig, 'Emil Ludwig zum 50. Geburtstag', *NFP*, 25 Jan. 1931 (Kl 1201); 'Emil Ludwig at Fifty', *Living Age*, Boston (Apr. 1931) (Kl 1200).

[3] Zuckmayer, 52–3; *BdFr* 50.

[4] *WvG* 325.

a few years later, it seemed too late). For the moment, nothing happened, and of course escape was not possible. When he returned to Kapuzinerberg the flood of congratulations had still to be faced, and none of those who received the expected smooth replies realized how deep had been his depression.

The inevitable telegram from the Kippenbergs he had received before leaving for Munich: 'we greet the honoured author whom the Insel-Verlag has counted among its own for 25 years . . . and we greet you, dear Stefan Zweig, most heartily with Goethe's words: *und so fortan!*' From the hotel he had replied, with words expressing something of his true feelings on reaching the 'ominous figure' of fifty. On the credit side were 'a gain in humanity, the possession of friendship, human trust—and in all these I find you both on the first page. May it remain so, unchanged, and may there be preserved, through the dark days of responsibility, what was begun in brighter and younger times.'[1] Rieger had prepared a bibliography of his works to date for special publication by the Insel, and one of the most touching letters he received was from him: 'I speak nothing but the most elemental truth when I say that without you I would today hardly have it in me to believe in anything in the world.'[2] A notable tribute appeared in the *Inselschiff* from Joseph Gregor:

> if I call your friendships those of a collector, your essays encyclopaedic, your collection that of a poet, then I must lend to your work all these qualities. . . . Meanwhile your building rises. . . . My admiration is . . . that you have had the power to construct a world in the midst of the worst of all possible worlds, . . . that you, who might have led a carefree life far from the cares that gnaw at our everyday existence, have gladly sacrificed this material fortune for the essential, for work. The fearful tragedy of the present will develop further. But a complete European figure is there in you, without need of Europe, in your gifts, your purpose, your influence, your connections, your successes.

[1] Telegram from the Kippenbergs, 28 Nov. 1931 (Arens[2] 132); letter to Kippenberg, same date (Sch).

[2] Letter from Rieger, 26 Nov. 1931 (ZE); *Bibliographie der Werke von Stefan Zweig, dem Dichter zum fünfzigsten Geburtstag dargebracht vom Insel-Verlag, 28 November 1931*, zusammengestellt von Fritz Adolf Hünich und Erwin Rieger, 500 Exx.

He knew Zweig would not be celebrating this day, but added: 'do not let yourself be overcome by this tragedy! . . . Scarcely a thing will be altered, in the quiet, inward work, in the new epoch into which you enter today.'[1]

Thanking Servaes for his good wishes, Zweig recalled that it was nearly thirty years since 'I first came up to the *NFP* office to hand in a manuscript to an editor, and instead found for myself a true friend to take with me into life. Thanks for that and for everything which I learned from you'—characteristically adding that he might ask his friend Friedenthal, then literary editor with Knaur, to try to get that house to publish Servaes's Goethe novel.[2] (We may note that he was also helping Felix Braun at this time, getting the Insel to publish his *Tantalos* and canvassing support for the award of the Bauernfeld Prize to Braun.) 'I have survived!' he wrote to Fleischer on 30 November, 'thanks for condolences and congratulations!'[3]

Perhaps most worrying at this time was the dark feeling that from every side there threatened encroachments on his personal liberty and freedom of action. His income was very largely dependent on sources outside Austria—the family business in Czechoslovakia, and, of course, his royalties, chiefly from Germany; and although after the Creditanstalt failure in Vienna in May and the subsequent financial restrictions in Germany he had been able to make adequate arrangements with Kippenberg for the best use of his mark income (only just within the law, he wrote in December: *salvavi animam meam*),[4] the uneasy feeling that restrictions

[1] *Inselschiff*, xiii. 1 (Christmas 1931), 7–10. The issue had a frontispiece photograph of Zweig, by Otto Skall; four poems of his ('Neue Fülle', 'Hymnus an die Reise', 'Lied des Einsiedels', and 'Der Bildner'); the bibliography (17–30), with less detail of the translations of his works; and a tribute from the Verlag (63), describing their fruitful association since the publication of *Die frühen Kränze* twenty-five years earlier: 'Stefan Zweigs lebendiger, von den grossen Menschen und Zeiten der Vergangenheit erfüllter und zugleich der Gegenwart zugewandter Geist hat uns aus tiefer Übereinstimmung mit unserem Wollen eine Fülle von Anregungen geschenkt.' It also announced the *Ausgewählte Gedichte* (Insel-Bücherei Nr. 422).

[2] Letter to Servaes, 30 Nov. 1931 (StB).

[3] Letters from Felix Braun, end 1931 (ZE); letter to Fleischer, 30 Nov. 1931 (Sch).

[4] Letter to Kippenberg, 9 Dec. 1931 (Sch).

over which he had no control were closing in on him was a contributory factor in his depression.

By the end of the year he was in Paris. His unease had communicated itself to Friderike, who in her New Year's greeting to him wished for him as good a 1932

as is possible with the influence the surrounding atmosphere has on you. I would myself so love to be able to give you peace, but I am not as thoughtful as I was, for I cannot any longer find my own equilibrium in sitting still. The house is no longer sufficiently home for me: I have little to say in it, I have no right of ownership, it is too big for me, too broad a cloak over a soul that often shivers. That I set my mind to make it easier for you and to reconcile my duties, you know, and this I promise.[1]

She too had to get away and try to find relief in work. As Suse was still in Switzerland, she spent part of January there, calling on Rolland (whose pretty new secretary, a Franco-Russian, charmed her—an omen for her own future that she perhaps fortunately overlooked), and starting her preliminary studies for the biography of Pasteur that Rolland wanted her to write.

I think much on Rolland [she wrote from Les Rasses, near Sainte-Croix in the Jura] and the changed atmosphere [in Geneva] . . . how true, and yet false, is his concept of the world. . . . A pity that you will not come here for a few days, I mean to him and to Geneva. It is in many ways once again the 'Heart of Europe', admittedly no healthy one, but one that is trying with more or less honesty to cure itself before it is given up for lost. If only you were prepared to buy a small house here, on the bank of the beautiful lake where flowers bloom in January. There are bad times coming. In nightmares I have already seen Hitler bombs falling on our house. Who would ever have thought that one would include the re-election of Hindenburg in one's prayers! And there is no time to be lost in taking decisions.[2]

For all his premonitions, she seemed to see more clearly than he what was to come. How different their lives might have been had he followed now her urging to 'take decisions'; but his tendency to evade made him put them off, and, though not too late, they were when finally seized too often in surprising and

[1] *BrW* 250. [2] *BrW* 252–5.

tragically wrong directions. In Paris now his own mood had once more changed, and he was 'as happy as a carp in fresh water'. There were more invitations than he could cope with, a radio talk, books to be signed, autograph auctions to be attended, and a stream of friends—Schalom Asch, the Masereels, Julien Cain, the Luchaires, Benaroya 'my Bulgarian biographer', Duhamel, Valéry, Jean-Richard Bloch (for whose book in its German version, *Vom Sinn unseres Jahrhunderts*, he was writing a Foreword), Roger Martin du Gard (whose *Thibault*—'enfant légitime de Jean Christophe . . ., admirable hymne à l'homme libre'—had so enchanted him in 1931). But he complained that his own work suffered: 'I would take delight in staying for two months, but I cannot work without a secretary, it is the old *Misere*. If only I had someone with me to whom I could dictate . . . I should have done twice as much with half the expenditure of effort and not had this continual nervous wish to get home.'

This somewhat peevish outburst prompted a sharp but just reply from Friderike:

the reproach that you have done too little work cannot be laid at my door. More, and more successful, books could hardly have come from your pen. You have grown in your books from year to year. The human being in you has perhaps from the routine become more sparing, but he will be restored to life if you can once more lose your preoccupation with petty details. You have not spared the worker in you. Since you have been with me, my dear, your work has *grown* in an unbroken chain; and even if I am not a stenographer I have given you in truth all the undisturbed surroundings an artist needs. This does not come by itself. Do not under-estimate it, by wanting to make a stenographer out of me, least of all now when my grey hairs are appearing. Embraces from your

Ex-Mumu.[1]

[1] *BrW* 255–6; letter to Rolland, 20 Mar. 1931 (Dum 325).

4

It passes;
And after, was all one.
The word fell sleeping, when that world awoke.
Karl Kraus

In May 1932 Zweig was invited to give a lecture in Florence, and the week he spent there was one of the most enjoyable of his life. At the frontier the customs did not even look at his luggage: 'I must have a face that inspires confidence.' His Italian hosts were respectfully attentive to his every want; he had a luxury room at the Excelsior, with a spacious balcony, and time to be alone, wander through the Uffizi, see his friends Enrico Rocca and Lavinia Mazzuchetti (his translator), sniff the reseda-laden air, and eat wild strawberries. The lecture, which he gave in Italian in the Palazzo Vecchio, was 'Der europäische Gedanke in seiner historischen Entwicklung', a theme close to his heart, and was one of his best. 'It was astounding', he wrote to Friderike, expressing his regret that she had not been there, and describing the 'heavenly hall of the Signoria', filled to bursting with over a thousand in the audience, all Italians. 'What wonderful women—grand événement artistique, I had to sign about 200 books, refuse invitations from the Podestà and every conceivable Marchesa and Principessa . . . the whole thing had an incredible cachet which I think could not be surpassed anywhere in the world . . . along with Moscow's Opera the most impressive experience of my ageing existence.' On his return he found an even greater honour awaiting him: an invitation, signed by Marconi, to lecture to the European 'Volta' Congress of the Moral and Historical Science class of the Reale Accademia in Rome that November. His work on *Marie Antoinette* and *Die schweigsame Frau* prevented him from attending in person, but his lecture, 'Die moralische Entgiftung Europas', was read in his absence (an adaptation, entitled 'Der geistige Aufbau der neuen Generation', appeared in the *NFP* on 20 November).[1]

[1] *BrW* 257–9. The lectures are reprinted in *Zeit und Welt*, 299–326 (*Der europäische Gedanke*) and *Begegnungen*; Reichner, Wien, 1937, 234–48 (*Die moralische Entgiftung Europas*).

It was, in a way, an Italian year, and these opportunities to speak in Fascist Italy on such European, internationalist, themes may have strengthened in him the thought that here was a possible counterweight to the threat developing in Germany (an idea which appealed to many Austrians in the early thirties). Certainly the naïve faith he still retained in the power of reason to halt the trend to totalitarianism was heartened at the time by his success in a personal intervention with Mussolini himself: a letter addressed directly to the dictator secured the pardon and eventual release of Doctor Germani, a former protégé of the murdered Matteotti, who had been imprisoned for his efforts to get Matteotti's children out of Italy. Zweig was immensely (and justly) proud of this, and wrote jubilantly to Rolland, on 17 January 1933: 'I have had in my view the greatest literary success of my life, greater even than the Nobel Prize, I have saved Dr. Germani.' Rolland congratulated him on the achievement, but was at pains to urge caution and scepticism: 'Certainly, Mussolini is clever! But I beg you, don't be taken in! . . . They want to "get" us . . . they won't get me. I don't at all like the game Emil Ludwig is playing with Mussolini. He affects independence, but goes to extremes of flattery.' But, even after the grievous disappointments of the succeeding years, Zweig still looked back at the end of his life on this letter, the only one he ever addressed to a statesman (indeed, the only time he ever emerged into the open in an active fight for freedom), as the one which brought him the greatest joy and satisfaction. (Friderike's considerable part in the drafting of it went unacknowledged.)[1]

'I can be thoroughly satisfied with this year,' he wrote to Kippenberg just before Christmas, 'it has taught me something (which indeed I might have learnt personally from you)—namely, that even after fifty the sun still stands high in the heavens, and one has perhaps even enough warmth to be able to pass it on to others. I hope you are as satisfied from a business point of view as I most decidedly am in these God-forsaken days!'[2] In November, in the new elections for the Reichstag, the Nazis

[1] *WvG* 313–15; *BrW* 267; letter to Rolland, 17 Jan. 1933 and Rolland's reply (Dum 133–4).

[2] Letter of 23 Dec. 1932 (Sch.)

had suffered losses (though they still remained the largest party, as they had been since July). In a short stay in Arosa in December he had finished the second act of the libretto, and Strauss was more than pleased with the way it was composing.[1] The taste of fame, in Italy and with *Marie Antoinette*, seemed to have lost its former bitterness, and his sense of failure to have passed. Arrangements were in hand for authorized editions of his works in Portuguese translation in Brazil; and he was thinking once again (as he had in 1928) of a visit to South America, to see a part of the continent he thought was spiritually much closer to Europe than was the North. He asked his Spanish translator in Buenos Aires, Alfredo Cahn, for suggestions for a two-month visit to the Argentine and Brazil.[2] Even during January 1933—a fateful month for Europe—he took great pleasure in the completion of the final act of the libretto. Strauss, renewing his gratitude to Kippenberg for the introduction of the poet who had written for him 'the best text created in comic opera since *Figaro*', said that, having now read *Marie Antoinette* and *Die Heilung durch den Geist*, he was ashamed to confess how little he had known of Zweig's work, and thought, when he considered the bubble reputation of Ludwig and the much-advertised 'tedious patrician' Thomas Mann, that Zweig's true value had not yet been appreciated. 'I felt immediately', said Kippenberg in reply, 'that I had arranged a happy marriage, and am delighted to hear it confirmed from both partners.'[3]

With Hitler's appointment as Chancellor at the end of the month, however, the tender plant of Zweig's optimism was withered. Of a sudden all seemed to go wrong: 'a kind of ill-will pervades the world now which is unbearable'. The film rights of *Brennendes Geheimnis* were not being paid for, and a lawsuit loomed; a group of unemployed actors in Berlin had started rehearsals for a completely unauthorized production of *Volpone*,

[1] *Str* 32.

[2] Letter to Koogan, 22 June 1932 (K); letters to Alfredo Cahn, 22 Oct. and 24 Dec. 1932 (Cahn).

[3] Letter to Ebermayer, 9 Jan. 1933 (*BdFr* 52); letter from Strauss to Kippenberg, 24 Jan. 1933 (*IAusst* 256) and Kippenberg's reply, 25 Jan. 1933 (Grasberger 344).

and when he agreed to it, on condition that critics were excluded (for Emil Jannings was then under contract for a production of the play), he was suddenly the object of attack in the German and then the Austrian press. 'One does not mind being the target of muck-slinging for things which are one's own responsibility, but merely because a book has sold 40,000 copies to be the object of such attacks is most upsetting,' he wrote to Ebermayer, 'and as one who has a horror of all publicity it makes me sick.' Telephoning Kippenberg on 3 February, he learned that the bookshops and theatres were deserted in Germany because of the political situation —'a grisly time, and yet perhaps better than those that are coming'.[1]

In Salzburg he had a sort of grandstand view of what was happening to Germany. The fact that from the Kapuzinerberg he could actually see Berchtesgaden became significant for him only later; but at the time there was no mistaking the meaning of the trickle of refugees, or of the Nazi agitators in the guise of 'tourists', who now made their way over the nearby border. Brutal force was now in command, and he knew in his heart that it would be a long time before reason and moderation would prevail. He expected from one day to the next a similar *Umsturz* in Austria. There were many in Vienna, and in Germany itself, who comforted themselves with the thought that this could not last long. Zweig, however, remembered the words of the director of the Wremya publishing house in Leningrad in 1928, when he had asked him why, since he regretted his earlier days of wealth, he had not emigrated immediately after the Revolution: 'who would have thought a thing like a republic of workers' and soldiers' councils would last more than a fortnight?' He saw now the same self-deception. The Reichstag fire on 27 February was for him the final confirmation, exposing Hitlerism for what it really was: the coincidence that the film of *The Burning Secret* was showing at the time throughout Germany, its placards for the Berliners standing in satiric juxtaposition to the event, served only to underline the grim reality.[2]

[1] *BrW* 266; letter to Ebermayer, 9 Feb. 1933 (*Heute* 20).

[2] *WvG* 331, 344. The following year the police confiscated copies of *Brennendes Geheimnis*—not because of the authorship but because a communist

Only two weeks before, at a dinner with Brockhaus and Ebermayer, Kippenberg had expressed the view that Zweig was unlikely to be caused any difficulties by the political changes (when someone mentioned that he was also part-owner of a factory, Kippenberg was jokingly incredulous that he could have yet *another*).[1] Zweig never forgot his astonishment when, just after the Reichstag fire, he suggested to his publisher that it would soon be all over with his books in Germany: 'you have never written a word against Germany or involved yourself in politics', said Kippenberg.[2] But, swallowing the Nazi medicine of 'order', he could not in the end avoid taking with it the purge of anti-Semitism. There began to fall now a silence between the two.

And silence was Zweig's watchword now, to the dismay of those who demanded a public stand, an open declaration of war on the forces of darkness. He put off his planned lecture tour in March in Scandinavia, which had been arranged by the Swedish-Austrian Society (Ginzkey stood in for him), to avoid any 'discussions' whether he had the right to travel abroad and make an appearance as a *rassenfremder* writer ('of foreign race'—a term much used by the Nazis): 'one must these days really strain every nerve not to be drawn . . . into politics and discussions'.[3] In a letter to Rolland in April he said: 'I pass in silence everything we have suffered morally, for even now, faithful to myself, I will not hate a whole country, and I know that the language in which one writes does not permit of separation from a people, even in its madness, or allow one to call down curses on it.'[4] Strauss, who maintained a blithe indifference to political régimes so long as they allowed him to get on with his work, but was understandably worried lest an incautious word from Zweig might affect the future of *Die schweigsame Frau*, was reassured by Kippenberg: 'Zweig has never been one of those who open their mouth in all directions, but he will in future be more reserved than ever and

pamphlet was circulating under its title cover (letter to Roth, undated, *c.* August 1934).

[1] *Heute* 24.

[2] *WvG* 332.

[3] *BrW* 270; *Str* 48; letter to Kurt Frieberger, 27 Mar. 1933 (*Sp* 74).

[4] Letter of 10 Apr. 1933 (Dum 179).

in complete retirement live only for his work.' (They had evidently met at the end of March.)[1]

Though he had refused the Scandinavian invitation, from this extreme reserve, Zweig nevertheless accepted one to Switzerland, to a veritable 'barrage of lectures' in Berne, Zürich, and Geneva, and enjoyed in March ten days of the calm atmosphere there. Already quite a colony of German refugees had formed in Switzerland: he saw Max Herrmann-Neisse, Ernst Toller (whose flat in Berlin had been ransacked by the Nazis), and Wilhelm von Scholz; and heard how the panic of the intellectuals was growing, how each day brought new attacks against Jewish writers. Signing his books by the hundred exhausted his fountain-pen, but he felt that he could not withdraw himself from people who were well disposed: 'there are millions now who are ready to hate and despise on a word of command'. He realized already that the total control of the German press by Goebbels meant that not even a line by him or about him would ever appear there again. Taking a walk from Basle over the French frontier he was touched by the policeman's recognition, 'mais votre nom m'est bien connu'—happily not in the sense these words would have held at the German border.[2]

Attacks on himself continued to unnerve him, and in early April he was particularly worried by one on the German radio by Schaukal. Striving to hold the middle way, he became more and more disheartened by the impossibility of the task. Friends like Gregor tried to cheer him up—'as if so great, splendid and admired a life's work could be even touched by a phrase on the radio!'—and to stress what they thought was the transitory nature of this phase. Joseph Roth, however, writing from Paris, was more alarmist, and urged him to wait quietly: 'do not protest in any form!' Both Gregor and Felix Braun, as also Rieger, suggested that his best plan was to get away from Salzburg for a time. Braun, indeed, came much nearer to Zweig's own feelings, and already in April expressed the thought that he should consider leaving Kapuzinerberg for good. 'It would not be flight, but

[1] Letter from Kippenberg to Strauss, 1 Apr. 1933 (*IAusst* 256).

[2] *BrW* 268–71.

simply the drawing of a natural conclusion and a reasonable action in the face of thanklessness and ill-will. . . . To stay in Salzburg from a sense of duty would have no point. If you do not return to Vienna, there are places enough in Europe which would be proud to be honoured by your presence.' He was not ready to draw this conclusion; but at the end of April spent a short time with Friderike at Cadenabbia preparing the first draft outline of his *Erasmus*.[1]

He had recently read, at Friderike's suggestion, Huizinga's book on this 'first of the Europeans', whose affinity with his own spirit struck him deeply, and whose position, in a time of equally fanatical warring of extremes, had been so like his own. To write his story now seemed the least he could do at such a time—and, himself an Erasmian, *homo pro se*, the most. 'I want to erect a small monument to him,' he wrote to Rolland in April, 'and he who can read will read the history of our times in analogy. No way remains for us to make ourselves heard except to write in symbols or to emigrate.'[2] But his unrest made it hard, his inability to concentrate was more and more disturbing, and a work which in happier days would have been finished in two months now stretched into six, even ten.[3] *En route* to Lake Como he met Walter Bauer (to whom he had advanced the cash to enable him to take a holiday in Italy); at a Bolzano hotel they ran into brownshirts. 'That has conquered', he said gloomily to Bauer, pointing to the jackboots outside the doors in the corridor; 'it will disappear again—but when?'[4]

The public withdrawal in April by the Third Reich of its citizenship from Thomas Mann, now in exile in Lugano, came as a shock more severe to him than to Mann himself (or to Hermann Hesse, who could think it even salutary for the true German spirit once more to be in opposition to official Germany).[5] But it was

[1] Letters from Gregor, 4 Apr. 1933 (ZE), Joseph Roth, 6 Apr. 1933 (Arens[3] 147), and Felix Braun, 6 Apr. 1933 (ZE); Fr 323.

[2] Fr 272; letter to Rolland, 26 Apr. 1933 (Dum 180).

[3] Letter to Ebermayer, 19 June 1933 (*BdFr* 55, *Heute* 114).

[4] Walter Bauer, Arens[1] 138.

[5] Letter from Thomas Mann, 24 Apr. 1933 (TMArch); letter from Hermann Hesse to Mann, 21 Apr. 1933 (*Briefwechsel*, ed. Anni Karlsson, Suhrkamp, Frankfurt am Main, 1968).

the burning of the books in Berlin on 10 May that plunged him into a personal situation more desperate than any that had faced Erasmus: for the world-wide attention this barbaric act attracted threatened to turn him into a hero and martyr, 'which I by no means am'. 'I would gladly have done without this advertisement,' he wrote to Servaes, 'you know I am a man who prizes nothing more than quiet'; there was nothing to be done, he said, but wait, wait, keep silent. Honour though it was to share this total literary annihilation in Germany with such eminent contemporaries as Einstein, the Manns, Werfel, and Freud, the 'martyrdom' was more painful to Zweig than the event itself.[1] And his silence brought him nothing but execration from those who urged action and protest.

To Felix Salten, who wanted him to attend the PEN Congress to be held in Dubrovnik at the end of the month, he expressed the view that German Jews should keep out of such demonstrations (for it was clear that the book-burning would figure prominently on the agenda), and he escaped again to Switzerland in an attempt to evade the necessity of a clear stand one way or the other.[2] When the official invitation came, Friderike was obliged to telegraph weakly: 'My husband away, will not attend', for she did not know what he had arranged with Salten. In the end he had to send a clearer telegram. On the train to Bad Gastein, on his way back, there was a highly awkward meeting with the 'new German' delegation travelling to Dubrovnik. He was polite, especially as Hanns Martin Elster, who had written so appreciatively of his work in 1922, was among their number; but the talk was of the weather.[3] The subsequent reports of disunity at the Congress (which at one point came to blows) sickened him, and he maintained his refusal to be drawn into the protest, as also later to vote for Jacob's resolution to the Austrian PEN Club disapproving their stand at Dubrovnik, and urging stronger protest against the treatment of writers in Germany. Ernst Toller's appearance at the Congress he particularly disliked, for he felt that by speaking Toller had diverted attention from the shameful

1 Letters to Servaes (StB) and Ebermayer (*Heute* 83), 11 May 1933; *WvG* 332–4.

2 Letter from Felix Salten, 13 May 1933 (ZE).

3 *BrW* 271–2.

fact that not a single one of the non-Jewish writers of Germany who were themselves unaffected 'dared to stand openly with us, their old comrades of many years. I find this silence much worse than the attitude of the Government, which after all is only carrying out its Party programme.' He contrasted Furtwängler's public stand for Bruno Walter and music with the cowardly silence of Hauptmann and the others, which could be interpreted only as condoning barbarism.[1]

The influence of his chess partner that summer was hardly salutary. Fuchs, who since the days of the twenties had become a constant companion of Stefan's when he was in Salzburg, and had done regular proof-reading for him, was a functionary of the Austrian Social Democratic Party, which, despite its strength, was becoming increasingly negative in its opposition to the current right-wing trends. His wife, who worked occasionally as a secretary for Zweig, was the daughter of a Social Democrat deputy. Now almost daily in his company, Fuchs's constant bitter condemnation of what he called democracy's betrayal of social ideas served to deepen Zweig's pessimism, and to shake his belief in the ideal of humanity which had so long been for him an article of faith.[2] Strangely enough, however—as though he knew it was the last time he would see it—he was enthusiastic about the Salzburg Festival, with Strauss, Bruno Walter, Wassermann, and many others, whereas in previous years his only reaction had been to complain of the *Rummel*.[3] Even this brief enjoyment, however, was marred by Strauss's apparently self-seeking complaisance towards the new rulers of Germany. One of his young women admirers from Germany was staying for a few days in Bad Reichenhall, but the only possibility for a meeting was on the frontier bridge at Gmain, between the two customs posts, for Nazi regulations now set a 1,000 mark premium on any journey outside the country, and he, of course, was not prepared to enter the Reich. They joked for a while under an

[1] Letters from Jacob, 21 June and 5 July 1933 (ZE); Leftwich 90; letter to Alfredo Cahn, 6 June 1933 (Cahn).

[2] Bauer 77; Fr[2] 156, 166; statement to the author by Friderike Zweig.

[3] Letter to Ebermayer, (? 5) August 1933 (*Heute* 150).

umbrella in the pouring rain on the bridge: but the incident symbolized for him what he had lost.[1]

His situation was agonizing, not least because he felt himself powerless to act. True, he was pressing for the establishment of a unified publishing house by all those (English, Dutch, Italian) who were issuing books now in the German language—apart from anything else, because it was beginning to be clear to him that he must find an alternative to the Insel-Verlag for his own works. But even a tentative effort to get himself in print in the *émigré* world brought nothing but more attacks, this time from the exiles who saw him as a sycophantic collaborator with Nazism, and he quickly withdrew his name from Klaus Mann's *Sammlung*, to which he had promised an extract from *Erasmus*.[2] His somewhat petulant refusal to pay his local taxes in Salzburg—which brought him a lawsuit and a fine of 100,000 Schillings—was a singularly pointless demonstration. He found it possible, now and then, to consider the ominous developments in Europe merely a passing phase, a postponement of the ultimate achievement of a world-state, a 'world-Switzerland'.[3] But inwardly he knew the trouble was more deep-seated.

He lacked, and knew he lacked, the calm resolution of a Thomas Mann; realizing this was a time for decision, he yet could not bring himself to take it. All he knew was that he must get away from Salzburg for the coming winter, perhaps to South America (where he had invitations for lectures) or to Rome. 'At all events I shall shut up the house for the winter,' he wrote to Ebermayer on 10 June, 'unless circumstances compel me to give it up altogether. Much, alas, has changed here, not least inwardly, my joy in developing my home, my collection . . . is completely dead, I am thinking of making my life simpler and thus more mobile, to leave my homeland (though the pressure for this certainly did not come from within).' And later that month, bemoaning his inability to concentrate, 'I need counterweights like music, people,

[1] Information from Helene Freifrau von Ledebur.

[2] Letter to Ludwig, 16 June 1933 (Sch); letters to Lissauer, 20 June and 21 Sept. 1933 (StB); letters from Klaus Mann, 19 May and 15 Sept. 1933 (ZE).

[3] Statement to the author by Friderike Zweig; letter to Robert Faesi during 1933 (Faesi, op. cit. 1307).

and it is Rome or London that attract me most, only not to drift into some corner of émigrés. . . . One must seek in the world a substitute for what one has lost at home (for the German language is my home, indissolubly).'[1] He was not yet thinking of an actual emigration, but his exclusion from the homeland of the language seemed far worse than that, and he could not see how anything productive or lasting could come after this spiritual uprooting.

By September *Erasmus* was still not finished, and he needed two or three months more, somewhere 'where one does not feel politics too near'. Paris was impossible, for he would be overwhelmed with so many friends, and the busy, profitless discussions of the army of refugees there. Where better than London? He remembered his last visit, over a quarter of a century before, and it suddenly seemed as though the coolness and reserve of the English, then so repellent, would now be exactly what he needed. The British Museum could provide every reference likely to be wanted for his work. And, best of all, in England, still outside the European political mêlée, the *émigrés* were less immediately obvious. On 20 October his bags were set down in the lobby of Browns Hotel.[2]

[1] Letters to Ebermayer, 10 June and 22 June 1933 (*BdFr* 54–5).

[2] Letter to Lissauer, 19 Sept. 1933 (StB); *WvG* 345.

VII. London 1933–1940

'Now each man stared straight into the glass eye of history.' Georg Kaiser

'I often seem to myself like a man who spends his nights in the cemetery on the grave of his departed wife.'
Zweig to Paul Zech, September 1936

I

'When I try to think where is the best place for you outside Austria, the answer is England.'
Camill Hoffmann to Zweig

This was to be a temporary stay only, in so far as he had planned these months of uncertainty at all; but it was significant that, instead of remaining in an hotel as he normally did on such journeys, he rented a flat before the first week was out, at 11 Portland Place. The first step into emigration had been taken. The cool equanimity and reserve of the English, which had once so irritated him, he now found a soothing contrast to the nervous agitation, the *ewige Hetze*, of the Continent. It was wonderful to be left to oneself, among civil, disinterested people, in a 'courteous and hateless atmosphere', to be able to work steadily in the 'blessed British Museum, where one does not feel political stupidity and one can still concentrate'. Blessed too the undisturbed pleasures of the English in their 'cats, football and whisky', the contrast of their simplicity with the complications of the Central Europeans. He had once again given up smoking. Now *Erasmus*, which had been such an unconscionable time in the early months of gestation, rapidly reached completion.[1]

In a sense the book was something of an autobiography, a 'veiled self-portrait'.[2] He saw himself in the same predicament as his subject: striving to hold the balance, to be the man of the middle way, the way of humanity, to understand the conflicting parties without losing impartiality, and therefore detested with equal passion by both. 'You describe in it', wrote Thomas Mann, 'to some extent the myth of our existence . . . and the justification of the apparent ambiguity under which we suffer and which has made me, at least, almost as hated by the émigrés as by those "in there".'[3] Zweig described the book to Rolland as a profession of faith, an attack against fanaticism in all its forms, 'that bastard of the mind and of violence'; to Rudolf Kayser as the tragedy of the gentle, weak man in the middle, submitting to the fanatics, 'mirroring something of my own inner destiny'; to Strauss as 'a quiet hymn of praise to the anti-fanatical man, to whom artistic achievement and inner peace is the most important thing on earth . . . my own way of life symbolized'.[4]

Not everything in London appealed to him, for he felt that the *émigrés* there were gravely in error both in their ceaseless attacks on the Third Reich (which lost effect by constant repetition) and in their unremitting attention, in books and articles, to the Jewish problem (which in his view defeated its own end by tending to create something that in many countries did not exist). To his mind, working and writing for effect against Hitlerism demanded a loftier, more subtle method, a form that might penetrate to and be read in Germany itself. He saw *Erasmus* as such an attempt.[5] At the same time he felt it would be impossible for him to publish in Germany; and his plan for the book was first a private printing, to send to his friends, and then editions outside Germany only[6]—indeed, the plan of a 'gentle, weak man in the

[1] Fr 364–5; *WvG* 346–7; letter to Rudolf Kayser, 30 Nov. 1933 (*Sp* 76); letter to Rolland, 14 Feb. 1934 (Dum 184); letter to Roth, undated (? end 1933) (Roth).

[2] *WvG* 347.

[3] Letter of 8 Nov. 1933 (Mann *Br* i. 338).

[4] Letters to Rolland, 18 Dec. 1933 (Dum 203); Kayser, 30 Nov. 1933 (*Sp* 75); and Strauss, 17 May 1934 (*Str* 63).

[5] Letter to Cahn, 30 Dec. 1933 (Cahn).

[6] Letter to Kayser, 14 Dec. 1933 (*Sp* 76).

middle', and small wonder that its effect at the time, apart from the admiration of the converted, was virtually nil in the sense he had intended. Yet the book is one of his finest, both in its expression of his humanism (as significant now as it was then) and in its historical picture of his spiritual ancestor.

The historian may carp at inaccuracies of detail [wrote Wallace K. Ferguson in 1935]; he may complain, and with reason, that the background is out of focus; . . . yet he will be forced to recognise that the face is the face of Erasmus, even though the voice may occasionally seem the voice of another. By some gift of intuition or creative imagination, Stefan Zweig has succeeded in realising for himself and in reproducing for his readers, from a fund of historical information somewhat less than adequate, a very understanding picture of a man whom many more erudite scholars have failed to understand at all.[1]

He was six weeks this time in London. The pressure of his forebodings remained strong, for he recognized only too well the lack in the German of that gift of moderation with which the French and the English were blessed: 'he alternates always between self-contempt and self-glorification, and when this latter becomes practically a state religion, the future must really hold trouble'.[2] He knew in his bones what was coming to Austria and the rest of Europe, yet could not bring himself to burn his boats. Six months earlier, on the very day of the Burning of the Books, he had told Rolland that he had said goodbye to his house, his collection, his books: 'let them take the lot, I don't care. On the contrary, I shall be freer when all this life no longer weighs on my shoulders . . . all that is for quiet years that proceed at a snail's pace—in times like ours one must have one's shoulders free.'[3] Yet now, in London, he had a fearful and crippling sense of insecurity when he thought of Friderike and all that he loved left at Kapuzinerberg. He toyed with the idea of moving permanently to England, but agonized in his indecision.[4] The resolution, albeit temporary, was achieved by chance. In the British

[1] *Journal of Modern History*, vii (1935), 365 ff.

[2] Letter to Cahn, 30 Dec. 1933 (Cahn).

[3] Dum 180–1.

[4] Letters to Cahn, 30 Dec. (Cahn) and Kayser, 30 Nov. 1933 (*Sp* 75).

Museum his passion for manuscripts led him to glance through an account of the execution of Mary Queen of Scots, and with characteristic curiosity he began to delve further into her story: was she guilty of the crimes alleged? The books that he read were so contradictory that he felt impelled, as so often before, to go back to the sources and find out for himself. When he left for Austria again on 1 December he had made up his mind to return to London to write a *Maria Stuart*.[1]

First, however, it had become essential to find a publisher outside Germany. In November a private letter of his to the Insel-Verlag had been published, without explanation and without his knowledge, in the Leipzig *Börsenblatt für den deutschen Buchhandel*: indeed, he first learned of it through an attack in the Vienna press describing him as a 'traitor to the émigés'.[2] That this could happen to one who had been so careful to avoid any kind of public utterance cut him to the quick, and in an access of almost demented fury he determined to break with the Insel. Kippenberg's later personal letter of apology—the incident had occurred while he was away sick—could not move him, and he sent off a reply that must have given him the greatest pain to write, severing for ever their association of twenty-eight years. 'My life is there, but honour is more important', as he said to Joseph Roth. Once the heat of the moment had passed, he realized that such a link was not in fact to be broken overnight. Before leaving London he had felt constrained, in view of the publicity, to issue a statement through the Jewish Telegraphic Agency making it clear that he was severing his connections with Germany; but from Salzburg in December he told Kayser that, despite the desolating thought of the break-up of his life's work, he did not wish to sunder at one brutal stroke the closely interwoven ties of so many

[1] Letter to Kayser, 30 Nov. 1933 (*Sp* 75); *WvG* 347.

[2] The letter appears to be that in issue 240 of the *Börsenblatt*, pp. 787 f.; in it he expressed his surprise that Klaus Mann's *Sammlung* was by no means the purely literary journal Mann had led him to expect, but on the contrary overwhelmingly political (quoted in Matthias Wegner (ed.), *Exil und Literatur: Deutsche Schriftsteller im Ausland, 1933–1945*, Bonn, Athenaeum, 1967). Many *émigrés* felt, like Klaus Mann, that Zweig was falling over backwards 'to avoid offending Goebbels' (letter to Zweig of 15 Sept. 1933).

years—rather he would make a pause, against his better judgement, and see whether the next few months would again subject madness to reason. It was a situation without parallel for him, and he had no idea of the legal position over his rights.[1] But he showed his grasp of the realities it implied by negotiating at once in Vienna for publication of his works there.

He persuaded Herbert Reichner, editor of the *Philobiblon* journal and therefore well known to him, to start his own publishing house; and thereby ensured, at any rate for a time, his survival in the German language. The Reichner Verlag, based in Vienna, was set up early in 1934; on Zweig's insistence, and contrary to the publisher's own inclination, it was incorporated also in Leipzig and Zürich, so that theoretically, and to some extent in practice, its books were available in the Reich itself (a circumstance also not likely to endear Zweig to the *émigrés*). The firm was not, as many thought, owned or directly controlled by Zweig, who had resisted the temptation to provide finance. He was content to leave policy to Reichner, as long as he retained the final say on production and format of his own books; and to facilitate this he secured the appointment of Emil Fuchs as a special assistant to Reichner. For the latter, of course, the venture was an attractive one, with the prospect of publishing all the future works of a very successful author and of reissuing his earlier volumes, which had been such a gold-mine for the Insel; in fact it was only under pressure from Zweig that he could be brought to add other authors, such as Trebitsch, to his list. His business methods, however, were not always to Zweig's liking, and the information provided to the author by Fuchs, as his 'private spy', often produced in the years that followed hard feelings and sometimes acrimony.[2]

All this was arranged in a few short weeks in Vienna before Zweig returned to London in February 1934. But his apparent decisiveness in the business enterprise concealed a restive consciousness that, far from holding the middle way of detachment,

[1] Letters to Kayser, 30 Nov. and 14 Dec. 1933 (*Sp* 76–7), and Roth, undated, end 1933 (Roth).

[2] Statements to the author by Friderike Zweig; Homeyer 83.

he had been forced like Erasmus into a corner from which all exits were equally open to attack. There was a prospect of considerable financial loss over the break with the Insel (he had heard that Fischer in a similar position were demanding 200,000 marks for the surrender of Jakob Wassermann's rights); yet no amount of argument could convince the fierier spirits like Roth, who saw everything in black and white as far as the Nazis were concerned, that it was not money that worried him, but the need for a little time to find a gentlemanly and dignified way out.[1] He realized that Kippenberg himself had not been responsible for the gaffe which had precipitated his decision, and could not bear to hurt his old friend by over-hasty action. The definitive edition of *Erasmus*, now to be published by Reichner, he thought might be preceded by a limited edition dedicated to Kippenberg on the occasion of his birthday, and in February 1934, while still in Vienna, he wrote the Insel chief a very understanding letter:

> tell me quite frankly your views (when you have read the manuscript) —you will see anyway that there is not a single word in the whole book to which objection can be taken. But I understand every reservation one must have today, and would propose two alternative forms of dedication: either outright to you, with your full name and the date (which would be the freest and fairest), or merely 'A gift and sign of friendship, on 22 May, 1934', so that only the initiated know who is concerned, and others, with no name mentioned, will simply pass over it. I leave it entirely to your free choice, I am determined that—as far as I can ensure it—you should suffer no unpleasant surprises from my side. We plan a book here of great beauty, with Holbein initials and woodcuts, so that the bibliophile character of this edition is particularly stressed . . .; there will be no review copies sent to newspapers, only to friends and to those who inquire at *Philobiblon*.[2]

The plan was not realized, but the attacks on him continued for his apparent compromising with the Nazis.

The feeling that he could not win, that whatever action he took would bring him only vilification from either friend or foe, was a reflection of his indecision in his personal affairs. There was a

[1] Letters to Roth, undated, end 1933–early 1934 (Roth).

[2] Letter of 13 Feb. 1934 (Sch).

fundamental conflict within him, still unresolved, between his intuitive knowledge of the fate that would overtake Austria and his reluctance to abandon her completely. The deep force of his personal crisis and his premonition of the future combined to urge him towards a complete break with the life he had hitherto led—indeed, he had had the feeling, as he took the flat in Portland Place, almost of returning to his beginnings in Kochgasse, as unknown in London as he had been then in Vienna, starting afresh. But it was a half measure: Austria was still his home; Friderike, Suse, and Alix still his family; above all, the German language in which he thought and wrote was still preserved for him in Vienna. In reality he was still avoiding the issue.

The half-way house had seemed, in the relative peace of London, for a short while to succeed. Alone there, he had felt uncommonly well, seeing few people, 'but the best—Shaw, Wells, Schalom Asch' (he was long to remember the urbane but deadly cut-and-thrust of a lunch-time duel between the British writers); and it had seemed to him, as he wrote to Ebermayer, that he had overcome this crisis *ad personam*. In December he had received an offer, 'financially quite fantastic', to go to Hollywood for ten weeks (friends told him that the film moguls would go as far as tripling the money offered, so badly did they want him); but he refused it, despite the 'moral effort required to let so much money go down the drain'.[1] His work was going well again, and he had made excellent progress with *Maria Stuart* at the British Museum. It seemed he could have all this and Austria too: to be able, as it were, to commute between this new life and the old. But his visit to Vienna was to jolt him out of this complacency and face him with the necessity, at last, of a clear decision.

It chanced that he was there, from 12 to 16 February 1934, during the days of the *Heimwehr–Schutzbund* conflict and of the Dollfuss Government's attack on the workers' flats in Floridsdorf. Living in the Hotel Regina and going quietly about his business, he in fact saw and heard absolutely nothing of this in person, and was surprised, when he wished to proceed to Salzburg, to

[1] Letter to Ebermayer, 2 Jan. 1934 (*BdFr* 56); *WvG* 357; letter from Ernest Bloch, 5 Jan. 1934, quoting a letter from Mrs. Deborah Lewin, Los Angeles (ZE).

find the resultant strike had stopped all trains. When they were running again, on 17 February, he left for home, with a certain uneasiness, but not yet fully appreciating the significance of what was happening (as was so often the case, to be a few streets away from such events meant that one knew less than the newspaper-readers on the other side of the world).[1] At Kapuzinerberg a pile of correspondence and the *Erasmus* proofs awaited his attention, and he worked very late into the night. On such occasions his manservant knew better than to wake him, unless specifically instructed: but that morning he had to, for the police were at the door. Hurriedly pulling on his dressing-gown, Zweig found himself confronted with perhaps the most fantastic situation of his life: the officials, polite but firm, had orders to search his house for hidden arms of the *Schutzbund*. He was astounded, for he had (as was well known) never entered the political fray, nor published anything that could remotely be described as political; and the veriest idiot of the *Schutzbund* would in any case scarcely have chosen a house on a hill, with only one access, as a secret arms cache. Pale and tense, he could only say: 'Please look for yourselves.'

It was evident from the perfunctory and somewhat embarrassed way in which they did so that they had little faith themselves in the credibility of their mission. Their only find was an old Army revolver in one of his wardrobes: issued to him in 1915, it had, of course, never been used, and, as he demonstrated to them, he had no idea even of how to load or unload it. They duly confiscated it, and in half an hour were gone. But the incident was decisive for Zweig. He began almost at once to pack a few necessaries, resolved to leave immediately, and this time for good. His most sensitive nerve had been touched, that of his personal freedom, and he reacted 'as though against a deliberate insult'. He learned later that the search had been merely *pro forma*: Nazi pressure on the officials of western Austria had increased alarmingly, and it was felt necessary to make a show of impartial firmness in order to try to control them (though the commission set up for the purpose was heavily biased towards the *Heimwehr*,

[1] *WvG* 348–51; *Str* 60.

and headed by the later notorious Seyss-Inquart). At Friderike's prompting the *Landeshauptmann* (the same Rehrl who had had his hand forced over the dispensation for their marriage fourteen years earlier) came to call on Zweig in person on his next visit to Vienna, to explain and seek his indulgence. But now he was determined to take the earliest possible train out of Salzburg, to Paris and London.[1]

In the compartment he found Robert Neumann, also on his way into exile, but for more directly political reasons, and told him with bitterness what had happened. 'The Salzburg police that morning had looked for an allegedly hidden machine-gun under the bed of this out-and-out pacifist, this hater of all weapons. But he prophesied that this non-existent machine-gun would one day begin to shoot, and that was why he had chosen exile.'[2] A woman journalist who sought an interview with him on the train was repulsed—an understandable but unwise act, for the result of this (and possibly of some incautious remarks he made later at Julien Cain's) was an article in the French press attributing to him sentiments of an anti-Dollfuss character. Reported to the Ballhausplatz by the Austrian ambassador, this led to rumours in Vienna that he had 'fled' because of the 'February events', and to a full-scale investigation, the immediate outcome of which was an order to the *NFP* not to accept his material. Rieger, whose help he enlisted, was eventually able to intervene with Hofrat Ludwig, the successor of von Winternitz at the Ballhausplatz, and to satisfy the authorities.[3]

For it was nothing more than the truth that the political developments were not the real reason for his departure. He had in fact been asked by the Austrian Government to collaborate (as

[1] *WvG* 352–3; *BrW* 306; Fr 365–6; Fr[2] 166–7; statement to the author by Friderike Zweig; *Bildb* 103. *Landeshauptmann* Rehrl was well disposed towards Zweig; during the Second World War he was nominated by the opposition movement against Hitler as 'Politischer Beauftragter' in Wehrkreis XVIII (Salzburg) (Peter Hoffmann, *Widerstand, Staatsstreich, Attentat—der Kampf der Opposition gegen Hitler*; Piper, München, 1969, 423).

[2] Neumann, 114–15.

[3] Statements by Rieger to Friderike Zweig; letters from Rieger, Vienna, 12 and 16 Apr. 1934 (ZE); letters to Roth, 27 and 28 Mar. 1934 (Roth); letter to Kippenberg, Easter Saturday 1934 (Sch).

Werfel was already doing) on propaganda for Austria's independence, and felt ill at ease over his refusal.[1] This is not to say that the Vienna shooting left him unmoved, or that its significance escaped him. One of the many letters he wrote on that last night in Salzburg, before the search, was to Alfredo Cahn:

> The days in Vienna are growing terrible; it is the victory of the fascist idea, and this will lead tomorrow to that of the National-Socialists. For us, to whom violence in any direction seems mad, the air is heavy in such times, and often I have a terrible premonition that all this represents only the preliminary skirmishing of a war a thousand times more frightful.[2]

But the final straw was the intrusion, into his private world, of officialdom, for which all his life he felt intense antipathy, and the menace he saw it now presenting in Austria to the possession he valued above all else—personal freedom. Back in London, his first act was to send a formal notification to the Salzburg authorities that he had now given up his residence there.

2

> '*My dear friend! You are not an émigré, do not make yourself one voluntarily! . . . Do not leave the soil from which everything has grown for you!*'
>
> Csokor to Zweig, August 1934

Friderike had been unable to move him to a more rational reaction, and, as always, the practical consequences were hers to see to. She had been more and more alone in these last years, engrossed in maintaining the house (in itself by no means a part-time job) as the base she felt he needed, stilling his *Postnervosität* while he was away, but with her strong and positive character necessarily developing her own interests; unlike Stefan, she was an organization person, and was indefatigable in both local and international associations in the social and humanitarian fields. For all his gentleness and kindness, he had taken very much for granted what she had done for him, as a clock passes unnoticed until it stops ticking. Though she followed him now to

[1] Vallentin 65–6. [2] Letter of 17 Feb. 1934.

London, and stayed for a short while, bringing with her a few things which might help to re-create his life over there, such as the Blake drawing of King John, the fact remained that to wind up their affairs in Austria was not something that could be done as quickly as buying a train ticket from Salzburg to London.[1] There is no doubt that she was willing, indeed wanted nothing better than, to join him in England ('I would love to live with him in London and have a house there, anything rather than be separated from my husband', she told Joseph Leftwich that spring).[2] Had she not, indeed, as early as 1932, with a premonition of coming disaster more vivid then than his, spoken wistfully of a move to Geneva?[3] But, with the best will in the world, it was not possible for her to cast loose with the same readiness as he, and it was natural that her love for her homeland, though not deeper than his, should make her hesitate longer. In his impatience to start anew he failed to recognize that at heart she was with him; and there now began to develop a rift between them that the sensitive Rieger, in far-off Vienna, was quick to notice from their letters.[4] Stefan began to persuade himself, when, far from well, she went back to Salzburg in March, that she was leaving him to face the future alone, that she could not, or would not, tear herself free from the ties of Kapuzinerberg. As yet unspoken, the thought was there: a real break with the past might include a break with the companion of so many fruitful years.

Unwittingly, Friderike was herself to prepare the path for this. Her main care was to see that his work on *Maria Stuart* should prosper. The research was almost done, and he needed now a secretary to begin dictating the first draft. A girl recruited through the Austrian embassy proved unsatisfactory; through Franz Neumann, Friderike then found one apparently admirably suited. Charlotte (or Charlot) Elisabeth Altmann, a tall twenty-six-year-old, granddaughter of a rabbi, had emigrated to England from Frankfurt with her brother Manfred in 1933. (Her father,

[1] Fr 366–7.

[2] Leftwich, *Liber Amic* 59.

[3] Cf. also *BrW* 273, para 2 of letter of 27 May 1933.

[4] Letter from Rieger, 4 Mar. 1934 (ZE). Other letters from him at this time show that, contrary to Friderike Zweig's memory (Fr 369), he did not come to London to join them.

a hardware merchant formerly of Kattowitz, died a year or two later, and her mother then joined the children in England.) A well-educated girl, Lotte had already stayed for a month in England three years earlier; and after she had spent the summer months of 1933 at Whittingham College, Hove, her English was fairly good, though she had little knowledge of other languages. Now living in north-west London, she seemed ideal for Stefan's purposes; and before Friderike went back to Austria Lotte was in daily attendance at Portland Place, where the new *Betrieb* could begin. A 'silent woman', serious and earnest, she became a devoted admirer of her employer, who, very naturally, began to find her uncritical willingness to follow his every whim a not unwelcome change from what he considered Friderike's reluctance to fall in with his plans.[1]

His euphoria in the following months, once he had got over the unpleasantness of the Paris allegations, was quite surprising. London was wonderful, 'one lives just as one pleases, miles removed from politics', he wrote to Kippenberg on Easter Saturday, telling him that he was making energetic progress with *Maria Stuart* and that it promised to be a 'solid, worthwhile book'. He felt better in himself than he had for years, and the reserved, tactful, and friendly manner of the English, the total absence of passion, was as beneficial as a sanatorium after the excitement of Vienna and Paris.[2] Lotte accompanied him on a visit to Scotland, where he wanted to see for himself the background to his book. He had begun to learn again, like a schoolboy, he told Roth, with all the uncertainty and curiosity of youth: and in his fifty-third year the presence by his side of a young woman was doing him good.[3] The rush of untoward events in Austria and Germany—the introduction by Dollfuss of a corporate state in May, the Roehm bloodbath at the end of June, the attempted Nazi *putsch* in Vienna, and the murder of Dollfuss followed by Mussolini's move of troops to the Brenner in July—

[1] Fr 368; Home Office papers.

[2] Letter to Kippenberg, Easter Saturday 1934 (Sch); letter to Strauss, 26 July 1934 (*Str* 69).

[3] Letter of (?July) 1934 (Roth). Cf. also Fr 370.

all seemed like manifestations of another world, outside his 'sanatorium'. His letters to Rolland that summer speak only of the peace and passionless atmosphere of England; the problems of Europe are forgotten in the delights of Covent Garden, or Shakespeare in the Regent's Park open-air theatre.[1] Everything fitted his notion of a new life. Even in Paris in February, on his way to London, he had seemed to Antonina Vallentin absurdly youthful: 'I feel on the threshold of a new adventure,' he had told her, 'it is sometimes a good thing for old gentlemen like me if a great shock comes to jolt them out of their rut.'[2] In one letter to Rolland now he went so far as to express his gratitude to 'Mr. Hitler' for having given his life a new *élan*, and freed him from the dangers of becoming too bourgeois: this crisis, he thought, would be as salutary for him as that of 1914, which tore him loose from the soft and gentle life of Vienna.[1]

True, his political pessimism remained boundless; but precisely because he felt Europe to be on the brink of war he seemed to be living more intensely, holding on tenaciously to the last vestiges of freedom and offering up every morning 'a prayer of thanks that I am free and in England'.[3] 'It is wonderful', he said one day to Leftwich as they strolled up Kingsway to the Strand, 'to walk about the streets and feel that no-one is looking to see what Party badge you have in your lapel.'[4] Though a political cloud, no bigger than a man's hand, began to gather over *Die schweigsame Frau* (the instrumentation of which Strauss had now virtually completed), he remained calm: had not Strauss received Goebbels's personal assurance that there was no black mark on his file? On 2 August—the very day of Hindenburg's death and Hitler's assumption of the Chancellorship as *Führer*—Strauss wrote: 'I can inform you in the strictest confidence that you have been "under observation" in London and that your admirable conduct has been judged "correct and politically unobjectionable".' For the moment his gnawing fear of the future was suppressed, and he could even quite calmly plan a short return visit to Austria in August after ten days in Switzerland. But Salzburg

[1] Dum 184.
[2] Vallentin 66.
[3] Letter to Roth (?July) 1934 (Roth).
[4] Leftwich, *Liber Amic* 59.

was finished for him. The old hunger for far-off places had returned, 'to see the world once again before it crashes about our ears'.[1]

To remain silent and stand aloof from events, to get on quietly with his work, seemed for once to be justified. A long letter in June to Professor Fanto, in charge of the costumes and décor for the opera's forthcoming première at the Sächsisches Theater, Dresden, was devoted to imaginative and most detailed suggestions and a long description of the background: mercantile England 'combined with the memoirs of Casanova and the caricatures of Rowlandson'.[2] Despite the unhappy February experience, Zweig twice returned to Salzburg from Switzerland in August for brief visits. Strauss, forbidden by the Nazis to accept an invitation to conduct *Fidelio* at the Festival that summer, was nevertheless able to attend for the performance of his *Elektra*; and their meeting after the opera, in a gay circle which included the conductor Clemens Krauss, gave the opportunity to discuss the possible casting for *Die schweigsame Frau*. Krauss also suggested a few alterations to the text to improve its voice-suitability.[3] Strauss, who was prepared to make all kinds of concessions to National-Socialism to remain free for his work (and was not personally in a very secure position under the regime, for his son had married a Jewess, his publisher was a Jew, and of his librettists one was now a Jew and the predecessor not entirely 'Aryan'), had recently accepted the presidency of the *Reichsmusikkammer*. In blissful *Kunstegoismus*, however, he was now pressing Zweig to produce a further libretto for him; and in the course of the summer Zweig sent him an outline on the theme of peace at the end of the Thirty Years War—though, at the same time, more realistic than Strauss, he said he was quite prepared for it to be handed to another to work up, to avoid political trouble for the composer.[4] All in all, it was a time of optimism

[1] *Str* 70; letter to Roth (?July) 1934 (Roth).

[2] Letter of 26 June 1934 (Sch); *Str* 69.

[3] Information from Helene Freifrau von Ledebur.

[4] *Str* 73–7. In Zweig's outline, entitled *24. Oktober 1648*, the libretto was in fact later written by Joseph Gregor, introduced to Strauss by Zweig, and became the opera *Friedenstag*.

for him—quite unwarranted, and, for a character such as his, decidedly unhealthy.

A long typewritten letter to René Schickele from Salzburg in August expressed his feelings.

So much has changed, I see that I was too indulgent towards Russia, which invented psychological terror and the propaganda machine, instruments which now cross Germany like a steam-roller. I simply think that it is our task, not like the journalists and polemic-writers to attack every *single* manifestation, but to proceed against the *causes* themselves. I have made an attempt in this sense with my *Erasmus*, the man who defends himself firmly against every form of fanaticism, against every attempt to reduce thought to a common norm (whether fascist, communist or national-socialist). Perhaps it is old-fashioned . . . to defend the concept of [individual] freedom; but at any rate I try to do so in my private life. I tie myself to no party or group, am dissolving my publishing connections with Germany (slowly and without any ostentation, which I hate), and [this phrase added in pencil][1] am quitting Salzburg; but everything I do I try to do *quietly*, and would prefer to be attacked for it rather than to be praised. There is nothing of the so-called heroic in me. I was born a conciliator, and must act according to my nature. . . . I can work only from the connective, the explanatory; I cannot be a hammer, nor will I be an anvil.[2] So we are a very few, who occupy the most thankless and most dangerous post—in the middle, the no-man's-land between the trenches, the non-combatants who do not shoot but continue with their ploughing. What holds us together is not to be seen, but is thereby perhaps a stronger link than slogans and congresses; and a secret feeling tells me that we act rightly if we remain true to humanity and renounce the temptation to take sides.

Promising Schickele a copy of *Erasmus*, he continued that the book was grossly misunderstood:

my concept was in no way to raise neutrality to the status of a principle, but merely to show by an example what enormous moral demands it

[1] No doubt to avoid upsetting the worthy Frau Meingast, who still stayed on as his secretary at Kapuzinerberg.

[2] Goethe's words:

Du mußt herrschen oder dienen:
Hammer oder Amboß sein.

can make on a man and to what a tragic position a man of independence must come in times of mob madness. I am going back now to London. I was here only for two days, which I spent very happily with Toscanini. . . . [There was added a pencilled P.S.] Only not to become uncertain, I say to myself every day. I hear from both Italy and Germany that enthusiasm is gradually beginning to wane. It will be a long time before people there begin to act, but they are already starting to think and that is the first step.[1]

He was indeed caught in the cross-fire between the trenches. To only a very few intimates, like Csokor, Braun, and Schickele, did he reveal his mind, and his quiet, unostentatious search for obscurity, his *Abseitsstehen*, appeared to the world at large merely cowardice. There were murmurs among the *émigrés*, and later strong pressure from them, against his apparent collaboration with the enemy in allowing *Die schweigsame Frau* to go forward to its production in Dresden. He was urged on all sides to make a public protest against its presentation in Nazi Germany. But, apart from his aversion to such forms of public gesture, his impartial spirit felt it unjust to make difficulties for Strauss, who was, after all, at seventy, considered by many as Germany's greatest living composer, had spent nearly three years on the work, and had behaved towards him with the greatest correctness, friendship, and even courage. And, though the situation was painful for him, he let events take their course, in silence.

As he learned later, his silence and inaction made more difficulties for the rulers of the Reich than would have any protest. Strauss, almost the only remaining star in their cultural firmament, whose adherence they greatly prized, insisted that the name of his Jewish librettist should not be concealed, and the result was a controversy, at the top, of some acerbity, with Goebbels arguing that Zweig was a non-political man and his libretto unobjectionable, and Rosenberg accusing the Propaganda Minister of deviation from the principles of National-Socialism. The *Führer* himself had in the end to decide, and after lengthy conferences towards the end of September personally gave Strauss his authorization for the production, in spite of its offence against

[1] Letter of 27 Aug. 1934 (Sch).

the law forbidding any theatrical performance in which a Jew participated.[1]

It was impossible, of course, for Zweig to remain completely silent. A particularly insidious attack on Strauss in *Der Stürmer* ('if he wishes to use Jewish collaborators for his coming works we shall have to draw conclusions which are not very pleasant') he felt he could not let pass without comment, and through Leftwich he issued a statement to the press, explaining that as soon as the Hitler regime came to power he had tried to withdraw his work, but, finding the contract gave him no release, had arranged many months before that all his royalties should go to constructive relief work among German Jewry. He attended a number of the performances of the Vilna Yiddish Theatre during its visit to London in 1934, and spoke at a reception for the company at the Whitechapel Art Gallery: 'If Jewry has been able through thousands of years to resist oppression and attack, it is because even in time of danger Jews gave the best they could, realising nothing would be gained by returning hate for hate. The Jewish way must be to go on creating positive values to enrich both Jewish life and the world.' But as far as he could he remained out of the limelight. At the opening of the London season by the Palestine Hebrew Theatre *Ohel* with his *Jeremias*, which the *Observer* thought better Zionist propaganda than a hundred speeches, cries of 'Author!' went unanswered, for he had taken a gallery seat to avoid having to appear on the stage.[2] And he kept away from the main stream of the emigration, whose eternal necessity to be in opposition, always against something, seemed to him tragically sterile. It made no sense, he said in another letter to Schickele in the autumn, to waste one's strength in dashing the head against the cell walls; one should rather try to preserve it, and, following Cervantes's example, 'concentrate on writing good books in this invisible prison'.[3]

[1] *WvG* 334–42; Robert Welsch (Leftwich xvii). It is interesting to note that Goering, whose sister-in-law had translated some of Zweig's works into Swedish, was a great admirer of Zweig and owned copies of most of his books (statement to the author by Friderike Zweig).

[2] Leftwich 93, 95–8.

[3] Letter of 26 Oct. 1934 (Sch).

He had meanwhile worked hard on *Maria Stuart*, and as it neared completion his previous optimism and delight in London waned. Now the Englishman's sublime indifference seemed merely a desire to avoid mention of disagreeable things, and his sympathetic approach to conceal a profound lack of feeling for the problems besetting the foreigner. London began to bring a 'mortal ennui'. It was still a good sanatorium for the nerves, but 'in the long run the white walls of a sanatorium become insupportable'.[1] For over a year there had been pressing invitations to undertake a lecture tour in South America, where his books had won a wide and enthusiastic public, but he hesitated to go so far afield. It was high time for a change of scene, however, and he decided to accept a similar invitation from the U.S.A. It happened that Toscanini and Asch were to travel there too, and they arranged to take the *Conte di Savoia* together from Villefranche in January 1935.

For the preceding month Zweig moved to the Hotel Westminster on the Promenade des Anglais in Nice, where he planned to put the final touches to *Maria Stuart*. He of course needed Lotte for this, but he felt that propriety demanded a written invitation from his wife. He therefore asked Friderike to do this, and herself join him in Paris before Lotte arrived; as always, she fell in with his wishes. When the three arrived in Nice, Friderike noted, with an amusement somewhat tinged with bitterness, that Lotte had registered an enormous trunk through, slightly to Stefan's embarrassment, for in past times he had always insisted on Friderike's travelling with only hand luggage when she accompanied him. The secretary occupied a smaller room on the same corridor as theirs, and Friderike looked after her, getting her to do her work on the airy balcony of their room and inviting her to join them on their excursions.

There were many friends on the Cote d'Azur at the time: in addition to Asch and Toscanini, André Maurois, Jules Romains, Stravinsky, and Wells made it a microcosm of the Europe he loved, and of his closer friends there were Schickele, Joseph Roth, and Hermann Kesten. The days brought hard work but the

[1] Letter to Rolland, 4 Oct. 1934 (Dum 184).

evenings pure delight in such company. Lotte was with them everywhere: at a Toscanini concert in Monaco, on occasional motor drives along the Corniche. Stefan treated her with apparent indifference, often to the point of rudeness, in front of Friderike (when Friderike pointed out a beauty spot to her, he said: 'Waste of time, it means nothing to her'); but Friderike became aware now for the first time of the situation she had herself brought about. Returning unexpectedly to the hotel, after securing papers necessary for Stefan's United States visa—there was some question about his actual place of residence—she was shocked to find them in each other's arms. At her insistence he sent Lotte away for the last few days before his departure on 10 January. His embarrassment was profound, but he could not bring himself to clarify, even to himself, his intentions and desires. As Friderike, her heart heavy, was seeing him off on the boat, a letter arrived for Stefan from Lotte, in her banishment in a pension in the French Alps, and he passed it to Friderike unopened, as though to relinquish the responsibility to her. Though it expressed regret at having upset his wife, the letter was an open declaration of her love for him, which the temporary absence had done nothing to diminish. It was clear to Friderike that Lotte was determined to get what she wanted, and thought that she alone understood Stefan's needs. But when she sent the letter on to him in America, he wrote promising to give up Lotte on his return.[1]

3

'The librettist I liked better than the composer.'
Max Brod to Zweig

There was no escaping the press conference when they arrived in New York on 19 January 1935, but the reporters tried fruitlessly to get him to speak out against Hitlerism. Joseph Brainin described later his exasperation at Zweig's resistance: 'persistently I tried to draw him out of his shell, intent on extracting from him a quotable condemnation of Hitler's barbaric persecution of the Jews. My efforts proved vain.' But he continued: 'it was only

[1] Statements to the author by Friderike Zweig; Fr 371–8; Fr² 159.

a few days later, when I met him privately, that I caught a glimpse of his tortured soul', his real face—that of a disillusioned man trying frantically to hold on to a Europe that no longer existed, but which he refused to mourn as dead. In truth, as Zweig said in a letter to Leftwich at the time, his fear was that words from him might affect the fate of the Jews still left in Germany. 'They are hostages, and anything we who are free say or do will rebound on these defenceless people. We must do nothing now that involves a personal political demonstration.'[1]

The air of America, which he was visiting for the first time since 1912, certainly acted as a tonic; but he noted that it was not easy for *émigrés* to support exile here. The most successful were those who spoke the universal language of music. One of his concerns on this visit, apart from negotiating the American rights for *Maria Stuart* with Huebsch of the Viking Press (the Queen of Scots also formed the subject of some of his lectures), was to try to get support for a project he had tried in vain in England to bring forward: the establishment of a Jewish monthly publication, in which might appear the best creative work by Jews in all languages. He envisaged this as a dignified counterweight to the demagogic propaganda that threatened to destroy Europe; 'we must never permit ourselves to descend to the intellectual level of our opponents', he told Brainin. But he made no headway in this during the short stay of three weeks. Certainly at the press conference it was not a subject the reporters wanted to hear about.[2]

After his return he could spend only ten days in London, for the proofs of *Maria Stuart* awaited him in Austria with Reichner. Despite his promise to Friderike, he made no move to dismiss Lotte. From Salzburg, where he stopped for a few days, he wrote once again to Strauss, suggesting that the opera should be withdrawn, but the preparations were too far advanced. Strauss, who some months before had seen no difficulty in continuing their collaboration ('by the time the things are finished, in a few years,

[1] Joseph Brainin, *National Jewish Monthly*, Apr. 1942, 254, 285; Leftwich 95, 97.

[2] Brainin, op. cit.; solicitor's letter to the Home Office, 29 Nov. 1938 (Home Office papers).

the world will probably look different'), was still confident, but somewhat more cautious. 'If I have the good fortune to receive one or more texts from you, then it is agreed that no-one will learn of it . . . nor that I am composing a libretto of yours. Once the score is finished, it will go into a safe which will be opened only when we both feel the moment suitable for a performance.' Zweig, however, feeling such covert action unworthy of Strauss's standing, continued to press him to find another librettist; but he could make no progress against the old man's Bavarian obstinacy. 'There is no [other] poet who can write me a usable text', the composer wrote, '. . . after [Hofmannsthal's] death I thought I would finally have to give up, but chance (can one call it that?) led me to you. And I am not giving you up, not even because for the moment we have an anti-Semitic government.' From Vienna, in March, where he was working hard correcting the proofs of *Maria Stuart*, Zweig the collector reminded him of his promise to let him have the manuscript pianoforte score, which of course he would show to no one. Still worried, however, about the political consequences for Strauss, he suggested they should take the precaution of ante-dating it to when it was actually begun, i.e. before the *Machtergreifung*, and while he was still in Vienna a month later he succeeded in getting Strauss, who would not hear of Faesi or Lernet-Holenia, at least to consider Joseph Gregor as his successor, discussing with Gregor 'Semiramis' as a possible theme.[1]

Like Strauss, Kippenberg was trying to convince himself that the present regime in Germany was a transitory phenomenon only, but his cordial letters to Zweig, telling him, for example, that *Marie Antoinette* was still in print with 2,000 copies on his shelves, failed to move him, though Zweig was as always very grateful to hear from him. 'You know', he had told him from Nice in December, 'that this interruption was among the most painful burdens I have had to bear in matters intellectual', and he stressed how he regretted the non-fulfilment of his plan to dedicate *Erasmus* to Kippenberg, which would have made clear to the world that no conflict between them had been at the root of this

[1] *Str* 92–120.

'pause' in their collaboration.[1] But his talk of a 'pause' was merely because he knew that this was what his friend wanted to hear: for he was already convinced in his own heart that it would be more than that. '*Maria Stuart* will be finished this week', he wrote from Vienna on 5 April; 'the book looks splendid, but—I probably need say no more to the master of the Insel.' The pleasure he took in it was clouded by a painful feeling of nostalgia for the old familiar colophon, and he hoped, he said, one day to see it again on his books. A meeting they planned in Linz had unfortunately to be cancelled, and of course it was impossible for him to agree to join the Kippenbergs at the Dresden première of *Die schweigsame Frau*, now fixed for 24 June: the theatre promised to be full of high Party functionaries, and his presence would have given rise to all sorts of 'superfluous comment', but he felt content that 'so worthy a godfather would be present at the christening'.[2]

The Reichner production of *Maria Stuart* was indeed fine, and the book achieved instant popularity. Distribution in Germany itself (despite the *Führer*'s authorization of the opera) proved fraught with difficulties: 'the Jewish firm of Reichner must in future be stopped from flooding Germany with prospectuses which press on us the works of Stefan Zweig and other Jews', blustered *Die Neue Literatur* in its December number; but sales in America reached the 200,000 mark by the end of 1935.[3] Felix Braun liked Stefan's change from the 'psycho-analysis' of his previous biographies to a more straightforward historical interpretation, and urged him to write more in this vein: 'therein lies an essential part of your gifts'. For an authority on the period like Conyers-Read there was a certain irritation in Zweig's 'calm assurance of certainty about facts which have heretofore been regarded as far from certain', and his apparent assumption of 'almost god-like insight into the motives and impulses which lay behind the facts'. For the even greater authority J. E. Neale,

[1] Letter from Kippenberg, 25 Feb. 1935 (ZE); letter to Kippenberg, 20 Dec. 1934 (Sch).

[2] Letters to Kippenberg, 5 Apr. and 6 May 1935 (Sch); letters from Kippenberg, Mar. 1935 (ZE).

[3] Letter to Ebermayer (?24) Dec. 1935 (*Heute* 646); Wulf 277.

however, the book was to be compared with Lytton Strachey's *Elizabeth and Essex*, for 'character and psychology are legitimate evidence in human story, and it may be that the littérateur, who is more skilled in handling this evidence, will arrive at sounder conclusions than the historian; provided always that he does not run foul of documentary evidence, rightly interpreted'. He thought that Zweig, sensibly refusing to sit on the fence over the controversial question of the Casket Letters, had come down on a side not incompatible with the evidence (though he took issue with Zweig's view of the Babington Plot: 'in these days it is a licence permitted only to Mr. Belloc to present this plot as one of Walsingham's devilish schemes'.) He paid tribute to the book's 'brilliant qualities', with 'many descriptive passages to be scored and many sentences that one would give a good deal to have written'.[1]

The effort of completing this manuscript the previous year had for a moment left Zweig tired of 'biography-fabrication' and its 'fashionable success'.[2] But before long he was seized by the idea of a follow-up to *Erasmus* in a study (suggested to him by Pastor Jean Schorer of Geneva) of the fanaticism of Calvin, and the heroic opposition of another great but lesser-known humanist, Castellio. After a short stay in Austria, therefore, to see *Maria Stuart* finally through the press, he planned to spend some time in Switzerland to make a start on the research. But the visit to Vienna dragged out longer than intended. His mother had been very ill, and (though filial piety had never been his strong point) a sense of duty kept him by her side. His teeth too were giving him trouble, a longish course of treatment proving necessary with the Vienna dentist whose patient he had been for many years—another tie, small but important, with the homeland he was trying to abandon. His short stay in Salzburg had strengthened in him the feeling that Friderike, in a sentimental and misplaced patriotism, was determined to oppose his move to London, and

[1] Letter from Felix Braun, 19 Apr. 1935 (ZE); Conyers-Read, *Yale Review*, xxv (1936), 609–12; J. E. Neale, *Saturday Review of Literature*, New York, xii, 31 Aug. 1935.

[2] Letter to Schickele, 26 Oct. 1934 (Sch).

was dragging her feet over the processes of liquidating their life at Kapuzinerberg. He even held against her her intervention with *Landeshauptmann* Rehrl, who now came to Vienna especially to try to explain to him the background to the house search.

The resultant, unnecessary, bitterness darkened once more his outlook, and the old pessimism began to gain the upper hand. Ebermayer, meeting him in the Hotel Regina for the first time since 1933, saw the crisis of the marriage as at least as important as that of the world in Zweig's resolve to finish with his old life. Though his eyes lit up when he heard of the opposition to the Nazi regime nursed by Ebermayer and his friends, nothing could shake his sadness and gloom. 'I cannot for ever sit and stare at a wall', he said—the wall of Germany looming ominously over against Salzburg; but Ebermayer realized that not only his way of life but his marriage itself was dissolving in the 'conflagration of these years'. From Switzerland in June Zweig poured out all his bitterness in a letter to Fleischer, now in London: 'I view the conditions in our homeland with the utmost pessimism, and if I had been able to have *my* way I should long since have been your neighbour. But I have had to struggle heavily with sentimental opposition . . . F. is making things . . . terribly difficult for me. . . . I have set myself the autumn as a final deadline. Then the decision must be taken.'[1]

The sudden death of Moissi while he was in Vienna was hardly calculated to lighten his mood. The previous year he had once more been drawn into the world of the theatre, when Pirandello had invited him to translate his latest play *Non si sa come*; and Moissi himself, keen to play the lead, had pressed him further when they had met in Zürich. By October 1934, alongside the work on *Maria Stuart*, he had completed the translation, and rehearsals were ready to begin the following March for the production of *Man weiß nicht wie* at the Vienna Volkstheater. On 22 March, however, before they could start, Moissi was struck down in Zürich by pneumonia, contracted while filming in Rome. Like his predecessors in the honour of holding the Iffland

[1] Fr[2] 167; *Heute* 491–2; letter to Fleischer, 20 June 1935 (Sch).

Ring, Kainz and Matkowsky, he died in the very moment of appearing in a Zweig play.[1] Remembering those other disasters, Zweig thought it a dark omen indeed. But, as then, he tried to seek comfort in new work.

Arriving in Zürich on 9 May, he took a small suite in the Hotel Bellerive on the Utoquai, at the side, for the lake frontage apartments were too expensive. He sought obscurity, as usual, but it was pleasant to find that the owner, when she heard his name, offered immediately to reduce the price by three francs a day. Lotte had remained in England, and he arranged for his old friend, the publisher Carl Seelig, to provide a secretary, whom he hoped to keep fully employed, for he started at once his research for *Castellio*, in the library. In the evenings he would be in one of the cafés, the Odeon, Terrasse, or Select: 'urbane, sensible, *bon viveur*', Klaus Mann remembered, 'always ready to help, warmly interested in the work and worries of others', as 'eminently pacifist' as ever. But Walter Bauer, to whom he was perhaps closer, saw the deep pessimism beneath this exterior. 'It may be', he said once to him, 'that I shall one day stand before your door without a possession in the world.'[2] Remembering that Thomas Mann's sixtieth birthday was approaching, he asked Friderike to forward from his collection the manuscript of Goethe's poem *Will einer sich gewöhnen*, so that, although he was unable to honour the occasion by a public tribute, it should privately at least not pass unmarked.

How often have you taught me as a master, strengthened me as a man, as a character [he wrote, sending the poem], and carried me through my own uncertainties by your splendidly upright bearing! . . . To express all this in worthy and essential form needs more than a letter, it should be formed as a considered oration, a confession or a book. But what this hour, these constricting times refuse us will one day be expressed in more just and suitable form, and then perhaps

[1] *WvG* 165–6; letters and telegram from Pirandello, 2, 11, 23 Sept. and 7 Oct. 1934 (ZE); Fr 301. The approach from Moissi, as shown by the correspondence with Pirandello, was in 1934, *c.* Aug., not 1935; there is no confirmation of the earlier meeting with Pirandello in Paris mentioned by Friderike Zweig.

[2] *BrW* 275; *Wendepunkt* 314; Walter Bauer, Arens[1] 139.

our witness will show how much you have meant to our generation as man, leader and example.[1]

The approach of the 'Dresden Day' for *Die schweigsame Frau* gave him increasing concern. Though there was nothing he could do to affect the outcome, he still cherished a small hope it might yet be put off. But he tried, as he said to Fleischer, to regard it as a purely historical affair, something finished 'before the Hitler war' (it was self-evident to him that Hitler meant war) 'and therefore a thousand years old'. At the rehearsals Strauss insisted to Karl Böhm, the conductor, that the text was more important than the music, and was prepared to reduce his *mezzofortes* to *piano* to ensure that the singers' words could be heard. With Maria Cebotari as Aminta, the opera promised well, and Strauss was delighted with the rehearsals. Although both the *Führer* and Goebbels, according to rumour, intended to grace one of the performances with their presence, none in fact of the Party bosses attended the première on 24 June; and the royal box at the Sächsisches Theater was occupied by *Reichsstatthalter* Mutschmann, with Blomberg and a number of other army officers in the other boxes. The Intendant had tried to omit Zweig's name from the programme, but had had to yield to Strauss's furious insistence, and the text read: 'Freely adapted by Stefan Zweig from Ben Jonson.' All seats were sold, Katharina Kippenberg reported to Zweig, and the opera was acclaimed on all sides as a tremendous success, not least due (and here a number of music critics[2] dared on the morrow to agree with her) to the delightful libretto. At a reception afterwards, in the Rathaus, Strauss, on Mutschmann's right hand, beamed in triumph.[3]

Other reports reaching Zweig, however, were not so enthusiastic, and conflicted a good deal one with another. As might be expected in his present mood, he tended to believe the adverse critics:

[1] *BrW* 275; letter to Thomas Mann, undated (TMArch).

[2] One wrote: 'Der Text war von einem Mitglied jenes *Zweiges* der deutschen Literatur verfasst, der jetzt nicht mehr genannt werden soll' (Friedenthal, Arens[1] 213).

[3] Letter to Fleischer, 20 June 1935; *Str* 158, 175–6; letter from Katharina Kippenberg, 27 June 1935 (Sch).

one thing is certain [he wrote to Friderike], it is *much* too long, and second, *maddeningly difficult*, i.e. quite the opposite to what I had imagined. . . . Parts are apparently outstanding, and the first act well integrated, but then, like *Arabella* and *Die ägyptische Helena*, it goes over into the tedious. His powers seem to be intact, but his dynamic is lacking. . . . Of all the difficult operas of Strauss, this seems to me the most difficult.

He thought—as has indeed proved the case—that it would enjoy only a sort of half-life, like *Die Frau ohne Schatten* and *Helena*, brought out on occasion but not a permanent item in the repertoires, and probably quite impossible for small stages, thereby completely confounding his original hopes for it. He noted also, among the critics, a certain animosity towards Strauss himself, a sign, he thought, of the way things were going now in Germany, and this seemed to be underlined by the pointed absence of Goebbels from the première.[1]

In this his instinct was right, for even before he had written the letter to Friderike the blow had fallen. After only one more performance, thinly attended, the opera was ordered to be withdrawn and was banned throughout Germany. Early in July came the news of Strauss's resignation as President of the *Reichsmusikkammer*. The Gestapo, on the watch for ammunition to further the cause of the Party purists in this affair, had intercepted a letter to Zweig in which Strauss, with his usual *insouciance*, had not only urged him once again to start on another libretto but had also expressed himself rather too freely on matters political. Confronted with the letter, he had no option but to resign. Though the opera was given in Zürich, Graz, and Prague later, and even in Italy, it is not clear whether Zweig ever saw it. (Strauss towards the end of his life still thought it the best comic opera since *Figaro*, and considered the E major finale one of his best melodic inventions.)[2]

There was nothing to do but immerse himself in work. The research for *Castellio* was making headway, and, Seelig's

[1] *BrW* 276.

[2] *Str* 141–2; 169–74; letter from Strauss to Johannes Franze, 1 Apr. 1947 (Grasberger 461).

secretarial help proving unsatisfactory, he sent early in July for Lotte to come over from England. In a 'plethora of difficulties' he found the 'old reliable pleasure in the God-given children's game of covering a stack of white paper with ink, in the illusion that thereby something important and valuable is achieved'. His letters to Friderike were somewhat curt in tone. Discussing plans for a working holiday together later in the summer, he was against her suggestion of Bad Gastein—altogether too near Salzburg, and he would be compelled continually either to come down to see people or receive them there; already journalists were seeking him out for a statement on the Strauss affair. He gave his orders on 15 July: 'arrive Salzburg on the morning of the 29th, *Falstaff* that evening' (it was possible that Huebsch, his American publisher, on a visit to Europe, might be able to join them), 'the following day see Toscanini and then off to get down to work as soon as possible', not to Gastein but to Marienbad, Frau Meingast to come along. On no account would he stay longer in Salzburg, where the 'onslaught of all these people tires me and their interests, after all, are not mine'.[1]

Ebermayer spent two days with him and Lotte in Pontresina just before he left, going for long walks with them and taking tea at which Fräulein Altmann presided charmingly. He found Zweig personally energetic and optimistic, but politically more pessimistic than ever, forecasting years before the Nazi horror would end, and even a world war. Rudolf Binding joined the party on the evening of 27 July, and Ebermayer was struck with the effect of his talk on Zweig, reinforcing his sense of coming disaster. 'All very fine, a splendid chap this Binding. But all the same, he wrote a poem on Hitler!' Zweig confided to Ebermayer that his marriage would soon be dissolved, and that he would definitely settle in London. After a farewell coffee together on 28 July, Ebermayer saw them off on their several trains, she to London and Stefan to Salzburg, grasping his two hands as the train drew out as though he knew this would be their last meeting.[2]

The month of August spent with Friderike in Marienbad (at

[1] *BrW* 277–8; letter to Katharina Kippenberg, 29 June 1935 (Sch).
[2] *Heute* 564–8.

the Villa Souvenir, on the Waldquellzeile) was more harmonious than might have been expected. Yet, although he avoided any outright confession of his feelings, Friderike could no longer have any doubt that this was the end of their life together. He had always taken his freedom for granted, and felt, naïvely, no need to explain or elaborate his relations with Lotte. He was content to let the situation take care of itself, and could quite calmly suggest to Friderike that they should continue to take holidays like this together from time to time. Ever anxious to avoid a scene, he could not bring his hand to put the pistol to her head. It was fortunate that she too had work on hand, the biography of Pasteur which had occupied her since her visit to Geneva three years earlier. That he was able to lose nearly a stone in weight while in Marienbad was not entirely due to his literally frenetic work on *Castellio* or the beneficent waters of the spa. He dreamed still of a completely new life: if he could not find it himself, then perhaps vicariously in a novel whose hero takes the plunge. Describing this idea to Rolland (the novel never in fact materialized), he said he was profoundly moved by the 'call to begin again instead of merely continuing'.[1]

4

> *'God offers to every mind its choice between truth and repose. Take which you please—you never can have both.'* Emerson

From Marienbad Zweig and Frau Meingast left the train in Vienna, leaving Friderike to go on alone to Salzburg. He found his mother very much better, indeed extraordinarily lively and insisting on going out at least twice a day, so that his decision—at last taken—to settle in London caused him less twinge of conscience in her regard. He gave her his word (and undoubtedly meant it, provided he could keep himself entirely free) that he would never abandon Friderike. With Reichner things were going well and orders flowing; and the news from Germany

[1] Statements to the author by Friderike Zweig; *BrW* 278; Fr 378; letter to Friderike Zweig from Frau Meingast, 30 Aug. 1935; letter of 22 Aug. 1935 (Dum 206).

that Jewish or part-Jewish firms like Fischer and Ruetten & Loening were about to liquidate or transfer to 'Aryan' hands brought him a melancholy satisfaction over his own prudently early disengagement. It was good to see Rieger again, Gregor and Bertha Zuckerkandl, and he was able to attend a birthday dinner for Csokor (as with Thomas Mann, a private present had to take the place of a published tribute).[1] A few days in Switzerland thereafter were enough to complete the assembly of the material and illustrations for *Castellio*; and arriving back in London, via Paris (where he saw Roth again and Masereel), on 26 September, he felt pleased once again to breathe the quiet and congenial air of England.

'They have only one aim here, to keep out, and that is mine too as a writer.' He could even be gay at times. Taking Hermann Kesten for a bus-ride through London, he raised his hat as they passed the Bank of England, saying: 'I always salute her as I pass; there is the home of half the world's money.' Joking with Kesten and Ernst Toller over tea with rum in the Café Royal, he argued with some of his old good humour that an author should avoid irony, love his time, his public, his heroes.[2] In truth, however, his life was a muddle. An all too correct appreciation of the way the world was going had, in theory, led him to a clear resolve to start again in England, 'to defend my work and my freedom'. But he could not seem to achieve what he wanted. There were deep forces within him which made him more dependent on the roots of his Austrian homeland than he would admit to himself. Outwardly, too, the repeatedly expressed sorrow of his many close friends there at his departure caused him a sense of shame at abandoning them, and his constant desire to avoid giving hurt blunted the edge of his decision.[3] It was a *Verwirrung der Gefühle* more painful than that of the hero of his *Novelle*, and resulted in the utmost confusion in dealing with the practical problems. And the unfortunate Friderike became more and more the scapegoat. Without telling her, he had begun to make arrangements for

[1] *BrW* 279–80; statement to the author by Friderike Zweig.

[2] Home Office papers; *Brw* 287; Kesten, *Poeten* 148; Kesten, *Dichter* 73–4.

[3] *BrW* 283–4.

the sale of a great part of his collection of manuscripts, and of the unique catalogues, several thousand in number, which she had so carefully maintained for him over the years; but on the other hand he would give her no advice or clear instructions on the disposal of Kapuzinerberg and its contents. In such a time of turmoil it was, in fact, extremely difficult to get rid of such a property, its lack of a motor-road in the age of the automobile proving in particular a serious drawback. He blindly told himself, however, that she alone was at fault, believing her still unwilling to uproot, and continued to blame her for his own inability to settle into the new life. Yet at the same time he wanted her to be on hand in Austria, to be near his mother.[1]

The *Betrieb*, because of this indecision, remained necessarily divided between Portland Place and Kapuzinerberg, the bulk of his correspondence still arriving at the latter, and having to be dealt with by Friderike and Frau Meingast; and his inner confusion was reflected in the constantly conflicting instructions he sent. Now she was to deny he was in London, now to say he had moved there for good. In October 1935 he began to look around for a more suitable flat, 'a *Provisorium*, a place of safety, an address, somewhere I can keep my most important things permanently. Salzburg can remain as long as it gives you pleasure —as a summer residence and in fact as long as it lasts in the other sense, I have no intention of depriving anyone of their homeland.—I have only one wish: peace in the world and at home.' Depressed over the outbreak of the Italo-Abyssinian war, he responded sharply to her pressure to know more about the new flat (for obviously decisions on their effects in Salzburg depended on this): 'there is still time, for no-one can foresee what the next months will bring. . . . I beg you, do not announce decisions— I am dependent on my work and on the fate of the world and *my* proposals are therefore the more important. But I know nothing except that I can finish the book [*Castellio*] in six to eight weeks.'[2]

When he found what he was looking for (it was round the corner, at 49 Hallam Street, in a building just being completed,

[1] Fr 379; *BrW* 280, 283. [2] *BrW* 284–6, 288.

so there was no hurry to move), he announced his intention of coming over to Salzburg to sort out what could be transferred. But Friderike's desperation can be imagined when she heard that in fact he would cross to Paris first (where Jules Romains was marrying his secretary, as Rolland had done—another omen), then go to Vienna, where he begged her not to hold him up ('I must get down sharp and concentrated to my work . . . at 55 one must be sparing with one's time'), and over to Italy and Nice.[1] But at least she had some idea of the size of the Hallam Street flat, and could get on with the sad selection of what would go into it from Kapuzinerberg. She was able to join him for a while in Nice in January 1936, before following the shipment over to London later in the month, so as to have everything ready before his own return. As she landed at Dover the Immigration Officer told her he was proud to have admitted Stefan Zweig's wife to England. She tried her best to make the new study in Hallam Street a replica of the old, with the same red carpet and a Masereel landscape over the bookshelves (which, however, held only a tenth of his former 10,000-volume library).[2] When he returned by air to Croydon from Paris on 14 February, it was virtually ready for him; but he spent two more weeks at Portland Place, kept indoors by typically ghastly English weather, to finish off *Castellio*, and also to put up Masereel, who was over for a few days. It was not until 6 March 1936 that he was able to report his change of residence officially to the police (the demands of officialdom, though of a more genial character here, could nowhere be denied). Friderike stayed as long as she could, but early in May had to return to Salzburg, where so much needed her attention. Her pleading, and that of many of his friends, that he should change his secretary had had no effect (for so gentle a character he could sometimes show a surprising obstinacy); and Lotte stayed on, at £5 per week, this also meeting official requirements of regular employment for her residence permit. When Friderike left, Stefan had still not faced the issue between them.[3]

[1] *BrW* 280–1.

[2] *BrW* 289; Leftwich, *Liber Amic* 59; Fr 381–2.

[3] Home Office papers; letter to Schickele, 26 February 1936 (Sch); card to Guido Fuchs, 2 Mar. 1936 (StB); Fr 379.

His relationship with Rolland began to reflect now his own uncertainties. Though their correspondence continued unabated, he held against Rolland his defection from the cause of humanism in his whole-hearted endorsement of Russian communism. As early as October 1934, replying to Schickele's similar misgivings, Zweig had thought that 'we stand more in his spirit than he does himself, since he . . . approves everything in Russia and excuses everything, even suppression'.[1] Rolland's seventieth birthday was due in January 1936, and a full year before his more devoted adherents in France, such as Jean-Richard Bloch, began to plan a suitable celebration of this jubilee, to which they naturally expected Zweig to contribute both financially and in person.[2] At the best of times he would have preferred to keep out of such public demonstrations: now, the markedly extreme line that this would obviously take made it all the more distasteful to him. On his way back from Switzerland in September 1935 he had been able to see Rolland. Calling on him at Villeneuve (it seems that this was in fact their last meeting), he was greatly disappointed with the outcome. Rolland looked tired and old, and seemed himself somewhat concerned over what was being planned, though Zweig's efforts to persuade him against presiding over such a purely political manifestation were unavailing. Zweig determined, for himself at any rate, to take no part; but in Paris a few days later, *en route* to London, he avoided a meeting with Bloch, and left other friends, like Masereel, who counted on his support for the celebration, unaware of his real feelings about it. (His unwillingness to hurt his friends frequently brought more pain and trouble than a direct and honest approach would have done.) 'Well, I've done my duty,' he had written to Friderike after seeing Rolland, no doubt referring to a financial contribution—the easy way out—'and I don't have to be forced into an affair which goes against my inner convictions.' Up to a week before the three-day jamboree, at the end of January 1936, the organizers were still counting on him to appear as one of the speakers, and his refusal, when he was forced to spell it

[1] Letter to Schickele, 26 Oct. 1934 (Sch).

[2] Letter from Jean-Richard Bloch, 12 Jan. 1935 (ZE).

out, came all the harder.[1] Though he never lost his respect and admiration for Rolland, and published a tribute on the day ('Dank an Romain Rolland', in the *Pester Lloyd*, in translation in the preceding week's *Vendredi*),[2] their ways diverged now more and more. Their correspondence too became more sparse, sometimes even not without a sharp note, as when Rolland complained at his selling Beethoven manuscripts without telling him beforehand, or (more upsetting to Zweig) appeared to be taking Friderike's side in the latter stages of their marital crisis.

Zweig had finally mastered his hesitations about going to South America, chiefly because, his main interest being in Brazil, the Brazilian Government had sent an official invitation, but also because the International PEN Club Congress, to be held in Buenos Aires in September 1936, afforded not only a convenient opportunity but also a free sea passage. This became one fixed point in an otherwise fluid time. It was not surprising that, *Castellio* once sent off to Reichner, little creative work came from his pen. The once steady flow of essays, articles, and reviews was now a trickle; the *Pester Lloyd* a substitute for the *NFP* (though the latter, without his prior knowledge, and somewhat to his annoyance, brought out an extract from *Castellio* in May). He did not, however, forget Freud's eightieth birthday, and assembled a number of suitable names to be associated with the 'Gratulationsschrift' he published in the *Pester Lloyd*. Freud, sending him his thanks, noted that in all Zweig's 'Panoptikum', his gallery of remarkable people, he was, if not the most interesting, at any rate the only living person, and added: 'In biography, as in analysis, there are phenomena which may be grouped under the heading of "transference".'[3]

Symptomatic perhaps of Zweig's state of mind was an excursion in the genre of the film. Ebermayer had succeeded, towards the end of 1935, in buying back for him from Orplid-Film, Berlin, the rights of *Angst*, and by the following May a French

[1] *BrW* 281–2; letter from Masereel, 16 Jan. 1936 (ZE).

[2] *Pester Lloyd*, 26 Jan. 1936 (Kl. 1188); *Vendredi*, 24 Jan. 1936.

[3] *BrW* 290; Stefan Zweig, 'Sigmund Freud zum 80. Geburtstag', *Pester Lloyd*, 3 May 1936 (Kl 1344); letter from Freud, 18 May 1936 (Freud *Br* 422).

version, *La Peur*, in which Gaby Morlay was to star, arrived in a script which he thought quite good in parts. When Robert Neumann, now also in London, suggested they might collaborate on a film script for a *Manon Lescaut*, the idea appealed for a while, and they completed it during the early months of 1936. (The script was never used, and leafing through it twenty years later Neumann was surprised that the yellowing pages showed no stain from the 'best butter' in which it had been 'baked'—'all the same, a style, a bearing, a touch of greatness in it'.) But Zweig lacked, as Friderike has noted, the necessary enthusiasm for the cinema as an art, and both *Lescaut* and later *Das gestohlene Jahr* remained merely sidelines.[1]

More important for him was a project to assemble his scattered works of the past into new editions with Reichner. The three essay trilogies had been published in 1935 in one volume as *Baumeister der Welt*; this year he wanted to unite the *Novellen*, legends, and *Sternstunden* in two volumes of *Gesammelte Erzählungen*, one containing the three rings of the *Novellen* chain, the other as a 'kaleidoscope'. Then would follow a volume of selected essays, on people, cities, and books, which would bring 'the opus more or less under one roof'. But working at such a distance from Reichner, and in the distracted confusion of his personal affairs, he was unable to give this the attention it deserved, and the *Erzählungen* volumes greatly displeased him when they finally appeared in the autumn. They had no over-all title, merely *Die Kette* and *Kaleidoskop*, which he felt would mean nothing to the new readers he hoped to attract, while his old public, thinking to find something new, would be disappointed. It made him long again for the old days with the Insel.[2]

Castellio gegen Calvin—ein Gewissen gegen die Gewalt, which appeared in May 1936, also suffered from his disorganization, though he blamed Reichner for pressing him too hard. The review copies were out before he discovered an historical error in the section on Bernardo Ochino: quick reprinting of a whole section was necessary to correct the main edition, but the

[1] *BdFr* 57; *BrW* 286–7, 290; Neumann, 117–18; Fr 224.
[2] *BrW* 292, 303–4.

immediate effect was spoiled of a work which, following *Erasmus*, was for him an essential statement of his philosophy. Warm tributes from Mann, Feuchtwanger ('delighted to see you have so unmistakably come down on our side'), and Felix Braun could not console him. The English edition with Cassell, which went to press while he was in South America, was an even more desperate disappointment, for it gave prominence to the portrait of Calvin rather than to that of Castellio, and in the translation of Eden and Cedar Paul (whose work was always regrettably slapdash) the emphasis was so great on the fanatic that the humanist, the true hero, was virtually eclipsed.[1] In German the book aroused some animosity in Switzerland, and he regretted having included the name of Calvin in the title (so much so, in fact, that he held up the French version, intending to revise the text, and this was not published until 1946, when it touched off a bitter controversy worthy of the sixteenth century itself).[2]

It was a sad outcome, for the book was more than a restatement of *Erasmus*. It dealt with 'the problem of problems: how to unite freedom with order',[3] and in fact brought more of a message of hope for the future in stressing that moderation outlasts fanaticism, however entrenched the latter may appear. If Erasmus represented Zweig as he really was, Castellio is a portrait of him as he would like to have been.[4] (To Rolland in July he wrote that to crush the enemy of dogmatism it was necessary to create 'a fanaticism of anti-fanaticism', a pacifism not sheep-like but aggressive and active. But it was not in his nature to be a fighter of this kind.)[5]

Depression returned now more frequently. There were many letters from Jewish friends still left in Germany, which, though they merely confirmed his jeremiads, were none the less greatly disturbing in the horrors they revealed. Appeals for his help

[1] Letter to Roth, 2 June 1936 (Roth); letters from Feuchtwanger, 29 May, and Felix Braun, 30 May 1936 (ZE); letter from Thomas Mann, 30 May 1936 (Mann *Br* i. 417); *BrW* 304.

[2] *BrW* 293. Cf. Schorer, *Jean Calvin et sa dictature*.

[3] Zweig's notes (*Ausst* 81).

[4] Zweig said this himself in a letter to Joseph Roth in 1938.

[5] Letter of 30 July 1936 (Dum 203–4).

from those who had escaped but were destitute increased. He was often exasperated by the 'incessant dunning', but in fact did much to assist, quietly and unobtrusively. His frequent subventions to Joseph Roth, to keep his head above water in France, served unfortunately only to sink it further into brandy. (An anguished plea from the writer H. E. Jacob for bail to the tune of 20,000 Austrian schillings, when he was held in 'investigatory arrest' in Vienna by the Schuschnigg regime, had, however, to be refused—he was not as rich as his friends thought.)[1] As he worked on the legend of the Menorah, *Der begrabene Leuchter*, the modern predicament of the Jews troubled him immeasurably; and it was characteristic that, though he knew they would survive the oppressions of the day as they had those of past ages, he felt his generation too old, as he said to Leftwich, to start again. 'We no longer have the great spiritual strength of our ancestors,' he wrote in a symposium *Whither Jewry?* organized by the London periodical *Dos Yiddishe Wort*, 'the only way of fighting the new hatred is from within . . . by finding the road back to ourselves.' In private, however, he doubted whether his generation could take this hard road.[2]

'One would like to crawl into a mouse-hole and never see a paper again', was his comment on reading the news of the troubles in Palestine. Reviewing Roger Martin du Gard's *Été 1914*, he foresaw that the history of Europe now (unless at the last moment it came to its senses) would not repeat the heroic epic of 1914, but be merely 'the document of an immeasurable collective fatigue and of an indifference, no longer explicable by logic, to our own destruction'.[3] Yet—confused as ever—he could sometimes summon up an extraordinary optimism, forecasting an end to the 'mischief' in another six months to Paul Zech (who had reached the Argentine, and whose choice of South America as a refuge greatly surprised him at this time).[4]

Friderike meanwhile had still been unable to find a buyer for

[1] *BrW* 285, 287–8; letters from Jacob, 15 Apr. and 15 June 1936 (ZE); *BrW* 290.

[2] Leftwich 93–5.

[3] *BrW* 291; Stefan Zweig, '1914 und heute', *Zeit und Welt*, 336.

[4] Letter to Zech, end 1935 (*Ged* 18).

Kapuzinerberg, and was getting no help from Stefan. An offer from a religious order in Munich he had told her to refuse, apparently because of the delay in finalizing the deal. When he came over to Austria, in the middle of June, mainly to see his mother again and to deal with Reichner's proofs of the *Kaleidoskop* volume, he travelled via Zürich, and could not be held for more than a night at Salzburg, where he expected to find his mail and papers reduced to the essentials, so that he could get through them quickly. Though she went with him to Vienna for a few days, their future was still unclear. His conviction that she was opposing his will persisted; but she did not wish to disturb his forthcoming voyage to South America, which she hoped would bring a more reasonable frame of mind, by pressing him now for decisions.[1] In a letter at the end of July to Gisella Selden-Goth (a kindred spirit in the field of music-collecting, whom he was glad to know had secured the Mahler items from the April sale of part of his own collection), he described the opposition he had had to cope with from 'near relations who always condemned my so-called pessimism and wished to bind themselves to the homeland the more strongly as my own desire to get away grew. I almost forget the wonderful years I lived there, in the bitterness I have experienced. Already last year I felt a mysterious enhancement of pleasure when I realised that the Toscanini world was on the point of disappearing.'[2]

As for Klaus Mann, so for Zweig, there was something macabre about the Vienna of those days, which they saw clearly as living on borrowed time. But no one, least of all Friderike, would listen to the Cassandra. He spoke of refuge in work, and indeed was not idle; but he had nothing major on hand, and could not settle to more than a further addition or two to the *Sternstunden*. Most of July he spent with Lotte in Ostende, always a favourite resort, and succeeded in persuading Roth, about whose drinking he was seriously concerned, to join them. He had a tremendous admiration for Roth's work, which he thought greater than his own ('a genius, like Verlaine, like Villon!'), and hoped, with

[1] *BrW* 293–4; statement to the author by Friderike Zweig.

[2] Letters to Gisella Selden-Goth, 18 Apr. and 31 July 1936 (*UB* 13–15).

Hermann Kesten's help, to save him from himself by this change of scene, buying him new clothes and trying to restore his self-respect. Lotte remained discreetly in the background, living in a separate hotel. To Irmgard Keun, who met them there, Zweig seemed the very image of the film-fan's conception of a famous writer—'worldly, elegant, well-cared-for, with a gentle melancholy in his dark gaze . . . a castle in Salzburg and a lady-like secretary'.[1] It was a peaceful interlude, which did a lot to restore his humour before the time came, on 31 July, to return to London to pack for his South American journey.

5

'Simply the most magical thing there is on earth . . . a land for me.' Zweig to Friderike

The strength of his curiosity about South America may be judged by the fact that he had actually accepted an invitation to attend a PEN Congress (it was the only one ever to see him). He was given his Brazilian visa as a guest of the Government, and their proffered hospitality both flattered and surprised him. His books, in particular the *Novellen* and the *Baumeister* essays, had in fact achieved much greater popularity in Brazil than he had realized; at first in both authorized and pirate editions, but now properly launched at the hands of the enterprising house of Guanabara, who had had the sole rights since 1932 and had probably prompted the Government invitation. Ernst Feder recalled visiting no house in Brazil in which the works of Zweig were not represented. There was no hope, therefore, that his condition on accepting, namely that there should be no official receptions or publicity, would be met: for the Brazilians he was *the* star of European literature, and all stops were to be pulled out for this visit. He was to be glad of his prudence in packing tails and white tie.[2]

He embarked at Southampton in the Royal Mail liner *Alcantara* on 7 August. It was only a few weeks after Franco's insurrection

[1] Kesten, *Poeten* 149–50; Irmgard Keun, Arens[2] 197–9.

[2] *BrW* 291–2; letter to Editora Guanabara, Rio de Janeiro, 21 July 1936 (K); Fr 328.

in Spain had begun, but the scheduled stop in Vigo was not cancelled, for there were refugees to be picked up. He was one of the few who ventured ashore there, and once again was able to see something of a revolution at close quarters: the town was in Franco hands and recruitment for his forces in full swing, the new uniforms and vehicles reminding him of similar scenes in Italy and Germany years before. But shipboard life gives a marvellous detachment, and he put Europe's troubles out of his mind in his enjoyment of the voyage, with daily exercises on the upper deck and swimming in the pool, his fellow passengers quite different from his usual associates and telling him a lot about Brazil. The thought came to him of the contrast this 'floating sanatorium' presented to the tiny ships of the discoverers of the New World, and in his last letter to Friderike from on board he included in a list of books he wanted sent to London one on Magellan, whose story he determined would be his next major work.[1]

The reception in Rio, after the unforgettable morning entry into the great bay, was worthy almost of royalty or a visiting head of state. Met at the port by representatives of the Ministry of Foreign Affairs, and the Austrian ambassador from Buenos Aires acting as *chargé* in Rio, he was whisked off to a magnificent four-room apartment in the Copacabana Hotel, a car and an 'attaché' from the Ministry at his permanent disposal. A tight and exhausting programme had not only been arranged, but also published in all the papers, and he was mobbed by journalists on the first round of visits, to the Presidents of the Academy and the Brazilian PEN Club, and the Foreign Minister. The following days were a fantastic whirl, the Brazilians cramming in as much as they could in their desire to show this high-priest of European letters every aspect of their capital and their life, and to accord him every honour. He was received by the President of the Republic, dined with the Foreign Minister at the Jockey Club, gave lectures in French at the National Musical Institute and the Academy of Letters (where queues two streets long waited in vain long after the 2,000 available seats had been taken), and got

[1] *BrW* 295–7; Home Office papers.

severe cramp from signing his name hundreds of times a day, the highest in the land wanting his autograph or a picture. He visited the 'paradise' of the islands in official launches, made tours in 'his' car with 'his' attaché (which included Petropolis—'the most beautiful country I have ever seen'), and was overwhelmed with gifts and invitations. On a visit to São Paulo, at its famous prison the band drawn up for his inspection (two-thirds of its members murderers) broke into the Austrian national anthem in his honour; he visited the Snake Institute and saw a coffee plantation; he made daily 'news' in the papers, and his photograph was everywhere. The mad round almost tore him apart, he wrote to Friderike, and he was losing a kilo a day: but 'Brazil is *unbelievable*, I could howl like a dog at the thought of having to leave'. The beauty, colour, and splendour of Rio he found indescribable, the people enchanting, and the total absence of any race problem amid such a mixture made it to him a paradise on earth, where he could wish to stay for years. 'One thing is sure, this is not my last time here.'[1]

Probably only the charm of Brazil and its people could have made Zweig forget his native shyness and abhorrence of the limelight. The genuine warmth of their reception and the lavish extremes of hospitality left a very deep impression. In his lecture at the Academy of Letters, 'Dank an Brasilien', he expressed the thought that the world's centre of gravity had long since moved away from Europe: perhaps this young country with so clearly a great future, which seemed to have absorbed the culture of the Old World into the vitality of the New, might afford that hope for humanity he feared was stifling in Europe. Certainly his address on 'L'Unité spirituelle du monde' showed optimism about the future victory of the world's moral unity over its tendencies to self-destruction.[2] All the same, as he climbed exhausted on to the boat for Buenos Aires, he felt glad that he had not undertaken to speak at the PEN Congress, and could remain in the shadows after the over-strong light of Rio. Duhamel, with whose wise humanity he felt such affinity, and Emil Ludwig were on board,

[1] *BrW* 297–301; De Souza 16.

[2] De Souza 16–18; Stefan Zweig, 'Dank an Brasilien', *Zeit und Welt*, 156–7.

and made the journey congenial; but he began to look foward to the return voyage and getting down to some work of his own.[1]

Conscious that his fare had been paid by the PEN Club organizers, he attended dutifully, although the Congress stretched out interminably, with consecutive translation into three languages, and allowed almost no break. He refused to accept the chairmanship, and managed to survive without speaking more than once. Here the attentions of the press amounted almost to persecution. He was particularly incensed to see his picture headlined as 'weeping during Ludwig's speech', when in fact, overcome by the efforts of the Congress to present him and the German writers in exile as martyrs, he had rested his head in his hands precisely to defeat the photographers. The rivalry between Duhamel and Romains for the office of International President, and the ill-concealed animosity between them, distressed him, as the friend of both; but he could not succeed in reconciling them. The proceedings were rent by controversy between right and left, but he tried his best (standing to one side, and therefore the confidant of all) to abate the friction by diplomatic action in the *coulisses*. He took a somewhat cynical view of the numerous resolutions urging peace on the world—a hollow achievement to which no amount of applause could give substance.

There were countless invitations, both to speak and to dine, but he left all this to Ludwig, whose vitality and encyclopedic knowledge he greatly admired; he preserved his good humour by escaping to eat alone in the local *picheros*.[2] Buenos Aires was a disappointment after Rio—it might have been Birmingham or Genoa, he thought, with its lack of pictures and palaces—but an evening at Alfredo Cahn's, whose wife at his request prepared an *arroz a la valenciana*, and where he could meet his publisher Antonio Zamora of *Claridad*, was a memorable pleasure. Cahn recalls how, placed at table in face of one of his bookcases, Zweig asked if one of the books might be reversed: it was *Deutscher Geist*, a collection of *Kulturdokumente der Gegenwart* by Lange Danzig and E. A. Dreyer, and he did not want to spoil his appetite

[1] *BrW* 301. [2] *BrW* 301–3; Parandowski, 40–1.

by so antipathetic a sight. Cahn also remembered Zweig's envy of his library, now that his own collection was in dispersal. The popularity of his works in Argentina, though not as great as in Brazil, was still considerable (every day he found in his hotel room a bunch of red roses, homage from an unknown reader of *Carta de una desconocida*), and Cahn was charged by the Government to request him to write a biography of the national hero San Martin—should he refuse, then Ludwig was to be approached. Cahn was greatly disappointed when Zweig, pleading his preference for the defeated rather than the victor as hero, felt that to accept would merely show vanity on his part, and was even more chagrined when Ludwig, whose work he considered far below that of Zweig, and the man himself an empty publicity-seeker, took up the challenge with gusto, saying *his* biography would make San Martin a world figure. (Not without a certain *Schadenfreude*, the translator noted that, despite Ludwig's great splash in the Congress hall, his works in Argentina fell off noticeably in the following years, whereas those of Zweig doubled and trebled their sales.)[1]

The flood of new impressions, especially his enthusiasm for Brazil, had greatly lightened Zweig's outlook. Paul Zech, now living in Buenos Aires, one of the oldest friends of his youth, but who had not seen him for many years, thought, as he saw him off on the *Almanzora*, that he had taken a 'considerable step nearer reality', although he did not mistake in their conversations the burden of melancholy Zweig carried with him. 'I often seem to myself like a man who spends his nights in the cemetery,' he said once, 'on the grave of his departed wife. What has died away from me in these last years is immeasurable.'[2] But on the return voyage he worked well, both on a series of essays on Brazil (which appeared later as *Kleine Reise nach Brasilien* in the volume of selected essays) and on his first sketch for *Magellan*. He seemed in excellent spirits when he landed at Southampton on 6 October,

[1] Manuscript account (Cahn); Cahn, *Stefan Zweig, Amigo y Autor*, 115–16, 124. The correspondence with Cahn indicates that the Argentinian request for a biography of San Martin may in fact have been made in 1938—or possibly renewed then.

[2] *Ged* 21.

laden with costly gifts from Brazil which were followed soon by still further consignments.[1]

6

Leave me, ye memories! Alone, alone
And nameless must I go out in the world;
House, let me free! *Das Haus am Meer*, II. ix

At Vigo he had received a letter from Friderike, who had been at Hallam Street for some time, getting things in order for his return, and cataloguing the much-reduced library. Lotte had been in attendance. Their relations had been unstrained, but cool; for Friderike could not fail to remark the challenge which underlay the younger woman's approach to her. Nothing of this, of course, was allowed to appear in her letter to Stefan: she hoped with all her heart that he was returning fit and rested, undisturbed by news from Europe, and his new inner wealth proof against any devaluation (the franc had just been devalued).

Here you will find everything in order. It was a great joy for me to live here again and to feel you closer despite the distance over the sea. I shall be leaving again on the 12th or 13th. I shall come to meet you at Southampton, so as to miss as little as possible of you. There is much to tell, but all unimportant beside my curiosity to hear your reports by letter enlarged.

But her hopes of a change in him proved vain (part at any rate of their week together he spent at the Langham Hotel), and although when the time came for her departure the word divorce had not arisen, she knew this was the beginning of the end. He had actually pressed her to go, saying he needed room to put up Rieger and Masereel; yet he seemed full of contrition when he saw her to the station.[2]

The following months indeed brought much sorrow. His letters were full of despairing outbursts, the feeling that the whole world was against him. The mess made by Reichner of the *Erzählungen*, and that of Cassell with *Castellio*, were just two of an apparently unending succession of exasperations; even the

[1] Fr 330; *BrW* 300.

[2] Fr 382; Fr[2] 187; statement to the author by Friderike Zweig; *BrW* 303.

parcel of his favourite goose liver she sent for his birthday was held up by the Customs and arrived late. Things were moving at last over Kapuzinerberg—but too late. 'The last four years seem like forty,' he wrote, envying her ability to summon up enthusiasm for people, 'and have made me correspondingly older inside.' 'At 55 and after 35 years' work one gets a little tired of these continual difficulties and complications. I would be happy to lead a quiet anonymous life somewhere and get off this chariot which never stops.' Salzburg—and Friderike—became a 'complex' which no self-analysis could remove: he wanted to be rid of them, but felt darkly that roots once cut off could not be restruck. Unable to carry through what, in practical terms, should have been a resettlement of no difficulty for one of such wealth and standing, he began to see himself as the epitome of his race, the wandering Jew; and moods of self-pity alternated with his outbursts against the blows of fate.[1] For the Jews who were actually the target of these blows, his legend of the Menorah, *Der begrabene Leuchter*, published early in 1937, brought much solace. 'Perhaps the eternal hunting of our people over the earth has a meaning,' he had written, 'that the holy appears to us holier still with distance, and that our heart becomes ever more humble in our dire extremity.'[2] His own suffering was only vicarious, but paradoxically all the harder to bear, and he convinced himself that he too was wandering, rejected, homeless.

On his first arrival two years before he had made inquiries with Carr of the Foreign Office about naturalization (and he would pursue this in due course); yet now he bought 10,000 dollars' worth of U.S. Savings Bonds, asking Huebsch to keep them for him.[3] And the old stand-by of work—he was deep in *Magellan* by the end of the year—which prospered only with frequent changes of scene, merely underlined for him now his rootlessness. Travel, once the essential stimulus (and still effective, he found as he finished a second draft in Naples in January), now became also a penance, the sharper because self-inflicted. He continued to

[1] *BrW* 304–5.
[2] Stefan Zweig, *Der begrabene Leuchter*; Reichner, Wien, 1937, 38–9.
[3] Home Office papers; letters from Huebsch, December 1936 (ZE).

rail against the 'machine', when the levers that controlled it were in his own hands. The fear of growing old had always been with him. His fiftieth birthday had already seemed a watershed; at fifty-five he thought the road led ever more steeply downhill. Still vigorous in body, with scarcely a grey hair, he looked to Friedenthal already a broken man, moving restlessly up and down the room, one hand gripping the other's wrist in a nervous movement that was becoming characteristic, full of prophecies of doom. The effort to conceal this outside his intimate circle—and on his travels he successfully maintained the image of the elegant man-of-the-world, the famous author, circulating from Paris to Naples, Rome to Milan, as at home in the world of the arts as in the salon of the crown princess of Italy—served only to strengthen his feeling that he belonged to a generation that was finished.[1]

In such a frame of mind the apparent onslaught of the outside world made his decisions, when they were forced on him, verge sometimes on the irrational. Inevitably, Friderike was full of questions about the house, which he had made clear to her when she left London was to be got rid of without delay, but which she meanwhile could not maintain or heat on the allowance he was giving her. When he returned to Hallam Street from Italy in February 1937, intent on finishing off *Magellan* and starting on a novel, his irritation at these disturbances was beyond bounds. Unable from a financial point of view to stay at Kapuzinerberg, Friderike had found temporary quarters with her old friend Yella Hertzka in Vienna; Johann, the manservant who had been with them for seven years, proved unamenable to taking her orders in Stefan's absence, and returned to Salzburg from Vienna without her leave, so she was forced to send him his dismissal via the police lodger in Kapuzinerberg. When she wrote to Stefan suggesting a pension for him, he flung back: 'I have been fighting for three years not to have the Salzburg house complex still in my head. That is why I wanted to finish it at all costs. The Johann affair is now yours. So please cook it yourself.'[2]

[1] Friedenthal, Arens[1] 214; *BrW* 306–9; Fr 318–19. Cf. also Treb 375, Zuckmayer 53.

[2] *BrW* 310; Fr[2] 168; statement to the author by Friderike Zweig.

Faced with a virtual ultimatum from Lotte, he determined not only to 'finish' Kapuzinerberg but also to make a legal formalization of his finances *vis-à-vis* Friderike (though he still baulked at the word divorce). She was charged not only with having ready all the papers for the sale of the house and the final disposition of effects, but also with arranging a meeting with lawyers, so that in May he could clear the lot in two days' stay at Salzburg and at most a week in Vienna. It was incredible, and tragic, that one who had all his life bent lovingly over the records of others should so carelessly and in such senseless haste deal with his own, that the bibliophile and collector should cast so many treasures to the winds in a matter of days. He was persuaded that his haste was a reflection of the dangerous flux in the world: the political situation was 'catastrophic', the Stock Exchange down-turn at the end of April 'the greatest financial crash in years', even Warburg the banker was giving up his house and taking a flat to be more mobile (though Friderike, he observed tartly, 'so absorbed in Salzburg things', would probably not have noticed all this). In fact, however, it was the reflection of his instability and of the contradictions within him. Felix Braun, admiring his 'positive action in carrying out decisions recognised as necessary', had no conception, close friend though he was, of the divided and unhappy spirit the smooth front concealed.[1]

The house went to a Frau Gollhofer for 63,000 schillings, probably less than half its true value. 'Dr. Zweig,' commented a Salzburg paper, 'although never politically active, had not felt at ease in Salzburg since the February days of 1934, has lived a great deal abroad and has now taken up permanent residence in London. These circumstances caused him to get rid of his property for a relatively small sum.' Friderike, in order to make the legal proceedings as smooth as possible, had chosen a friend of Stefan's as her lawyer. She was to be greatly surprised at her husband's behaviour over what she had thought was purely a financial and administrative arrangement. After the documents had been signed, they returned together to the Hotel Regina, where he was staying, and he flung himself on the bed in a mood of

1 *BrW* 310–12; letter from Felix Braun, 25 Apr. 1937 (ZE).

apparently acute depression: it was clear that to him the agreement meant their final separation, and he seemed already stricken with remorse.[1] Bewildered, she returned the same night to Salzburg, where she received the following day a long letter from him.

In it he stressed that he felt no bitterness.

I would not like you to think this has been a happy hour for me—on the contrary, I am writing this in the night, sleepless and full of thought of the good time that is past. We have both made mistakes, and I wish it could have turned out otherwise—by God, I feel nothing but sadness over this outward farewell, which for me inwardly is not one, perhaps even bringing us closer together when all the pettinesses and troubles of a more intimate life are gone. I know, without being vain, that it will be bitterly hard for you to be without me—but you are not losing much. I am no longer the same, have become a misanthropic withdrawn man whose only remaining real joy is in work. . . . I feel these times as the most horrible pressure. Forgive me at all events if through this kind of pessimism I spoiled many an hour for you, but you know I have never made things easy for myself and make it hard for others to be joyful in my company, except in rare happy intervals. . . . I am full of faults and inadequacies, but one thing you know, I have never forgotten anyone I have ever loved, and how should I become a stranger to you, who stood closest to me. . . . Please, never harbour the thought that you have somehow 'lost' me, and do not worry about other people. If they condemn me, they are partly right, but on the other hand they have no idea what I have suffered through the Salzburg complex.—You however no-one will condemn, and whoever is on your side will always be dear to me.[2] . . . I am convinced that this was the right way out, yet I feel a deep pain . . . the best time is gone for ever and we lived through it together, much of it in real happiness and for my part in blessed work. . . . Think of me only as your best friend—may there often be opportunity for me to show this, and forgive me all the pain this separation has caused you. . . . I thank you for everything, and forget nothing of the good communion of these years, and will *never* forget it.[3]

[1] Unidentified Salzburg paper, 1937; *BrW* 312; statement to the author by Friderike Zweig; Fr[2] 168.

[2] Roth, on a visit to Austria, was deeply incensed at Stefan's treatment of Friderike, and left him in no doubt of his feelings; but Zweig maintained his great regard for him—his 'unhappy love affair', as he called it.

[3] Letter of 12 May 1937 (*BrW* 312–14).

On his way from Vienna to Zürich, where Lotte was awaiting him, his train stopped at Salzburg, and he met Friderike briefly at the station. His resolution once more weakened, and he begged her not to think that he was bound to Lotte: if she would come with him, as far as Zell am See, could they not send a telegram to the lawyers and cancel the agreement? In fact he held her on the train, much to the alarm of Joseph Roth and her daughters, who had accompanied her to the station but had left them alone together. The telegram was sent when they stopped at Zell and she got out to return to Salzburg; but it was in vain—her lawyer was on leave, and action was not immediately possible. He had wanted her to follow him to Zürich as soon as might be; once there, however, his mood swung round yet again (from the desire to avoid a scene with Lotte, Friderike suspected), and he telegraphed to the contrary. Though the agreement was merely a scrap of paper, detailing financial arrangements which it would have been simple to disregard, and nothing so binding as divorce proceedings, he obviously saw it as a final separation; but could not bring himself positively to decide, veering now one way, now the other. As so often, he let circumstances decide for him, and, once he was back in London with Lotte, the die was cast.[1]

Friderike now had to make her own dispositions. Everything seemed to indicate staying in Austria—not only Stefan's wishes (as far as these could be made out) but also the fact that the girls were now established in careers there, Alix in a travel bureau and Suse as a photographer. She therefore took a villa near Salzburg, in the Nonntal, in the children's name, because she understood Stefan did not wish her to be officially domiciled in Austria (the lawsuit pending over his non-payment of the Salzburg taxes was apparently the reason for this). Much furniture and other effects from Kapuzinerberg had to go into storage for lack of room, including her collection (some 600 volumes) of Stefan's works, original and in translation, which the Insel-Verlag had edited specially for her with printed dedications, the manuscripts of the successive drafts of his earlier works, and (most treasured item of all) the *Jeremias* manuscript of 1917, with his poem to her.

[1] Fr[2] 170–1.

But she settled as best she could, and was touched that Stefan sent her, as a welcoming present, the Goethe 'Mailied' which had for so long hung on his wall. He too seemed to have found a certain equilibrium.

> The tension between us had finally to be ended [he wrote at the end of June]. Your urge to independence is too great—not that you were not spiritually in the right—but too great for me and I had no strength left for the unspoken contradictions. Even at the last moment of regulation you could not trust me: perhaps you were right, for I no longer trust myself . . . since I see that my oldest friends like Roth, Rolland (for political differences) are estranged from me, and it is perhaps really difficult to be with me—the blow four years ago was actually deeper for me than you realised. It is better, I hope, the way things have turned out, for at least you have peace and security and in addition, I swear to you, my most cordial friendship which will show itself far beyond the mere letter.[1]

He continued to write, as of old, every few days, describing the 'machine' which had caught him up once more: a television interview, a reception at the Austrian embassy for the Vienna Philharmoniker, a memorial evening for Drinkwater, the Philadelphia Ballet with Margarete Wallmann, a Bruno Walter concert—all in addition to a great deal of work: conferences for *Magellan*, still not in final form, two new *Sternstunden*, proof-reading the essay volume, and a start on the new book, the novel on which he almost despaired of concentrating. But all this was like a drug to avoid the necessity of clear thought. Even a resolve to make provision for Friderike in the event of his death came to nothing. Fuchs, visiting London on Reichner affairs, was, he wrote to Friderike, to be given a sealed letter to hand to her after his death, 'with certain arrangements and assurances which I do not wish to make public elsewhere'. This letter never came to light, and indeed Fuchs told Csokor later that he did not receive it, presuming that Stefan feared difficulties with Lotte. He wanted to include Friderike in his summer plans, but her suggestion of the Salzburg Festival was out of the question for him ('you still will not believe that Salzburg has been a nightmare for me for

[1] Fr² 187–8; *BrW* 314, 316–17; statement to the author by Friderike Zweig.

four years'); and after he had spent a month at Marienbad again they were able to meet in Lucerne. Though not their last meeting, it was the last time they were really together.[1]

It is idle to speculate whether the course of events might have been changed. Had Friderike in fact followed him to Zürich, there would without doubt have been a most painful scene, which, though Lotte might have received her *congé*, would have left Stefan —quite unable to stand life with the independent Friderike any longer—completely at the end of his tether and brought his instability to the point of desperation. As things were, his *laissez-faire* chimed with his pessimism over the world situation to make him feel more than ever the homeless wanderer and member of a lost generation. The wonder is that he contrived to survive so long.

7

'He that hath Wife and Children, hath given Hostages to Fortune; for they are Impediments to great Enterprises, either of Vertue, or Mischiefe.'
Francis Bacon: 'Of Marriage & Single Life'

Magellan was now as good as finished, but Zweig spent part of January and February 1938 in Portugal with Lotte before finally sending off the proofs. He had taken great trouble in selecting illustrations, and the result was a book of great distinction, not only in the standard edition but also in a limited edition of 100 signed copies, bound in half-leather and with special illustrations and maps. Both this and the essay volume *Begegnungen mit Menschen, Büchern, Städten*, which came out at the end of 1937, maintained for the outside world his façade of calm superiority to events and a superb indifference to the world crisis. 'I envy you your ability to defend yourself by work of beauty', wrote Freud; Thomas Mann admired the splendour and riches of *Begegnungen*; 'the days when one encounters a Zweig', said the pianist Alfred Cortot, 'are to be marked by a white stone in the life of beings who have respect for ideas or curiosity for intelligence'.[2]

[1] *BrW* 315–20; Fr[2] 188–9; *Ausst* 83 and photograph.

[2] Letters from Freud, 17 Oct. 1937 (Freud *Br* 430), Thomas Mann, 14 Nov. 1937 (Mann *Br* ii. 32), and Alfred Cortot, 13 Oct. 1937 (ZE).

But his sense of the approaching assault on Austria was strong. Alarmed by the negotiations between Lord Halifax and Hitler in November, he had paid a quick visit to Vienna; as he embraced his mother, he had felt that it was for the last time, and he was saddened by the apparently unshakable optimism of friends like Csokor.[1] Early in March he reproached Toscanini, who had refused to conduct at the next summer's Salzburg Festival, for abandoning Austria too soon, 'while she is still defending herself . . . the only effect will be that Furtwängler and Strauss will turn Salzburg into a German festival city'. But a few days later, almost exulting in the pessimism 'which at least gives me the strength to withstand events', and in his wise decision to get out in time, he saw everyone—too late—'trying to escape by the same door . . . even including my wife and her daughters who have just set up that gigantic house[2] in Salzburg and, against my will and my advice, have anchored themselves financially there'. In a matter of days came the *Anschluss*.[3]

For Friderike it was a disaster. In January she had gone to Paris with Suse, mainly for the chance of seeing Stefan again on his way back from Portugal, but also for Suse to gain experience abroad in her photographic work, leaving Alix at Nonntal. She had stayed on, taking a flat first near the Étoile and then in the rue de Grenelle, unconscious of the approaching storm, and when it broke she was too paralysed to return. The ground was suddenly cut from beneath the new life she had just begun. Before joining her in Paris Alix packed and prepared for shipment the remaining treasures from Kapuzinerberg, both in store and in the Nonntal villa; but they were eventually seized by the Gestapo and auctioned—a heart-breaking loss. Her decision to stay in Austria—for which consideration for her daughters was mainly responsible, but which she thought also met Stefan's wishes—had been fatal.

[1] *WvG* 365–6; Csokor, *Sp* 109.

[2] It was in fact a modest enough villa, the annual rent for which Friderike had secured by letting rooms to wealthy American visitors to the Festival in the 1937 season.

[3] Letter to G. Selden-Goth, 3 Mar. 1938 (*UB* 45); letter to Fleischer, 7 Mar. 1938 (Sch).

Stefan, despite his protestations of having foreseen it all, was deeply wounded by the event, most of all by worry about his mother, still in Vienna. He vented his feelings in self-justification to Fleischer:

My brother, as a Czechoslovak, will probably emigrate, with heavy financial loss . . . my wife was at the moment in Paris with one daughter and does not want to return, what will become of her money, of the lavish house she so foolishly set up there, God and Goering alone know. You remember how desperately for years I protested against staying and settling there. . . . It is the same with Reichner. . . . I pleaded with him to convert into a limited company here. He has left everything in the lurch . . . poor Fuchs has the greatest difficulties in having to answer for everything.[1]

Reichner too had been paralysed by the blow. Two weeks after the *Anschluss* Frau Gregor wrote to ask Zweig to intervene with him: her husband's book was about to appear, and the desperate Fuchs could not get a word out of his chief, who was nevertheless being assured by the new regime that all that was needed was the appointment of an 'Aryan' lawyer to take charge of the business. What was chiefly worrying Reichner was not so much the advent of an anti-Semitic regime as his recent publication of a book by Schuschnigg. Finally, after a few more weeks of indecision, he fled to Zürich. His defection knocked away one of the main props left to Zweig's life: his outlet in the German language.[2] Though his work on the novel had been progressing well, he felt now like an actor playing to an empty theatre: 'the sense', as he wrote to Lavinia Mazzucchetti, 'of writing in German into the void'. It was possible before long to make arrangements with Gottfried Bermann-Fischer, who had set up a German-language house in Stockholm after the take-over of S. Fischer in Germany; but Zweig never really recovered from this loss of both homeland and language at one and the same time. 'Trained pessimist' though he was, the catastrophe had exceeded his worst fears.

Not only my mother still there, and my friends [he wrote to Schickele in April], not only that my whole opus is trodden once more into the

[1] Fr. 384–6; Fr² 191–4; letter to Fleischer, 28 Mar. 1938 (Sch).
[2] *Bildb* 97; letter to G. Selden-Goth, 18 May 1938 (*UB* 49).

ground—it is also the loss of almost the sole remaining circle of effect, the plunge into emptiness. If it was just a matter of 'lasting out', as you put it, one could summon up the strength. But on top of that the continual need to start again with a head bespattered with the thousand filthy stains of outside existence—passport questions, place of residence, family problems, life problems. One gets often very tired. . . .[1]

Nevertheless he worked with a will to help those less fortunate than himself. Hallam Street became a sort of welfare office, providing all kinds of services for dozens of Austrians—finding jobs, publishers for their books, entry permits, cash. Trying to get a post for Robert Braun in London, he wrote to Eugenie Hirschfeld: 'if only you knew how many letters I write and *how* few I have so far really been able to help—it makes me despair'. He appealed, successfully, direct to the Queen Mother for help for the refugees; organized an appeal to Russia to accept a number; and himself sent regular monthly subventions to Ernst Weiss, after the writer reached Paris, until his suicide in 1940.[2] 'Helping on all sides, though I am unable to help myself. . . .' For, well off though he was, his own case was by no means easy in terms of the hated 'outside existence'. He remembered the words of a Russian exile: 'Once a man had only a body and a soul. Now he needs a passport too if he is to remain a man.' Till now Zweig's Austrian passport had sufficed (it had been renewed only fifteen months before). Now he, and Lotte too, must join the dreary queues at the Home Office to secure a substitute for that essential qualification for membership of the human race. And although he had been based in England for over four years, his absences had been frequent and prolonged; he found he would have to sit out a few more years yet before naturalization could be entertained.

They were granted Certificates of Identity in August—the very month when, in Vienna, his mother died, with none of the family at her side (her nurse, an 'Aryan', was forbidden to spend the

[1] Lavinia Mazzucchetti, *Novecento in Germania*, 271; letter to Schickele, 22 Apr. 1938 (Sch); letter to Liesl Monath, 4 July 1938 (LM).

[2] Letter to G. Selden-Goth, 6 Apr. 1938 (*UB* 46); Robert Braun, *Sp* 84; *BrW* 328; statements to the author by Gertrud Isolani and Friderike Zweig; letter from Robert Neumann, 22 June 1938 (ZE); Kesten, *Poeten* 148–9.

night in her house if a Jewish man were present). 'I do not hesitate to confess', he wrote in *Die Welt von Gestern*, 'that from the day when I had to live on foreign papers or passports I never again felt as though I completely belonged to myself. . . . On the day I lost my passport I discovered, at 58 [he was actually 57], that one loses more with one's homeland than just a circumscribed spot of earth.' His image of himself as a homeless wanderer became sharper—and not only homeless, but rejected and forgotten, for it hit him hard when, applying at the Home Office, he found his name was quite unknown to the clerks dealing with his case.[1]

What was to be done, what to be made of his life? His ideas were in constant flux. In June he had been firm against abandoning Europe for the New World: 'we must at all costs avoid suddenly wanting to make a home out of America, which till now was more of a curiosity for us than an ideal—radical changes are now completely out of the question for our generation'. Almost in the same breath he told Rolland that he was thinking of emigration to South America, yet probably agreed when Rolland said he could not see him installed in Brazil: 'it is too late in our life to strike deep roots there. And without roots one becomes a shadow.' In July, again, he told friends in New York that America was a hundred times preferable to London, and it was only the need to secure his naturalization that was keeping him in England.[2] He had accepted an invitation for a lecture tour in the U.S.A. for the end of the year, and in October, after the disaster of Munich had piled Pelion upon Ossa, seemed to be influenced by the many letters he received from friends who had settled there and were successfully starting a new life. At the same time he spoke of revisiting Brazil the following summer, and in fact secured a visa for that country in May. Like a bird fascinated by a snake, he was transfixed by the world's headlong rush towards war. 'One has almost forgotten that there was once

[1] *WvG* 369–74; Home Office papers; *Ausst* 83; Fr 386; letter to G. Selden-Goth, 14 July 1938 (*UB* 53).

[2] Letter to G. Selden-Goth, 4 June 1938 (*UB* 52); letter from Rolland, 24 June 1938 (Dum 185); letter to Liesl Monath, 4 July 1938 (LM).

an Austria,' he wrote after Munich, 'the time storms by so quickly, one wave overtakes another; we are already no longer alive, but enclosed in the coffin of history.' He was fond of quoting Rilke's words of 1915: 'Überstehen ist alles', 'to survive is everything': but increasingly felt that his generation could not find in itself the capacity for survival. 'We are too Erasmian . . . to prevail against these men who have a battering-ram in place of forehead and brain. Against those possessed by the mania of nationalism only those themselves possessed can stand: we are poisoned by our humanity.'[1]

Unable to solve this essential problem, he could nevertheless take certain steps before the visit to America. One was to start and press forward the official process for British naturalization. After concocting a long letter, through his solicitors, to the Home Office, detailing his residence periods in England since 1933, his movements and activities, he sent in his application in December, with, as referees, Archibald G. B. Russell (his friend since the far-off days of William Blake in 1906), Newman Flower of Cassells, William Rose, and Lord Carlow (whom he had recently met through Anthony de Rothschild and Louis Golding).[2] The other—more painful, but already foreseen—was to propose to Friderike a formal divorce.

Though he did not, it seems, yet consider marriage with Lotte, the latter's position was equivocal; and though she too had applied for naturalization, the uncertainty of the times made it essential that he should be truly free to look after her. The Concordat reached by Schuschnigg with Rome just before the *Anschluss* had barred further marriages by dispensation with non-Catholics, and also permitted the invalidation of existing ones on application by relations. Alfred, at Stefan's behest, was prepared to do this; but before embarking on such a distasteful course he offered Friderike the alternative of formal freedom through the courts, and told her he was prepared to be the 'guilty party'. He was undoubtedly moved by a deep, hardly conscious urge to be

[1] Home Office papers; letter to Guido Fuchs, 8 Oct. 1938 (StB); letter to Koogan, 31 Oct. 1938 (K); letter to Alfred Wolfenstein, 15 Oct. 1938 (*Sp* 86).

[2] Home Office papers.

rid of her completely, the feeling that a new life required this total break; and his letters in recent months had been increasingly irritable, sometimes even violent in tone. She was at first reluctant to agree, for British naturalization, which he would undoubtedly be granted in due course, would of course also be invaluable for her as his wife; and she appealed to Rolland to use his influence to persuade Stefan at least to defer this step. It was in vain. He would have none of Rolland's arguments, and was not to be shaken, condemning what he called Friderike's *Oesterreicherei*. In the end she could not withhold her assent, for she had been grievously disturbed by the unbalance which his letters had shown ('c'est déjà de la folie', she had said in one letter to Rolland), and felt that the only hope for him now, as it had ever been, was to feel himself untrammelled. It was agreed that mental cruelty would be the grounds offered; and evidence was given by Alix of Stefan's habit of locking himself away in his room and refusing to speak to the family. The procedures did not drag out, and the decree absolute was granted on Christmas Eve, just before he left for America.[1]

It seems incredible that with such a deeply troubled spirit, and in the face of the, to him, cataclysmic events in Europe, he could complete a 400-page novel. Begun after his return from South America, already in second draft by the time of the sale of Kapuzinerberg in 1937, it was worked and re-worked through the Spanish Civil War, the *Anschluss*, and Munich (no fewer than eleven volumes are extant of his notes, manuscripts, and successive drafts). Though perhaps not the 'great Austrian novel' he had dreamed of, its scene—the distant days of the Habsburg Monarchy—and its theme—the disasters to which unthinking pity for another can lead—were a profoundly personal expression of his two obsessions: nostalgia (which only the Portuguese word *saudade* can express) for his homeland, and his regard (in which pity played a part) for Lotte. A valiant blow, therefore, in a new battle with the daimon, though the catharsis was to prove in-effective. He hesitated a long time over the title: the expression

[1] Fr[2] 206–7; letter from Friderike Zweig to Rolland, 5 May 1938 (Dum 135–6); statement to the author by Friderike Zweig; Home Office papers.

'pity' seemed too direct in German, as did Felix Braun's suggestion of 'compassion'; and he settled finally on *Ungeduld des Herzens* ('the heart's impatience')—though it appeared as *Beware of Pity* in the English version and in the successful film[1] later made of it. He arranged for its publication in German with Bermann-Fischer in Stockholm and Allert de Lange in Amsterdam; but, realizing he was now only 'an author in translation', was doubtful of its appeal to the Anglo-Saxon taste, which from the financial point of view was all-important. (Here he was wrong, for both American and English editions sold well: Cassells reprinted three times in a week, and the novel was one of his biggest successes in England.) Sending it to Koogan, his Brazilian publisher, however, he thought it would interest a larger public than had his previous works there. Ernst Weiss, harshly unmindful of Zweig's generosity to him, and unaware of the personal character of the book, thought it pure plagiarism ('I rediscovered one of the characters of my inflation novel, in slightly damaged form'); but to Rolland it was an excellent novel, 'débordant de sève jusqu'à l'excès'—although he thought it too long by half, its creative fullness squandering the material for another whole book, a Balzacian epic of the conquest of the Kekesfalvas by the Jew Kanitz.[2]

'Our client is due to leave for the U.S.A. on 17 December,' said his solicitors' letter to the Home Office, 'where a lecture tour has been arranged for him and where he has been asked by the Theatre Guild . . . to assist in the production and rehearsing of one of his plays.' It was the end of the month, in fact, before he could leave. He looked forward to lunching with Thomas Mann, now in Princeton, N.J., but otherwise there promised to be few spare moments. In his tour, which lasted through January and February 1939, he gave no fewer than twenty-five different lectures and readings in cities from coast to coast (including also Toronto), and had to spend twenty nights in trains between

[1] Starring Lilli Palmer and Albert Lieven, directed by Maurice Elvey, 1946.

[2] *Ausst* 85; letter to Schickele, 22 Apr. 1938 (Sch); letter from Felix Braun, 6 Aug. 1938 (ZE); letter to Koogan, 31 Oct. 1938 (K); Kesten, *Poeten* 148; letter from Rolland (Dum 214).

them. There was little time to take note of the sinister developments in Europe (the German press campaign, leading up to the occupation of Prague, was in full swing), but even at this distance there was no escape: Hitler's raucous tones issued from a fellow passenger's radio on the train from Houston. From San Francisco he wrote to Gisella Selden-Goth to say he expected to leave again for Europe on 3 March: 'probably the worst mistake I can make'.[1]

8

'I will *not see and survive a second war.*'
Zweig to Felix Braun

To Duhamel, who came to see him in London shortly after his return from America (and who thought the Hallam Street flat, though nicely furnished, cold and depressing), Zweig's pessimism seemed overwhelming: he was convinced of Hitler's invincibility. The swallowing-up of Czechoslovakia in March was simply one more step towards a war too horrible to contemplate, or, worse still, towards a bloodless Hitler conquest of all Europe. The end of an era, he felt clearly, was approaching, and 'rotten bones' like his would not survive to see the next.[2] 'To believe in a collapse in Germany', he wrote to Felix Braun, 'is madness. . . . We should have the courage to admit to ourselves that we (no less than our ideals) are something that is finished, a piece of history. . . . To see clearly and yet not despair, that, my dear friend, is what is fitting to our years.' And though he added that there was no going back—even if through a miracle it were possible, they would never find the old homeland again—and said he was determined not to see or survive another war,[3] yet he still felt it his duty to stay at his post, to record the catastrophe, even if he

[1] Home Office papers; letter from Thomas Mann, 28 Dec. 1938 (Mann *Br* ii. 73); Fr 406; letter to Wolfenstein, 15 Oct. 1938 (*Sp* 86); *WvG* 363; letter to G. Selden-Goth, 9 Feb. 1939 (*UB* 57). Two of the lectures ('Das Geheimnis des künstlerischen Schaffens' and 'Geschichtsschreibung von Morgen') are reprinted in *Zeit und Welt*.

[2] Dum 185; letter to Guido Fuchs, 11 May 1939 (StB).

[3] Letter of late summer 1939 (*Sp* 87–8)—probably early July, since it was written before his move to Bath.

could do nothing to avert it. Hearing of the suicide of Ernst Toller in New York in May, he said to Leftwich: 'this is not the way'.[1]

At a time, however, when—at long last—all free Europe and England too were beginning to brace for resistance to Hitler, Zweig's horror of violence prevented him from lending his arm to the struggle. The 'great European', as Jules Romains called him in a noteworthy address in Paris that spring,[2] nowhere gave a clear call to courage, even if he could not call to arms. True, he joined Fred Uhlman's 'Free German League of Culture', and, on the platform with Kingsley Martin and Wickham Steed, spoke his tribute at its Conway Hall meeting in memorial to Toller and Roth. (Like Verlaine, with whom Zweig had once compared him, Roth had succumbed in Paris to alcoholism in May, and his death had affected Zweig very deeply.)[3] At E. M. Forster's request he sent a generous contribution to the National Council for Civil Liberties. He also lent his name to Thomas Mann's proposed 'German Committee', which planned to distribute fortnightly brochures within Germany written 'by representatives of the German spirit for the German people' ('it is our duty and our obligation to use our influence', said Mann).[4] But his constant cry was that he was too old, too tired, and even his efforts to help the other refugees began to fall off. The numbers 'pressing in' on him grew to the point where he felt he had to flee from London, at first for a week or so at a time, then in the summer to consider a permanent move.[5] Even an old friend like Ehrenstein, who had reached Brissago and was sending desperate appeals for help in getting into France, or at least an intervention with publishers to get him some money, found a deaf ear and was driven to exasperation by Zweig's bewailing of his own fate:

[1] Leftwich 90.

[2] *Stefan Zweig — Grand Européen*; reprinted in translation Arens², 295 ff.; published in the U.S.A. in English (Viking Press) and French (La Maison Française) Nov. 1941.

[3] Uhlman 217; *Daily Worker*, 24 June 1939.

[4] Letter from National Council for Civil Liberties, July 1939 (ZE); letter from Thomas Mann, 26 May 1939 (TMArch).

[5] Letter to Guido Fuchs, 28 Apr. 1939 (StB).

you, the author of *Jeremias* . . . are not only completely free but could even help me with the income from the Jeremiad! . . . Remind [the old] Stefan Zweig that, although without him I might never have got into the *Kriegsarchiv*, he without me would hardly have got out to Switzerland! . . . You at least still have in German a novel and a drama, and even if it is sad that your main works are missing because you did not set up Reichner in Switzerland, remember that you are a world house and that your books are a success in every other language!

Zweig began to speak of the new tides of refugees as nothing but beggars, mostly second-raters, weaker brethren 'who had delayed too long'.[1]

His letters were 'terrifyingly depressing' to friends like Felix Braun, and even the cheerful courage of Masereel could not shake his pessimism. The artist's fiftieth birthday was due in August, and Zweig, in addition to planning an exhibition of his work in London for the autumn, had recast his 1923 essay to accompany von der Gabelentz's comprehensive bibliography of the printed works, which was to appear with Vorms in Paris.[2] But when Masereel joked 'perhaps we'll meet one day in a concentration camp', Zweig seized on this and was for ever repeating the thought, seriously, to his other friends. Louis Golding thought his eyes looked sad and curiously frightened.[3] As before, there were not wanting those who saw nothing but abject fear and cowardice in his attitude. In an article for Tcherikover's new Yiddish periodical in Paris *Oifn Sheideweg* (*Au Carrefour*), dealing with the position of Jews in political life, he had taken the sensible line (as indeed did Max Brod in the same issue, though for different, Zionist, reasons) that nothing had so promoted the anti-Semitic movement as the prominence of Jews in politics: 'it is not by pushing forward, but by deliberately holding back, that a man reveals his moral strength'. Professor Jack Isaacs, of London

[1] Letter from Ehrenstein, 22 June 1939 (ZE); letter to G. Selden-Goth, 12 July 1939 (*UB* 60–1).

[2] The war prevented publication, but von der Gabelentz printed the essay twenty years later in his *Frans Masereel*; Verlag der Kunst, Dresden, 1959.

[3] Letters from Masereel, 29 June and 11 Aug. 1939 (ZE); from Felix Braun, 15 July 1939 (ZE); and to Braun, ? early July 1939 (*Sp* 87–8); Louis Golding, *John o' London's Weekly*, 19 Mar. 1948.

University, who knew Zweig quite well, told Leftwich he thought there was a good deal to be said for this view, purely as expediency, but feared there was a strong element of 'inner cowardice' in it. In any case, it was hardly an appropriate message for the times, and Zweig's innate aversion to the strident and assertive, which had always earned him misunderstanding, was now more than ever branded by the 'men of action' as contemptible.[1]

The old anodyne of work could still be tried. Though most of the fragments, drafts, and notes which had filled his desk had been destroyed in the final clear-out of Kapuzinerberg, he had carefully preserved those for the 'great Balzac', the project that had been with him for over thirty years and which he had always conceived of as to be the crowning work of his life. Was this not the time, at last, to get down to it? It would take a year or two's work: but the time for minor subjects seemed past. It was essential, however, to get away from London and the continual pressure of people there. In July he moved with Lotte to Bath, which they had visited earlier for ten days, and whose peace and beautiful countryside, reminiscent in some ways of the Salzkammergut, made great appeal. They stayed at first at Lansdown Lodge, a boarding-house in Lansdown Road, where her brother Manfred and his wife Hannah came occasionally to see them, but where otherwise their withdrawal was complete. In the last two months of peace the change of scene and absorption in a major work seemed, as they always had in past days, to be restoring him after the spiritual and material exhaustion of London. His notes, already several hundred pages accumulated over the years, grew steadily, the flags and references in Balzac's works multiplied, and he began to sketch the first draft. Between whiles he prepared another *Sternstunde*, on the death of Cicero—'another who was killed by dictatorship, who dreamed of order and stood firm for justice'. Felix Braun was overjoyed to hear that at last the Balzac was in train: 'this is your unique task, to write such a work, no writer of the world is so much your own as he . . . your early essay will now be fully instrumented'. His life in Bath (like that of 'a crumbling stylite') seemed happy for a

[1] Leftwich 96–7.

while; Huebsch, who came for a visit in July, was dragged off on long walks—'we English have become very military now'.[1]

It was a summer of sunshine, like that of 1914. But whereas then few people had any premonition of war, now hardly a soul could doubt that the next was at the gate. For many, particularly in England, it was almost a relief, to be welcomed as ending the tensions of the last six years; in France too, though not so often, the cry was heard 'il faut en finir'. But for Zweig, infinitely depressed, feeling himself old and broken, it could only be the end. The signing of the Nazi-Soviet Pact on 23 August and the march into Poland on 31 August were merely the last nails in the coffin of Europe. Worse, the concentration camp he had so often foreseen loomed for the 'enemy alien', even in England: and while his own position, not without connections, might save him from internment, Lotte's was more dubious, and he feared for her health (she suffered from asthma) under such conditions. His Certificate of Identity had just been renewed, but his naturalization had still not come through; he felt, all the same, it was incumbent on him to take every measure possible to protect her, and on the day after Hitler's attack on Poland—while England still seemed to hesitate in her declaration of war—he applied for their marriage licence. On 6 September the civil ceremony took place in Bath, Hannah Altmann and a solicitor Ingram acting as witnesses.[2] 'Don't think I am still a lover', he had said once to Friderike about his feelings for Lotte; but, although pity (that dangerous sentiment he had described in his novel) undoubtedly entered into his motives for the marriage, her faithful devotion to him and the companionship she offered had resulted on his part in a deep warmth of regard and affection. Friderike, still in Paris, received a letter from them both, asking her to forgive them and not to regard her friendship for them as at an end. Later came a legally endorsed declaration from Stefan, with the express wish that she should continue to bear his name. At the

[1] *WvG* 390–1; Leftwich 86; letter to Felix Braun (? early Sept.) 1939 (*Sp* 89); letter from Braun, 12 Aug. 1939 (ZE); letter to Liesl Monath, 2 Sept. 1939 (LM); letter to Kesten, 12 June 1939 (*Exil* 104).

[2] Home Office papers; *BrW* 320; Fr 388; *WvG* 392–3.

end of the month the couple moved to a house of their own: Rosemount, on Lyncombe Hill, with views a little like those of Kapuzinerberg, and Friderike was invited ('how pitiless is the heart of a man!') to be their first guest—though she never went.[1]

His work on Balzac, in the first days of September, seemed pointless. His first concern must be to try to secure his position, and in letters to the Home Office and to those he thought might be able to help, like Wells and Desmond Flower, he tried to hasten the process of his naturalization. He had been provisionally graded 'B' as an enemy alien (i.e. not to be interned, but with restrictions on his movements); and to be able to speak at Freud's cremation in Golders Green on 26 September he had to plead for special dispensation to leave Bath. The procedures of the Tribunal set up to examine individual cases were inevitably slow—'remarkable that even after six years they are still not convinced of my "harmlessness", so I must stand a few more weeks in the corner like a naughty schoolboy'—but what hurt him most was the movement restriction, the 'degradation' of having to appear in person at the police-station and give detailed reasons and timing whenever he wanted to go away. It was his old hatred of officialdom with its encroachment on the liberty of the individual; and the result was that he would not apply, even when it meant missing the memorial meeting for Freud held later in London.[2]

For a short while, as in the early days of 1914, his deeply rooted pacifism appeared to have changed to a more militant view. 'We are in practice too old,' he wrote to Guido Fuchs, 'but I am somewhat disappointed that so few Austrians, Jews and Czechs have volunteered for the Army; they all want to get into the BBC or obtain permits to work, even the twenty- and thirty-year-olds. An Austrian Legion would have had more effect than all the speeches and articles—it is really painful that I at 58 cannot set an example.' To Leftwich also he deplored his age: people would say that he knew well enough he would never be accepted if he volunteered for army service, but that was how he felt about

[1] Fr 388; Fr[2] 208.

[2] Home Office papers; letters to Guido Fuchs, undated (? Sept.) and (? 5 Oct.) 1939 (StB); letter from Robert Neumann, 11 Nov. 1939 (ZE); Leftwich 87.

it. 'I can't understand a single Jew of military age not joining up to fight Hitler.'[1] He corresponded with Hugh Walpole about possible service in the newly formed Ministry of Information, which he suggested should start a German-language paper, and stressed in his letters to the Home Office the authority his name could exert for propaganda purposes abroad, especially in the neutral countries, if his offers of service to the Government were accepted. But until his 'white-washing' by the Tribunal had been completed, and his naturalization put through, there was nothing for him, and he languished inactive in Bath.[2]

Another lecture invitation to the U.S.A. had to be refused, although he hoped to be able to make a proposition in 'a few months'.[3] He pulled every string he could find in his efforts to hurry up the Home Office. To Wells, who said he would intervene on his behalf with Lord Winterton, he stressed that the delay of over a year since his application was published in the press had given rise to rumours that there must be some mysterious reason for it, and that these had been strengthened by the restriction on his movements: not only was this embarrassing and discrediting, but it also made him feel useless

> in such a decisive moment of history. I hope not to appear presumptuous in stating the purely statistic fact that from all writers in the German language not one has today a larger public in all languages of the world than myself and that only very few could have such an influence in neutral countries on both sides of the ocean. . . . Nothing is more painful than to be obliged to be idle in a time where everybody's service is a moral duty.[4]

Wells, sending his letter on to Winterton, endorsed his case strongly, saying that Zweig would be placed by many critics alongside Maugham or Galsworthy: 'this sort of thing injures us with the American intelligentsia and especially with the Jewish

[1] Letter to Guido Fuchs, undated (? Sept.) 1939; Leftwich 86.

[2] Letter from Hugh Walpole, 7 Sept. 1939 (ZE); letter to Home Office, 12 Sept. 1939 (Home Office papers).

[3] Letter to Harold R. Peat, New York, 19 Nov. 1939 (copy in ZE).

[4] His letter was in English. His knowledge of the language was never strong, and it is not known who helped him iron out here the quaintness of expression usually to be found in the many letters he wrote in English during the war.

side of it (very influential with the press) and what good it does except to gratify the xenophobia of some old fool on a tribunal, I cannot imagine'. Leftwich spoke with Humbert Wolfe, and Desmond Flower wrote to the Home Office. But despite this strong support, no exception was made in his case. It was not until 12 March 1940 that the Certificate of Naturalization was finally granted, Lotte three days later making her declaration of British nationality as his wife.[1]

9

'What more is life worth now—condemned to write in German and therefore finished in a world that belongs to that other Germany?'

Zweig to Körmendi

It is doubtful whether Zweig's brief flare of enthusiasm for the fight could ever have lasted long, even if his offers of service had been immediately accepted. As it was, condemned to inactivity and feeling hemmed in by the official restrictions, his sense of uncertainty returned. Even in the first days of mobilization he had been quite unreasonably incensed when his train for London from Bath was halted at Oxford and he had to miss a rendezvous with Friedenthal at Paddington.[2] During the first months of the 'phony war' he felt glad that he was not concerned with propaganda, in which field England seemed to him highly incompetent and even misguided. He had the feeling that government circles in England, as opposed to those of France, wanted to avoid any discussion of the re-establishment of Austria: 'the fact that they have thrown us into one pot with the Germans, while describing the Czechs as friends, seems to me a sign one cannot overlook'. The 'surprising discovery' by the Tribunal in December that he was not after all a Nazi was cold comfort.[3] Depression, heavier than ever before, returned to settle on his shoulders, an indescribable sadness, he told Leftwich, 'a kind of Job's despair, who asks God why he gives all to the wicked'.

[1] Home Office papers; Leftwich 87.

[2] Statement to the author by Richard Friedenthal.

[3] Letters to Guido Fuchs, undated (?Sept.) and 13 Dec. 1939 (StB).

News of what was happening in central Europe, and the plight of the refugees, increased his melancholy: he could hardly bear to open his mail, knowing beforehand what it would contain. The sense of belonging to a lost generation, that could not possibly survive the coming years of confusion, hatred, and bitterness to see a fairer world, once more dominated his mind; and he began to consider an autobiography—not an egocentric narrative, dwelling on his works and successes, but the story of the time he had lived through, which history, with that artistry he had often recorded, had brought to a dramatic close on 1 September. 'I will depict Vienna and the Jewish Vienna, the war and our fight in the war, our rise and downfall since Hitler, the humiliations, the life of the "sans patries". I will call it "My Three Lives", because I feel that I have lived in three different ages.' This he thought should be his task now, rather than the Balzac which would anyway take too long; and it was his main distraction while he remained buried away in Bath, trying to avoid 'plaguing my friends with my unnecessary presence'.[1]

The end of an era. It seemed fitting that Jethro Bithell should plan an anthology of modern German verse, and it was a melancholy pleasure to give his advice, suggesting Lissauer should be represented 'for curiosity value', as well as Lernet-Holenia and Max Herrmann-Neisse. The inclusion of some of his own poems drove home once more the bitterness of exile from his mother tongue (though of course the *Collected Poems* had been out of print long before 1933). The news of René Schickele's death in France in February was another symptom of finality. In one year Roth, Toller, Freud, Schickele![2] And, as he collected his memories of that earlier war, and thought of how much he had been able to achieve then, 'united in brotherhood with the best men of the time in all countries across all frontiers', he felt humbled. Then the symbol had been Jean Christophe; now his preoccupations were expressed in Martin Du Gard's *Thibault*, to which he often referred—Jacques's condemnation of war, and especially Antoine's resignation in the face of death, even without the hope of an

[1] Leftwich 86–7; letter to Liesl Monath, 30 Dec. 1939 (LM).

[2] Letters to Bithell, 15 Jan. and 12 Feb. 1940.

after-life.[1] 'Courage et surtout patience', Masereel had written, 'Hitler n'est pas éternel!' Zweig felt he could summon up neither the one nor the other. 'The good meat of life we have eaten it up', he wrote (in English) to Fleischer, '. . . silly old chaps which speak of the good old times.'[2] Even the message of optimism in Irwin Edman's *A Gleam of Light in the Darkness* (which he translated with Friedenthal as a 'finger exercise' during the long blackout evenings of January) failed to inspire him.[3]

Friderike, aware of his deep depression, took now a typically vigorous step to try a cure with the old remedy—a change of scene. In February, with the help of Duhamel and Julien Cain, she started the wheels turning for him to give a lecture in Paris, and he travelled there early in April. His choice of subject surprised her, for she had not known that he had started his autobiography.[4] It was 'Das Wien von Gestern', a theme prompted by the pathos of Vienna's tragic fate under the Nazis, and filled out by the sharper memories he was now recalling. The attendance surprised him, for the Théâtre Marigny—no small auditorium—was crammed, and hundreds were turned away. He praised the city of his birth for its tolerance, and as a place where one could breathe 'world air', without the feeling of being caged in 'one language, one race, one nation or one idea'. Contrary to Goethe's words, 'a man should neither rule nor serve'—he must above all remain free.[5]

There was not enough time to arrange a repeat, but he was able to give three talks on Radio Paris, in which, as in his 1914 essay, he spoke to his friends and spiritual compatriots in the enemy countries who had to remain silent. Rolland was in Paris at the time, but they did not meet. For Friderike the few days they could spend together were a great joy, but she realized, not only from the lecture and the radio talks, that the visit had not

[1] Letter to Körmendi, 21 Jan. 1940 (StB); Dum 326.

[2] Letter from Masereel, 4 Oct. 1939 (ZE); letter to Fleischer, undated, 1939 (Sch).

[3] *Ein Schimmer Licht im Dunkel*; Schriftenreihe 'Ausblicke', Bermann-Fischer, Stockholm, 1940.

[4] Fr 391–3; *Bildb* 105.

[5] Stefan Zweig, 'Das Wien von Gestern', *Zeit und Welt*, 132, 144.

had the effect she had hoped for. Although he took the opportunity of some research for the Balzac study, he became absorbed by the story of André Chénier ('who foresaw Napoleon as we foresaw Hitler'), taking Friderike with him to visit the grave in the Picpus cemetery.[1] At all events, she felt that only change and new projects could help him, and when, just after his return to Bath, invitations to visit South America were renewed, she pressed him to accept.[2]

Lee van Dovski, meeting him in Paris for the first time since Utrecht in 1929, found the change remarkable. The 'aristocrat' had disappeared, his Jewishness was more prominent, the delicate hands transformed and covered with dark hair. It was the physical reflection of the deepest depression of his whole life. For a brief while, he wrote to Paul Zech that spring, he had hoped to swing out of it, to look beyond the uncertainty of life in emigration, the forcible separation from people who meant much to him, like Carossa or Ricarda Huch, the terrible losses among the Jewish community; to believe that one day the clouds would lift and light once again shine down into the darkness. 'From the earliest days of my youth I strove only to stress the "European man", the "European mind". Is that lost, totally and irrevocably, after the century-long efforts of our great minds?' Now his whole being cried out that it was—gone, past, *vorbei*. 'The hatred that surrounds the world in blackness eats its way forward like a pestilence, of which the doctors know only that it takes a toll far heavier than that of plague or cholera.'[3] There seemed nothing he—or especially his generation—could do to stop it. In conversation with Cain in Paris he foresaw the tragedy which was to overwhelm France, and urged his friend (in vain) to escape while there was still time.[4] To Ludwig, in a farewell letter before his friendly rival sailed for the U.S.A. at the end of May, he said he was hesitating over accepting the South American invitation, not from fear of the crossing, but from the feeling 'that I ought not for a second time, as I did then in Switzerland, to view events

[1] Fr[2] 212–15; Fr 225; Dum 130. [2] Fr 394.
[3] Lee van Dovski, *Liber Amic* 28; *Ged* 27–8.
[4] Letter from Julien Cain to Friderike Zweig, 1946.

only from the outside'. But by the time of the fall of France, a blow that hit him harder than the *Anschluss*, he thought he would probably go—'though things look so frightful that a well-aimed torpedo-shot would to my mind be the best answer'.[1]

Actual emigration further west, to either North or South America, he seemed to have ruled out. In March he had written to Kesten that to leave Europe now would mean that one would never return. 'Here we can fulfil a duty, merely by our presence. America would swallow us up.' Meeting him in Paris, he went further: 'an intellectual who leaves Europe now betrays her'.[2] Even after the fall of France he told Fleischer that Bath gave him the first feeling of home he had had for years, happy with his books and papers together: the only thing that frightened him was the thought of the possible invasion and what would follow it—'the Nazis shall not find me alive!'[3]

It hardly seemed worth the tedious battle for the necessary U.K. exit and U.S. transit visas for the visit to South America, and right to the last moment he was undecided whether to go. There seems no doubt, however, that he regarded the journey purely as a visit and, if he did go, intended to return to England. Heinrich Eisemann, an old friend of his autograph-collecting days, finally secured at his request reservations on the Cunard liner *Scythia*, sailing early in July for New York from Liverpool; but when he telephoned the news, Zweig said he could not travel. The next day, however, he rang Eisemann again and asked him to accept the bookings. 'I could not decide . . . for a long time, but now it has become pressing, highly pressing, to try to take some action [in South America],' he wrote to Leftwich just before departing, 'everything depends now on the New World. . . . I hope to be back home by the end of October . . . on the journey I shall work on my autobiography.' Manfred and Hannah Altmann, with Eisemann, saw them off from Euston. In

[1] Letter to Ludwig (?30 or 31) May 1940 (Sch); letter to Fleischer, 19 June 1940 (Sch). Cf. also *BrW* 321.

[2] Kesten, *Poeten* 151.

[3] Letter to Fleischer, undated (Sch).

the pressure for reservations the only berths available in this last-minute rush had been on a lower deck; but on their arrival on board the captain was happy to offer so distinguished a couple his own cabin.[1]

[1] Statement to the author by Heinrich Eisemann; Leftwich 82.

VIII. The Last Years 1940–1942

'What think you of the dire fate that has brought us to birth in these times? . . . For myself I see no other course but to emigrate, forsake my home and go wherever Fortune bears me. . . . When, on the threshold of our century, a new world rose from the waves, the gods destined it as a refuge where men shall till free fields under a fairer sky, while the cruel sword and a shameful plague doom the ruins of Europe.'

La Boétie to Montaigne, *c.* 1560

'The game of chess in which he was engrossed led him to make one careless move after another; and despair, which had long looked over his shoulder, finally guided the hand which could not take back the sacrifice. He realised that he was checkmated, or rather: he thought he was. It was the daimon of impatience that overturned the board.'

Felix Braun, *Das Musische Land*

I

'Emigration implies a shifting of one's centre of gravity.' Zweig to Thomas Mann

Zweig's intention had been to make his transit of the United States as short as possible, and embark for Brazil by the first available ship. The end of the battle in France, however, had left Friderike and her daughters, as well as many other friends, in a serious plight, and he felt he should lend his aid to the efforts being made by the refugees already in America to obtain entry visas for the large number who wished to cross, as well as to other forms of help. With Lotte, he put up at the Wyndham Hotel on West 58th Street, and it was nearly a month before they left New York.[1]

When the threat to Paris became clear, Friderike had been able, just three days before its occupation by the Germans, to make her way south to Montauban. Suse and their spaniel Schuschu (the last of Kaspar's puppies), neither of whom were fit, joined friends in one of the rare taxis that could be found for the journey; Friderike and Alix, with what little luggage they could carry, had to join the crowds at the station, where by a miracle they succeeded in finding room on a train. The arrival of a number of foreign embassy staffs in Montauban, and the presence among the refugees there of people who in the past had had to do with the Salzburg Festival, inspired Friderike to suggest to the Mexican ambassador a blow for his country's tourist trade by granting visas for a suitable party of artists: her approach appealed to Señor Rodriguez, for Zweig's name was as well known in Mexico as in the other Latin-American countries, and visas were eventually granted for over a hundred. Meanwhile, the efforts of Stefan and the others in the United States had also been successful: President Roosevelt authorized the grant of U.S. visas for about a thousand 'intellectuals in danger', and sent a personal representative to Marseille to deal with the applications. Making her way there, Friderike was able to include not only herself and her daughters but also the latter's husbands, who, having served for a time with the French army, had now secured their demobilization. Visas were one thing: actually to leave Vichy France quite another, for exit permits required both Vichy and German approval. A clandestine crossing into Spain would first be necessary. After many vicissitudes, including crossing the Pyrenees on foot, the party reached Lisbon about the middle of September.[2]

Since leaving Paris Friderike had been uncertain of Stefan's own movements. Her relations in New York, to whom she had written from Montauban, were able to give him her address there, and thereafter cables and letters kept them in touch. The terrible events

[1] Letter to G. Selden-Goth (July) 1940 (*UB* 64).

[2] Fr 394–5; Fr² 215–31; *BrW* 321–2.

in France had shaken him, and although when he arrived in New York he announced his firm intention of returning to Bath once the tour was over ('where I have all my possessions, my books, and hoped to live out my life in quiet'), by the end of July he was already wondering whether he would ever see Rosemount again—'j'ai tout laissé et je n'ai même pas pu prendre mes cahiers de travail [Balzac] avec moi'.[1] He expressed to Jules Romains, who had also now reached America, some bitterness over the 'enemy alien' marking in his passport, which brought him dark looks from immigration officers; and he contrasted England's indifference towards intellectuals with the respect they had always earned in France. His baggage had been searched at Liverpool as though he were a common criminal.[2] To Thomas Mann, soon after his arrival, writing in admiration of his *Lotte in Weimar*, which he had reviewed in glowing terms before leaving London, he said that England in the first months of the war had made him feel helpless and useless, with the internment of the enemy aliens (both Robert Neumann and Eisemann were in camps), the 'fifth column' agitation, and the growing resentment against all those with a German-sounding name; but he hoped *rebus bene gestis* to return there, without adding to the number of the displaced and homeless or increasing the burden of the others. He had had to leave the almost completed manuscript of the Balzac study behind, he said, 'but is it not more important to save oneself for the work one can still do rather than for that half-done or already completed?' In a later letter he said he was quite determined to return to England, unless Mosley became dictator there—in which event America would equally be no long-term refuge—but for the moment he was trying to put out of his mind the question of *Wohin*: 'either the storm blows itself out or one ends oneself'.[3]

[1] *BrW* 322; letter to G. Selden-Goth (July) 1940(*UB* 64); letter to Fleischer, 22 July 1940 (Sch).

[2] He told Romains, in fact, that his Balzac manuscript had been confiscated there: 'they must have thought there were military secrets in it' (Romains, 'Les Derniers Mois et Dernières Lettres de Stefan Zweig', *Revue de Paris* (Feb. 1955), 4). A copy of part of the manuscript was, however, with him in America and Brazil.

[3] Letters of 17 and 29 July 1940 (TMArch).

'Formerly writer, now expert in visas', half his time was spent in the interminable efforts to get help for friends and acquaintances—the affidavits, permits, money so desperately needed—but he was trying to work as well, continuing with the autobiography.[1] 'We are after all participants in one of the greatest transformations of the world, and so long as I cannot bear witness in the artistic sense (creatively) I will at least do so in the documentary.'[2] He also wrote two articles for the *New York Times* on 'The Effects of War on the Future of Writing', and sought some relaxation in collaboration with Berthold Viertel on the film script from his unfinished *Postfräuleingeschichte*. (Their agreement was to share equally the costs of agents' fees, etc., but any eventual profits were to go to Viertel, Zweig professing no interest in its future.)[3]

The apparent firmness of these sentiments was soon belied. He tired quickly of the efforts needed, dealing with the 'authorities' he hated so much, to secure the salvation of Friderike and the other refugees, and was always stressing the precariousness of his own situation, with only a transit visa for the United States. He could, no doubt, have extended this, but felt unable to summon up the strength necessary for pressure on the authorities; and even before the Washington decision on visas for the 'intellectuals in danger' had come through, he went ahead with his reservations on the *Argentina* sailing for Rio on 9 August. He was letting himself be driven, once again, by circumstances which with determination it would have been quite possible to alter. This inner uncertainty and weakness showed itself in an increasing irritation at the apparent inability of others to help themselves. He persuaded himself that the plight of Friderike and her family (still, as far as he knew then, in unoccupied France) was due to their failure to secure foreign visas in time (though this was in fact far from the case).[4] It was not till nearly a month after his arrival in Rio that he heard that she and the others were at last on

[1] Kesten, *Exil* 179; letter to G. Selden-Goth (summer) 1940 (*UB* 65).

[2] Letter to Thomas Mann, 29 July 1940 (TMArch).

[3] *Blätter der Internationalen Stefan-Zweig-Gesellschaft*, 8/10 (Oct. 1960), 14–17; *Ausst* 88; letter from Viertel to Friderike Zweig, undated.

[4] Letter to Siegfried Burger, *c.* 15 Aug. 1940.

the way across the Atlantic: he had been able to telephone her in Lisbon, transmit funds, and arrange for one of the Portuguese ministers, whom he knew, to give her some assistance there. With a large party of the intellectuals who had qualified for U.S. visas—the Werfels, Alfred Polgar, Golo Mann, Heinrich Mann and his wife, and Buzislawsky among them—she finally secured passages on the Greek vessel *Nea Hellas*, and arrived in New York on 13 October.[1]

For Stefan and Lotte the change of scene to South America was naturally beneficial. 'We are ashamed that we are here in a country at peace and unbelievably beautiful', wrote Lotte in English to Fleischer; though Stefan added, 'I wish I would be again in Bath'.[2] His reception in Rio, where they arrived on 21 August, was warm, but not on the quasi-royal scale of four years earlier, for he had written to Koogan, his publisher, to emphasize his desire to lead as quiet a life as possible, and treat the visit as a 'holiday', by which he meant being able to work in seclusion.[3] Although, therefore, some lectures had been arranged (one, in French, was on 'La Vienne d'autrefois'), the publicity about his arrival and stay in Rio was restrained. He attended a PEN Club dinner in September, and was able to see the friends he most cared for, such as Jaime Chermont and Mello-Franco; but was otherwise free, not only to get quietly on with the autobiography, but also to travel and see more of Brazil, in readiness for another project he now had in mind—the expansion to book form of his 1936 essays on this 'country of the future'. To this end he regarded his lecture tour to Argentina and Uruguay merely as a three-week excursion, after which he would return to Brazil for the remainder of the year, before going back to the United States and (eventually) England.

During September and most of October he managed to sink himself in this work; and between lectures, Spanish lessons three times weekly to prepare himself for the 'excursion', and visits to São Paulo and Ouro Preto, was able to some extent to put out of his mind the subjugation of Europe and the apparently overwhelm-

[1] *BrW* 323–4; Fr 395–6; *Wendepunkt* 409.

[2] Letter of 9 Sept. 1940 (Sch).

[3] Letter of 22 July 1940 (K).

ing threat to England. But he could not entirely suppress the gnawing thought that what he had left in Bath might be destroyed, and that he might not be able to return. Condoling with Friderike on the death of the younger of her two brothers, Arnold, he wrote: 'it might have been better for him to have stayed in Europe, it is still a good place to die in (not to live in). I am almost certain that everything I have in England, my books, my manuscripts, my savings, will be lost, but at least I have passed a good year far from the daily terror and I hope to continue the last years of my life somewhere—God knows where?' A short stay in Teresepolis, where a pension owned by a Czech family served traditional delicacies, did something to cheer him before he left for Buenos Aires by air on 26 October.[1]

Alfredo Cahn (often known as 'Alfredo Zweig' or 'Stefan Cahn' because of his single-minded devotion to the master) was delighted to be able this time to welcome him in his own right, rather than as merely another PEN Club visitor. He made use of the occasion of his own birthday on 28 October to invite a representative selection from the literary, artistic, and scientific circles of Buenos Aires to a supper party, and was impressed by the way in which Zweig took pains to neglect none of the guests, speaking now English, now Spanish, French, or German. It was characteristic that, when he was received by the Argentine Foreign Minister, Zweig refused any form of honour, asking instead (successfully) for visas for three German refugees. Four lectures had been arranged in the capital. The first, in the Colegio Libre de Estudios Superiores, attracted several thousand people: police control was necessary, traffic to the school barred, the hall emptied of some of its seats to give more standing room, and loudspeaker relays to adjoining rooms arranged. A delegation of young people approached Cahn before the lecture started, to plead for a repeat, to which Zweig after some hesitation agreed; and as he went up to the lectern the first thousand seats for the next performance had already been sold. Among those standing were a former Vice-President of the Republic, two senators, one of the leading political party chiefs, and several professors. Zweig acquitted

[1] De Souza 30; *BrW* 323–4; letters to Siegfried Burger, Sept. and 20 Oct. 1940.

himself well in Spanish, and the 'miracle' of a foreign author speaking in the vernacular enhanced the sensation. He felt like a famous tenor when he had to be shut in a small room after the talk to protect him from the crowd. 'Never before or since', wrote Cahn, 'has Buenos Aires seen anything like it.'[1]

In Cordoba, where with Cahn he spent the night of 7 November, there was a similar scene. As there was no opportunity to repeat the lecture, the joint hosts, the Press and Jockey Clubs, arranged for loudspeakers outside the theatre where he spoke, which was packed. He was thoroughly exhausted after further talks in Santa Fé, Rosario, and again in Buenos Aires, where he spoke in English to the British Community Council and in German to the aid organization for German-speaking Jews—not so much from the performances themselves as from the overwhelming hospitality of the Argentinians, and the effort of keeping up conversation in Spanish, which, despite his lessons, never became easy for him. The fact that such a well-known European author was actually visiting the interior brought people from far and wide to see him; invitations, receptions, sightseeing crowded each day; he found it impossible to pay for anything himself. At Santa Fé, in fact, he felt he could not keep up the pace, and tried to cancel the Uruguay visit. His hosts there, however, would not be put off, offering double fees and the cost of the air passage, and he could not let them down. He flew to Montevideo on 13 November, gave the contracted radio talk, and was back the following day, to fly off to Rio again on 15 November.[2]

He had given the proceeds of the English and German lectures to the welfare organizations concerned, but the income from the tour remained substantial, and it had been a most remarkable experience, with three weeks of impressions almost as crowded as had been those of Brazil in 1936. But even before the Montevideo trip his depression had quickly returned. In his mail was news of the death in an air crash in Brazil of Hernandez Catá, the Cuban ambassador and a gifted writer who had become a close friend. Zweig felt himself almost responsible, for he had recommended

[1] Manuscript account (Cahn); Kesten, *Aufbau*, New York, 27 February 1942, 15. Cf. also *BrW* 330.

[2] Manuscript account (Cahn); *BrW* 325–8.

to the people in São Paulo that they should invite Catá to lecture, and it was on the return journey from there that the tragedy had occurred. And there was news too of the suicide of Ernst Weiss: death seemed to take only the best. 'I think I will never get back to Europe,' he wrote to Friderike, 'and everything I have there, my books and above all my Balzac (three-quarters written and prepared) are lost, as well as all the lands in which I had roots, for the English and American world is not mine. . . . At least, in order to be sure of a country where one does not have to beg for visas, I have ensured a permanent visa for Brazil.' Back in Rio, where he hoped to spend at least a month in quiet work, he found it hard to settle, with the thought recurring that publication in German was vain, that he could never strike roots again, that he was old. 'You at least have two more years to go till sixty,' he wrote to Friderike on her birthday in December, 'while I am on the last of the fifties. When I applied the other day for a police identity card, the nice young lady wrote: "Hair, grey." No wonder.' He refused to believe that the Balzac material could be sent on from England through the censorship; and the news of the bombing-out of Cassells in London, with the destruction of their entire autumn production, including his own *Tide of Fortune* (twelve *Sternstunden*), confirmed his fears that his possessions in England were a write-off. Moreover, the wartime financial restrictions introduced by the British began to make him think that his circumstances were straitening—or at least to say so, in and out of season.[1]

What concentration he could muster he devoted to the preparation of the book on Brazil. Leopold Stern, who had just arrived in Rio from Europe, and was assembling impressions for his own book, remembered joining him on a 'voyage de documentation' on the *bonde*, the Rio trams, and dividing the spoils afterwards (Zweig would use the story of Pedro II's personal tram-car, while he would take the anecdote of the origin of the phrase 'Vai comprar um bonde').[2] The Brazilian Government were keen to

[1] *BrW* 328–9.

[2] Leopold Stern, *Rio de Janeiro et Moi*, Editora Civilização Brasileira, Rio, 1942, 255–61.

further Zweig's project, which promised valuable publicity for the country, and offered him considerable facilities, especially for travel to the northern states which he had not yet seen and which he proposed to visit on his way back to the U.S.A. The summer heat of Brazil was not conducive to work, though it had the advantage of making him lose weight. His Christmas wishes to Friderike were gloomy. Rosemount was as good as lost: 'Bristol is being bombed daily and we are as near as Brooklyn is to New York—no, much nearer. But at least one's bones are away.' He had had no word from any of the friends left behind in that 'hell'—Fleischer, Felix Braun, Warburg, and the others—and was unable to help them. 'People who make "literature" today or are able to speak, I cannot fully understand: it seems to me more like a human defect than a virtue (but perhaps art is really always determined by defects).'[1]

Absorbed by Brazil as a subject, he intended to leave the autobiography until his return to North America. The thought of New York, however, with its inflated population of refugees, was repugnant: there were nearly three hundred people he knew there, who would all be offended if he did not see them, and he felt he could stand company only in small doses.

> It exhausts me to have to see five or six people every day. . . . The telephone went from morning till night in New York and Buenos Aires; what I fear is that people over-estimate me, I would be expected to get Huebsch to publish their books, arrange introductions to papers etc. etc., when if I can do something I do it spontaneously. . . . I am not blessed with the wise economy of Mann, who can get rid of people after an hour—with me they all stay three.

He besought Friderike, therefore, not to tell anyone he was coming, so that he might have a week or so in New York dealing with his own affairs, and be able to find a place, not too far away, perhaps in a small university town with a good library, where he would be able to work in peace and choose his company.[2] But his plans wavered, the uncertainty of life was too great, and despair was not far beneath the surface. 'To survive,' he wrote to Zech on 12 December, '. . . yes, that could be everything. But will one be

[1] *BrW* 330–1. [2] *BrW* 330–2.

able to summon the patience for it?' He was glad that few people remembered or were able to reach him on his fifty-ninth birthday; yet the solitude and the almost total break in mail communications with England brought terrible depression. As a Christmas and New Year's card he printed a translation he had just made of a stanza from Camoens' *Lusiades*:

> Weh, wieviel Not und Fährnis auf dem Meere,
> Wie nah der Tod in tausendfalt Gestalten!
> Auf Erden, wieviel Krieg! Wieviel der Ehre
> Verhaßt Geschäft! Ach daß nur eine Falte
> Des Weltballs für den Menschen sicher wäre
> Sein bißchen Dasein friedlich durchzuhalten
> Indes die Himmel wetteifern im Sturm,
> Und gegen wen? Den ärmsten Erdenwurm![1]

2

> *'Not for peace have we been the chosen among the peoples. Wandering is our habitation, sorrow our soil, God our home in the ages; . . . suffering is your holy heritage.'*
> *Jeremias*

Early in January 1941 Zweig set off with Lotte for the tour of northern Brazil and the return to the United States. They saw Bahia, Pernambuco, and Belém, where he spent ten days completing the final draft of the book, to be called *Brasilien—Land der Zukunft*. He had planned to avoid too rapid a change from the heat of Brazil to the northern cold; but once in Florida they in fact travelled by air via Washington to New York, arriving on 23 January. Though he had promised to advise Friderike, with the change of plan she had received no message, and was astounded, calling at the British Consulate to collect a 'navicert' for heavy luggage expected from Europe, to see Stefan step from one of

1 'Ah woe! How much distress and danger on the sea, how near us death in myriad forms! On land, what strife, what commerce odious to honour! Would there were but one corner of the globe secure for man to live out in peace his brief existence, while the storms of the heavens vie—against whom? the miserablest worm on earth!'

Letter to Zech, *Ged* 37; *BrW* 331; Fr 402. The poem was sent to Zech, Wittkowski, and Gisella Selden-Goth, among others.

the lifts. He had reported with their passports half an hour after their arrival.[1]

It was a coincidence which seemed to both of them to hold a deep significance. For Stefan, who now spent nearly three weeks in New York before finding the quieter retreat he wanted, it was strangely calming to discover that an affinity he had thought lost still remained between them, and that chance or destiny had led them to a meeting which, premeditated, might well have been a difficult one. Whereas he had hitherto carefully avoided a confrontation between Friderike and Lotte, he now found he could consider their meeting with equanimity. For her part, Friderike, who had always thought to see the hand of destiny in her relations with Stefan, was surprised to find in her heart no animosity towards Lotte, whose quiet devotion she saw was now such an important part of Stefan's life. On the contrary, she felt greater understanding for her and sympathy in her worry over her family caught up in the London 'blitz'. Their lives had not merely grown apart but had developed more sharply the contrast of former years: she was more active than ever, extrovert, thriving on contacts with people, while Stefan sought to retire ever deeper into his shell. In her modest rooms in Greenwich Village it was she who now enjoyed the student-like independence he had once wanted for himself. Yet, though Stefan never risked leaving her alone with Lotte, the three achieved for a few months a relationship of balance and cordiality which helped him immeasurably at first, not only in concentrating on *Brasilien* but also in ideas for new work.[2]

As he had foreseen, New York (he stayed again at the Wynddam Hotel) was quite impossible to work in, and although he completed a *Novelle*,[3] and *Brasilien* was soon more or less finished, the final version needed less distraction. He settled on New Haven, Connecticut, where Yale's excellent library would be at his disposal, and on 11 February moved into the Taft Hotel there.

Within three weeks he was able to send the book in sea-mail

[1] *BrW* 331–2; Fr 402; Fr[2] 236–7.

[2] Fr 402–4; *BrW* 332.

[3] *Fishermen on the Seine*, published only in English (Harpers, Feb. 1941).

instalments to Koogan in Rio, so that the Portuguese version could appear at the same time as those in English, German, and other languages; had written another *Novelle*; and was deep in research for a short study of Amerigo Vespucci, the mystery of whose 'baptism' of America had suddenly intrigued him. Working in the Yale library was a 'boon and comfort', and a subject like Amerigo the only possible isolation from the horror of world events. He was near enough to New York to get there easily when necessary, but far enough away to escape the pressure of people; at the same time, there were a few good friends and acquaintances in the area—Schalom Asch, Henrik van Loon, Thornton Wilder. There was a great deal of typing to be done, both for the *Novellen* and for *Brasilien*, copies of which had to be prepared for English, French, Spanish, and Swedish translation, and Alix was pressed into service to help Lotte, against due payment. For a short while the wheels of the 'business' seemed to be turning again as of old.[1]

He was not deceived, however. There were too many influences at work against any such return to bygone happiness. When he had first arrived the previous year the Americans' blind optimism and lack of preparation against the coming onslaught had appalled and dismayed him: like England before her, the U.S.A. was surrendering her outer bulwarks of defence, with no appreciation of the danger, and sticking her head in the sand of an unreal neutrality that was doomed in advance.[2] Now it seemed even worse. 'It will be the most terrible year in world history, and whoever is not lucky enough (as most are) to feel indifference to what does not directly affect him, suffers most horribly. I *know* what is coming, and it often drives me to distraction.'[3] He thought that even Switzerland would fall to the Nazis, and arranged to cash and divide with Friderike a joint insurance policy they had had for many years there.[4] To his sharp sense of the world disaster was added private grief. That spring came the

[1] *BrW* 333–4; letters to Koogan, 11 and 22 Feb. 1941 (K); letter to Fleischer, 22 Feb. 1941 (Sch).

[2] Letter to Thomas Mann, 29 July 1940 (TMArch).

[3] *BrW* 334.

[4] Statement to the author by Friderike Zweig.

news of the deaths of Max Herrmann-Neisse in London, of Oskar Loerke in Berlin, and, most shattering of all, of Erwin Rieger in Tunis—'one more piece of the past has gone, he was always loyal, and a true friend'. 'The emptiness grows quickly around one, and one tells oneself that Roth and all the others took the more sensible road' (he was convinced that Roth's drinking had been a form of suicide).[1] Hotel existence, too, was steadily wearing him down. 'Better to live in tents and hotels and to be free!' had been his cry after the *Anschluss*;[2] now the nomadic life, in happier days a welcome relief, pressed heavily and increased his unrest. Finally, Lotte's health gave some cause for concern. Her asthma remained troublesome, and the sudden change to a North American winter had given her influenza and a succession of colds. He was still longing to return to England, but it was clear that if, as he now thought, this was out of the question, they would before long have to seek a less extreme climate. By the time *Amerigo* was completed, at the end of March, he was already planning to return to Brazil, perhaps in June before the American summer got too hot, hoping by that time to have completed the autobiography in its main lines. But then, in spite of all he had said about the impossibility of New York, he took the surprising, and unfortunate, decision to exchange the Taft for the Wyndham again.[3]

Inevitably, he was drawn once more into the sphere of refugee aid. The 'Emergency Rescue Committee', headed by Frank Kingdon, in which Erika Mann, Kesten, and, of course, Friderike were active, pressed him to speak at a dinner to raise funds for its work. Having somewhat reluctantly agreed, he found the preparation of the ten-minute speech extremely difficult. 'I do not want to say a word that could be interpreted as encouragement for America's entry into the war, no word that announces victory, nothing that justifies or glorifies war, and yet the thing must have an optimistic ring.' He found the American method of passing round the hat distasteful, and the political intrigue behind

[1] *BrW* 334–5; letter to Zech, 22 Apr. 1941 (Sch).

[2] Letter to G. Selden-Goth, 21 Sept. 1938 (*UB* 55).

[3] Letter to Fleischer, 26 May 1941 (Sch); letter to Koogan, 28 Mar. 1941 (K).

the scenes even more so. But it went off successfully.[1] Later Jules Romains proposed to the Committee that its work might be helped by the formation of a 'European PEN Centre' in New York—a sensible suggestion, for the London and New York PEN Clubs were obviously not up to the task of giving adequate aid to the refugee writers who, in many cases with no knowledge of English, were in severe straits. This did not prevent opposition from the existing Clubs, who regarded it as disruptive of the PEN organization; but despite the quarrels it went ahead, and Zweig was glad this time to be asked to speak at the opening of the Centre on 15 May.

He dwelt in his speech (which was later broadcast to Europe in English and German) on the tragedy that the persecuted should have to share the language of their persecutors, that crimes against the spirit of freedom were being conceived in the same idiom in which the sufferers thought and spoke. 'It is for us today, us who can still speak, to maintain unshakably erect, in a confused and already half-destroyed world, our belief in moral strength, our trust in the unconquerable spirit, despite everything.'[2] Thanking Claudio de Souza, the President of the Brazilian Club, for his message of support, he wrote that it had been read before an audience of 1,000, and that $5,600 had been collected for aid to refugee writers.[3] On 4 June he gave a cocktail party at the Wyndham for all his Austrian and German friends. It was a rare departure from his customary retiring ways, and significant of the deep sympathy he felt for his fellow refugees, even though he had himself never known the hardships to which most of them were exposed. ('It goes without saying that you are cordially invited', he told Friderike, and she was proud to be able to show publicly that their divorce had not diminished their affection for each other.)[4]

But his activity on behalf of the refugees—and it was much more than these few public appearances led people to believe—was an expression rather of his own inner despair than of any real hope for the future. 'You are only just starting a life in exile', he

[1] Fr 404; *BrW* 336.

[2] Romains, op. cit. 6. Zweig's speech was published in *Aufbau*, New York, 16 May 1941, 3.

[3] De Souza 32.

[4] *BrW* 337.

had said to André Maurois the previous year. 'You will see how, little by little, the world refuses itself to the exiled. . . . You will know a life which is no longer *our* life, and which is hardly worth the effort of living.'[1] Klaus Mann, happening to meet him on Fifth Avenue not long after the cocktail party, noted with some alarm how strange and wild Zweig (not at first seeing him and thinking himself unobserved) appeared in demeanour and glance: he was unshaven, and deep in thought, clearly not very pleasant thought. Accosted by Mann, he pulled himself together 'like a sleep-walker who hears his name', and in a trice was once again the old Stefan Zweig, the elegant and worldly man of letters, friendly and interested. But Mann could not forget that first, despairing look.[2]

Zuckmayer, visiting New York from his Vermont farm about this time, and invited to dine with Zweig in a French restaurant, was also struck by the unrelieved pessimism of this man, not yet sixty, still in excellent health and untouched by the struggle for existence which was the usual lot of the refugee. 'However war comes out,' said Zweig, 'a world is coming to which we don't belong.' Remembering their dinner together at Schwarz's in Munich on his fiftieth birthday, he said he thought sixty was enough; when Zuckmayer laughed and said 'We must get to 90 or 100, so that we can once again see decent times', he rejoined, with an infinite sadness, 'They will never come again, never for us. We shall be homeless . . . what sense is there in living on as one's own shadow? We are only ghosts—or memories.'[3] Earlier in the year, writing to Ludwig to congratulate him on reaching sixty, he had asked him to show by his example that this age need not necessarily mean decline, but, on the contrary, the expectation of 'new puberties, in the spirit of Father Goethe'.[4] The joviality was forced, and as he himself approached this threshold

[1] Maurois, Preface to De Souza, *Les Derniers Jours de Stefan Zweig*, Ed. Quetzal, Mexico, 1944, 13–14.

[2] *Wendepunkt* 431 (also in Arens[2] 201–2). Zweig in fact always hated shaving himself: Mann, writing after his death, may have thought to see more in his appearance than was there.

[3] Zuckmayer, Arens[2] 245–6.

[4] Letter to Ludwig, undated (?early Feb. 1941).

of age its significance as the end of life took increasing hold of his mind.

It was ironic that one who was falling ever deeper into despair should just now join the oracles contributing short articles to the *Readers Digest* series 'Profit From My Experience'. In two pieces in the July issue ('What Money Means to Me' and 'Never Hesitate!') the man who was unable to solve his own problems could advise his readers that 'our real security lies not in what we own but in what we are and what we create out of ourselves'; and 'one should never hesitate to obey the first impulse to give support, because a word or deed of compassion has real value only in the moment of utmost need'.[1]

Despite the distractions of New York he managed to get a good deal of work done on the autobiography: but this too was with a sense of ending, an artistic rounding-off of a life that was finished. 'What can we do with our pen?' he wrote, in English, to Fleischer towards the end of June.

> I have finished my book on Brazil and a little study on Amerigo Vespucci and am working on my autobiography. . . . There will not be much of private things in this reminiscence. It will be a large outlook and let us hope I can finish it within this my sixtieth year. Perhaps it will be the last I can say to this world from which I willingly would take leave. . . . I am very sad, you know I have a black liver and a too far-seeing eye; suffering from the today I see already in the same time the sorrows of tomorrow; the victory even will be spoilt to us all by the convulsions of the post war world. . . . I wish I could give you more courage than I have myself.[2]

It was already high summer, and very hot. It seemed necessary to make a concentrated effort to break the back of the work, in surroundings more congenial than those of an hotel room, before they escaped to the mild winter of Rio. At the end of June he moved with Lotte to Ossining, N.Y., renting a small villa at 7 Ramapo Road. Jules Romains wondered at his choice of this 'banlieue sinistre', which was hardly likely to lighten his dark mood. It was determined primarily by the fact that Friderike, whom he wanted to be able to consult frequently over the book,

[1] *Readers Digest*, July 1941. [2] Letter of 25 June 1941 (Sch).

had moved there some weeks before; installed nearby, he could readily tap her own memories, and Alix could help with the typing. For Lotte the move brought her nearer her niece, Eva, her brother Manfred's daughter, who had recently been evacuated from England and was boarding at a school in neighbouring Croton. There began now a frantic, almost desperate, month of hard work, a daily stint in the midsummer heat of eight or nine hours. Stefan seemed as though he were working against time, against some deadline known only to him; Lotte strove to keep pace, as though to prove to others and to herself that her health was no handicap. When Friderike remonstrated with Stefan that she would not be able to maintain this murderous effort, he replied that the absorption in work would be good for her health.[1]

Was there a deadline? Had he taken a decision which he told no one about? To Romains, who saw a great deal of the couple during June and July before his own departure for Mexico, they gave the impression, in spite of their frenzied work, of being physically and morally broken—indeed, Zweig wrote to him later of a 'breakdown' at this time. 'I thought when I married a young wife I was assuring a modicum of gaiety for my later years,' he said once, 'and now here I am obliged myself to sustain her.' Remembering afterwards the last time they met at Ossining, in the middle of July, Romains was convinced that there had been some crisis, 'une épreuve spécialement cruelle', but had no idea what it could have been.[2] It seems likely that it was in fact the renewed close association with Friderike, and the memories awakened by their work together on the autobiography, which occasioned the tension. He visited her frequently in the rooms she occupied in the Hildebrandts' bungalow in Ossining, and on one occasion avowed in desperation that he wanted to stay with her, never leave her again.[3] But it was too late. The realization that he was committed, tied irrevocably to Lotte, that the line was unerasably drawn between the second and third of his 'Three

[1] Dum 338; Fr 407–8; Fr² 239; statement to the author by Friderike Zweig.

[2] Dum 338; letter from Romains to Friderike Zweig, 15 June 1947.

[3] Statement to the author by Friderike Zweig.

Lives', and that he could never go back to what had been, must have been overwhelming for a spirit that so hated to be fettered.

The testimony of René Fülöp-Miller is significant for this crucial period. One of Zweig's oldest friends, since the days in 1905 when the older man had been so encouraging over his first poetic efforts, Fülöp-Miller had also found refuge near Ossining, and spent many an evening in discussion with him about a comprehensive work on Death on which he was engaged. Only later did it strike him how interested Zweig had been in poisons and their lethal dosage, and in the psychology of the final hour, turning the conversation again and again to these aspects of the subject.[1] In a letter to Zech about this time, referring to the suicides of Weiss and Hasenclever, Zweig said: 'They lost patience. Should one therefore deplore them and accuse them of betrayal? I should be the last to do so.'[2] We can have no doubt that the feeling had grown in him that his life was at its end, and that the thought of suicide—not for the first time—was now never far from the surface. But no one can say for certain exactly what was in his mind as, at the end of July, the autobiography virtually finished, he tooked reservations on the *Uruguay* due to sail for Rio from New York on 15 August. 'Back to South America on the old work and lecture business,' he wrote to Kesten just before sailing, 'and I hope from there to fix my immigration later. . . . Auf Wiedersehen unten oder oben.' To Romains in Mexico he spoke of his 'psychic depressions', and the feeling of indecision which had weighed him down for months. 'On the one hand it would be madness to return to England, where morally I am a foreigner and still a little the old "enemy alien"; on the other, there are difficulties in living abroad without the possibility of settling somewhere—my position becomes more and more absurd.' Romains would one day return to France, America would have been merely an episode for him: he, however, would never again have a homeland, 'et le provisoire semble devenir pour moi le définitif'.[3]

[1] Fülöp-Miller, Arens[1] 167–8. [2] *Ged* 29–30.

[3] Letter to Kesten, 15 Aug. 1941 (*Exil* 196); letter to Romains, 11 Aug. 1941 (Romains, op. cit. 7–8); letter to Eisemann, 22 July 1941 (*Ausst* 89).

To Koogan, who had suggested that, since he wished to live quietly in Brazil, it would be best to rent a small villa in Petropolis, he wrote to give his date of arrival, and said this seemed a good idea: he was very tired, and their one dream was of being able at last to rest. 'Ne dites rien avant à personne.' A little later he said that though they had at first thought of an apartment in Rio, the idea of changing again in the hot weather in December was repellent. 'We have been months, more than a year, in hotels, and you can imagine how much we long to stay in one place, chez nous.' He spoke of learning Portuguese, which should not be difficult as he could already read it well.[1] To Fleischer he wrote at length in English on 7 August, expressing his fatigue and the destruction of his life by the war, 'because we with our sixty years will be too old for this new world to come'. The autobiography would perhaps be his last book, for he felt completely exhausted.

> This nomadic life from hotel to hotel . . . the lack of real rest and concentration begins to disturb me seriously—if I could only see a future life and a real past! Shall I ever see the Bath again? . . . I suddenly begin to feel like an old man—is it the shadow of the sixtieth year? I would like to live forgotten on a forgotten place somewhere and never to open more a newspaper. Most of the emigrees have settled down here, only my self and Lotte are wandering and wandering without to see a final rest. . . .[2]

The few days before sailing he spent in New York, once more at the Wyndham. There were farewells to his closer friends, such as Berthold Viertel and Joachim Maass; Friderike came from Ossining to spend with them the day before departure; and they visited Eva at Croton. There seemed a finality in these goodbyes. To Maass Zweig appeared highly nervous, complaining of the idiotic formalities required for a journey these days, irritable and obviously heavily overworked. Returning to the hotel after dinner with him and Lotte at a Viennese restaurant, Zweig left them abruptly in the bar, saying he had to lie down; and Maass heard Lotte's despair over Stefan's condition—she had no idea

[1] Letters to Koogan, 1 Aug. 1941 and undated (*Nouvelles Littéraires*, Paris, 44e année, No. 2036, 8 Sept. 1966, 7).

[2] Sch.

what was wrong with him, and said she felt powerless to help. 'What can I do in fact for him', she asked sadly, 'except allow myself to be dragged along with him?' When they went up to say goodnight, he was calmer: as of old, he talked to Maass about his own work, and praised warmly the hospitality of Brazil, which he said seemed almost like a home to him. As Maass rose to leave, he surprised him by the suggestion that he might take with him the Remington portable typewriter they had been using for some years: he would not need it any more, it seemed sensible to travel light and buy Lotte a new one the other end. Sensible, indeed: but Maass felt that for a writer to give away a machine with which a series of important manuscripts, including the autobiography, and so much of his correspondence had been set down signified more than merely a travel convenience. On the last day, alone with Friderike for a while before they went up to Croton, his face fell into that fixity of expression she had noticed often in the previous weeks, and he said: 'Do you realise we shall probably never meet again?' He quickly recovered, and seemed strengthened when she replied that she would go to the ends of the earth to see him; but she never forgot the way in which he had said this. Eva and Ben Huebsch saw them off on the *Uruguay*.[1]

3

'Time gives the pictures, I only speak the words to accompany them.' *Die Welt von Gestern*

Invited to speak at the 17th International PEN Club Congress in Stockholm in September 1939—which was, of course, cancelled by the war—Zweig had prepared as his theme 'Die Geschichte als Dichterin': history as artist, poet, dramatist, the unsurpassed mistress of every form of art, from the drama of the isolated historic moment—the *Sternstunde*—to the colossal canvas of the French Revolution or the slowly unfolding epic of the rise and fall of a civilization. He compared historic truth to an artichoke, from which successive layers can be peeled seemingly

[1] Joachim Maass, Arens[2] 208–15; Fr 412–13; statement to the author by Friderike Zweig.

without ever reaching the inner core: history must therefore always be to a certain degree artistic invention, *Gedichtetes*.[1] The concept governed his approach to the autobiography. With his ingrained aversion to the limelight, he would not dream of giving to the world a purely personal tale: but the story of his generation as reflected in his own life, of the unprecedentedly swift succession of apocalyptic moments in Europe to which he had happened to be witness—this was worth telling. History herself had made the frame, a triptych of the most violent contrasts, separated by the turning-points of 1914 and 1933, and had drawn, for him at least, a firm line at the end in 1939. It was his role, as one who had chanced to stand at the epicentre of these earthquakes, to colour in the panels and complete her work of art. And since truth must be partly *gedichtet*, it seemed even a positive advantage that, in self-imposed exile from Bath, he had scarcely the smallest aid to memory—no books, no notes, none of the vast correspondence he had received from the humble or the mighty, and few contemporaries whom he could consult.

My Three Lives, as he had first considered entitling it, would not suit this concept, and he was for some time uncertain how to express it in a title. In letters to Cahn he canvassed a number of possibilities: *Wir*, *Eine geprüfte Generation*, *These Days are Gone*, *Die unwiederbringlichen Jahre*, *Ein Leben für Europa*, *Vida de un Europeo*. To call it a triptych, though it would naturally fall into that form, seemed inappropriate, since the outbreak of war in 1939 made a clearly defined end, 'and my experiences since then seem less important, indeed thoroughly insignificant in comparison with what others are having to live through'.[2] It was not till October, when he finally completed the work in Brazil, that he decided on *The World of Yesterday*.

Reading the first draft of the early chapters in Ossining, Friderike remarked on the almost total exclusion of personal detail in his description of Imperial Austria, that world of security: he gave the impression that he and his fellows lived happily in an Arcadian world, an atmosphere of serenity in which art reigned supreme, when, as they both well knew, the inadequacies and

[1] *Zeit und Welt*, 329–36. [2] Letters of 19 Sept. and 18 Oct. 1941 (Cahn).

hypocrisy of the educational and social system were full of dangers for the adolescent. His shyness, he told her, had made him erase a chapter he had drafted on this delicate subject. In Brazil, however, he overcame this—to her mind—almost Anglo-Saxon reserve, and inserted the chapter *Eros Matutinos*[1] (though we can only guess at what personal experiences can have contributed to it). 'Zweig, the admirer, pupil and patient of Freud,' in Kesten's words, 'was far too shy to write a real autobiography. His extreme modesty made him recoil from the naked.'[2] Throughout the book, in fact, the seeker after anything more than the most general of personalia is disappointed. Zweig's concern is to describe the world he saw, not himself; the people he mentions by name are those he knew or met who helped shape that world, rather than the personalities of his life in their own right. There is no mention of Friderike, scarcely an indication even that he was married until the last pages, when he alludes to a second marriage; practically nothing on his family background, save in the most generalized terms as typical of his whole generation; not a word of Lotte, Rieger, Felix Braun, or Fleischer. On the other hand, the world of the mind, the historical picture of Europe between 1880 and 1939, are drawn in with bold, broad strokes that combine personal reminiscence with sensitive perception of the true current of events. Facts and dates are few, and, as we have seen, often not strictly accurate; but, as in his biographies, the historian as artist—the instrument of history herself as artist—succeeds as few others have done in conveying the feel and the atmosphere of a period. *Die Welt von Gestern*, though not a source-book, will remain of extraordinary value for this.

'It is the third time', he wrote to Guido Fuchs, 'that what has been built up has collapsed behind me; and it was a pale satisfaction to preserve at least in written form the life that once we lived. What I could do for the old Austria was mainly to evoke a picture of what it was and what it meant for European civilisation.'[3] The man who considered himself above all a European, a citizen of the world, found that his homeland, after all, meant more to him than he thought, now that it was lost; and his love for it shows

[1] Fr 409–10. [2] *Poeten* 146. [3] Undated letter (? Sept. 1941) (*Sp* 91).

more clearly in this book even than in *Ungeduld des Herzens* or his 1940 lecture on the Vienna of yesterday. But the burden of *Die Welt von Gestern* is its finality: September 1939 marks the end of the past, the ruin of the work achieved. 'A new world began, but how many hells, how many purgatories had to be crossed before it could be reached!'[1] It is clear that he did not expect, himself, to see it. In *Die Geschichte als Dichterin*, admitting that our times make it hard to take a balanced view, he could still stress that in the long run the apparently senseless makes sense, that the lesson of history should be one of courage to face the present rather than of despair. In his autobiography there is no such message of hope. 'Choose and speak for me, ye memories, and at least give some reflection of my life before it sinks into the dark!'[2] An air of fatalism pervades the book, not merely in such matters as the ominous deaths of Matkowsky, Kainz, and Moissi as they prepared to act in his plays, but also in the acute dilemma throughout his life between clairvoyance and powerlessness. Long before others, he saw what was coming; more than others he felt the helplessness of the individual in the tide of events. Fatalism, and an infinite nostalgia: the united Europe of which he had dreamed, and which, for a few short years between the wars, he had thought to be dawning, had retreated behind the clouds of barbarism, and he at least would never see it re-emerge.

4

> *'Everything is so far away here and the war so horribly protracted that one simply cannot encompass its consequences. Then it will be all one, what one has endeavoured, and a completely new life will have to be begun if one has the strength.'*
>
> Zweig to Friderike, October 1941

Though Zweig sometimes spoke of the autobiography as his last work, and its whole tenor made it seem like the final effort of a life he considered at an end, it is by no means certain that when he left New York for Brazil he had made any clear decision. Since he thought it impossible to return to England, Brazil, the only

[1] *WvG* 395. [2] *WvG* 12.

country for which he had at the time a permanent residence permit, offered the best chance of a life of retirement and peace, and relief from the 'homeless wandering' to which he thought he was condemned. Lotte's health should be improved, especially if they lived higher up in Petropolis. That the move would take him further away than ever from his remaining friends seemed, in his exhaustion after the intensive work of July and August, not to trouble him: indeed, the solitude beckoned. He foresaw that America would before long be drawn into the war, one way or another, and the thought, as he wrote to Friderike from on board the *Uruguay*, of having once more to go through a war as a foreigner oppressed him. Yet we find him at the same time telling Gisella Selden-Goth that his journey to South America was simply to be able to stay in one place for a while, after so much wandering, for he hoped later to return to the United States for good. He would still say, too, that he longed for a return to England: they had often considered it, he wrote about this time to Guido Fuchs, 'but my house is crowded' (with evacuees), 'I could not work there, and work is the only thing which can sustain one in these ghastly times'. Huebsch and others in the U.S.A. tried, in fact, to obtain transit visas for them for the return journey to England, which in principle should not have been impossible; but without success.[1]

His reception this time in Rio contributed to his uncertainty. Though he had been stringent in his messages to Koogan not to tell anyone he was coming, it was gratifying to find that the boat was met not only by Claudio de Souza but also by Aranha, from the Foreign Affairs Ministry. Zweig was disconcerted, however, when Aranha, after a brief greeting, turned quickly away fom him towards the man he had really come to meet, a Japanese diplomat.[2] Settling for a few weeks in the Hotel Central, until a suitable country villa could be found, he detected a certain lack of warmth in some of the Brazilian friends who had been so enthusiastic on

[1] *BrW* 338; letter to G. Selden-Goth, 15 Aug. 1941 (*UB* 71); letter to Guido Fuchs, undated (? Sept. 1941) (*Sp* 91); statement to the author by Friderike Zweig.

[2] Letter to Koogan, 1 Aug. 1941 (*Nouvelles Littéraires*, 8 Sept. 1966, 7); information from Ferdinand Burger; De Souza 33.

his previous visits. *Brasil—Pais do Futuro* was published shortly after his arrival, and although already in New York he had received a congratulatory telegram from one of the ministers who had read the manuscript, and the book, prefaced in the warmest terms by Afranio Peixoto, had many good notices, his panegyric of the 'Land of the Future' did not meet with an entirely enthusiastic reception. In not a few quarters it was more than cool, and in some actively hostile. His personal popularity ensured a welcome with most Brazilian readers, but some were disappointed to find so little mention of the achievements of which they were most proud, namely in the technical and architectural fields, and so much stress on the exotic and picturesque, of which they tended rather to be ashamed. One reviewer went so far as to write: 'one might have thought that an enemy of Brazil had written this book'. There were murmurs too that Zweig had worked on a well-paid commission from the Vargas government.[1] And, though he had his visa, he found Brazil as irritating as any other country in its official requirements for documentation formalities, extending even to fingerprinting, which for him represented the ultimate intrusion on the liberty of the individual. Brazil, in sum, was not the welcoming home he had hoped for: he still felt himself the *émigré*, condemned to move through the world like a mendicant, requiring police permission merely to exist. The prospect of recovering his equilibrium and 'fighting the moral fatigue which has come over me in these last months', as he put it in a letter to Romains, seemed as remote as ever: 'I am more of a European than I thought.'[2]

At all events, he pressed forward with the move away from Rio; and was able soon to rent from Mrs. Margarida Banfield, the American wife of a British engineer, a small villa in Petropolis, at 34 rua Gonçalves Dias. It lay about 2 kilometres from the town centre, just off the Rio road; though it had only two small bedrooms, a living-room and a kitchen, and a tiny garden at the

[1] Manuscript account and letter of 19 Sept. 1941 (Cahn); Fr 412, 414–15; Ernst Feder, Arens[2] 219. Stefan Zweig, *Brasil—Pais do Futuro*, trans. Odilon Gallotti; Editora Guanabara, Rio de Janeiro, n.d. (1941).

[2] De Souza 34; information from Ferdinand Burger; letter to Romains, 2 Sept. 1941 (Dum 338).

back, it was attractively sited on a hill, and from the roofed-in balcony at the front afforded a pleasing view across a small valley, with one or two shops and a small café in the road opposite. It was with a great feeling of relief that they moved in on 17 September, and for the first time for over a year were able to unpack and stow their suitcases. He had taken it only for six months in the first instance, but it was at last a point of rest. Life there was at first glance like paradise, with cheap 'heavenly' coffee, a maid and a gardener at their service for five dollars a month, and a refreshing stillness, in a place 'as deserted now as Ischl in October', the people cheerful and friendly. 'If I can succeed in forgetting Europe here, regard all my possessions, house, books as lost, be indifferent to "fame" and success and thankful only to be permitted to live in such a divine countryside while Europe is desolated by hunger and misery, I will be content.'[1]

To the young writer Viktor Wittkowski, with whom he had become friendly in Rio, he said that he intended in this retirement to devote himself to the 'astringent happiness of work after weeks of deconcentration'; and besides finalizing the draft of *Die Welt von Gestern* he began actually to plan a short *Novelle* as a diversion.

> On the whole my decision to leave America cannot be valued too highly [he wrote to Friderike on the day of their move]; one lives here nearer to oneself and in the heart of nature, one hears nothing of politics, and however much egotism there may be in this, it is after all self-preservation in both the physical and spiritual sense. We cannot pay our whole life long for the stupidities of politics, which have never given us a thing but only always taken, and I am ready to restrict myself to the smallest space if it will only give me peace for work.[2]

There was something Austrian about the people here and about the landscape of this 'miniature Ischl'. Ernst Feder, formerly Chief Editor of the *Berliner Tageblatt*, moved into a house nearby on 1 December, and the families became close friends. Lotte made progress with her Portuguese, and was soon able to instruct the

[1] *BrW* 339–40; information from Mrs. Margarida Banfield.

[2] Letter to Wittkowski, 17 Sept. 1941 (Sch); *BrW* 341.

maid, very willing but totally unskilled in anything more complicated than manioc and black beans, in the little she herself knew of the culinary arts. It seemed an unrelieved blessing to be able to 'stay put' for months on end, with nothing to do with 'authorities' or the body public. 'An old Goethe, a Homer and a Shakespeare I obtained out here are enough for immediate reading, and I can borrow more—though in truth the libraries of New York are irreplaceable for me.' In the evenings he went for walks, or played through with Lotte master chess games from a book he had bought (prompting the theme of the *Schachnovelle* he was sketching out).[1]

It was idyllic, but his pessimism and the deep restlessness of his spirit soon rose to the surface again. He could not forget Europe, and his 'self-preservation' brought with it a sense of guilt. De Souza, also now resident in Petropolis for the summer months, noted with his doctor's eye the melancholy and distress which showed during a pause in their conversation or at a moment of distraction, and Zweig's vain attempts to escape the inner anguish he felt. He would try to interest himself in questions of minor importance, speak on his walks with anyone he met and interrogate them in detail on the thousand problems of their humble lives. De Souza remembered his asking once to be driven out to Caxambu, where new works were in train for the water-supply of Petropolis, and the apparently deep interest he took in the very dull scene of trench and pipe, so far removed from his own intellectual activity. His was a case, the Brazilian thought, of psychic allergy in a hyperergic condition.[2]

Zweig was acutely aware of the unnaturalness of his position: neither one thing nor the other, a German writer without books, 'a Coriolanus who hates the country whose language he must use', British on paper only, unable to identify himself with the person described in his passport, and with the feeling that he could never again achieve a proper order or stability in his life. He felt like Keats, whose name was 'writ in water'. 'It is not only plants and

[1] *BrW* 341–2; letter from Lotte Zweig to Romains, 29 Sept. 1941 (Romains, op. cit. 10); letter to Siegfried Burger, undated (?end Sept. 1941).

[2] De Souza 42–3.

teeth that cannot live without roots, a man is no better off.'[1] The solitude he had sought so eagerly, the 'burial alive' he had thought so preferable to the bustle of New York, began before long to oppress. Though the mails to and from the United States were good, those with Europe were of necessity sparse and irregular, and the man who had once boasted that his daily correspondence was bigger than Goethe's now often found that the postman passed him by. In America he had felt that he could not abide to be with people. Now he was really alone (for apart from Feder, the Chilean poetess Gabriela Mistral, and De Souza, all close neighbours, he saw virtually no one in Petropolis; there were only occasional visits from Stern, Koogan, and Wittkowski; and Friderike's brother Siegfried Burger never suceeded in getting the necessary permit for the journey up from Rio); but he felt all the more keenly the absence of his friends and the intellectual stimulus of their company.

All his life he had been torn by the conflict between his need for solitude and a thirst for human contact, and this had been supportable, even fruitful, so long as it was possible to change at will from one to the other. Now he was condemned, it seemed, to isolation, the physical relief of which made all the sharper his mental anguish over the horrors of the times. The war, he could see clearly, was only now at its beginning; years, irreplaceable years, would have to pass before he could hope once again to be settled; and it would destroy to the last atom everything the previous generation had built. The only answer for him would be a new work, something big like the *Balzac* (but his papers for that had still not reached him), or an Austrian novel (but this would need study of the newspaper files of ten years, possible only in New York, where he did not wish to return in the foreseeable future). The feeling swept over him once more of the hopelessness of writing in German into empty space, and of the isolation of his position in the depths of South America, a European cut off from the world he had thought and lived in and from the books that meant so much. His capacity to produce, without

[1] Letter to Cahn, 19 Sept. 1941 (Cahn); letter to Romains, 28 Oct. 1941 (Romains, op. cit. 12).

the fuel of human contact and of his cultural heritage, would be 'snuffed out like a light without oxygen'.

These were the feelings he expressed in a letter to Friderike only a few weeks after the move to Petropolis: and he wondered how long this 'contemplative pause' could last.

> I would be much tempted to write about Montaigne, in whom I am now reading a great deal with great enjoyment—another (better) Erasmus, a completely comforting spirit. But out here there is practically nothing about him, and I do not even know whether I could obtain the books in America—one needs to absorb the whole atmosphere of the time in order to understand the man within it.

To those whose imagination made them feel the sufferings of others Montaigne advised withdrawal, standing to one side; but Zweig thought his own attempt to do this could not succeed. 'A few percent more egotism and less imagination would have helped me much in my life: now one cannot change oneself.'[1] Friderike, who had now moved back to a small apartment in New York, felt she must do all she could to encourage and help him to some new absorbing work. With her access to the libraries he so sorely missed (she thought later that she had been wrong to write to him so enthusiastically about them) she was able to send him a select bibliography on Montaigne, and later one or two of the books themselves, including that of Gide. She also suggested Da Ponte as a subject; but he said that if he could write at all it would be where his heart lay—Balzac or Montaigne.[2]

Towards the end of October *Die Welt von Gestern*, after considerable rewriting, was finished. He asked Wittkowski to check the typescript for him, for in this form, he wrote, he could see nothing: 'clarity comes for me only with the first galleyproofs, and with the Insel I could afford the luxury of treating them, both for style and content, as a manuscript. Those days are gone.' By 20 November he had sent it off to Bermann-Fischer (in America) and Huebsch. He had thought at first of publishing the German-language edition in Brazil, for to his pessimism Bermann-Fischer's Stockholm house seemed a hazardous venture, and the expense

[1] *BrW* 343–5; letter to Romains, 28 Oct. 1941 (op. cit. 12). Cf. also Treb 389.
[2] *BrW* 345–6.

in the United States would be prohibitive; having in the end decided on Stockholm, he remained prey to the worry that the copy the publisher sent to Sweden had been lost. But at any rate, 'that stone has been rolled away', as he wrote to Friderike, in the phrase he had so often used for the works of earlier days, and he could try to think of something new.[1]

A source of particular despair at this time was the realization of what was being done to the Jews in Europe. Stories began to filter through indicating a genocide surpassing all previous manifestations of anti-Semitism, and his horror, coupled with the feeling of guilt at his own escape, was beyond bounds. Asked to speak at a meeting to raise funds for Jewish war victims, he said he felt heavy at heart that he should be shown such friendship while others were suffering:

> we as human beings, and especially as Jews, have no right in these days to be happy. You cannot imagine what is happening in Europe. We must not think that we are the few just men who have been saved from the destruction of Sodom and Gomorrah because of our special merits. We are not better, we are not more worthy than all the others who are being driven and hunted over there in Europe.[2]

The prospect that the occasion of his sixtieth birthday might be celebrated publicly in Brazil at such a time revolted him, and he begged Koogan to do all he could to keep it quiet.

> I have never felt greater resistance to being fêted here, I who have escaped what England and the other countries must expect. . . . It is not the moment to be on view, and each of us who keeps his person in the shadows does well by his confrères. . . . For me the ideal would be for no-one to know this day and for me to be able to work on here in the shadows. For the Jews there are no more honours in these days, it is enough to survive.

His Jewishness was a matter of feeling rather than of religious belief. He had felt compelled to refuse an invitation to give the reading at the *Yom Kippur* on 1 October in favour of someone more worthy, for, as he wrote to Rabbi Dr. Lemle, 'like most

[1] Letter to Wittkowski, 20 Oct. 1941 (Sch); letter to Cahn, 18 Oct. 1941 (Cahn); *BrW* 346.

[2] Leftwich 88–9.

Austrians I was brought up in the most lax fashion in matters of faith and would not be able to overcome a feeling of uncertainty in an assembly of real believers'.[1] But his feeling for the suffering of his people was no less deep for that, even though it was for him only a part of the wider picture of the sorrows of humanity itself.

He had implored Friderike too not to remind anyone of his birthday, and was dismayed, though very touched, to hear that Romains was planning a *Festschrift* for the occasion. 'It is no time for festivals, and my friends, where are they? Unreachable, like Rolland and Masereel, or under the earth like Roth and Rieger; and one does not feel well disposed towards oneself.' It was an 'ominous day', and just as ten years earlier he had escaped to Munich, so now he arranged to take a car trip with Koogan to avoid any possible visitors—'if anyone should chance to remember it'. They had intended to drive to Friburgo, the Swiss colony, but the road was so bad that they spent the day in Teresopolis.[2] There were a few telegrams from America and England (including one from Newman Flower of Cassells), from Cahn in Buenos Aires, and (the only one within Brazil) from Soares, Minister of Foreign Affairs. Presents were not numerous but gave him much pleasure: Romains's *Festschrift*, the text of his 1939 lecture on the *Grand Européen*, with a specially written Dedication, in a limited edition bound in handsome leather and published simultaneously by Viking in English and the Maison Française in French; from Koogan a delightful little wirehaired fox terrier named Plucky; from Lotte a complete *Balzac* she had discovered in one of the bookshops of the rua São José; from Wittkowski a Taine essay, nostalgic reminder of his doctorate studies nearly forty years earlier. Friderike's present of the books on Montaigne she had found in New York arrived a few days afterwards.[3]

The 'melancholy day' was successfully negotiated, and his letters sounded an unusually cheerful note. 'You sent me your

[1] Letter to Koogan, undated (?Nov. 1941) (*Nouvelles Littéraires*, 8 Sept. 1966, 7); letter to Rabbi Dr. Lemle, undated (?Sept. 1941).

[2] *BrW* 345–7.

[3] *BrW* 347; Romains, op. cit. 13 and Arens[2] 295; letter to Wittkowski, 28 Nov. 1941 (Sch); telegram from Soares (K); manuscript account (Cahn); Flower 179.

aid in a very dark moment', he wrote to Romains. Thanking Wittkowski that evening, he said his work was moving more actively forward, on three or four things at once—Balzac, a *Novelle*, Montaigne, a novel[1]—'one must seek relief in work from the loneliness of life'. The little dog settled down at once, and, indeed, as he wrote to Friderike, lent their house for the first time a real air of home. His pedigree, 'as long as your arm, does not impress us who claim descent from Abraham as much as his good training—an animal is anyway a good substitute in times when humans are repulsive. . . . From the details of dog and Balzac you will see that with my increasing scepticism I am trying more and more to regulate my life on the long term.' Similarly, to Cahn he said that while in the early days of the war he had been unable to occupy himself with anything other than small, day-to-day work, he had now turned to more protracted subjects, several at once, and something would soon gain the upper hand.[2]

In reality, however, he simply could not look into the long term. He seemed afraid to make promises, afraid to take responsibilities upon himself. Even for such a close friend as Masereel, who was trying to get a visa for Colombia, and whose presence would have done him so much good, he made no attempt to intervene with Brazil. The fear of growing old (he had begun a hormone treatment while in the United States, which it was doubtless impossible to continue in Brazil) had always led him to a somewhat unrealistic view of age. In the autobiography he had quite often, no doubt unconsciously, overstated his age at the time of various incidents in his life; and in the *Novellen* he was writing now—*Die spät bezahlte Schuld* and *War es er?*[3]—his description of the protagonists seems significant. At fifty-six, the *Hofschauspieler* Peter Sturzentaler is presented as an old and broken man, while Betsy, the narrator of *War es er?*, her husband retired

[1] There was no trace of this after his death.

[2] *BrW* 347–8; letters to Romains (op. cit. 14) and Wittkowski (Sch), 28 Nov. 1941; letter to Cahn, 30 Nov. 1941 (Cahn).

[3] Left in Koogan's care, these have so far (1970) been published only in Portuguese (Guanabara, 1949, and Delta, 1953), under the titles *Divida Tardiamente Paga* and *Seria Êle?*, save for a shorter and considerably altered version of the latter in English, under the title 'Jupiter' (*Colliers Magazine*, 3 July 1943).

from the British government service and her sons grown up and gone, is thirty-two. Once, it is true, discussing with Feder man's greatly extended life-span today in comparison with former times, he had said that he at sixty would be quite capable of piloting an aircraft (and smiled when Feder rejoined that he would not care to be his passenger).[1] But already in 1931, in *Die Heilung durch den Geist*, he had written of Mary Baker-Eddy: 'Sixty-one —an age when indifference and fatigue first come over a human being, for how much longer can one be effective, and for whom?'[2] Fatigue was already upon him; indifference scarcely, rather a pervading despair that so many 'hells and purgatories' were to be crossed and so many years to pass before a new world would dawn.

He felt himself to be like the writer Mörner, in Jakob Wasserman's story *Der unbekannte Gast*, which he had just borrowed from the shelves of a neighbour. Mörner, 'in middle, or rather, advanced age', suffers an 'inexplicable change in his mental balance', is suddenly quite incapable of continuing a work just begun; and he tells his friends:

> When a man like me no longer believes in the importance and necessity of his mission, he is quite simply the most superfluous being on earth. . . . All reality becomes for him a greeting of ghosts, his spirit cannot grasp the depth of the abyss yawning before him. . . . If the stone one is quarrying falls to dust, if the torch one has lighted from the great fire of the world gives forth no flame but only scraps of red paper, then it is bad, worse than bad, it is the end.

And he asks his friends just to tolerate him: if it comes to the worst, he will try not to be a burden. The story dated from 1922, and Zweig must already have been familiar with it, as he was with all Wassermann's works. It may be, as Feder suggested later, that he felt drawn to it now, not for Mörner's rehearsal of the world's ills and for its description of a psychological state so exactly like his own, but because it in fact described a cure: the 'unknown guest', a doctor, agreeing with Mörner's diagnosis, can yet instil

[1] Ernst Feder, 'Stefan Zweigs letzte Tage', *Aufbau*, New York (?early) Mar. 1942.

[2] Stefan Zweig, *Die Heilung durch den Geist*; Insel, Leipzig, 1931, 267.

in him an optimism, the will to open his eyes to see that the times are no more out of joint than they were ten, a hundred, a thousand years ago. 'If your own eye be undestroyed, then the world is undestroyed! Lift up your eyes! Grasp the immense, the sweet, the painful, the blossoming, the enormous overflowing richness!' For Zweig to read this again may indeed have been a last attempt to save himself.[1]

That it failed is evident from a poem he wrote now, sending copies to Friderike and one or two of his distant friends. Its theme was the contented resignation brought by age and awareness of the coming darkness. The words concealed his despair, but expressed clearly his conviction that sixty was indeed the end of life.

Der sechzigjährige dankt

Linder schwebt der Stunden Reigen
Über schon ergrautem Haar,
Denn erst an des Bechers Neige
Wird der Grund, der gold'ne, klar.

Vorgefühl des nahen Nachtens
Es verstört nicht — es entschwert!
Reine Lust des Weltbetrachtens
Kennt nur, wer nichts mehr begehrt,

Nicht mehr fragt, was er erreichte,
Nicht mehr klagt, was er gemisst
Und dem Altern nur der leichte
Anfang seines Abschieds ist.

Niemals glänzt der Ausblick freier
Als im Glast des Scheidelichts,
Nie liebt man das Leben treuer
Als im Schatten des Verzichts.[2]

[1] Ernst Feder, 'Letzter Rettungsversuch', *Hüben und Drüben*, *Beilage zum Argentinischen Tageblatt*, xlii Jahrg., Nr. 1622, 1 June 1947.

[2] 'The dance of hours hovers more gently over hair already grey; for only with the beaker's tilting does its golden ground shine clear. The feeling of approaching darkness disturbs not—rather it lifts the burden! Only he can know the purest joy of observation of the world who desires no more for himself, who no longer asks what he achieved or complains at what he has missed, for whom

5

> *'Probably for years there will be no peace other than that inner peace, which we must strive to secure with all the strength of our soul, in defiance of all the daimons of outer unrest.'*
>
> Zweig to Robert Faesi, 1939

That he should have been led to Montaigne just now was apparently a matter of chance. Shortly after his installation in Petropolis he had discovered in the cellar a dusty edition of the *Essays*, 'a great find', he wrote to Fülöp-Miller, adding that their reading was absorbing him above all else. But this 'chance'—like his discovery of Verhaeren and Rolland—bears all the marks of having been 'determined from within'. It was not his first meeting with the *Essays*, but at twenty their message had meant nothing to him. Montaigne belonged, he now realized, to those writers whose significance can be appreciated only after the passage of time, after experience of life and its disappointments; and the problem for Montaigne—how to remain free and unaffected by the chaos of his times—was now precisely Zweig's own. It could not, he felt, be merely chance that among the few books left to Ernst Feder from his former library was the best complete edition of the *Essays*, or that one of the foremost experts on Montaigne, Fortunat Strowski, whose book was one of the important entries in the bibliography prepared by Friderike, was just now in Brazil.[1]

'Then as today the world torn apart, a battlefield, war raised to the apotheosis of bestiality', ran his notes: 'in such times the problems of life for man merge into a single problem: how can

ageing is but the gentle beginning of his farewell. Never shines the prospect freer than in the gleam of departing light; never is life loved more truly than in the shade of resignation.'

The poem was sent to Friderike Zweig and Zech, among others. It has been reproduced many times, notably Fr 295, Bauer 79, *Bildb* 119, Arens[2] 337, Arens[3] 249, and is included in the collected poems: *Silberne Saiten*, ed. Friedenthal; S. Fischer, Frankfurt am Main, 1966, 160.

[1] Fülöp-Miller, Arens[1] 168; *BrW* 347; letter to Wittkowski, undated (?early Dec. 1941) (Sch); letter to Kesten, 15 Jan. 1942 (*Poeten* 141, *Exil* 199); Friedenthal, Arens[2] 349.

I remain free? How can I break loose from the snare. How free myself from fear. How preserve myself in a time of bestialisation of humanity.' Montaigne in his tower was a 'brother in destiny' with Zweig in his retreat in Petropolis. '1593. Gets tired. Death. Tower. A single path to walk. The walls. From there look out over everything.' The parallel between the sixteenth century and the twentieth became for him ever more striking. Then, as now, a great burgeoning of the human spirit, explorations, discoveries, frustrated and cast into chaos by internecine war. And every line of Montaigne seemed to express the stoic determination, that Zweig so desperately wanted in himself, to preserve the inner self against the onslaughts of the world. His study would not be a biography, but would concentrate only on this (to him all-important) aspect of Montaigne's philosophy.[1]

'We were always a small minority,' he had written to Romains with his thanks for the *Festschrift*, 'we, the men of good will; our isolation only becomes more marked when the tide of great events flings others into the herd. The important thing for us is not to show our disenchantment, or only in a form readable and visible for the happy few, as did the good Montaigne who in my solitude replaces for me my distant friends.'[2] But it was not in his nature to be able to forget what was happening to the world: his tower could never be like Montaigne's, his isolation never complete. It was all very well listening only to the Brazilian news on the radio, and casting the newspaper aside after only a glance: there was no escaping the hammer blows of each succeeding turn in events.[3] He had foreseen that the United States would not be able to keep out of the war, but Pearl Harbour on 7 December and the overwhelming Japanese offensives that followed it were more shattering than anything he could have imagined, and plunged him into complete despair. His work seemed pointless, and to be condemned to think and write in German the greatest curse of all.[1]

[1] Friedenthal, Arens[2] 348–9; letter to Kesten, 15 Jan. 1942 (*Exil* 199); letter to Romains, 22 Jan. 1942 (op. cit. 17).

[2] Letter to Romains (op. cit. 14), 28 Nov. 1941; Dum 339.

[3] *BrW* 345.

[4] Letter to Wittkowski, 13 Dec. 1941 (Sch).

Here all is still and quiet [he wrote in English to Friderike a week after Pearl Harbour]; . . . but also this country will be involved one day . . . I have a lease till to the end of April, but alas, time runs with frightening rapidity. How far it seems to me that I had a house, my books and I know already that all this is gone for ever. . . . Petropolis will loose in the next two months its solitude and I am rather frightened by the thought of meeting people again—I do not like to talk now, because nobody can understand our position. One must have gone through things by own experience.[1]

To De Souza, who invited him to a PEN Club dinner at the end of the month, he described himself as a person who had lost everything in life he held most dear, and said he found it impossible to take part in such festivities while so many were suffering in Europe: it was a case of conscience. He was, he said, in mourning for Europe.[2] His inability to concentrate on work of any kind terrified him. On the last day of 1941, writing to Wittkowski after they had missed each other at a rendezvous on Christmas Eve, on one of his rare visits to Rio, he said he felt the extension of the war—making it the first truly world war—represented history's greatest catastrophe: people would not, or could not, grasp this, nor that from its corpse all kinds of spiritual and physical pestilences would arise. 'When I read that, for us in 1941, victory is promised for 1943 or 1944, the hand that holds the paper trembles with horror.'[3] Visiting Feder that evening, the memory of his Far East journey in 1909 made him speak of the Japanese successes as though he were an expert. 'I know how important these things are. I know the area exactly.' All was again uncertain for him. He was more than ever sure that he would never see Europe again, but also that he could not find a stable existence in Brazil. 'Still, we have this bungalow for four months more, and I try not to think further ahead than that.'[4]

He could not find for himself that 'inner citadel' of which Goethe had spoken and which Montaigne had defended so well against the chaos and brutality around him. And no further flight

[1] *BrW* 349.
[2] De Souza 36–7.
[3] Letter to Wittkowski, 31 Dec. 1941 (Sch).
[4] Feder, Arens[1] 161; letter to Siegfried Burger, undated (?late Dec. 1941).

was possible. 'Now, above all at my age,' he wrote to Zech in January, 'if one has given thought to flight, there is only one single possibility, that of flight into the very depths of the soul. A dangerous and a very painful journey.' It would be stupid and dishonest to say 'Be of good cheer, things will get better.' No: 'we need courage of quite a different kind'.[1] In a letter to Kesten he spoke of the 'fine courage' needed to await in patience the outcome, 'that "afterwards" which I would actually be curious to experience'.[2] But his heart failed him at the thought of the years the war would last, and the longer years before its legacy could be eradicated or the destruction made good both physically and spiritually. In Montaigne, whose example had seemed so apposite, he now dwelt on the passages dealing with death. 'Ce n'est pas la recepte à une seule maladie, la mort est la recepte à touts maulx. . . . La plus volontaire mort, c'est la plus belle. La vie despend de la volonté d'aultruy; la mort de la nostre.'[3]

'Above all at my age', he had said to Zech (who was in fact nearly a year older)—once again we find in him the notion that he was at the end of the road, that this was the end of his generation, and that the future must be left to the younger. To some Austrian visitors he said he wished he had remained in Brazil from the time of his first visit: he was too old now to adapt himself to a new life.[4] On 8 January came a letter from Roger Martin du Gard ('the best letter I have read since years') which expressed exactly his own feeling 'that we in our age have only the charge of spectators in the great play (or better tragedy), that the others the younger one have to play her part. Ours is only to disappear quietly and in a dignified way.'[5]

He continued to work a little, from habit and 'without intensity'. His study of Montaigne began to take shape, and the *Schachnovelle*—something, perhaps, of wish-fulfilment in its story of an Austrian lawyer's power of resistance to the pressure of the Gestapo—was finished early in January. Although it is one of his

1 Letter of 4 Jan. 1942 (*Ged* 38). 2 Letter of 15 Jan. 1942 (*Exil* 199).

3 Montaigne, II. iii ('Coustume de l'Isle de Cea').

4 Letter from Dr. and Mrs. Kris, São Paulo, to Friderike Zweig, 1 Mar. 1942.

5 *BrW* 351–2; letter to Wittkowski, 20 Jan. 1942. (Sch). Cf. Dum 326.

best *Novellen* (and, in Ben Huebsch's version, the only one really well translated into English), he seemed to have little confidence in it: 'my beloved but unfortunate format, too long for a newspaper or magazine, too short for a book'. It was the only time he had taken a theme directly related to current events: yet he thought it too abstract to win a wide public and, surprisingly, the theme too remote. He had sent the typescript to Feder, asking him, as an expert in the arts of both chess and literature, for his comments and criticism. When they met on his balcony on the evening of 8 January, he was full of Martin du Gard's letter, reading it to Feder almost with joy at its confirmation of his own feelings. Feder pointed out that his creative power was as great as ever—the *Schachnovelle*, the autobiography just sent off for publication, *Amerigo* about to appear; but he merely smiled and shook his head, remarking: 'Yes, there was at one time a certain lustre in what I wrote.'[1]

Had he already taken the decision to put an end to a life he regarded as finished? If he had, he kept it well concealed, both from those who saw him during January and February and from distant friends in his letters. We cannot overlook, however, a strong indication that already, early in February, his mind was made up. To Zech, enclosing a holograph copy of *Der sechzigjährige dankt*, he wrote on 4 February:

> I have at last been able to finish the work on the story of my life, and believe that with it I leave behind a document which will show what we wanted, attempted and experienced, we, the generation of writers who bore perhaps the heaviest burden of fate for centuries and centuries. . . . *What further commitments I have laid on myself you will shortly hear, perhaps direct, but perhaps also indirectly through that medium I have always hated* [this latter expression clearly meant radio].[2]

Even without the benefit of hindsight, the significance of these words seems umistakable. But to no one else did he go so far; and indeed it is always possible, when we consider the Hamletian indecision he had shown at the major cross-roads of his life of the

[1] Letter to Kesten, 15 Jan. 1942 (*Exil* 199); Feder, Arens[1] 156–7.

[2] Sch. (Author's italics.)

last eight years, that here too, and here most of all, he could not yet from one day to the next see his action clear.

To Friderike, the same day, there went a letter (in English) of almost serene sadness.

There is season now in our Ischl but I live not less retired than before, reading, working and walking with the little dog which is very sweet, not so intelligent as Kaspar was but very affectionate as if I would have him already for years. Letters become more and more scarce, everybody has his own worries and one does not like to write if one has nothing important to tell—and what in our little and reduced life is still important in comparison with the world-events. . . . Reading is my best help and only reading good old, if I may say, *proved* books, Balzac, Goethe, Tolstoy; but what we miss is good talk with people of our level. Most of the people we meet do not understand what is going on and coming, they believe that the coming peace will be but a continuation of the peace-time; one must have gone through certain things to understand them and Europe is mentally as far to them as China has been to us in the last terrific times. . . . I am not yet sure if I can rent the bungalow longer than April, in the case of a changement I shall let you know it in good time. . . .[1]

His reply to Martin du Gard a few days later described the natural beauty of the isolation in which he lived, and recalled that Bernanos was in a similar situation, content with little so long as he could remain free; but he stressed the cruel lack of books and friends, and the feeling he could not overcome of being still a homeless wanderer—'I still am silly enough to think always of "returning".' He looked forward to seeing the other's Journal in print one day: 'it will be more precious even than Gide's . . . I should like to be able to live thirty years more only to read it . . . the idea of seeing you again one day remains one of the few wishes I still permit myself'.[2]

Such relative serenity was, however, an infrequent mood in these days of January and February. He could not overcome his inner restlessness. Though in fact there was no obstacle to renewing the lease of the villa, he professed himself uncertain about it. To Feder, who was the one to see most of him at this time, he

[1] *BrW* 353–4. [2] Letter of 9 Feb. 1942 (Dum 327).

seemed 'like a bee sucking bitterness from every blossom' (he who had once been the cross-pollinator of so many flowers of European culture). He set his face firmly against anything which might in the slightest degree encourage to optimism, and reacted only to the negative, with a violence that was striking. That Brazil too would one day be involved in the war was self-evident to him, and he was nervous about the extent of Nazi penetration of South America.[1] According to some reports, he was the target for anonymous letters from Nazi sympathizers in Brazil, and there was malicious gossip abroad that he was not really married to Lotte, which, as Gabriela Mistral noted, worried him a great deal.[2] He had increasing recourse to tranquillizers and sleeping pills, for although Lotte's asthma was better at this altitude, she coughed continually, perhaps because of the smoky stove in the villa, and he could get little natural sleep for this reason alone, apart from his own troubled mind.[3] He had never been able to support sickness in others, and had always run away from it: now there was no running away.

6

'The only one of the Rights of Man left to a chap is: to croak how and when one pleases . . . and to be let alone at it, without a "helping hand".'

Amok

Feder remained quite certain that up to 16 February no fatal decision had been taken. The carnival in Rio was to start on Saturday, 14 February, and in the previous week Zweig announced his intention of going down with Lotte to see it, on the Monday, perhaps staying over Tuesday. It was arranged that they would drive down together with Feder on Monday morning. Later that week he was greatly disturbed by an article in a Brazilian paper alleging that a promise he had made to friends in Brazil to write a biography of Santos Dumont had not been kept,

[1] Feder, Arens[1] 154–6.

[2] Gabriela Mistral, interview in *Aufbau*, New York, 31 Dec. 1954. There is no direct evidence for the reports of the anonymous letters.

[3] Information from Mrs. Margarida Banfield.

because he did not wish to recognize the priority of Dumont over the Wright brothers, and thus prejudice the popularity and dollars he had earned in America. This was a considerable perversion of the truth: the suggestion of the biography had indeed been made, but he had done no more than describe it as interesting, and had not given any undertaking. (It is reported, though there is no firm evidence, that he had also been approached to write a biography of Vargas, and that in this case he had not concealed his view that the President was a personality of little importance; if true, a journalistic attack on this score might have been understandable.) At all events he felt that he should publish a reply, and on the Sunday spent some time with De Souza preparing his statement in Portuguese, weighing the wording suggested by his friend with meticulous care. (De Souza, no doubt unwilling to air what would have been a painful subject in Brazil, refers in his memoir of Zweig only to their translation together of 'a letter in French on a literary subject', but there seems no doubt from Feder's account that it was in fact the draft reply to the newspaper attack.)[1]

He was much exercised by the matter, and in the car with Feder on their way down to Rio the following morning asked his advice whether he should publish his reply. It seems, however, that the draft was destroyed, for no trace of it was afterwards found, and it never reached the editor. In it, again according to Feder, he explained that his reason for not undertaking the biography was his lack of technical knowledge, and he expressed the hope that a future biographer would not omit to mention Dumont's two letters to the Brazilian Academy of Letters (of which he was a member), in which he protested against misuse of the flying-machine for warlike purposes.[2]

Apart from this, Zweig appeared during the car journey to be restored in humour. He spoke to Feder of a suggestion he had received from the *Readers Digest* that he should prepare, as a puzzle for the readers, a short summary of some well-known work

[1] Feder, Arens[1] 158; De Souza 48–9.

[2] Feder, Arens[1] 158–9 and article 'In Memoriam Stefan Zweig', 1943 (journal unidentified).

of world literature, concealing the author and origin; and seemed taken with the idea, saying that he had already thought of some possibilities, such as Balzac's *Colonel Chabert*, the story of which he proceeded to relate in some detail. Feder recalled afterwards that, some weeks before, he had maintained the view to Zweig, when they were discussing the question of suicide, that the alleged wave of suicides after Goethe's *Werther* was nothing more than a *fable convenue*, and had suggested that Zweig should undertake an investigation of the legend. In their discussion then Zweig had given no indication that suicide was in any way a preoccupation with him; and certainly now, in his lively talk of the *Digest* proposal and his obviously keen interest in such a minor piece of work, he could not, in Feder's view, yet have reached any irrevocable decision. And he seemed more cheerful and self-controlled. As they reached the suburbs of Rio and caught their first glimpse of the processions of gaily costumed children he exclaimed with almost boyish enthusiasm at so pretty a sight. Sharing the brilliant spectacle with his wife seemed to give him much pleasure, and Feder thought that she too was a little brighter and less reserved than usual. They dropped him off at the Hotel Botafogo, and appear to have spent the rest of the day with De Souza amid the whirl of the carnival in the streets of Rio, Zweig making notes, which were later destroyed.[1]

They spent the night at De Souza's apartment. The following day, Shrove Tuesday, would, of course, be the high point of the carnival, and they had decided to stay on to see it. At breakfast-time, however, Zweig was seized with horror to read the newspaper headlines of the fall of Singapore two days earlier: 'No further resistance possible. Whole British Empire hears news with deepest mourning.' And also on the front page: 'Germans about to mount powerful attack through Libya towards Suez Canal.' The contrast with the gay pictures of the carnival processions which he had been watching himself only a few hours before plunged him into a deep depression, and although he gave no outward sign of his feelings he announced his decision to return

[1] Feder, Arens[1] 159–60 and article 'Stefan Zweigs letzte Tage', *Aufbau*, New York (?Mar.) 1942.

at once with Lotte to Petropolis and see no more of the carnival. He had promised to take Koogan's little daughter to the children's ball that day, but left the family at the door of the theatre, walking off with Lotte to the Praça Mauá to catch the bus for Petropolis, thrusting through the crowded street and square in the din of the shouting and singing and the blare of the bands. 'Riam, riam!' shouted the masked figures as they passed: 'por que vão assim tristes? Viva a folia!' It was a scene like that in his *Phantastische Nacht*. But his ears were closed now to the voices of life: he had decided to end it.[1]

Though De Souza, Koogan, and Feder wondered at his sudden change of mood they had no suspicion of how deep it went, or that this unexpected return to Petropolis was the first step in his final preparations. Nor, in the following days, did anyone else detect the slightest sign of what was afoot. He travelled once more to Rio with Lotte, probably on Thursday 19 February, to see Dr. Malamud, his solicitor, and deposit with him a copy of his will; and he called the same day on Koogan to leave with him a packet 'for safe keeping'. Neither friend remarked anything unusual in these actions, or in his demeanour. In the packet, which Koogan stowed in his office safe unopened, were some valuable drawings, including one by Rembrandt, and autographs, together with a letter in French addressed to Koogan, dated 18 February:

Before all I must thank you for all the kindness you have shown me during my life and ask your pardon for all the trouble I cause you by my death. You know how tired I was of life after losing my homeland, Austria, and could not any longer find true life in my work, living as a nomad and feeling myself grow old more by my inward sufferings than by the years.—I have left with Dr. Malamud a copy of my will deposed in New York during my stay there, and I give you now some further personal wishes. I should like to be buried in the Rio de Janeiro cemetery in the most modest and discreet fashion. . . .—As for the manuscripts which will be found, nothing apart from a small Novelle is finished. The Balzac, the Montaigne, a novel I started, are all in the stage of preliminary sketches. Have them anyway looked through by Viktor Wittkowski, against a fee. I still have a typed original

[1] De Souza 53–6; Feder, Arens[1] 160–1.

copy of my autobiography. Take it for your firm—perhaps it will serve for an original edition or for a translation: it is the last copy and I am not sure that the others are not lost.— . . . Ne me plaignez pas, ma vie était anéantie depuis des années et je suis heureux de pouvoir sortir d'un monde devenu cruel et fou. Gardez-moi un bon souvenir; j'étais toujours fier et reconnaissant de votre amitié fidèle et dévouée.

But this would not be read until after his death.[1]

On the same day, 18 February, he wrote to Friderike a letter of infinite sadness, between the lines of which can be read his decision:

Dear Friderike,

I have not more to write you than kindest thoughts. There was now the fantastic carneval in Rio but my mind is far away from festivities and more distressed than ever. There will be never return to all bygone things and what is expecting us will never give more what those times had to afford us. I am continuing my work but with a quarter of my strenght [*sic*]; it is more continuing an old habit than really creating. One must be convinced to convince, to have enthusiasm to stimulate the others and how to find this now! All my best thoughts are with you and I hope your children find good opportunity to work and to go ahead; they will still see the better world after this one. I hope you are in fairly good spirits and in perfect health and that Newyork with its variety gives you at least sometimes of his artistic wealth—here I had but nature and good books, old good books which I read and reread again.

Yours ever,
Stefan.[2]

Despite the somewhat faltering English there is no doubt that he wrote 'had' in the last sentence, though obviously he did not yet wish to make clear to Friderike what he had decided to do.

Back in Petropolis in the evening of 19 February, he sat down to write to Romains. It was the last letter to this old friend, one of the few remaining true representatives of the Europe he knew he would never see again. Though again not specific, it made clear to Romains, when he received it after the news of his death, the desolation of his spirit:

[1] Information from Abrão Koogan; letter of 18 Feb. 1942 (*Nouvelles Littéraires*, 8 Sept. 1966, 7); Fr 431; *Bildb* 125.

[2] *BrW* 356.

How I miss you in this hour! . . . I am a few years older than you, and as these past years were so charged with anxieties I often ask myself where the fountain of youth is to be found. All I have been able to give was thanks to a certain interior *élan*; I could seize the imagination because I was seized myself and that produced a warmth that could communicate. Without faith, without enthusiasm, reduced to the sole power of my brain, I walk as though on crutches. . . . I envy you your inexhaustible energy: for myself, I bend before each gust of wind, and the only strength I could find to sustain me was by withdrawing into myself. A tree without roots is an uncertain and wavering thing. . . . One does not like to write when one knows that letters will arrive cooled off by the length of their journey—and here I feel myself completely isolated, whole weeks go by without a single letter. . . .

Referring to the carnival, he added:

I could not let myself be swept along by this wave of pleasure and drunkenness; how one would have enjoyed in the old days seeing a whole city dancing, walking, singing for four whole days without police, without papers, without business—a multitude made one by joy alone![1]

'In the old days'—now such a spectacle was merely a symbol of the triumph of the lower instincts over the world of the mind.

7

What is there more, that I lag and
pause and crouch with unshut mouth?
Is there a single final farewell?
Walt Whitman, 'Songs of Parting'

Had Lotte already agreed to accompany him in this last act? There seems no doubt that her devotion was such that she would follow him to the end. All the same, there may have been hesitation. She went shopping as usual on the morning of Saturday, 21 February, and in fact bought rather more provisions than was normal: whether this represented indecision on her part, or was merely to avert suspicion, it is impossible to say. Friday he had spent getting his papers in order, and later that day the smoke rose

[1] Romains, op. cit. 19.

from a sizeable bonfire in the little garden at the back of the villa.[1] In his determination to conceal his intention, he made no farewell visits, except to call on Strowski, who was at the time staying in an hotel in Petropolis—but Strowski was out. The Brazilian writer Braga, whom he had known in Paris and liked, happened to telephone on Saturday to ask if he might call the following day. 'Demain je suis occupé', said Zweig. 'Et dans la semaine prochaine?' 'Dans la semaine prochaine nous ne serons pas là.' Braga had heard that they might be visiting Minas Gerais, and thought Zweig was referring to this. After a slight pause, Zweig added: 'Je suis heureux de vous entendre.' He was grateful for this opportunity to say a quiet goodbye to a friend, without betraying what he had in mind. Similarly, he rang De Souza on Saturday, not, as the latter would have expected, to arrange a meeting or to invite him over, but merely to exchange a few words—adding 'Je suis heureux de vous parler'. De Souza equally did not grasp at the time what this meant.[2]

The Feders they wanted to see again, and Lotte rang them on Saturday morning to ask them round that evening: to Frau Feder's counter-invitation she said they still had work to do, and would prefer to be the hosts, expecting them about eight. Feder has left the following account of that last evening together:[3]

As I came up with my wife about that hour to the verandah of his house on its steep slope, he sat writing at the open window of his study. It surprised me, for he did not usually work in the evenings.

—'Are we too early? Do we disturb you?'

—'No, not at all,' he said, with noticeable embarrassment. I did not suspect that I had surprised him in the act of writing his farewell letters.

We were together for four hours that evening. I had never seen him so sad, so completely crushed. The shadow which had always hung over him and darkened the natural brightness of his eyes was denser than ever before. I have always agreed with Rabelais that

[1] Information from Mrs. Margarida Banfield. [2] Feder, Arens[1] 162–3.

[3] What follows is an amalgamation, using Feder's own words in the author's translation, of his article Arens[1] 163–5, and of that in *Books Abroad*, vol. 17, 1 (Jan. 1943), 3–9 ('My Last Conversations with Stefan Zweig'), complemented by the article in *Aufbau*, New York (?Mar.) 1942 ('Stefan Zweigs letzte Tage').

'laughter is the natural state of man.' But I never laughed with Stefan Zweig. That night there was scarcely a smile.

'I have slept very little these last few nights,' he began. 'I have been reading a great deal,' [and he mentioned Bainville's *Life of Napoleon*, recalling] many incidents from it and [making] comparisons between the French Revolution and the present world upheaval. 'Would you like to have the book?' he asked me. I noticed that a large part of it had not yet had the leaves cut, and I said, 'Why, you haven't finished it yourself!'—'I don't expect to,' he said. And he insisted on my carrying off the two volumes. He knew that I was making a study of the French Revolution.

I had brought with me a little essay of mine, *Meeting at Weimar*, which he had expressed the wish to see before publication. Even in spite of the strain he must have been undergoing, he read it through as we sat there with his usual attentiveness, and then, apologising for not always agreeing with me, made some keen comments and criticisms.

I asked about a novel on the inflation period which he had told me something about. He had laid it aside some time before because he had not been able to secure precise dates and intimate details of that period. He spoke of Austria, and how much reason there still had been in the Germanic-Slav mixture of peoples there.

He spoke of his work on Balzac. 'There is no great Balzac biography. Those who attempted it all died before they could complete the work. I talked to Bouteron in Paris. He too will not write it. And for me also it is impossible.'

He gave me back the four volumes of my Montaigne which he had borrowed.

—'Have you got a complete edition now?'

—'Yes,' he murmured uncertainly, he had already written two chapters.

In the volumes he returned, the preface seemed to have interested him especially. There were two passages he had marked. One of them described Montaigne at the Royal court, 'lost in the crowd and observing.' In the other, Montaigne himself, distinguishing between the Mayor of Bordeaux and the man Montaigne, wrote: 'It is my opinion that you should lend to others and give only to yourself.' . . .

I assured him that his powers were undiminished, and that it was his duty to go on writing for the pleasure and profit of his many readers. 'But the trouble is,' he said, 'that when I used to write I was happy and full of enthusiasm. Now that's all gone.' . . . 'I used to be able to see my books through the press. I would correct the proofs five or six times. Now I have only my translations. They're my adopted children, and of course I love them, but they aren't quite the same thing as children of my own blood.' . . .

Now and then he used the phrase 'to die of the war,' as one dies of disease.

At the time I did not know why he returned the *Montaigne*, or . . . Bainville's *Napoleon* . . ., or why his wife, when he accepted my invitation to a game of chess, gave him a long surprised look. I suggested it because I thought the game which he loved so much would divert him from his gloomy thoughts. It was actually no particular pleasure to be his opponent at the board. I am a weak player, but his knowledge of the art was so moderate that it was hard for me to let him win occasionally. . . .

It is almost midnight as they accompany us back to our house. I go on ahead with Stefan Zweig. He mentions that a friend of his in Colombia, whose book on South America he has shown me, has been appointed Education Minister and has replied to his congratulations by inviting him to visit Bogota. I say: 'You ought to go,' and as our wives catch up with us, to Lotte: 'We have just planned a joint expedition to Colombia. Will you come too?' My wife thinks that such a journey in wartime is not without its dangers. Lotte contradicts her: but her own journey from England was not exactly pleasant. 'I shall not make that journey,' says Zweig. . . .

He gives me his hand once more, smiling, in farewell. He feels that his mood oppresses us: 'So, forgive me my black liver!' With these words and a deeply sad glance he disappeared into the darkness of the magical summer night, and from my many meetings with him this picture remains dominant and clear before my eyes.

The letters Zweig had been writing before the Feders' arrival had been numerous. Those directed to the ordering of his affairs were couched in terms very much as though he were simply leaving on a journey, with no direct reference to the terrible decision he had taken. But their import would be clear enough when they reached the addressees. To the Director of the town library of Petropolis he wrote in French:

I do not have my library here, this most necessary tool for my work has been lacking for years: there are only a few books which chance and friendship have accumulated in my home. But I should be happy if you would choose some for your beautiful library, which has been so useful for me and which demonstrates your respect and your love for books and letters. May it grow and develop and give to others as much pleasure as it did to me![1]

And to Cardoso Miranda, the Prefect of Petropolis, 'cher confrère':

I have to thank you for the good hours I have been able to pass in your admirable town. If I dared for a third time to build a house, in an attempt to rebuild my life which has been cut off from the roots of its birthplace, it would have been here and nowhere else. But how good it was to live, to work here amid a generous and peaceful nature; my last glance from my window was once more to embrace the supreme beauty of the countryside! Permit me also to thank you personally for your great friendliness. . . .[1]

'I am so awfully sorry,' he wrote in English to Mrs. Banfield,

but we have taken another decision than to rent your nice house again—you cannot imagine how tired one gets at sixty to live without his own house and wandering around.—All the little expenses, light, telephone, wages for Antonio and the maid ect ect will be paid by the executors of my will here in Brazil (Dr. S. Malamud or Abrão Koogan). I have also given orders that of my clothes ect somewhat should be given to this honest and kind people who made my stay in your house still more agreeable to us.—Kindest regards to your husband and your boys! Yours, Stefan Zweig.

About Plucky my executors will decide—if you want him really you have but to inform them; I know that he would have a good time with your boys.[2]

To his 'cher ami' Koogan he was more explicit.

Excuse me if I cause you trouble and work, but I was at the end of my strength because of this nomadic life and the bad state of health of my dear wife. I ask you that my burial should be as modest and private as possible. The small debts of my household are to be paid from what remains here. In the closed drawer will be found my balances and my testamentary dispositions. Dr. Malamud will, I hope,

[1] Facsimiles in the papers of Leopold Stern, Rio de Janeiro.

[2] Original in possession of Mrs. Banfield, Rio.

take charge of the legal affairs. In my will (and also that of my wife) I have authorised him and you to act as my executors for all my affairs in Brazil.—I would ask you also to send the letters off by air mail as soon as possible. And I thank you with all my heart for your good friendship, wishing the best for you, your wife and your child. Votre ami jusqu'à la dernière heure. . . .'[1]

To Wittkowski he also, despite their common language, wrote in French, no doubt to avoid any suspicion on the part of the Brazilian authorities (Brazil's decision early in February, with the rest of the South American republics, to break off diplomatic relations with Germany and Italy was expected any day to be followed by her declaration of war on the Axis). He explained that he had asked Koogan to let Wittkowski look through the manuscripts,[2] completed and uncompleted, he was leaving behind, mentioning in particular the *Schachnovelle* (though three copies of this he had sent off by registered post that day to Viking, Bermann-Fischer, and Alfredo Cahn) and the *Novelle, War es er?*; and he asked him to take special care that the remaining copy of the autobiography was preserved, as that sent to Sweden was quite possibly lost.

The other things are partly in the form of first sketches (alas, the Montaigne) and alas again, the Balzac, which is only the skeleton of the big book I would have written if the war had not prevented me (it was the first of two big volumes). If you find something which Koogan could keep, let him do so—destroy the rest!—I will ask Koogan to give you some remuneration from my royalties during your work of classifying; I do not believe in a great posterity for these things, it is just an instinct of preservation, a sentimentality.

As in the letters to Koogan and others, he repeated his complaint of great fatigue after these years of wanderings: 'when my sixty years sounded it was for me like a call: rest, since you cannot finish what was your real work, the great Balzac'. And he added that, anyway, it was significant that all those who had wanted to

[1] *Nouvelles Littéraires*, 8 Sept. 1966, 7.

[2] Sch. Wittkowski thought this charge effectively appointed him Zweig's literary executor, and there ensued a somewhat acrimonious correspondence with Dr. Altmann, the controversy conducted partly in public. Cf. letter from Wittkowski to *Aufbau*, New York, 28 May 1943.

take the measure of this giant had recoiled from the work required to treat 'cet héros du travail'. 'Je me sens très heureux depuis ma décision—la première fois depuis ce jour de septembre qui détruisait mon monde.—Courage! Vous êtes jeune! Vous verrez encore la vague se relever!'[1]

That, having taken the decision, he felt happier, calmer, more at ease, there is no doubt. In a farewell letter to Fülöp-Miller, written in these last few days, he recommended to his friend a careful rereading of Montaigne, and quoted once more from that essay which he had read so often himself: 'La vie despend de la volonté d'aultruy; la mort de la nostre. . . . La réputation ne touche pas une telle entreprinse: c'est folie d'y avoir respect. Le vivre, c'est servir, si la liberté de mourir en est à dire.'[2] At the outset of the war he had been able to repeat Rilke's words of 1915—'to survive is everything'; now, feeling himself too old to await the rise of the wave, he could exercise that right which Montaigne justified. In a world in which freedom for the individual seemed at an end, he could still remain free by this last act: here and here alone was to be found that inner citadel he had sought in vain, 'un port tresasseuré, qui n'est iamais a craindre'. 'When you get this letter I shall feel much better than before', he wrote to Friderike on the Sunday morning.

You have seen me in Ossining and after a good and quiet time my depression became much more acute—I suffered so much that I could not concentrate any more. And then the security—the only one we had—that this war will take years, that it would take ages before we in our special position could settle again in our home was too depressing. I liked Petropolis very much, but I had not the books I wanted and the solitude which first had such a soothing effect began to become oppressive—the idea that my central work, the Balzac, could never get finished without two years of quiet life and all books was very hard and then this war which is not yet at his hight [sic]. I was too tired for all that and poor Lotte did not have a good time with me, especially because her health was not the best. You have your children and with them a duty to keep up, you have large interests and an

[1] Sch.

[2] Fülöp-Miller, Arens[1] 168. The quotation is from Montaigne, II. iii ('Coustume de l'Isle de Cea').

unbroken activity. I am sure you will still see the better time and will give me right, that I with my 'black liver' did not wait any longer. I send you these lines in the last hours, you cannot imagine how glad I feel since I have taken the decision. Give my love to your children and do not complain me—remember the good Joseph Roth and Rieger, how glad I always was for them, that they had not to go through these ordeals. Love and friendship and cheer up, knowing me quiet and happy

Stefan.[1]

These letters are our only clue to his state of mind that Sunday, and, the servants who lived out being off for the day, there were no witnesses to what actually happened. The morning was obviously spent in final ordering of his papers: the bankbooks for their modest accounts in Brazil, some cash, small bequests to Koogan and his nephew by marriage, Ferdinand Burger, were placed tidily with their wills in the drawer of his desk. He posted off a short undated note to Ferdinand, enclosing a little cash for him: 'I had the feeling that it was only embarrassment that prevented you and the family from coming up here. As I am just putting my affairs in order I am sending something for you—unfortunately it is Sunday, so I cannot register it, but I hope it arrives.' The manuscripts and drafts he enveloped, marked 'Pas toucher! Tous ces manuscrits (en grande partie inachevés) ont à être remis à Senhor Abrão Koogan, Editora Guanabara, que j'ai prié de les garder et faire reviser par Mr. Victor Wittkowski Hotel Russel Praia Russel', signed and left on a chair in the corner. On the fly-leaves of Romains's birthday gift, the leather-bound volumes in English and French which Romains had dedicated in his own hand, he added 'et donné par lui à son ami Abrão Koogan, 21.2.1942', and these he placed in a prominent position on the desk.

The letters he had written were stamped, the pencils on his desk sharpened, books he had borrowed marked for return to their owners. There remained only one thing: to write an open declaration, his last act of authorship, to set a fitting seal on a life devoted to letters and spirit of freedom, a conclusion of honour

[1] *BrW* 357.

and artistry. It was headed in Portuguese, *Declaração*, but otherwise written in German:

> Before parting from life of my own free will and in my right mind I am impelled to fulfil a last obligation: to give heartfelt thanks to this wonderful land of Brazil which afforded me and my work such kind and hospitable repose. With every day I have learned to love this country more and more, and nowhere else would I have preferred to rebuild my life from the ground up, now that the world of my own language has been lost and my spiritual homeland, Europe, has destroyed itself.
>
> But after one's sixtieth year unusual powers are needed in order to make another wholly new beginning. Those that I possess have been exhausted by the long years of homeless wandering. So I hold it better to conclude in good time and with erect bearing a life for which intellectual labour was always the purest joy and personal freedom the highest good on this earth.
>
> I salute all my friends! May it be granted them yet to see the dawn after the long night! I, all too impatient, go on before.

This signed and dated, and left prominently on the desk, they were ready. That afternoon, some time between midday and four o'clock, they took massive doses of veronal and lay down together for this last sleep, Stefan in shirt, tie, and trousers, Lotte in a flowered kimono she had donned after a bath. The bottle of mineral water they had used bore the ironic label *Salutaris*. Little Plucky, the terrier, lay down too, outside the room, to wait patiently for his master to awake and take him for the evening walk. There was four-leaved clover in a vase on the sideboard.[1]

[1] H. E. Jacob, 'Aus den Polizeiakten von Petropolis', *Neue Zeitung*, Wien, Feb. 1952, and *Sp* 101; information from Mrs. Banfield, Ferdinand Burger, and Abrão Koogan; Stern, *passim*; *Nouvelles Littéraires*, 8 Sept. 1966, 7. The *Declaração* has been reproduced several times in facsimile, notably in *The World of Yesterday*, Cassell, London, 1943, and Arens[3] 32.

8

> *'Many men of feeling, throughout the world, must have meditated, the day when they learned of this double suicide, on a responsibility which is that of all of us and on the shame of a civilisation that can create a world in which a Stefan Zweig cannot live.'*
> André Maurois

On Monday morning, 23 February, the servants were not surprised when the Zweigs did not appear: it was not unusual for them to be up late into the night, and their standing orders were that they were not to be disturbed in the mornings. Antonio went off to his work as usual, the woman about her duties in the house. She knocked at the bedroom door later in the morning, but receiving no reply thought the couple still slept. At about three in the afternoon Claudio de Souza telephoned, intending to suggest a walk to Zweig; the maid said they were still sleeping, and de Souza assumed she meant their siesta. But when Antonio returned, and there was still no reply to a knock, he became alarmed. Trying the door, he found it locked. He climbed on to the roof, removed some tiles and looked in, to discover with horror what had happened. The police were called and began their investigation, not without some suspicion that more lay behind this apparent suicide than met the eye: in the current delicate political situation for Brazil, the death in unusual circumstances of refugees from the Axis powers needed some explanation. As it happened, an acquaintance of Zweig's, the French architect Alfred Agache, on his way down to Rio, stopped to call at the house and was told the news by one of the detectives coming down the steep steps: horrified, he rushed off to De Souza, who came back with him immediately, together with Leopold Stern, whom they had alerted by telephone. Stern, the only one who knew German, was able to translate the *Declaração* and satisfy the magistrate when he arrived of the tragic truth, so that no autopsy was found necessary.[1]

All three were deeply moved. De Souza, thinking that the Zweigs had no relatives in the country and that the PEN Club

[1] Information from Mrs. Banfield; De Souza 64–5; Jacob, op. cit., *Sp* 102–3; Stern 9–21.

PLATE 8

ZWEIG MEMORIAL, BAHIA, BRAZIL

of Brazil was their only family, took on himself the sad duties of a next-of-kin. One of his first acts for his dead friend, so distinguished a guest of Brazil, was to telephone to General Pinto, Chief of Staff at the presidential palace, to ask that President Vargas be informed immediately and his permission sought for a state funeral. Despite Zweig's last wish in his letters to Koogan, which of course became known only later, De Souza, and indeed all official Brazil, felt that nothing less than state honours were due to the author of *Land of the Future*. Vargas, once assured that the Zweigs were not Catholics, readily gave his authorization.[1]

The tragedy had aroused great publicity, and the state funeral the following day was without parallel in the history of Brazil for an *estrangeiro*, bigger and more moving even than any for a Brazilian writer, save only that of the statesman Ruy Barbosa. The coffins, laden with flowers, were placed on biers in the main school of Petropolis, Grupo Escolar Pedro Segundo, where Carauta de Souza, President of the town's Academy of Letters, held an address before a distinguished gathering which, though it could number none of Zweig's older friends and only the very few recently close to him—De Souza, Feder, Koogan, Stern—included the President in person, Ministers of State and numerous official and academic delegations. For the last journey to the cemetery Admiral Peixoto, representing the President, the painter and dramatist Raul Pedrosa, the Prefect Cardoso Miranda, Academician Professor Clementino Fraga, and Leopold Stern were among the pall-bearers. As the cortège passed, in brilliant sunshine, through the town, the shops spontaneously closed their shutters and a great multitude followed. It had been decided (though it seems doubtful whether Zweig would have approved) that the ceremony should be according to the Jewish rite, and at the graveside, not far from the mausoleum of Emperor Pedro II, Rabbi Dr. Lemle and Cantor Fleischmann officiated. As the coffins were lowered a dark cloud passed over the face of the sun and there was a heavy shower of rain, which ceased at the moment the ceremony reached its close.[2]

[1] De Souza 65–6; Jacob, op. cit., *Sp* 104.

[2] Jacob, *Sp* 105–6; letter from Feder to Friderike Zweig, 4 Mar. 1952; De Souza 72; Stern 113–15; Leftwich 89.

Epilogue

'Almost a paradigm of European influence is the figure of Stefan Zweig—at least he may count as the precursor of those who must come if we are to succeed in saving our spiritual world from the general chaos.' Erwin Rieger

'A man reveals his true being only in what he creates.' Stefan Zweig, *Das Geheimnis des künstlerischen Schaffens*

'His work remains to us, and one can still find in it reasons for loving life, in spite of everything.' Frans Masereel

'A morte de Zweig e um choque para todo o Brasil', said a Brazilian friend, who had not even known him, to Feder. His fame there and the immense popularity of his works brought countless tributes in the press of Brazil. On 2 March, the 'seventh day', the Jewish community of Petropolis held a meeting of mourning, at which Rabbi Lemle spoke and Miss Haberer sang from Händel in English. On 15 April the PEN Club of Brazil held a memorial meeting in the noble rooms of the Academy of Letters in Rio, attended by the diplomatic corps, including the British ambassador, and the most distinguished from the ranks of Brazilian society and letters, and addressed by De Souza as President of the Club, Miranda, and Feder.[1] There were similar meetings in New York and London.[2] Throughout the free world the sense of loss was overwhelming; to the refugees from Hitler,

[1] Feder, Arens[1] 152; letter from Feder to Friderike Zweig, 4 Mar. 1952; De Souza 5–6.

[2] The London PEN Club meeting could not be held until 23 July 1942, in the Rudolf Steiner Hall, with Herman Ould in the chair. It was addressed by Robert Neumann and G. B. Stern, and Berthe Grossbord gave a reading from Zweig's

especially, the tragic event was both a shock and an enigma, for Zweig—wealthy, secure, darling of publishers the world over—was the last man they would have expected to take his own life. 'He seemed so robust,' wrote Rolland, 'so assured of existence and knowing how to safeguard it from all dangers.'[1]

The way in which the news was transmitted that Monday served only to deepen the mystery for those who had known him. His *Declaração*, rendered on the spot into French by Stern and thence into Portuguese by De Souza (both in an understandably emotional state), reached the Brazilian press and the international wire services in an inaccurate and incomplete form, which gave the quite false impression of a self-centred, even cowardly, act, founded only in despair. 'Personal freedom' became 'human liberty *and my own*', and the optimistic note in the penultimate sentence of 'the dawn after the long night' was entirely omitted.* Since the original document was reproduced in facsimile in most papers in Brazil, the error was soon noticed, and (in a country poised then between peace and war) became the subject of a heated political debate, with accusations of suppression, in the interests of an Axis 'fifth column', of Zweig's faith in the ultimate victory of the Allied cause. De Souza was at pains, in an interview with *O Globo*, to explain that he had dictated his translation directly from Stern's verbal French, and that it was taken down by a 'third person' as he spoke: his lack of knowledge of German had prevented him from spotting the omission, and he remembered that the pencilled pages of the version for which the correspondent of the *Jornal de Petropolis* made himself responsible (for distribution to his colleagues in Rio and to the DIP agency) ended at the 'affectionate adieu'. He defended himself strongly against the imputation of pro-Axis sentiments, and stressed the anti-Nazi spirit of the PEN Club.[2]

works. At the meeting in New York on 28 Feb. 1942, held under the auspices of *Aufbau*, the editor, Manfred George, was in the chair, and the speakers included Emil Ludwig, Ferdinand Czernin, Klaus Mann, and Berthold Viertel; Eleonore von Mendelssohn gave a reading from the works.

[1] Letter to Andrée Jouve, 25 Feb. 1942 (Dum 136).

[2] Cuttings, undated, from *O Globo* and *Correio da Manha*, Rio de Janeiro (end Feb.–early Mar. 1942).

* See Note at end of chapter, p. 357.

But it was some little time before the text of the original reached the U.S.A. or England, and the effect of this defective translation in the first weeks was regrettable. For all the sincere tributes to Zweig's humanism and devotion to the cause of freedom, many could not see his suicide as other than a defection from the ranks, and therefore a triumph for the other side. He had always been right, so far, in his pessimism, thought Zuckmayer: was it possible that he was right again now, and that the struggle was hopeless?[1] Thomas Mann, with all respect to Zweig's deep and gentle humanity, and his goodness, which had helped so many to live, saw only the tragedy that these qualities were not robust enough to survive the darkness and greet the dawn (even after the full text of the declaration was known, he held to the view that suicide was a dereliction of duty, in selfish disregard for the discouragement it would exercise on the refugees—though he was to see it otherwise after the suicide of his son Klaus seven years later).[2] Emil Ludwig, in a typically flowery letter of farewell in the 27 February memorial issue of the New York refugee paper *Aufbau*, found the deed frankly incomprehensible: he had understood Toller, but he could not understand Zweig, whose character, philosophy, and circumstances should have made him, of all the refugees, survive the longest.

> Why did you not follow the example of our master [Goethe] who, with the enemy in his land, pressing to his very door, turned to study the geology of China?

> One is silent before the majestic finality of such an act [wrote Bruno Frank in the same paper], the motives for which can rarely be fully recognisable. And one's thoughts turn to those comrades who, under externally more difficult circumstances, are obliged hourly to combat despair. Let us hold together, let us help one another materially and morally, that no more shall fall before we see the light.

Alone of the contributors to that issue of *Aufbau*, Heinrich Mann and Lion Feuchtwanger (neither particularly enamoured of

[1] Letter to Friderike Zweig, 26 Feb. 1942.

[2] *Aufbau*, New York, 27 Feb. 1942; letter to Friderike Zweig, 15 Sept. 1942 (Mann *Br* ii. 281–2).

Zweig during his life) understood instinctively that he had not in fact despaired of the ultimate victory of humanity.[1]

'He always seemed so strong, and yet was weaker than I, as is now revealed', wrote the gentle Felix Braun to Friderike from his lonely cottage in the English Lake District; 'he could bear it no longer, and just as an impatient boy . . . gives up a game which means everything to him, so he, the unhappy one, threw away his life, without a thought of what that life had meant for us'.[2] 'He was overwhelmed by the past,' said a *New York Herald-Tribune* editorial, 'and by the realisation that all he had held most dear had been wantonly destroyed.' The New York *Sun* recalled an interview he had given in July 1940, in which he had said that though exile did not kill the body, it killed the power of creation: when that was dead the life of the body did not seem to an artist worth living.[3] 'He was an exile in time from the 19th century,' ran the London *Times* obituary on 25 February, 'and his death may perhaps be attributed to his weariness in wandering.' 'If even this man, ready with help to his last breath, doubted the final victory of the cause of justice,' wondered Csokor, 'what remained for us, living spiritually and materially on the brink of the abyss?'[4]

The reasons for a suicide must always remain an enigma, for who can know what passes through a man's mind in the last hours? It is the custom for those who remain this side of the divide to speak of the balance of a suicide's mind being disturbed: that is to say, we regard the deliberate choice of death as a kind of madness—though the awe with which we approach the act invests it often with a kind of heroism. The outward causes of such a decision often seem plain enough, particularly in the case of a suicide pact, when a man and a woman under the pressure of events, either private or public, reach the end of their tether. But the matter is usually more complicated. In the case of Stefan

[1] *Aufbau*, New York, 27 Feb. 1942. Other contributors were Hermann Kesten, Franz Werfel, Walter Mehring, Alfred Polgar, Berthold Viertel, Lothar Wallenstein, and Paul Stefan. The issue also carried an extract from Zweig's translation of Verhaeren's poems *Hymnen an das Leben* ('Die letzte Sonne'), and a short appreciation of his life and work (including the defective translation of the *Declaração*).

[2] Letter of 25 Mar. 1942.

[3] Quoted in *The Jewish Journal* (? end Feb.) 1942.

[4] *Sp* 110.

Zweig we may discern something like a mosaic of reasons, no piece complete in itself, each dependent on the others if the picture is to be seen whole.

Before all, we must recognize that the depressions to which he was subject throughout his life—almost pathological in their intensity—brought with them a certain predisposition towards suicide. Even as a young man at the university he had once spoken of the courage which would be needed to put an end to one's life, and said that he would himself be capable of such courage if ever he felt that his life had lost its sense.[1] Twice during his life he had urged Friderike to join him in death, when in the grip of especially deep depression. In his personal struggle with the daimon he managed almost always to gain the upper hand, to subject the forces of violence within him (as he said to Jules Romains) to his self-control. People admired his cleverness, the good timing he showed in the conduct of his life: 'il a su faire régner la sagesse dans sa vie à lui', thought Romains. Few suspected that there were occasions when the daimon could not be controlled, and that then his sense of defeat became an urge to self-destruction, an urge in particular, like Kleist's, to seek a companion in suicide. The positive strength of Friderike's character was enough, on those two earlier occasions, to divert him from the abyss. The third time she was not there, and Lotte's gentler nature, melancholy and readier to despair, could not allow her to do otherwise than 'be dragged along with him'.

In earlier years, we must also not forget, he had had a 'cure' to hand for his depressive states. Though he would complain of the shackles of the 'business', it had always been possible for him to cast them off at a moment's notice, to take off from his 'springboard' and wander freely through the world, seek out from his enormous circle of friends those who suited the mood of the hour, or simply plunge into areas of human activity hitherto unknown to him—a 'Zufuhr an Leben und Leidenschaft' which would quickly restore him. Ideas for new work would flow, the

[1] Hans Müller-Einigen (*Jugend*, 329–31) has reconstructed a romanticized account of a conversation with Zweig on these lines; there is, however, no reason to doubt the fact.

zest for taking up old projects would return. But in Petropolis no such escape was possible. He was in a corner, from which there was only the one way out. And in fact it is difficult to avoid the conclusion that, perhaps even consciously, he had actually sought out this impossible position. He had convinced himself that, at sixty, his powers were exhausted, that the rootlessness, the 'years of homeless wandering', of which he spoke continually, must be ended: in choosing the virtually complete isolation of Petropolis, he was deliberately cutting himself off from the one thing that could have saved him—the possibility of movement and change. The ideal of personal freedom, the 'connecting thread' of his life's work, had, in fact, meant for him nothing more than freedom to move and to exchange one ambiance for another, to still his inner restlessness with new scenes and new people. Without such change he could not maintain his extraordinary application to the work which was his whole life. With friends, or with those he loved, like Friderike and Lotte, he could never establish a quiet and peaceful relationship without quitting them at frequent intervals; once alone, however, in an hotel room in some provincial town, he rapidly felt the need to seek out company again. In the last months in Brazil the freedom to change was lost—seemingly of his own volition.

This is the centre-piece of the mosaic, but of itself it begs the question. It is only by fitting the other pieces round it that we can begin to see an explanation for so apparently irrational a decision by so wise a mind. Robert Dumont, whose perceptive *Stefan Zweig et la France* contains the only detailed study so far made of Zweig's correspondence with Romain Rolland, felt that these letters—perhaps the only ones in which he expresses himself without reserve—give a clue to the enigma.

> Behind the author of great editions, whose success and material achievement are the envy of so many of his colleagues, there stands concealed a disappointed artist, a creator ill-content with his work, despairing of mastery in the higher genres and of showing himself worthy of the models he reveres—a little-known aspect which may help to explain the fatal act of Petropolis.[1]

[1] Dum 216.

That a feeling of failure, of retribution demanded by fate for a success he had not deserved, was present in his mind is very possible: his renunciation of the task of the 'great Balzac' may indeed be an expression of this. Certainly a sense of hopelessness in his work was strong in him. The loss of his 'homeland of the German language' had been a keener blow even than that of Austria and of Europe itself. The thought that his intellectual labour, his 'purest joy', could survive only in translation, was shattering.

It seems unlikely that Lotte's health weighed materially in his decision. She was physically fairly robust, and her asthma had in fact improved since their move into the mountains. There were certainly, however, times when he must have felt that the young wife who, he had hoped, would lighten his declining years was but an additional burden, in a condition which would never really improve. Pity was for the main part in his regard for her: in urging her to join him in death, to be the Henrietta Vogel to his Kleist, he may well have seen the act as one of compassion. But, above all, he needed, like Kleist, a companion in death, to 'free him from the loneliness of the last second'; we may doubt whether he saw in Lotte, as Kleist saw in Henrietta, a sick woman 'already dedicated to death'.[1]

Unlike Castellio—the man he would have wished to have been—he lacked the prop of a religious faith to sustain him. 'Ces êtres hypernerveux, agités, incertains,' Olivier had said of the Jews, 'ont besoin d'une foi qui les tienne.' Perhaps, as Felix Braun thought, it would have needed but a slight impulse, from the right hand, to have awakened belief: for Braun, it was Zweig's great misfortune that his spirit had remained so firmly closed against it.[2] Zweig's ideal had been very much of this world—the cultural unity of Europe—and his life's work a conscious programme to that end. When the tide of barbarism swept away the Europe in which this ideal could still be sought, he had nothing left. Politically he had been a quietist: he had seen internationalism not as a political programme but as the sum of individual, personal links forged in friendship. The intellectual leaders of

[1] Stefan Zweig, *Der Kampf mit dem Dämon*, 222.

[2] Letter to Friderike Zweig, 26 Feb. 1942.

Europe, of every country of Europe, had been his friends: now they were either gagged in 'inner emigration' or cast-out wanderers like himself, if not already in the grave. He had never been a fighter, and to join the ranks of those who, like Werfel, or Thomas Mann, urged meeting violence with violence could be only a betrayal of his ideal.

His essentially pacifist nature would not allow him to see the war as a struggle between right and wrong, between the forces of darkness and the angels of justice and freedom. For him it remained an unmitigated disaster for the world, in which untold numbers would be persecuted, tortured, and killed, and the vicarious suffering which assailed him in his safe retreat had become unbearable. 'A few percent more egotism and less imagination would have helped me much in my life; now one cannot change oneself.'[1] There was no joy in his heart as he read of German losses in Russia: such deaths represented no victory for him, and he was as deeply affected by them as by the stories of the sufferings of the Jews in Central Europe. The horror of the war as such had bitten deep into his soul. Each report of violence and death, no matter to which 'side' it referred, deepened his depression.

Humanism, he had written in *Erasmus*, was constantly threatened by the unreason of passion; humanists must be ready for sacrifice in the certain knowledge that 'time and again in history a tidal wave of fanaticism, swelling from the primeval depths of the human unconscious, will sweep over and burst all banks. . . . It is their moral duty to stand firm and see it through without being confused at heart.'[2] 'Every wave, no matter how powerfully it rises, must fall again', he had said a few years later. But he had become convinced that this new tide of bestial inhumanity, spreading ever more swiftly over the globe, would be many years in the turning, and that his generation would not see it recede. Schooled as he was in pessimism,[3] his worst predictions of disaster,

[1] *BrW* 345.

[2] Stefan Zweig, *Erasmus von Rotterdam*; Reichner, Wien, 1934, 18.

[3] The phrase is from a letter to Liesl Monath, 4 July 1938: 'Ein so gelernter Pessimist ich bin, diese Katastrophe hat mein Vorgefühl noch arg übertroffen' (LM).

right from the time of his first encounter with Mussolini's Fascism in 1921, had been more than fulfilled; now, after the blows of Pearl Harbour and Singapore, with Brazil about to be involved in a war literally on a world scale, it is not difficult to understand his despair. The night would indeed be long before the dawn. And his sense of the artistry in the historic process, sharpened as he completed *Die Welt von Gestern*, made him see it as only fitting that his own life, one of a generation that was finished, should be ended now. The legacy of Erasmus would have to be left to other hands, to a new generation: 'we ourselves have too little of the maniac, of the fanatic, in our ideals, we are too Erasmian, too Alexandrine, to prevail'.[1] Like Castellio at the end of his long struggle with Calvin, he was tired. Hitler, like Calvin, would win. While the human element of history had always fascinated him—the great *Sternstunden*, the turning-points where all depended on a single human being—he had long since recognized its essential amorality, which neither punishes evil deeds nor rewards good, but rests in the last resort on force rather than on justice. Though he had not forgotten the equally valid lesson of history, that every attempt to corral the whole world into a single system is doomed to eventual failure, he had not the strength himself to await the turn.

There was a sharp dichotomy in almost every aspect of the character of Stefan Zweig. Reared in a world of security, never knowing real hardship or any substantial material loss even when its security disappeared, he was consumed all his life by an inner restlessness, and was ever sensitive to the slightest movement of the apparently firm ground beneath his feet. He was indeed, in Werfel's words, 'not born to take it easy'.[2] Intensely curious about every aspect of human life, he could be the most gregarious of men, the veritable 'apostle of the religion of friendship' that Rolland acclaimed: yet he could not bear society for long and was ever on the move to escape, only then to long once more for the company of congenial friends. Impulsive and impatient, remaining in many ways a spoilt child, he yet was capable of

[1] Letter to Alfred Wolfenstein, 15 Oct. 1938 (*Sp* 86).
[2] *Aufbau*, New York, 27 Feb. 1942.

sustained concentration and the most diligent application to his work. His love for music was deep, but he was rarely relaxed or patient enough to sit a concert out. His disposition was kind, unselfish, and gentle, and his charity noble, as countless friends in less fortunate circumstances could bear witness; but the violence and passion latent in him could not always be concealed or controlled, and there was more than a touch of sadism in his attitude towards women, who loved him more than he felt he deserved. He could be gay, light-hearted, but the 'black liver', the intense depressive states, would always return.

His deeply pessimistic nature, with his capacity for imagination, lent him the vision of a prophet—'my sense of premonition of political disaster troubles me like an inflamed nerve'[1]—but he showed himself weak in taking the personal decisions such insight demanded. A famous man and an effective public speaker, he shunned the limelight and refused honours, and would never 'use his elbow' or ask favours for himself. He gave the impression of a civilized, sophisticated man of the world, and certainly conducted the 'business' of his writing with an admirable professionalism; in reality he was shy and retiring to a degree, fearful even with close friends of disturbing them. In many ways a sceptic, he could nevertheless often be filled with a boyish enthusiasm, and the courteous façade, the apparent detachment with which he listened to others, concealed deep convictions.

His Bohemian/Italian descent, his facility in languages, and the degree of assimilation in which he grew up in Vienna made it easy for him to feel himself a European, rather than an Austrian or a Jew, as at home in Paris or Rome, Berlin or Prague, as in Vienna or Salzburg. None the less there were roots both in his homeland and in his Jewishness deeper than he realized himself, and their severing by the axe of the new barbarism was to wither the apparently strong plant of his internationalism. The man always admired as a *Lebenskünstler*, considered by Romains as one of the seven wise men of Europe,[2] was in fact very often prey to doubt and despair. He could never achieve in his life the calm integration of a Verhaeren or a Rolland, and it was his realization

[1] Letter to Roth, undated (? Apr. 1936) (Roth). [2] Arens[2] 344.

of this that perhaps accounted for the deep veneration in which he held these heroes of his youth and middle age.

A perfectionist in his work, for which no trouble or effort was too great, he remained something of a dilettante in life, tiring quickly of human relationships and shunning too close an involvement with others, happy only when he could feel free to break off and move on to new experiences. (When you met him, said Antonina Vallentin, no matter where it was, his manner suggested a suitcase in the next room half-packed ready for travel.)[1] He enjoyed adventure, the approaches of the 'unknown woman' attracted by his stories, and the *Schwärmerei* of the teenage girls at his lectures—but only in the knowledge that he could take the next train away. 'True freedom lies in the recognition of necessity', wrote Spinoza; Zweig, despite his great kindness and desire to avoid giving hurt to others, instinctively drew back from any relationship which threatened to make demands of necessity on him. His pity was too often of the weak and sentimental kind, 'no more than the heart's impatience to be rid as quickly as possible of the painful emotion aroused by the sight of another's unhappiness'.[2] Similarly, he sought to preserve his personal freedom, his civil liberties, by side-stepping, with the excellent sense of timing lent him by his remarkable foresight, the great political onslaughts of the time. At the end, when no further escape was possible, he had isolated himself from those who loved him, save only Lotte, and had to bow to the last great necessity of all.

He was acutely sensitive to the emotions of others, and had an uncanny capacity to feel vicariously their sentiments and sufferings. His soul vibrated, like a delicate seismograph, to the distant earthshaking of war. 'People speak so lightly of bombardments,' he wrote in one of his last letters, 'but when I read of houses collapsing I collapse with them.'[3] So strong, indeed, was this sympathetic feeling that in the last years it induced in him a sense of identification, against all reason, with those truly under the blows of fate. The citizen of the world had become the wandering Jew,

[1] Vallentin 58.

[2] Stefan Zweig, *Ungeduld des Herzens*; Bermann-Fischer, Stockholm, 1939, 228.

[3] Franz Werfel, Arens[2] 280.

the civilized traveller a mere nomad, the holder of a British passport a persecuted refugee. Still wealthy, he imagined himself poor; with his powers at their height, he thought himself declining.

A streak of fatalism was always strong in him, ill-assorted with his urge to be untrammelled and free. History he saw not only as an artist but also as a stern ruler, choosing men to carry out her decrees rather than herself being shaped and directed by men. He could observe her work of the past with delight, of the present with awe and trepidation, but her commands were not to be ignored, nor the strokes of destiny averted. That this in practice meant indecision, he himself recognized. 'You cannot imagine', he said once, 'what a joy it would be to know at once the position to take, the decision to opt for.'[1] Too often he let events take charge at crucial moments of his life, or, delaying too long, was forced along the wrong road. His aversion to any form of political or organizational activity, partly from shyness of publicity, was also rooted in this fatalism: what could men achieve in the face of destiny? What was to be, would be. His was essentially a passive nature, admiring, but unable to emulate, robust four-square figures like Jaurès and Verhaeren, or destiny-defying characters like Rimbaud and Magellan. 'Born a conciliator', he could not be a hammer, and would not be an anvil.[2] He could prophesy and warn, but unlike Jeremiah could not lead. Like Montaigne, he could only flee before the plague. The true hero for him was a Tersites, not an Achilles; a Castellio rather than a Calvin: not those who 'erect their transient empires over millions of graves and smashed lives, but those who, non-violent, submit to violence'.[3]

In earlier years there had been a positive quality in the way this philosophy had found expression in his works and in his life. *Jeremias* showed the energizing power of defeat, the ultimate superiority of vanquished over victor. Non-political, Zweig worked in his own way at 'the art of the possible', not by way of the high-sounding manifesto or the international congress but by practical personal application of the principle of international

[1] Vallentin 55. [2] Letter to Schickele, 27 Aug. 1934 (Sch).
[3] Stefan Zweig, *Castellio gegen Calvin*; Reichner, Wien, 1936, 27–8.

brotherhood and friendship. His life's aim was to be 'above party in everything', 'to understand even that which is most foreign, always to value peoples and times, figures and works in their positive, creative sense', and by this 'will to understand and to make understood, humbly but faithfully to serve our indestructible ideal: humane understanding between men, outlooks, cultures and nations'.[1] Alongside his major works stands an immense and varied opus in this sense: essays, introductions, appreciations of the work and significance of great contemporaries and great figures of the past, in Germany, France, Russia, the Anglo-Saxon countries, Belgium, Italy, Portugal, not merely in the world of letters but across the whole cultural board.

His studies of Balzac, Dostoevsky, Tolstoy, Fouché, Marie Antoinette, Magellan, Erasmus, Mary Queen of Scots, Rolland, Casanova, Verhaeren, Freud, Dickens, Nietzsche, Stendhal, Mesmer, Hölderlin, Kleist, were justly pillars of his fame. Less well known but of almost equal importance was the seemingly inexhaustible stream of his shorter interpretative writings—a panorama of European culture, suffused with deep understanding, and constructed with a critical competence few have equalled. Rousseau, Goethe, Jean Paul, Marceline Desbordes-Valmore; Sainte-Beuve, Beatrice Cenci, Rimbaud; Renan, Händel, Flaubert, Lenin; Verlaine, Byron, E. T. A. Hoffmann; Amerigo Vespucci, Baudelaire, Jeremias Gotthelf; Balboa, Cicero, Jens Peter Jacobsen, Wilson; Blake, Chateaubriand, Whitman, Victor Hugo; Lafcadio Hearn, Rouget de l'Isle, Mozart, Proust—the list might suggest the dilettante or the literary journalist, but in fact in every case, however short the essay or introduction, his judgement was based on thorough research, immensely careful preparation, and an intuitive ability to place his subject against the backcloth of European culture seen whole. More intense still was his observation of the contemporary scene, where personal acquaintance and often friendship with the leaders in many spheres made him unrivalled as interpreter. In the world of letters, Rilke, Thomas Mann, Hesse, George, Hofmannsthal; Drinkwater, Schalom

[1] Stefan Zweig, *Begegnungen mit Menschen, Büchern, Städten*; Reichner, Wien, 1937, 6.

Asch, Ginzkey, Tagore, Bazalgette; Carossa, Gorki, James Joyce, Dehmel, Joseph Roth; Schweitzer, Barbusse, Schnitzler, Jakob Wassermann; in the arts, Rodin, E. M. Lilien, Masereel; in music, Mahler, Busoni, Toscanini, Bruno Walter; on the stage Moissi and Kainz; in the 'great world' Rathenau, Jaurès, Herzl, Berta von Suttner, Lammasch—on all these, and on many lesser lights, he had a penetrating contribution to make, seeing their varied work as threads in the great tapestry of Europe's intellectual heritage.

His generation 'believed in the unity of Europe as in a gospel', but the First World War had destroyed the early child-like faith that it would ever be quickly achieved. Tracing the European idea in its historical development, in his lecture at Florence in 1932, he had noted the extraordinary simultaneity of the Romantic mood in many countries in an age of relatively slow communication. Byron and Mickiewicz, Pushkin and Hölderlin could express similar feelings quite independently of each other; the revolutionary spirit of the 1840s appeared simultaneously at different points through Europe. It was the germ of something like a 'common European psyche'. How much more then today, in an age which instantaneous communication has made an 'age of simultaneity', could one hope, despite the centrifugal tendencies of the nations and their internecine strife, that the European idea would seize men's minds, and that one day—not tomorrow, perhaps not even in the lifetime of his generation—a united Europe would be a reality.[1] Through unremitting toil, 'each at his post', the Tower of Babel would rise again, and on its summit the nations would be reunited, he had written in 1916;[2] we must stay at the post assigned to us, he could still say in 1940,[3] though by then the new world conflagration had made it clear that the effort would be harder and the road even longer than he had dreamed.

In the last resort, he wrote in his *Verhaeren*, the force which

[1] Stefan Zweig, 'Der europäische Gedanke in seiner historischen Entwicklung', *Zeit und Welt*, 301–26.

[2] Stefan Zweig, 'Der Turm zu Babel', *Europäisches Erbe*, 279.

[3] Letter to Kesten, 24 Jan. 1940 (*Exil* 130).

decides the effect of a man's work is the sense of responsibility: 'to be responsible, and to feel that one is responsible, is equivalent to looking at one's whole life as a vast debt, which one is bound to strive with all one's strength to pay off'.[1] Though often in his personal life he tended to evade responsibility, to escape from the involvement with others the generosity of his nature entailed, there was a clear *Verantwortungsgefühl* in his approach to his life's work, as though in truth he was striving with all his might to pay off the vast debt. There was a plan in his life, formed after the First World War when he settled in Salzburg. He had never tried to evaluate his work, he wrote in 1922:

> I give as much as I can—it is not for me to estimate its worth. But on the other hand I feel it an important obligation on me consciously and actively to develop that unifying, comprehensive element which—through the European mode of life of my early days, varied experience of the world and friendships reaching out beyond Germany's boundaries—has not been without effect; and thus myself to assist in the reconstruction of the old European community and to work against an isolation which would be as fatal for Germany as for her former opponents. A mere act of will cannot enhance one in one's art: it can however in one's moral bearing, in one's activity and one's passion to be of service. Herein I see a task for which I am by nature and destiny particularly suited, and I am comforted by the thought that my literary achievement, even if itself insignificant, may be of value in this sense of solidarity, perhaps even of greater effect in this invisible way than in the outward form of book or drama.[2]

In the last years it seems almost as though he saw his ideal as an unattainable Holy Grail, towards which man must ever strive, but which constantly recedes from his grasp. 'Only ideals which have not been worn out or compromised by realisation', he said in *Erasmus*, 'can continue to work in each new generation as the element of moral progress.'[3] The journey, not the arrival; as Goethe had said, only in striving can redemption lie. His pervading pessimism, deeper than ever before in the dark days at the end of 1941, had thus in fact an underlay of optimism: though he

[1] Stefan Zweig, *Emile Verhaeren*; Insel, Leipzig, 1910, 209.
[2] *DDh* 9–10.
[3] *Erasmus*, 226.

felt himself to be finished, his ideal, unrealized, would remain to inspire those coming after. He had seen Rolland's life as a work of art. 'A single great man who remains human saves, always and for all men, the belief in humanity.'[1] For his own life he could make no such claim; but, having borne witness to the world of yesterday which had ended in 1939, he could achieve a final work of art by his death, disappearing quietly and with dignity, in good time and with erect bearing. We may cavil at the reasoning; we cannot deny the courage of this last act.

That there are so few memorials to Stefan Zweig today would not have displeased this most modest of men. His grave, alongside Lotte's amid the cypress trees of Petropolis, is marked by an unadorned black marble stone, bearing only the names and dates in English and Hebrew. There is a tablet on the house of his birth in Vienna; the path ascending the Kapuzinerberg in Salzburg bears his name, as do obscure streets in Vienna and Rio de Janeiro. A bas-relief looks over a square in Bahia. A small but devoted band keeps his memory green in the International Stefan Zweig Society in Vienna. Perhaps the most touching and not least appropriate tribute is the most recent one: the naming after him of a new *B'nai B'rith* lodge, founded in September 1968 in the Rio suburb of Penha. The young men there, small boys at the time of his death, their fathers immigrant Jews, mainly from Russia and Poland rather than from Austria or Germany, saw in Zweig a son of Jewry who was at the same time in the van of the fight for all humanity, and recognized in his apparent failure and defeat a true victory in that struggle.

[1] Stefan Zweig, *Romain Rolland — der Mann und das Werk*; Ruetten & Loening, Frankfurt am Main, 1921, 260.

* The following were versions of the end of the message that appeared in the first few days, as compared with the original:

A Noite, Rio, 28 Feb. Assim, julgo melhor terminar a tempo uma vida que dediquei exclusivamente ao trabalho espiritual, considerando a liberdade humana e a minha propria como o maior bem da terra. Deixo um adeus afetuoso a todos os meus amigos.

PM, New York, 24 Feb. Therefore I believe it is time to end a life which was dedicated only to spiritual work, considering human liberty and my own as the greatest wealth in the world. I leave an affectionate goodby to all my friends.

(As in many other Brazilian papers, a facsimile of the original was carried alongside this 'translation').

Aufbau, New York, 27 Feb. Daher glaube ich, daß es an der Zeit ist, ein Leben zu beenden, das nur geistiger Arbeit gewidmet war und das stets die Freiheit und auch meine eigene als den größten Reichtum in der Welt betrachtet hat. Ein herzliches Lebewohl an alle meine Freunde!

Original

So halte ich es für besser, rechtzeitig und in aufrechter Haltung ein Leben abzuschließen, dem geistige Arbeit immer die lauterste Freude und persönliche Freiheit das höchste Gut dieser Erde gewesen. Ich grüße alle meine Freunde! Mögen sie die Morgenröte noch sehen nach der langen Nacht! Ich, allzu Ungeduldiger, gehe ihnen voraus.

APPENDIX TO CHAPTER V

Bibliography of Stefan Zweig's Works 1925–1929

ESSAY VOLUMES

1925	*Der Kampf mit dem Dämon* (Hölderlin, Kleist, Nietzsche)	Insel-Verlag
1928	*Drei Dichter ihres Lebens* (Casanova, Stendhal, Tolstoi)	Insel-Verlag

NOVELLEN, FICTION, AND OTHER PROSE WORKS

1925	*Angst* (revised, shortened edition)	Reclams Universalbibliothek, 6540
	Leporella (published 1929, see *Kleine Chronik*)	
(31 May)	*Die unsichtbare Sammlung* (see also *Kleine Chronik*)	*Vossische Zeitung*
1926	*Verwirrung der Gefühle* —*24 Stunden aus dem Leben einer Frau* —*Untergang eines Herzens* —*Verwirrung der Gefühle*	Insel-Verlag
1927	*Sternstunden der Menschheit: fünf historische Miniaturen*	Insel-Bücherei, 165
	**Erinnerungen an Émile Verhaeren* (republication of 1917 version)	Selbstverlag
	Die unsichtbare Sammlung (see also *Kleine Chronik*)	*Insel-Almanach*; Berliner Bibliophilenabend
	Der Flüchtling: Episode vom Genfer See	Bücherlotterie der Internationalen Buchkunstausstellung, Leipzig
1929 (27 Mar.)	*Rahel rechtet mit Gott*	*NFP*
	Joseph Fouché: Bildnis eines politischen Menschen	Insel-Verlag

* Reprinted in *Begegnungen mit Menschen, Büchern, Städten*; Reichner, Wien, 1937.

1929	*Der Zwang*; *Phantastische Nacht*	Roman-Rundschau, Nr. **19**, Wien
	Fragment aus einer Novelle	*Buch des Gesamtverbandes schaffender Künstler Oesterreichs*
	Kleine Chronik —*Die unsichtbare Sammlung* —*Episode vom Genfer See* —*Leporella* —*Buchmendel*	Insel-Bücherei, 408

PLAYS

1926	*Volpone* (adapted from Ben Jonson)	Kiepenheuer
1927	*Die Flucht zu Gott* (epilogue to Tolstoy's *Das Licht scheinet in der Finsternis*)	Felix Bloch Erben
1928	*Gelegenheit macht Liebe* (in collaboration with Lernet-Holenia, under pseudonym 'Clemens Neydisser')	Felix Bloch Erben
1929	*Das Lamm des Armen*	Insel-Verlag

REVIEWS

1925 (June)	Anna Dostoiewskaya: *Erinnerungen*	Die Literatur, Berlin
1925/1926	J. Meier-Graefe: *Dostoiewski der Dichter*	,,
	W. Michel: *Friedrich Hölderlin*	,,
	H. Schwarz: *Salzburg und Salzkammergut*	,,
1927	Paul Zech: *Rimbaud*	*Tagebuch*, Berlin
1929	*Aufmarsch der Jugend: Anthologie jüngster Prosa*	*Münchner Post*

ARTICLES AND ESSAYS

1925	*'Die Stadt als Rahmen (Salzburg)'	*Salzburger Festspielalmanach*
	'Romain Rollands Kindheit'	*Die Rampe*, Hamburg
(31 Jan.)	*'Die Monotisierung der Welt'	*NFP*
(31 May)	'Thomas Mann zum 50. Geburtstag'	*Berliner Tageblatt*
(June)	'An den Genius der Verantwortlichkeit (Thomas Mann)'	*Neue Rundschau*
(27 Sept.)	*'Marcel Prousts tragischer Lebenslauf'	*NFP*
1926	'Prolog (an Ariel) und Epilog (an Caliban) zu Shakespeares *Sturm*'	*Insel-Almanach*

* Reprinted in *Begegnungen mit Menschen, Büchern, Städten*; Reichner, Wien, 1937.

		'Internationalismus oder Kosmopolitismus'	*Literarische Welt*, Berlin
		'Liber Amicorum Romain Rolland' (with Duhamel and Gorki)	Rotapfelverlag, Zürich
		'Tagebuch eines halbwüchsigen Mädchens'	*Almanach des Internationalen Psychoanalytischen Verlags*, Wien
		'Romain Rolland'	*Leipziger Jüdische Zeitung*
		'An Wilhelm Schmidtbonn' (in *Chor um Schmidtbonn zum 50. Geburtstag*)	Deutscher Verlagsanstalt, Stuttgart
	(28 Mar.)	†'Irrfahrt und Ende des Pierre Bonchamps: die Tragödie Philippe Daudets'	*NFP*
	(5 May)	'Zum 70. Geburtstag Sigmund Freuds'	*Münchner Neueste Nachrichten*
	(29 June)	'F. A. Brockhaus: Beschwerde gegen einen Verleger (Casanova betreffend)'	*Berliner Tageblatt*
	(3 Oct.)	‡'Vorbeigehen an einem unauffälligen Menschen: Otto Weininger'	*Berliner Tageblatt*
	(4 Nov.)	'Ben Jonson'	*NFP*
	(28 Nov.)	'Zu Verhaerens 10. Todestag'	*Literarische Welt*, Berlin
	(2 Dec.)	†'Legende und Wahrheit der Beatrice Cenci'	*NFP*
1927		*'Marceline Desbordes-Valmore' (republication, augmented, of 1917 edition)	Insel-Verlag
		'Gedächtnis eines deutschen Menschen' (Ami Kaemmerer)	*Die Ausfahrt*, Verlag Silberburg, Stuttgart
		'Moissi im Gespräch' (in *Moissi — der Mensch in Worten und Bildern*, ed. Hans Böhm)	Eigenbrödler Verlag, Berlin
		‡'Léon Bazalgette'	*Europe*, Paris
	(1 May)	'Das Geheimnis der Beatrice Cenci'	*Magdeburger Zeitung*
	(7 May)	'Ben Jonsons Volpone in Deutschland'	*Leipziger Neueste Nachrichten*
	(12 May)	'Zu Emil Luckas 50. Geburtstag'	*Kölner Zeitung*

* Reprinted in *Begegnungen mit Menschen, Büchern, Städten*; Reichner, Wien, 1937.

† Reprinted in *Zeit und Welt*, ed. Friedenthal; S. Fischer, Frankfurt am Main, 1946.

‡ Reprinted in *Europäisches Erbe*, ed. Friedenthal; S. Fischer, Frankfurt am Main, 1960.

1927	(28 Sept.)	'Zur Entstehung des Volpone'	*Neue Zürcher Zeitung*
1928		'Brief an einen französischen Freund' (in *Buch des Dankes — Hans Carossa zum 50. Geburtstag*)	Insel-Verlag
		'Das Buch als Weltbild'	*Universum*, Leipzig
		'Bücherladen in London: Bermondsey Bookshop'	*Freie Volksbildung*
		'Shakespeare'	*Freiburger Theaterblätter*
	(25 Mar.)	*'Rede zu Ehren Maxim Gorkis'	*NFP*
	(20 July)	'Stefan Georges Stellung im deutschen Geistesleben'	*Die Literatur*, Berlin
	(16 Sept.)	*'Ypern'	*Berliner Tageblatt*
	(Oct.)	'Anmerkungen zu James Joyces Ulysses'	*Neue Rundschau*
	(Oct.)	†'Reise nach Russland' (three articles)	*NFP*
	(8 Nov.)	'Hans Carossa'	*Berliner Tageblatt*
1929		'Zutrauen zur Zukunft' (in *Die Frau von morgen, wie wir sie wünschen*)	E. A. Seemann, Leipzig
		'König der Juden' (in *Zeitgenossen über Herzl*, ed. Nussenblatt)	Jüdischer Buch- und Kunstverlag, Brünn; (English) *New Palestine*, New York
		'Byroniana'	*Frankfurter Zeitung*
		'Jüngste Generation der deutschen Lyriker'	*Literarische Welt*, Berlin
		'Lettres allemandes'	*Revue européenne*, Paris
		'Nach einem Jahr: Deutsch/Französische Gesellschaft'	*Deutsch/Französische Rundschau*, Paris
		'Un pur poète: R. M. Rilke'	*Revue européenne*, Paris
		'Sigmund Freud, der Siebzigjährige'	*Literarische Welt*, Berlin
	(11 Jan.)	'Moskauer Theater'	*Halle'sche Nachrichten*
	(30 July)	'Hans Franck'	*Münchner Neueste Nachrichten*
	(autumn)	'Siegfried Trebitsch'	*NFP*

FOREWORDS

1925		Renan: *Jugenderinnerungen*, trans. Hannah Szass	Frankfurter Verlagsanstalt

* Reprinted in *Begegnungen mit Menschen, Büchern, Städten*; Reichner, Wien, 1937.

† Reprinted in *Zeit und Welt*, ed. Friedenthal; S. Fischer, Frankfurt am Main, 1946.

		Hans Prager: *Die Weltanschauung Dostoiewskis*	Borgmeyer, Hildesheim
1927		*Paul Verlaine: Anthologie der besten Übertragungen*	Insel-Bücherei, 394
		Anthologie jüngster Lyrik, ed. Klaus Mann and Willi Fehse	Gebr. Enoch Verlag, Hamburg
		Max Brod: *Tycho Brahes Weg zu Gott*	Herbig
1928		Grigol Robakidze: *Das Schlangenhemd*	Diederichs
1929		‡E. T. A. Hoffmann: *Prinzessin Brambilla*	Aittinger, Paris
		Oskar Baum: *Nacht ist umher*	Reclam
		Richard Specht: *Florestan Kestners Erfolg*	Reclam

ESSAYS ON AUTOGRAPH COLLECTING

1925		'Die Welt der Autographen'	*Jahrbuch der deutschen Bibliophilen*
1926		'Echte und falsche Autographen'	*Autographische Rundschau*
		'Überschätzung des Lebenden'	" "
1929		'Neue Napoleon-Manuskripte'	*Philobiblon*, Wien

LECTURES (the few published out of a large number given)

1926	(29 Jan.)	†'Romain Rolland'	Meistersaal, Berlin
1927	(20 Feb.)	*'Abschied von Rilke'	Staatstheater, München
1929	(July)	†'Hugo von Hofmannsthal'	Burgtheater, Wien

TRANSLATIONS

1926	(May)	Verhaeren: 'Der Baum'	*Rheinische Blätter*
	(Dec.)	Verhaeren: 'An meine Augen'	*Inselschiff*
1928		Verhaeren: *Helenas Heimkehr*	Reclam

EDITIONS

1927		*Goethes Gedichte: eine Auswahl*	Reclam

FILM

1928		*Angst*	Orplid-Film, Berlin

* Reprinted in *Begegnungen mit Menschen, Büchern, Städten*; Reichner, Wien, 1937.

† Reprinted in *Zeit und Welt*, ed. Friedenthal; S. Fischer, Frankfurt am Main, 1946.

‡ Reprinted in *Europäisches Erbe*, ed. Friedenthal; S. Fischer, Frankfurt am Main, 1960.

Sources and Bibliography

No attempt has been made to give a comprehensive bibliography of the works of Zweig, for which the reader is referred to the full-scale work by Professor Randolph J. Klawiter, listed below.

UNPUBLISHED MATERIAL

	Abbreviations used in the footnotes
Correspondence received by Zweig, in the papers of the Zweig Estate, London	ZE
Letters to Friderike Zweig, from Stefan Zweig (not included in the published *Briefwechsel*) and others	
Zweig letters in the Handschriftensammlung, Stadtbibliothek, Vienna	StB
Zweig letters in the Deutsches Literaturarchiv, Schiller Nationalmuseum, Marbach am Neckar	Sch
Correspondence between Zweig and Thomas Mann, in the Thomas-Mann-Archiv, Zürich	TMArch
Zweig letters in the Ellen Key Archiv, Kungliga Bibliotek, Stockholm	KB
Zweig letters to Abrão Koogan, Editora Delta, Rio de Janeiro	K
Zweig letters to Liesl Monath, New York	LM
Zweig letters to Joseph Roth, photocopies in the possession of Friderike Zweig	Roth
Zweig letters to Alfredo Cahn, photocopies, together with Cahn's ms account of Zweig's visits to Buenos Aires, in the possession of Friderike Zweig	Cahn

PUBLICATIONS

ARAUJO LIMA, Claudio de. *Ascensão e Queda de Stefan Zweig*. Livraria José Olympio, Rio de Janeiro, n.d. (?1942).

ARENS, Hanns (ed.). *Stefan Zweig: Sein Leben, sein Werk.* Bechtle Verlag, Esslingen, 1949. Arens[1]

—— *Der grosse Europäer Stefan Zweig.* Kindler Verlag, München, 1956. Arens[2]

—— *Stefan Zweig im Zeugnis seiner Freunde.* Langen-Müller, München, 1968. Arens[3]

BAEDEKER, Peer. See EBERMAYER, Erich.

BARRICELLI, Jean-Pierre. See ZOHN, Harry.

BAUDOUIN, Charles. *Éclaircie sur l'Europe.* L'Abbaye du Livre, Lausanne, 1944. Baudouin

BAUER, Arnold. *Stefan Zweig.* Köpfe des XX. Jahrhunderts, Band 21, Colloquium Verlag, Berlin, 1961. Bauer

BIN GORION, Emanuel. *Ceterum Recenseo: Kritische Aufsätze und Reden.* Alexander Fischer, Tübingen, 1929.

BRAUN, Felix. *Das Licht der Welt: Geschichte eines Versuches als Dichter zu Leben.* Th. Morus-Presse im Verlag Herder, Wien, 1949. *Licht*

—— *Das Musische Land.* Oesterreichische Verlagsanstalt, Innsbruck, 1952. *Mus Land*

—— *Zeitgefährten.* Nymphenburger Verlagshandlung, München, 1963.

BRAUN, Robert. 'Erinnerungen an Stefan Zweig', *Buch und Leben*, Heft 10 (Okt. 1962), Europäischer Buchklub, Stuttgart, pp. 1–3.

BROD, Max. *Streitbares Leben: Autobiographie.* Kindler Verlag, München, 1960. Brod

CAHN, Alfredo. 'Stefan Zweig, Amigo y Autor', *Revista de la Universidad Nacional de Cordoba*, 2a Serie, Año VII, No. 1–3 (Mar.–Aug. 1966).

DAVIAU, Donald G. 'Stefan Zweig's Victors in Defeat', *Monatshefte* (Jan. 1959); University of Wisconsin, Madison, Wis., pp. 1–12.

DUMONT, Robert. *Stefan Zweig et la France.* Études de Littérature Étrangère et Comparée, No. 58; Didier, Paris, 1967. Dum

EBERMAYER, Erich. *Denn heute gehört uns Deutschland. . . .* Paul Zsolnay, Hamburg/Wien, 1959. *Heute*

—— *Buch der Freunde*, herausg. Peer Baedeker und Karl Lemke. Verlag Karl Lemke, München, 1960. *BdFr*

ELSTER, Hanns Martin (ed.). *Stefan Zweig* (Deutsche Dichterhandschriften). Lehmannsche Verlagsbuchhandlung (Lehmann & Schulze), Dresden, 1922. *DDh*

FAESI, Robert. 'Erinnerungen an Stefan Zweig', *Schweizer Monatshefte*, Jahrg. 41/12 (Mar. 1962), pp. 1301–10.

FEDER, Ernst. 'My Last Conversations with Stefan Zweig', *Books Abroad*, 17, 1 (Jan. 1943), pp. 3–9.

FISCHER VERLAG, S. *Vollständiges Verzeichnis aller Werke/ Buchserien und Gesamtausgaben, 1886–1956*. S. Fischer, Frankfurt am Main, 1956.

FITZBAUER, Erich. 'Stefan Zweig zur 15. Wiederkehr seines Todestages', *ÖGB Bildungsfunktionär*, Heft 56 (Mar. 1957), pp. 13–22.

—— (ed.) *Stefan Zweig: Spiegelungen einer schöpferischen Persönlichkeit*. 1. Sonderpublikation der Internat. Stefan-Zweig-Gesellschaft; Bergland Verlag, Wien, 1959. *Sp*

—— (ed.) *Katalog der Gedächtnisausstellung Stefan Zweig*. Salzburg, 1961. *Ausst*

FLOWER, Newman. *Just As It Happened*. Cassell, London, 1950. Flower

FREUD, Sigmund. *Briefe, 1873–1939*, herausg. Ernst Freud. S. Fischer, Frankfurt am Main, 1961. Freud *Br*

—— ZWEIG, Arnold. *Briefwechsel*, herausg. Ernst Freud. S. Fischer, Frankfurt am Main, 1968 Freud/Zw *BrW*

FRIEDENTHAL, Richard. 'Stefan Zweig', *Verbannte und Verbrannte*, herausg. Freier Deutscher Kulturbund, London (May 1942), pp. 4–6.

—— Nachwort zu: Stefan Zweig, *Balzac*. Bermann-Fischer, Stockholm, 1946.

—— Nachwort zu: Stefan Zweig, *Zeit und Welt, Gesammelte Aufsätze und Vorträge*. S. Fischer, Berlin/Frankfurt, 1946.

——Einleitung zu: Stefan Zweig, *Die Dramen*. S. Fischer, Frankfurt am Main, 1964.

—— Einleitung zu: Stefan Zweig, *Silberne Saiten, Gedichte und Nachdichtungen*. S. Fischer, Frankfurt am Main, 1966.

GEIGER, Benno. *Memorie di un Veneziano*. Vallecchi, Florence, 1958. Geiger

GRASBERGER, Franz (ed.). *Der Strom der Töne trug mich fort: Die Welt um Richard Strauss in Briefen*. Hans Schneider, Tutzing, 1967. Grasberger

GROSSBERG, Mimi. 'Die letzten Lebensmonate Joseph Roths', *Wort in der Zeit*, xi, 8–9 (1965), Stiasny Verlag, Graz, pp. 62–8.

HELLWIG, Hans. *Stefan Zweig: ein Lebensbild.* Wildners Kurzbiographien, Band 4; I. M. Wildner, Lübeck, 1948. H

HOMEYER, Fritz. *Deutsche Juden als Bibliophilen und Antiquare.* Schriftenreihe Wissenschaftlicher Abhandlungen des Leo Baeck Instituts, Band 10; J. C. B. Mohr (Paul Siebeck), Tübingen, 1963. Homeyer

INSEL, Die. *Eine Ausstellung zur Geschichte des Verlages unter Anton und Katharina Kippenberg*; Sonderausstellungen des Schiller Nationalmuseums, Katalog Nr. 15, herausg. Bernhard Zeller. Deutsches Literaturarchiv im Schiller Nationalmuseum, Marbach am Neckar, 1965. *IAusst*

INSEL-VERLAG. *Verzeichnis aller Veröffentlichungen, 1899–1924.* Überreicht von der Heller'schen Buchhandlung (Bukum A.-G.), Insel-Verlag, Wien, 1924.

JOUVE, Pierre-Jean. *Romain Rolland Vivant.* Ollendorff, Paris, 1920. Jouve

KESTEN, Hermann. *Meine Freunde die Poeten.* Kindler, München, 1959. *Poeten*

—— *Dichter im Café.* Knaur Taschenbücher Nr. 81, München, 1965. *Dichter*

—— *Deutsche Literatur im Exil: Briefe Europäischer Autoren, 1933–49.* Kurt Desch, München, 1964. *Exil*

KLAWITER, Randolph J. 'Stefan Zweig's *Novellen*: an Analysis'. Doctoral dissertation, University of Michigan, 1960.

—— *Stefan Zweig: a Bibliography.* University of North Carolina Studies in the Germanic Languages and Literature, No. 50; Chapel Hill, N.C., 1965. Kl

KRALIK, Heinrich. *Richard Strauss, Weltbürger der Musik.* Wollzeilen Verlag, Wien, 1963.

LANG, Wolf R. 'Stefan Zweig: Umrisse seines Lebens', *Buch und Leben*, Heft 11 (Nov. 1962); Europäischer Buchklub, Stuttgart, pp. 1–3.

LANGER, Norbert. *Dichter aus Österreich, Zweite Folge.* Oesterreichischer Bundesverlag, Wien, 1957.

LEFTWICH, Joseph. 'Stefan Zweig and the World of Yesterday', *Year Book III of the Leo Baeck Institute*; East and West Library, London, 1958, pp. 81–100. Leftwich

LEMKE, Karl. See EBERMAYER, Erich.

LIPTZIN, Solomon. *Germany's Stepchildren*. Meridian Books No. JP 19; World Publishing Co./Jewish Publication Society of America, Cleveland/Philadelphia, n.d.

LUCAS, W. I. 'Stefan Zweig', *German Men of Letters*, vol. ii, ed. Alex Natan; Oswald Wolff, London, 1963, pp. 225–48.

MANN, Klaus. *Auf der Suche nach einem Weg: Aufsätze*. Transmare Verlag, Berlin, 1931. *Suche*

—— *Der Wendepunkt: ein Lebensbericht*. G. B. Fischer, Berlin/Frankfurt, 1960. *Wendepunkt*

MANN, Thomas. *Briefe*: Band I—*1889–1936*, Band II—*1937–1947*, herausg. Erika Mann. S. Fischer, Frankfurt am Main, 1961, 1963. Mann *Br*

MAZZUCCHETTI, Lavinia. *Novecento in Germania*. Mondadori, Milan, 1959.

MECKLENBURG, Günther. *Vom Autographensammeln*. J. A. Stargardt, Marburg, 1963.

MÜLLER-EINIGEN, Hans. *Jugend in Wien: Roman*. F. Speidelsche Verlagsbuchhandlung, Wien, 1948. *Jugend*

NEUMANN, Robert. *Ein leichtes Leben: Bericht über mich selbst und Zeitgenossen*. Kurt Desch, München, 1963. Neumann

PARANDOWSKI, Jan. 'Erinnerungen an Stefan Zweig', *Wort in der Zeit*, vii, 11 (Nov. 1961); Stiasny Verlag, Graz, pp. 40–5. Parandowski

PRATER, Donald A. 'Stefan Zweig and England', *German Life and Letters*, xvi, 1 (Oct. 1962), pp. 1–16.

RAINALTER, Erwin H. Nachwort zu: Stefan Zweig, *Angst*. Reclams Universalbibliothek Nr. 6540, Leipzig, 1925.

RATHENAU, Walter. *Tagebuch 1907–1922*, herausg. Pogge und Strandmann. Droste, Düsseldorf, 1967.

RELGIS, Eugen. 'Los Ultimos Años de Stefan Zweig en Sudamerica', *Revista Universidad, Santa Fé*, No. 48 (1961).

RIEGER, Erwin. *Stefan Zweig: Der Mann und das Werk*. J. M. Spaeth, Berlin, 1928. R

ROLLAND, Romain. *Zwischen den Völkern: Aufzeichnungen und Dokumente aus den Jahren 1914–1919*, trans. Ré Soupault. 2 vols., Deutsche Verlagsanstalt, Stuttgart, 1954. *ZwV*

ROMAINS, Jules. 'Les derniers mois et dernières lettres de Stefan Zweig', *Revue de Paris*, 62e année, 2 (Feb. 1955), pp. 3–23.

SCHORER, Jean. *Jean Calvin et sa Dictature*. Grivet, Genève, 1948.

SCHUH, Willi (ed.). *Richard Strauss/Stefan Zweig: Briefwechsel*. S. Fischer, Frankfurt am Main, 1957. *Str*

SELDEN-GOTH, Gisella. *Stefan Zweig: Unbekannte Briefe aus der Emigration an eine Freundin*. Sammlung Dokumente zur Literatur- und Theatergeschichte, Band III; Hans Deutsch, Wien, 1964. *UB*

SOUZA, Claudio de. *Os Ultimos Dias de Stefan Zweig*. P. E. N. Clube do Brasil; Zelio Valverde, Rio de Janeiro, n.d. (1942). De Souza

—— *Les Derniers Jours de Stefan Zweig*. Préface d'André Maurois; Éditions Quetzal, Mexico, 1944.

SPECHT, Richard. *Stefan Zweig: Versuch eines Bildnisses*. Einleitung zur russischen Gesamtausgabe der Werke, Verlag Wremja, Leningrad; Spamersche Druckerei, Leipzig, 1927. S

STERN, Leopold. *La Mort de Stefan Zweig*. Editora Civilização Brasileira, Rio de Janeiro, 1942 (also in Portuguese: *A Morte de Stefan Zweig*, same publisher and year). Stern

TREBITSCH, Siegfried. *Chronicle of a Life*, trans. Eithne Wilkins and Ernest Kaiser. Heinemann, London, 1953. Treb

UHLMAN, Fred. *The Making of an Englishman*. Gollancz, London, 1960. Uhlman

VALLENTIN, Antonina. 'Stefan Zweig', *Europe*, 25e année, No. 22 (Oct. 1947), pp. 48–67. Vallentin

WOLFF, Kurt. *Briefwechsel eines Verlegers*. Scheffler, Frankfurt am Main, 1966. Wolff

WULF, Joseph. *Literatur und Dichtung im Dritten Reich*. Rowohlt Taschenbücher Nr. 809–11, 1966. Wulf

ZECH, Paul. *Stefan Zweig: eine Gedenkschrift*. Quadriga Verlag, Buenos Aires, 1943. *Ged*

ZOHN, Harry. 'Stefan Zweig and Contemporary European Literature', *German Life and Letters*, v, 3 (Apr. 1952), pp. 202–12.

—— (ed.) *Liber Amicorum Friderike Zweig*. Brandeis University; Dahl Publishing Co., Stamford, Conn., 1952. *Liber Amic*

ZOHN, Harry. 'Music in Stefan Zweig's Last Years' (with Jean-Pierre BARRICELLI), *The Juilliard Review*, iii, 2 (Spring 1956), pp. 3–11.

—— 'Stefan Zweig's Last Years: Some Unpublished Letters', *Monatshefte* (Feb. 1956); University of Wisconsin, Madison, Wis., pp. 73–7.

—— 'Stefan Zweig: Bericht und Bekenntnis', in *Wiener Juden in der deutschen Literatur*. Edition 'Olamenu', Tel Aviv, 1964, pp. 19–30.

ZUCKMAYER, Karl. *Als wär's ein Stück von mir: Erinnerungen.* S. Fischer, Frankfurt am Main, 1966. Zuckmayer

ZWEIG, Arnold. See FREUD, Sigmund.

ZWEIG, Friderike Maria. *Stefan Zweig: Wie ich ihn erlebte.* Neuer Verlag, Stockholm, 1947. Fr

—— (ed.) *Stefan Zweig/Friderike Zweig: Briefwechsel.* Alfred Scherz, Berne, 1951. *BrW*

—— *Stefan Zweig: eine Bildbiographie.* Kindler, München, 1961. *Bildb*

—— *Spiegelungen des Lebens.* Hans Deutsch, Wien, 1964. Fr[2]

ZWEIG, Stefan. *Die Welt von Gestern: Erinnerungen eines Europäers.* S. Fischer, Frankfurt am Main, 1955, 80.–90. Tausend. *WvG*

Index of the Works of Stefan Zweig

General Index